THE
PEARL
BEYOND PRICE

Other books by A. H. Almaas:

The Elixir of Enlightenment

Essence
The Diamond Approach to Inner Realization

DIAMOND MIND SERIES
Volume I: **The Void**
*A Psychodynamic Investigation of the Relationship
between Mind and Space*

DIAMOND HEART SERIES
Book One: **Elements of the Real in Man**

DIAMOND MIND SERIES: II

The PEARL BEYOND PRICE

Integration of Personality into Being: An Object Relations Approach

A. H. Almaas

Diamond Books  Berkeley, California

For permission to reprint excerpts, the author is grateful to the following:

Beshara Publications for *The Kernel of the Kernel*, Ibn 'Arabi, Muhyiddin, 1981 and for *Universal Man*, al-Jîlî, Abd al-Karîm, 1983; International Universities Press, Inc. for *Schizoid Phenomena, Object-Relations, and the Self*, Guntrip, Harry, 1969, for *The Self and the Object World*, Jacobson, Edith, 1980; The Hogarth Press and the estate of the author for *Schizoid Phenomena, Object-Relations, and the Self*, Guntrip, Harry, 1969; Jason Aronson Inc. for *Object Relations Theory and Clinical Psychoanalysis*, Kernberg, Otto F., © 1976; The Acorn Press and Chetana Private Limited for *I Am That*, Maharaj, Sri Nisargadatta, 1981; Basic Books, Inc., for *The Psychological Birth of the Human Infant*, Mahler, Margaret S., et al., © 1975 by Margaret S. Mahler; Harcourt Brace Jovanovich, Inc. for *In Search of the Miraculous*, Ouspensky, P. D., © 1949 by Harcourt Brace Jovanovich, Inc., renewed 1977 by Tatiana Nagro; Shambhala Publications, Inc. (300 Massachusetts Ave., Boston, MA 02115) for *The Experience of No-Self*, Roberts, Bernadette, © 1982; Jonathan Cape Ltd. for *Thinkers of the East*, Shah, Idries, 1971; A. P. Watt Ltd. for *Thinkers of the East*, Shah, Idries, 1971; William Morrow & Company, Inc. for *The Hollow Hills*, Stewart, Mary, 1973; Princeton University Press for *The King and the Corpse*, Zimmer, Heinrich, ed. Campbell, Joseph, Bollingen Series XI, © 1948, 1957, 1975 renewed by Princeton University Press; Columbia University Press for *Ego Psychology: Theory and Practice*, Blanck, Gertrude and Rubin, © 1974.

Cover photo: Statue of David from *The Sculpture of Michelangelo* by Umberto Baldini, photography by Liberto Perugi, Rizzoli: Milan, Italy. 1982

Cover design: Christine Molé

First published in 1988 by

    Diamond Books
    Almaas Publications
    P.O. Box 10114
    Berkeley, CA 94709

ISBN 0-936713-03-8 (cloth)   ISBN 0-936713-02-X (paper)

Library of Congress Card Catalog Number: 87-051720

Typeset in 10 point Garamond Light by MACAW
on a Macintosh computer, using JustText™ & output on a Linotronic 300

Printed in the United States by
    BookCrafters

INTRODUCTION

to the Diamond Mind Series

The Pearl Beyond Price is the second volume of the Diamond Mind Series. This series is a systematic presentation of a particular body of knowledge, which we call Diamond Mind, and its corresponding modus operandi, a way of working with people toward inner realization, which we call the Diamond Approach. The presentation is somewhat technical, and hence will be useful to psychologists, psychotherapists, educators and spiritual teachers, but is also accessible to the educated reader. This work is a response to an important need that is being felt in many quarters, a need for a spiritually informed psychology, or conversely for a psychologically grounded spirituality. This perspective does not separate psychological and spiritual experience, and hence sees no dichotomy between depth psychology and spiritual work. Through a creative critique and investigation, this system takes some of the elements of depth psychology, particularly those of ego psychology and object relations theory, and extends them into realms of the human psyche which are usually considered the domain of religion, spirituality and metaphysics.

This body of knowledge is not an integration or synthesis of modern depth psychology and traditional spiritual understanding. The inclination to think in terms of integration of the two is due to the prevailing belief in the dichotomy between the fields of psychology and spirituality, a dichotomy in which the Diamond Mind understanding does not participate.

The Diamond Mind knowledge is a multifaceted understanding of the nature of man, his consciousness or psyche, and the potential for expansion of his capacity for experience and inner development. These several points regarding the nature of this understanding will help to place it in context:

v

1. This knowledge includes an understanding of normal psychological functioning which also sheds light on some prevalent mental disorders. It adopts many of the findings of modern depth psychology, situating them in a more comprehensive view of man and also establishing their relevance for the pursuit of deeper truths about human nature beyond the levels psychology generally penetrates.

2. The psychological understanding is set within a metapsychological perspective that includes a broad outline of the domains of experience and functioning of the human psyche or soul. This metapsychology is not spelled out in any one of the volumes of the series, but is gradually developed throughout its several books.

3. This metapsychology is in turn set within a metaphysical outlook in which psychological experience is situated within a phenomenology of Being.

4. This work demonstrates that what is usually considered psychological investigation can arrive at dimensions of experience which have always been considered to be the product of spiritual practice or discipline. The psychological work is seen here not as an adjunct to spiritual practice, but as a spiritual practice on its own. This is the specific contribution of the Diamond Mind body of knowledge which prompted the idea of this series.

5. Not only can psychological investigation lead to realms of experience previously relegated to the spiritual, this work shows that when psychological understanding is refined by an openness to one's spiritual nature, such investigation, if pursued deeply, inevitably will penetrate into the realm of spiritual, religious or mystical understanding. In the course of such exploration one result is that many currently prevalent psychological dysfunctions such as some forms of narcissism and schizoid isolation, are revealed as direct consequences of spiritual alienation, which thus cannot be truly resolved by traditional psychotherapy.

6. This body of work includes a systematic understanding of the domain of spiritual experience, the realm of Being, that can be described in detail in modern psychological language. Thus it shows that this domain of experience need not be vague, symbolic or incommunicable. It also includes an exploration of the relationships between this domain of experience and the usual psychological dimension of experience, shedding light on the nature of ego structure

and identity. Thus the dimension of Being can be included in some vii modes of psychological research and investigation.

7. The presentation in the various volumes of the series attempts to illustrate methods of investigation, as well as the clinical and scientific bases for our conclusions, within a conceptually logical treatment of the various subject matters. However, because of the nature of the field of inquiry, the reader may well be aware of an experiential impact that cannot always be separated from the conceptual knowledge. This points to a particular quality of the Diamond knowledge: it is an experiential knowledge that is immediate and intimately human, but which can be elaborated conceptually.

It is my wish that this knowledge will be useful in refining and deepening our understanding of who and what we are as human beings. Perhaps it will make it possible for more of us to actualize our rich potential and to live more complete lives.

A.H. Almaas
Berkeley, California
November 1987

Dedicated, with gratitude, to
the **Diamond Consciousness**,
the inner guidance to the Land of Truth—

—and to Karen and Faisal,
who contributed greatly to the integration of this guidance;

—and to the students who, by trusting
its guidance, enabled its teaching to become a lived reality.

FOREWORD

The work that you have in your hands is quite extraordinary in that it
unfolds a comprehensive theory of personality grounded in a dimension of Being beyond our normal understandings of ego and identity.
For here a knowledge of the spiritual path of transformation appears
within, and is conjoined to, the modern context of western psychological process. Anyone with knowledge of the sacred psychologies at the
heart of the world's religious traditions will immediately recognize the
significance of this major work by A. H. Almaas.

The reader should be prepared for a stretch of mind as one
proceeds through the book. Our usual notion of "psychology" is
being expanded through Almaas' deeper spiritual perspective, namely,
his understanding of the essential nature of the human being. This
work is the first comprehensive account of the relationship of this
dimension, the spiritual ground of the individual, to the empirical
findings of developmental psychology. The structural theories of contemporary psychotherapy are reviewed and framed within this deeper
context, and this gives us a whole new perspective in which to appreciate the value and limitations of the state of the art on contemporary psychology.

Almaas' first task, which is taken up in Book I, is the full description and explication of the qualities and aspects of being. This may be
entirely new and unfamiliar territory to some readers. We hasten to
assure such readers that the states of being therein described should
certainly not be construed as mere concept or speculation, but should
be understood as a reality known through concrete experience, as at-
tested to by spiritual people throughout the ages. This subject, that of
the essential aspects of human beingness, Almaas unfolds in terms of
four categories: autonomy, beingness, personhood and contact. On
the other hand, those readers who are committed to a particular

xii religious path may find their understanding is being stretched because here the spiritual task is reflected in and through a new mirror for consciousness, the perspective of psychological process.

From the field of developmental psychology, new theories of human development have emerged as a result of extensive empirical research and experience. In particular, what has come to be known as the "object relations" approach has provided us with a very comprehensive explanation of the way in which our ego structures become formed and established, a process beginning in earliest infancy. In their findings, the emerging consciousness, as it comes to experience its objects, undergoes a process of shifting and transitional identifications, which being internalized, self-structure that consciousness, forming a self- and object-world. So from this empirical work, we not only learn of the origins of our ego identity, but why we come to perceive and relate to the world in the specific ways that we do. Almaas has recognized the importance of this research and has taken full advantage of these insights to explicate the psychological relationship to the dimension of being. This is the subject matter of Book II, and even if one has no prior acquaintance with object relations theory, the author offers a clear discussion and analysis of these principles such that one can readily grasp their import.

We hear today, from many quarters, voices questioning whether mainstream psychology has a view of man that fully appreciates his being and potential. Religious teachers, in particular, have grown hoarse telling us that we do not know or appreciate the depths of our own nature, who we really are. From Almaas' work, we can see just how and why we have lost contact with our own essence, and repressed our knowledge of it. We also see most clearly that the account of human maturation offered by developmental psychology, while most valuable from a certain standpoint, is based on a model of human maturity which is far too limited. This becomes especially clear when the problem of ego and identity is examined. Insofar as we have taken our own ego structures as a statement of who we are, we have, by that fundamental identification, effectively ordained the limits of our own growth and potential. We have also placed severe limits on our own powers of self-healing. As we are more and more beginning to appreciate, our ego-identity must be constantly defended, and that defensiveness is costly in that it blocks us from our deeper potentials.

Almaas demonstrates (1) how and why these ego-constructions tend to cut us off from our more essential states of presence, and (2) how essence can come to "shine through" these limiting structures, absorbing and integrating them into itself. If our more complete growth and healing seem to require a loosening or disidentification with ego constructions, how can this be done? The problem is that we think our ego is our "self," who we are. Our fear is that we will be left with nothing, and indeed, as Almaas shows, abandonment of defensive postures does first expose a state of deficiency. But this is only a step on the way to a deeper integration. As our capacities are assimilated to the personal essence, only then do we become fully human. Our notions of individuality, autonomy, maturity, are being revalued, seen no longer from the vantage point of ego, but rather from the ground of our own being. We learn that it is from the dimension of being that true integration takes place—not on the level of the mind, as is usually assumed by psychological theory. In developing this account in and through therapeutic process, Almaas has opened a new pathway toward the goal of the more complete realization of the person, the possibility of experiencing one's own essential being as a full presence without defensiveness. The author calls this the true experience of "I am."

With the evident need today for a spiritually-informed psychology, and the stirrings of a new field of "transpersonal" psychology, the foundational basis for this work is just now starting to emerge. Beginning with the contributions of Carl Jung and Roberto Assagioli, the new metapsychology takes as its startng point the existence and efficacy of this fundamental level of integrative being. This dimension can make its appearance within the therapeutic work when space and attention is provided for it, coming to be experienced intuitively as "inner guidance," a presence experienced in and through the ego-field. By such an alignment, a far greater potency is available for raising and assimilating the fixated, fragmented or fragmenting aspects of our psyche. This process itself comes to consciousness as spiritual development and moves to center us at a higher level of awareness, and the distinction between psychological process and spiritual development begins to disappear, leaving a wider and more unified view of human evolution. What is usually insufficiently appreciated is that Jung and Assagioli drew from the inner, more esoteric side of

xiv   soul-healing. Jung, in particular, tried to decode the forgotten symbols of many such traditions to show how being and psyche attempted to communicate so as to order and unify the materials of the inner world. It was from his reading of these sacred psychologies that Jung developed his account of the "individuation process." And now we are fortunate in that we are beginning to learn from teachers representing living spiritual traditions.

Almaas' account of the relation between ego and being broadens this metapsychology in bold new directions. We have already noted his extensive use of the insights of developmental psychology to elucidate ego-structure and ego-identity. But even more significantly, the psychospiritual work reveals itself as a path of personal realization leading to enlightenment. In comparison, Jung was under the impression that the absorption of the ego by the self meant an extinction of the personality, and he communicated that fear to his readers. But to Almaas, the person is supported by Being, and the "taking up" of ego-structure into Personal Essence actually represents the full development of human potential. This is fully unfolded in Book III, in his discussion of the development of "The Pearl Beyond Price," setting forth the dynamics of individuated enlightenment, an extraordinary conclusion to the entire work. We have been prepared for this by Almaas in his two previous works, *Essence — The Diamond Approach to Inner Realization,* and *The Void — A Psychodynamic Investigation of the Relationship between Mind and Space,* but here in this work we see his thought in its fullest development to date.

Almaas clearly has the personal knowledge and experience of what he writes. On the occasions when he has taught publicly, his audience has quickly come to appreciate that his teachings embody a lived and living reality. And the students with whom he has worked privately or in groups seem, from all indications, to have come to experience the process described. Thus the book that you have before you should be read as an actual account of a living meeting between spiritual and psychological wisdoms.

Lawrence M. Spiro, Ph.D.
Melia Foundation
Berkeley, California
December 16, 1987

PREFACE

When translators write prefaces to works they have translated, they often include technical discussion of the difficulties of rendering certain concepts or even whole categories of words into the new language without losing the sense of the original. This book was written in English, but is in a sense a translation from a body of experience which submits to verbal description less readily than do most categories of human experience, and which "loses more in the translation." Not only the nonlinearity of the subject matter, which is true of any human experience, but the nature of the states of Being described here, make unusual demands on the reader to hold in abeyance the desire for intellectual resolution. One must proceed through a large number of steps in this book to see the whole picture at once, and these steps are closely interrelated.

There are at least two books here: a relatively simple book dealing with the spiritual concerns of human life from the perspective of the question of individuation, and a more technical discussion, mainly in terms of object relations theory, of the psychological phenomena involved in the pursuit of a deep understanding of the nature of one's true being. The more "technical" discussion (which is found particularly in Book I Part IV and Book II Part II) is written on a level accessible to the serious layperson. For this reason, the psychologist reading this material may wish that the discussion were even more technical or detailed, and more integrated with the various psychological literatures referred to by Almaas. That, however, would be yet another book. Almaas does plan a future volume focused on explicating specific case studies in depth.

Almaas' primary discovery is that the development of modern psychology has made newly accessible a resolution of the age-old dichotomy of the spiritual life versus the personal life. Specifically, the

xvi   theories and techniques of ego psychology and object relations theory
       can, when pursued from a certain perspective, allow a modern *gnosis*
       or understanding which makes heretofore esoteric insight and realiza-
       tion more available to people who are living a normal life in the
       world. This body of work is in part a product of the line of discourse
       begun by Freud, who was the first Western thinker to attempt to think
       scientifically about matters previously relegated to the accidental, the
       irrational, the unknown and presumably unknowable within human
       experience. Freud responded with tremendous courage, intelligence
       and objectivity to Socrates' challenge to "know thyself." The subse-
       quent development of psychoanalysis and psychology into an exten-
       sive, purportedly scientific field has been useful and enlightening.

           However, we can say again that a reading of the literature often
       makes one feel that something has been lost in the translation. Specifi-
       cally, Freud demonstrated an unremitting curiosity and a profound
       understanding of the fact that our lives arise out of depths of which our
       conscious minds are ignorant; this awareness which informed *his* work
       is often lost in the construction of what seem to aspire to be total ex-
       planatory systems about psychological life. A second source, then, of
       Almaas' contribution is that quality of mind constituted by objectivity,
       openness to the unknown, and curiosity. This quality which he refers
       to as the Diamond Mind operates sufficiently powerfully to penetrate
       and finally "transcend" the conceptual systems within which books on
       both spiritual realization and psychology are generally written. This is
       both a blessing and a curse: a blessing in that a new understanding is
       reached which extends the limits of each of these subjects; and a curse
       in that from the point of view of either domain of discourse, this book
       can be difficult to place in context.

           An example of this problem is what we have in the course of work-
       ing on this book dubbed the "angels on the carburetor" phenomenon.
       Reading certain of the more technical chapters which are set mainly
       within the frame of reference of psychology, but which utilize concepts
       such as "essential aspects," can have the effect one might experience
       reading a manual on car repair about how to rebuild a carburetor:
       learning that one must take the carburetor apart, clean the pieces,
       replace certain gaskets and put the whole thing back together, and then
       get two angels to sit on top of the carburetor in order to make it work.
       (This metaphor is actually not accidental; qualities similar to what

Almaas calls the "essential aspects" are studied in esoteric Judaism
under the category of angelology.) For the psychologist reading this
material the concept of essential aspects might seem esoteric; I would
point out here that to a political scientist, for instance, concerned with
the actions of government leaders, explanations involving such concepts as the Oedipus complex might seem equally esoteric.

This book looks at what most of us take ourselves to be, the ego
identity, in terms of what is beyond it. Its subject matter is esoteric,
finally, only in the sense that the concept of justice, or philosophical
questions about existence and identity, are esoteric to a child. A difference between children and most adults is that children have a
sense of an expanding, transforming life ahead of them. They know
that they will change, and fundamentally; they know that they will
learn, grow and lose their childhood in favor of something else.
Regaining that openness is both a desirable way to begin reading this
book, and a possible product of reading it.

Alia Johnson
Editor

THE PEARL BEYOND PRICE

Table of Contents

BOOK ONE:
The Nature of the Pearl Beyond Price

THE
PEARL
BEYOND PRICE

The NATURE of the PEARL BEYOND PRICE

BOOK ONE

Table of Contents

PART I

THE
PERSONAL ESSENCE

Chapter One

The Man of Spirit and the Man of the World

At a certain age, very early on in life, each one of us becomes aware of himself or herself as a walking, talking, thinking, feeling being—in short, as a living person. It is such a luminous discovery, but it quickly becomes dull with familiarity. Then we live our lives as if we now know what it is to be human, as if maturing were only a matter of becoming more of what we think we are already. The mystery is gone, and life becomes tedious and repetitive.

In this book we want to lift off the veil of familiarity. We want to inquire into the mystery of being a human being, a person. We want to explore the potential of being human. What is the extent of this potential? What is a truly mature and complete human being like? How will he and she experience themselves and the world, and what kind of lives will they lead?

We begin our enquiry by contrasting two poles of human experience. At one end of the spectrum is the experience of what we will call "the man of the world," the individual who is busy living a personal life, trying to find personal fulfillment, working on strengthening and expanding himself. It is an accepted and approved concern for a human being, in most societies, to seek personal happiness, fulfillment and autonomy, in the process of building a personal life, as long as it is not at the expense of others. This has become the dominant view of man in modern societies. The personal life is the core of most human activities; what is called a public life is still a personal life, related to the person, and lived for persons. In our exploration we

8   will examine in a new light the conviction that living a personal life centered around the person is its own value and end.

Contrasted to the perspective of the man of the world is the view of what we will call "the man of spirit," which considers a higher spiritual reality to be the true and proper center of real human life. The most profound teachings regarding human nature, those of the most accomplished and liberated of human beings, of the founders of the major religions, spiritual movements and philosophical systems point clearly, unequivocally and exclusively towards the life of selflessness, egolessness and surrender to a higher reality. One teacher after another, one great religion after another, one moral philosophy after another, extol the life of spirit—in which personal life is subordinated to a higher spiritual reality—as the highest and most refined, most fulfilled and only true life for man. Humanity is exhorted to move towards making the personal life be governed by spiritual values, and towards embracing the universal and impersonal truths, which are beyond self and personality.

Thus, the main difference between the perspective of the man of the world and that of the man of spirit is that the first considers the separate personal self to be the center of life, and personal life to be its own value and end, while the latter makes a higher reality to be the center of life, and believes that the personal life must be subordinated in relationship to such a higher reality. In Luke 9:23 Christ states: "If any man would come after me, let him deny himself and take up his cross daily and follow me. For whoever would save his life will lose it; and whoever loses his life for my sake, he will save it."

In Islam, the Koran asserts a similar stance. For example, in the following passage, the statement is that dying for God is the right course, implying that the personal life in this world is not as important:

> And do not speak of those who are slain in Allah's way as dead; nay (they are) alive, but you do not perceive.
> Who, when a misfortune befalls them, say: Surely we are Allah's, and to him we shall surely return.
> Those are they on whom are blessings and mercy from their Lord, and those are the followers of the right course.

The Far Eastern spiritual traditions go even farther than the prophetic tradition in denying the importance of the personal life. In the Dhammapada, a major Buddhist canon, the Buddha states:

No one is higher than him,
who will not be deceived, who knows the essence,
who has abandoned desire, renounced the world,
and lives untouched by the flow of time.
[Translated by P. Lal, *The Dhammapada*, p. 72]

Nevertheless, the life of the man of the world consists largely of the fulfillment of personal desires. The personal self is the sense of being a separate entity. It is not only valued; its real existence as an entity is taken for granted by virtually everyone. This personal self has been the focus of study of Western depth psychology, ego psychology, object relations theory, developmental psychology, self psychology, etc. An eminent psychologist says in a book devoted to its study:

> While no one can agree on exactly what the self is, as adults we still have a very real sense of self that permeates daily social experience. It arises in many forms. There is the sense of self that is a single, distinct, integrated body; there is the agent of actions, the experiencer of feelings, the maker of intentions, the architect of plans, the transposer of experience into language, the communicator and sharer of personal knowledge. [Daniel N. Stern, *The Interpersonal World of the Infant*, p. 5]

Western psychology shares the common cultural perspective that the self is and must be the central axis of life. Its view regarding the personal self can be seen as the expression and crystallization of the view of the man of the world cast in scientific language. It considers mental health the expression of a strong, cohesive personal self with a separate sense of identity. The founder of self psychology puts it this way:

> Mental health is often defined by analysts, in harmony with the remark ascribed to Freud (Erickson, 1950, p. 229), rather loosely and extrascientifically as a person's ability to work and to love. Within the framework of the psychology of the self, we define mental health not only as freedom from the neurotic symptons and inhibitions that interfere with the functions of a "mental apparatus" involved in loving and working, but also as the capacity for a firm self to avail itself of the talents and skills at an individual's disposal, enabling him to love and work successfully. [Heinz Kohut, *The Restoration of the Self*, pp. 283-284]

10   The importance of the self for object relations theory in terms of understanding psychopathology can be seen in the words of James Masterson:

> However, this additional dimension of a focus on the self
> (defined as an intrapsychic entity), when kept in concert
> with the other perspectives of developmental object
> relations theory, can lead to a broader, more inclusive and
> comprehensive concept of the borderline and narcissistic
> disorders as disorders of the self. [James F. Masterson, *The
> Real Self*, p. 19]

An important part of our exploration in this book will be to study in
detail and in depth the findings of depth psychology, especially those
of object relations theory, and relate them to the spiritual perspective
of the man of spirit. In fact, such findings will aid us tremendously in
understanding the various levels of the spiritual view of man, as we
will see in subsequent chapters. In this chapter we are describing in
some detail the perspective of the man of spirit because it is less
known or understood. In Chapter Two, we will focus in more detail
on the perspective of the man of the world and its center, the personal self, by discussing how it is understood by object relations
theory.

The man of spirit not only subordinates the self to a higher reality,
but sometimes goes further to deny its fundamental existence. The
highest realization in Buddhism, for instance, is that ultimately there
are no separate, independent and intrinsically existing persons. The
Buddha repeatedly stated this as in the following passage from the
Diamond Sutra: "It is because no Bodhisattva who is a real Bodhisattva cherishes the idea of an ego-entity, a personality, a being or a
separated individuality." [Translated by A. F. Price and Wong Mou-
Lam, *The Diamond Sutra and The Sutra of Hui Neng*, p. 26]

Lao Tzu, the legendary founder of Taoism in China, the reputed
author of the Tao Teh Ching, equates trouble with the belief in the
individual self; in one of the stanzas in the book, he observes:

> People are beset with great trouble because
> they assert that there is an individual self.
> If they take nothing personally, then
> what can they call trouble?
> [Translated by Ni Hua-Ching, *Complete Works of Lao Tzu*, p. 9]

These two approaches to human life are diametrically opposed to
each other. The most well-known profound teachings about human

nature point one way, and humankind in general is going another way, or at least so it seems.

The contradiction between the two perspectives is not only an appearance; it is quite real and has far-reaching consequences for human life and for the course of human evolution. They are divergent paths, each with its own values, aims and consequences.

One might be tempted to believe that the spiritual teachings are simply the opinions or beliefs of certain individuals or religious systems, which are not meant to apply to all people. But this is far from the truth. All major spiritual teachings stress impersonality, universality, selflessness, egolessness and the denigration of the personal. It is true that the various traditions differ in their emphasis and outlook; but they all extol selflessness, egolessness and the surrender of personal life to higher reality. The Far Eastern traditions generally see the ultimate human nature as impersonal and universal. Enlightenment, and hence, liberation and fulfillment are seen to be the consequence of realizing that the individual is a mistaken idea and that his true nature is the ultimate truth, whether that is seen as God (Hinduism), Tao (Taoism) or the Void (Buddhism).

The prophetic religious traditions (Judaism, Christianity, Islam) consider the human being an individual soul who needs to live a life of surrender to God's will, egolessness, selflessness and virtue. Reward is understood to come in the afterlife. Jesus Christ, in his Sermon on the Mount, makes this clear:

> Happy are you when men insult you and mistreat you and tell all kinds of evil lies against you because you are my followers. Rejoice and be glad, because a great reward is kept for you in heaven. [The American Bible Society, *The New Testament*, p. 9]

However, the mystical side of the prophetic tradition tends to be closer to the Far Eastern view of the ultimate nonexistence of the person. Mystical Christianity conceives of God as the ultimate ground and being of the individual, as the following text clearly indicates:

> He is your being and in him, you are what you are, not only because he is the cause and being of all that exists, but because he is your cause and the deep center of your being. . .
> And thus, also, he is one in all things and all things are one in him. For I repeat: all things exist in him; he is the

12   being of all. [Edited by William Johnston, *The Cloud of Unknowing*, p. 150]

This view of the oneness of all existence in God indicates that the existence of a personal self is not ultimate, and that salvation is the realization of this oneness. The great Sufi author, Ibn 'Arabi, goes even farther and asserts that there is nothing but God:

> And for this the Prophet (upon whom be peace) said: "Whoso knoweth himself knoweth his Lord." And he said (upon him be peace): "I know my Lord by my Lord." The Prophet (upon whom be peace) points out by that, that thou art not thou: thou art He, without thou; not He entering into thee, nor thou entering into Him, nor He proceeding forth from thee, nor thou proceeding forth from Him. And it is not meant by that, that thou art aught that exists or thine attributes aught that exists, but it is meant by it that thou never wast nor wilt be, whether by thyself or through Him or in Him or along with Him. Thou art neither ceasing to be nor still existing. Thou art He, without one of these limitations. Then if thou know thine existence thus, then thou knowest God; and if not, then not. [Ibn 'Arabi, *"Whoso Knoweth Himself . . ."*, pp. 4-5]

As we see, these teachings are unanimous in their evaluation of personal life as less important than some "higher" realm. What does this mean? Does it mean that the majority of humankind are completely astray, are so wrong and ignorant and completely out of touch with their nature that they go in the exact opposite direction from where they should be heading?

Many people, of course, believe just that: that the life of the world is antithetical to the life of spirit and truth. In fact, most of the great teachers have stressed that the life of the world is not the religious or the true life. But let us not hasten to conclusions.

It is possible, of course, that the majority of humankind are astray, are on the wrong path to human fulfillment. However, this does not explain why they are all on the same path! Why is it that all humans are pursuing personal happiness, wanting to lead a personal life where self and individuality are valued and cherished? In other words, if the ultimate goal of the human being is the universal impersonal truths of Spirit, why is it that all humans end up with an ego, with a self and a personality? Can it be just a mistake, a colossal mistake? And if it is, then why is it made so universally?

In this book, our interest is to understand the nature of the human being in a comprehensive way, a way that makes sense of the normal experience of most individuals while retaining the deepest insights into human nature, as seen in the most profound spiritual discoveries of mankind. We will introduce an understanding about human nature by contrasting the view of the man of the world, the usual perspective of most people who take the person and the personal life to be the center of human nature and concern, with the view of the man of spirit, the spiritual perspective of most religions that man's nature is ultimately spiritual, and human life must be governed by selflessness and egolessness. The most extreme position of this latter perspective is that self and individuality do not have an ultimate or real existence. This extreme position, although not shared by many spiritual groups, nevertheless remains a common and central contention for the most advanced teachings of most spiritual traditions, especially the mystical ones. More specifically, we will contrast the experience of most people that they are separate individuals, entities in their own right, with the contention of many spiritual traditions that the ultimate reality is a state of oneness of being and unity of existence, and ex-plore the relationship between the two.

We are well aware that not all people who are interested in spiritual life consider the ultimate reality to be that of oneness or unity. The spiritual perspective covers a wide range, from the religious perspec-tive of living a life according to divine commandments, to the spiritual one of finding a connection to a higher reality, to the mystical view of uniting with God or realizing the oneness of existence.

In this study we will focus on the second and third views as the purest expressions of the man of spirit, and will use them in our contrast with the view of the man of the world. Which one of these we will be using at each point will be obvious from the context, when not stated ex-plicitly. So in developing our understanding of what a complete human being is, we will contrast these opposing points of view, that of the man of the world who believes in the reality and centrality of the personal self and that of the man of spirit who considers such a personal and in-dependent self not to have any ultimate value or reality.

Some might believe that these perspectives are not dichotomies, that one can be a self and a person and live a personal life in a spiritual and universal way. This is in fact the perspective of most

14   individuals who are either at the beginning of their inner journey, or are among the many people who consider themselves religious. We are here using "religious" in contrast to "spiritual." It is, furthermore, the social ideal of most human societies. However, regardless of the merit or truth of this perspective, it is still not the view of some of the most advanced teachings. These teachings make it very clear that to live a true and spiritual life is to abandon self completely. In fact, many teachings assert that there is no self in any real way. The Buddhist teachings, especially, emphasize this "no self" perspective. The Dalai Lama, the head of Tibetan Buddhism, writes:

> As I may as well emphasize again, the teachings of no-self-soul is upheld by all schools of Buddhist thought since all alike recognize the atman-view that is adhering to belief in some permanent soul-entity, as the root of all trouble. [The XIVth Dalai Lama, *The Opening of the Wisdom Eye*, p. 94]

Others might jump to the conclusion that maybe it is possible to live a selfless personal life; that is, to be a human person, living a true personal life of work, love and knowledge, but without having a self. But even this hope is dashed when we inquire deeply into some of the profoundest teachings. Selflessness means egolessness, which means absence of the person. The late Nisargadatta Maharaj, one of the most profound Hindu Vedanta teachers in India, puts it this way:

> There is no such thing as a person. There are only restrictions and limitations. The sum total of these defines the person. . . . The person merely appears to be, like the space within the pot appears to have the shape and volume and smell of the pot. [Sri Nisargadatta Maharaj, *I Am That*, p. 204]

These teachings unequivocally state that the universal truth or the impersonal spirit is just that; there is no self and no person. They are not saying necessarily that personal life is bad; what they are stating is something much more fundamental. The assertion is that there is no person or self, which negates the existence of a person who can have a personal life. According to this perspective a personal life, i.e., the life of a person, is false; it is unreal, only an illusion. Enlightenment then is seen as simply seeing through this illusion.

As we have mentioned, this is the teaching specifically of the Far Eastern spiritual traditions, those of Buddhism, Taoism, Zen, Vedanta and the various forms of Hinduism. In the prophetic tradition, the

Hebraic-Christian-Islamic teachings, the emphasis is not on the unreality or absence of self and personality, but on negating their importance and the importance of a life based on them. We will see later on
that the prophetic tradition does give some value to personal life, but
personal life is meant in a sense different from that of the man of the
world.

There are, of course, those who believe in the "true self" or the
eternal soul. But the true self is not taken usually to be personal. It is
seen as infinite and boundless and impersonal. It is certainly not the
personal self of the man of the world. In the case of the various
teachings of Hinduism, self is equated with the Impersonal Spirit. The
self is usually referred to as the "atman," and the impersonal spirit as
the "Brahman." Mircea Eliade, in his comprehensive study of Indian
spiritual systems, writes about the Upanishads, one of the main
spiritual texts: "The great discovery of the Upanishads was, of course,
the systematic statement of the identity between the atman and the
Brahman." [Mircea Eliade, *Yoga, Immortality, and Freedom*, p. 114]

A common resolution of the contradiction between the perspective
of the man of the world and the man of spirit that many people com-
placently live with is that human beings are persons who can sometimes experience eternity, universality and impersonal spirit. These
people usually take the view that they are the ego which sometimes
surrenders to a larger or more universal reality. But according to the
teachers who say that the true reality is impersonal and devoid of any
hint of ego or personality, we *are* the impersonal and universal spirit
or Being, always and forever. Sometimes we take ourselves to be a
person or an ego, but this is a transitory mistake.

Some people accept these profound teachings as true, but, unable
to resolve this contradiction, continue to live a personal life, which
they believe is somehow false, in the hope of one day transcending it
into the universal impersonal realm. And some actually do transcend
the person and the personal life, or so they say.

This, however, does not resolve or eliminate the contradiction.
Living the impersonal life of universal truth is clearly possible, as has
been demonstrated by some of the above quoted teachers. But this
does not explain away the question of ego, the pursuit of personal
happiness and the belief in personal life. Transcending a situation is
not necessarily the same as resolving it.

16   We see that it is possible to live a transcendent, impersonal and universal life. But what does this mean about being a human being? What is a human life then, from this perspective? Is it just a way station, a meaningless gap full of suffering between our origin as the absolute reality and the final realization of the same reality? This is exactly the import of many of the teachings.

But what an absurdity to think that we come from an absolute reality of impersonal truth, live a personal human life of suffering, and then go back to the selfsame absolute reality.

Of course, in the state of absolute impersonal transcendence there is no concern and no question about the contradiction. The mind is silent. There is stupendous peace and wordless contentment. This is taken to be the answer by some teachers; there is no question, so no answer is needed. Still, this not a true resolution. A true resolution must satisfy all parts of the human being, including the mind. A state of impersonal peace and stillness is not the answer. Whenever the mind is there the question is there too. The answer, if there is one, must be at all levels, and must satisfy all parts of the human being, even his logic, if it is going to be a complete answer.

This is not to reject or devalue the truth of impersonality and universality. This truth remains the ultimate reality, the absolute nature of man and of all existence. Still, we are exploring human nature and human existence in order to understand human life in its true perspective. We put our inquiry so far in the form of a question: is it possible to understand ego and personality in a way that gives a meaning to the orientation of most of humankind, without contradicting the spiritual perspectives?

The perspective of most spiritual teachings is that ego is a falsehood, and hence it must die for there to be truth. We will show that this is true, but that it is not the whole truth. We will show that the ego, with its sense of self and personality, has a truth hidden within its nature, a truth that is not necessarily visible from the transcendent and impersonal state. We will show that ego is a reflection of a truth, an attempt to imitate an absolute and eternal reality. In fact, we will explore how ego is nothing but a failed or aborted attempt at a real development. We will show that ego is a reflection, an imperfect one indeed, but still a reflection of true reality, the reality of the true human being. We will see that by understanding ego, rather than transcending it, we can understand and actualize the reality of what it is to be a human being. Only through this understanding and realization can we see what human life is.

We will see that this truth that ego tries to emulate is what most people are seeking in their personal life, and that realizing this truth of what it is to be a human being is the aim of humanity.

Humanity is in a sense astray, but there is a pattern to this way of existence which, when understood, reveals the true nature of the human being. Only this understanding will heal the schism and resolve the contradiction. The true human being, what we will call the Personal Essence, is the resolution of the contradiction. It is the integration of both points of view.

From our point of view, the man of spirit has half the truth, and the man of the world has the other half, concealed behind a reflection that is taken to be the truth. In our exploration we will discuss some of the eternal truths, which are known in some of the spiritual traditions, and are not revealed, but instead kept as precious secrets, given only to those who genuinely seek.

However, we will sometimes use the modern language of psychology, and the findings of ego psychology and object relations theory, to convey these truths in a manner appropriate to our time.

The approach we are giving here can be seen as radical from the above points of view. The Personal Essence, which is the subject of this book, is neither "spiritual" nor "worldly." It is the true human being, the personal presence that is devoid of falsehood, without being impersonal.

This is not envisioned as possible by many spiritual teachings, although it is not the personality of ego. However, it is what makes the nature of ego and its concerns intelligible.

An important consequence of the understanding of the Personal Essence is a new perception of the life led by most people, the perception of a spiritual truth or an essential element in the heart of all ego strivings. This means that in fact most of humankind are not astray in the usual sense of the word, but are after something real and precious. The difficulty lies in the fact that they do not know how to find it.

The qualities of the Personal Essence are those of fullness, autonomy, competence, respect, dignity, integrity, excellence, maturity, harmony and completeness, among others. There is very little

18   knowledge and guidance in the modern world about how to develop
into such a true human being. The result is that most of us settle for
an imitation or an incomplete development, which is the personality
of ego.

Understanding that ego is a reflection, or an imitation, of a true
reality makes it possible to connect to this reality. One need not go the
usual spiritual route of abandoning one's personal life and the values of
that life, but rather one must look deeply into those values and explore
the true reality that they are approximating. Most people are not willing
to abandon their personal life for a spiritual quest, not merely because
of attachment to ego, but because they sense a truth in the values and
aspirations of personal life. For such people, the overwhelming
majority of humankind, understanding the reality underneath ego is a
more accessible means of spiritual development than the traditional
methods striving after impersonal reality. This is not only because in
this method they do not have to abandon their personal lives and aspirations, but also because this path reveals the deeper values and truths of
those aspirations and strivings toward actualization.

The path of the Personal Essence not only brings about the development of the real human being, but also opens an easier way to the
realization of the impersonal universal reality. The reason that realizing the life of the Personal Essence is a more accessible path for
human beings than the realization of the absolute universal reality is
that the ego is a reflection of the Personal Essence, and hence ego
can be used as a stepping stone towards it. The reason the realization
of the Personal Essence makes entrance into the universal and impersonal realms much easier is that these realms are part of the natural
and spontaneous development of the Personal Essence.

The Personal Essence allows us to see the meaning and the potential of a fulfilled human and personal life, a life of truth, love, dignity
and harmony, which includes the usual human concerns of work,
family, creativity, accomplishments and enjoyments of all kinds.

One of the few teachers who has seen this possibility and given
it its due importance is the Indian teacher and philosopher Sri
Aurobindo, who was not satisfied with his transcendent and impersonal states of enlightenment, and who worked towards the actualization of a liberated human life. Writing about Sri Aurobindo and his
work, one of his students says:

It is not enough for us to find our individual centre without 19
the totality of the world, or the totality of the world
without the individual, and yet less to find the supreme
Peace if it dissolves the world and the individual—"I do
not want to be sugar," exclaimed the great Ramakrishna, "I
want to eat sugar!" And without the individual what meaning would all the marvelous realizations have for us, for
we are no longer then. [Satprem, *Sri Aurobindo, or The
Adventure of Consciousness*, p. 177]

This book is an exploration of the Personal Essence—its nature, and
its relation to the ego and to the transcendent impersonal reality. Our
method is the realization and development of the Personal Essence
through the understanding of its reflection, ego. The presence of ego
points to the reality of the Personal Essence, just as the existence of
false gold indicates the existence of true gold.

Chapter Two

Being and Ego

In most spiritual traditions and work schools, ego has had a bad name, being characterized as the devil, the tempter, the spoiler. It is typically held as the barrier against enlightenment and realization. Ego is the center of the world of illusion and suffering, a stumbling block against the realization of truth and enlightenment. Various teachings have thoroughly explored the ways ego functions to resist and veil reality, although the different teachings have varying perspectives on and descriptions of those functions.

Some teachings see ego in terms of its activity, which is primarily desire for future pleasure. This desire for pleasure, which entails avoidance of pain, involves rejecting the present situation and hoping for a better one. The cycle of ego activity is thus rejection, hope and desire; it is based on memories of past experience, and is directed towards the future. Thus ego, which here is an activity which resists the present moment, is clearly antithetical to the perception of the nature of reality, which involves being in the moment. Ego then is seen as antithetical to Being, and therefore for Being, which is the Supreme Reality, to be perceived and lived, ego activity must cease.

Other perspectives see ego as the belief in a self or entity. The activity of ego is taken to be the activity of a person—an entity—who has desires and hopes. So here ego is seen as taking oneself to be a person, separate from the rest of the universe, who was born to a set of parents, who was a child, who grew up, in time, to his present status of an adult who has his hopes, desires and goals. The belief that this separate individuality is one's identity, one's self, is seen by some teachings as the main barrier to the ultimate reality, which is an impersonal and universal Being, or alternately the Void. Enlightenment then is the insight that one is not really this separate individual, a realization which is equivalent to the state of unqualified Being, or nonconceptual Reality.

Buddhism regards ego as a collection of tendencies, "skandhas," which are taken by the mind to have continuity in space and time. Ego is then analyzed in terms of its constituent elements to show that it does not exist in any real way, and meditation practices are designed to lead the student toward an experience of the ephemeral nature of ego. The venerable Chogyam Trungpa, discussing ego development, states:

> This development is illusory, the mistaken belief in a "self" or "ego." Confused mind is inclined to confuse itself as a solid, on-going thing, but it is only a collection of tendencies, events. In Buddhist terminology, this collection is referred to as the Five Skandhas or Heaps. [Chogyam Trungpa, *Cutting Through Spiritual Materialism*, p. 123]

Others, like the Sufis, see ego as a collection of primitive impulses and conditioned patterns which appear to the "unenlightened" as a cohesive entity with its own consciousness and volition. The ego or self in its ordinary state, before Sufi development, is referred to as the "commanding self." Idries Shah states that:

> The Commanding Self is the origin of the individual controlled by a composite consciousness, which is a mixture of hopes and fears, of training and imagination, of emotional and other factors, which make up the person in his or her "normal" state, as one would ordinarily call it. [Idries Shah, *A Perfumed Scorpion*, p. 83]

In many traditions, then, there is an understanding of ego as somehow false or illusory. However, given the fact that this "ego" is in fact the main realm of experience of the "man of the world," whose plight we are considering in relation to the relevance to him of spiritual truths, and also given our idea that the ego is a reflection of a deeper essential reality, perhaps this "false" phenomenon is worth investigating in some detail. Why do all human beings develop an ego, and what is the relationship of that ego to spiritual development? We can find some part of the answers to these questions in the field of modern psychology.

22   The spiritual traditions view ego as a product of past experience, of what is called the personal history of the individual. Buddhist tradition presents a detailed description of ego, but has little clear notion of its development. In the West it was Freud who began the systematic study of personality. He formulated his description of the structure of the personality, which he called the psychic structure, at the beginning of this century. He identified the ego, superego and id as the parts of the structure, and investigated the relationship between these units in his attempt to understand mental health and illness. However, he did little investigation of how this structure developed.

It remained to modern depth psychology, in particular ego psychology and object relations theory, to make the structure of the ego and its development the main focus of a whole scientific field, that of developmental psychology. Object relations theory has become the most widely accepted and consistent branch in this field dealing with ego structure and development.

In this book we will use many of the concepts developed in object relations theory, because it provides a detailed understanding of the development of ego. This is useful to our exploration of the respective realms of the man of spirit and the man of the world, in several respects: first, it makes very clear the status of ego as a mental structure, from a more scientific viewpoint than the simple claims of the man of spirit; second, it makes possible a method of exploration in which this mental status becomes increasingly clear to students, thus making the realm of Being more available to experience; third, it is extremely useful for understanding and overcoming obstacles to inner realization faced by those on spiritual paths; and finally, it supports a model of human development in which spiritual development, that is movement into the realms of Being, is seen as a normal part of human life rather than an alternative endeavor incompatible with personal life.

Object relations theory begins with the observation that the biological birth of the human infant is not the same as the psychological birth of the individual. A seminal text in this field is Margaret S. Mahler's *The Psychological Birth of the Human Infant*. This work arises from the observation that the newborn infant has no sense of being a person, and that this sense develops gradually in the first few years of life, as the infant interacts with its environment.

It is striking to note here how thoroughly each of us takes for granted, as obviously valid, the sense of being a separate, individual entity, even though it is not a given in our original state, but a development out of an original state of undifferentiation and lack of awareness of self or other. The stubbornness of that belief, and the reasons behind that stubbornness, will become increasingly apparent throughout this book.

Heinz Hartmann, considered by some the "father" of ego psychology, called the original state of the infant the "undifferentiated matrix." This matrix is taken to contain, in an undifferentiated and undeveloped form, the innate predispositions and capacities which will in time develop into the ego with its sense of separate individuality. Mahler, who studied this development by observing children in an experimental setting, called the process of ego development "separation-individuation":

> We refer to the psychological birth of the individual as the separation-individuation process: the establishment of a sense of separation from, and relation to, a world or reality, particularly with regard to the experiences of one's own body and to the principal representation of the world as the infant experiences it, the primary love object. Like any intrapsychic process, this one reverberates throughout the life cycle. It is never finished; it remains always active; new phases of the life cycle see new derivatives of the earliest processes still at work. But the principal psychological achievement of this process takes place in the period from about the fourth or fifth month to the thirtieth or thirty-sixth month, a period we refer to as the separation-individuation phase. [Margaret S. Mahler et al., *The Psychological Birth of the Human Infant*, p. 3]

Three points stand out in this statement:

1. There is no sense of a separate individual at the beginning of the life of the human being.
2. The psychological birth of the individual is a psychological achievement resulting from the separation-individuation process, in the first three years of life.
3. This development happens in the relationship to the mothering person, the primary love object; i.e., it is within the context of an object relation.

The outcome of the separation-individuation process is not consolidated until the fourth subphase of this process:

> From the point of view of the separation-individuation process, the main task of the fourth subphase is twofold: (1) the achievement of a definite, in certain aspects lifelong, individuality, and (2) the attainment of a certain degree of object constancy. [*Ibid.*, p. 109]

Object constancy means, among other things, the capacity to see the other, in this case the mothering person, as a separate person in her own right. Thus the child is experiencing himself as an autonomous person interacting with another autonomous person. Object relations theory has established that this achievement is the result of certain intrapsychic processes; i.e., it is the result of the building of certain psychic structures through a mental process. Mahler writes about the main processes and structures:

> The establishment of affective (emotional) object constancy (Hartmann, 1952) depends upon the gradual internalization of a constant, positively cathected, inner image of the mother. This, to begin with, permits the child to function separately (in familiar surroundings, for example in our toddler room) despite moderate degrees of tension (longing) and discomfort. Emotional object constancy will, of course, be based in the first place on the cognitive achievement of the permanent object, but all other aspects of the child's personality development participate in the evolution as well (see McDevitt, 1972). The last subphase (roughly the third year of life) is an extremely important intra-psychic developmental period, in the course of which a stable sense of entity (self boundaries) is attained. [*Ibid.*, pp. 109-110]

The sense of an individual self depends primarily on the establishment of a well-integrated self-image. The two primary inner structures established in the process of ego development are the self-image and the mother-image:

> In the fourth open-ended subphase, both inner structures—libidinal object constancy as well as a unified self-image based on true ego identifications—should have their inception. [*Ibid.*, p. 118]

Thus the achievements of a separate individuality and of object constancy are the consciously experienced manifestations of the inner development of the self-image and an internalized image of the mother. In fact these achievements are the same thing as the development of the inner images. This is an important point for our study in this book, so we emphasize it. The achievement of a separate individuality depends on two conditions:

1. *The establishment of a cohesive self-image.* In fact, the sense of being an individual is nothing but taking oneself to be this self-image. In other words, the individual is a mental structure, a construct in the mind. Before this construct is developed, according to object relations theory, there is no sense of being a person.

2. *The internalization of a positively regarded image of the mother (the "good mother").* The individual, that is the self-image, is supported psychically by the presence of the mother's image; thus the child does not feel alone when physically separate from the mother. He feels supported by the presence of the mother's image, which gives him the sense of security which allows him to be away from her, and makes it safer to regard her as an autonomous person.

These formulations of object relations theory are significant for our study in that they contradict the common belief that being a separate individual is an incontrovertible fact of life. Most of us believe that we are already persons when we are born, small and dependent at the beginning, maturing and becoming more independent as we grow up. The above discussion shows that this is not the case, but that the sense of being an entity, of being a person, is a developmental achievement. In fact mental pathology is increasingly being seen as the disruption or distortion of this development. Mahler states:

> The principal condition for mental health so far as pre-oedipal development is concerned, hinges on the attained and continuing ability of the child to retain or restore his self-esteem in the context of relative libidinal object constancy. [*Ibid.*, p. 118]

In this book we will investigate the tremendous implications of the fact that the sense of being an individual is not only a developmental achievement, but is a feeling that results from identifying with a certain structure in the mind, the self-image. That is, to take oneself to be a person, separate from others, with one's own volition, is simply to identify with this construct in the mind. This self-image, this psychic structure, is nothing simple or superficial. It is complex and profound, and the identification with it is just as profound. For our purposes,

26   however, it is crucial to remember that regardless of how completely the self-image has become part and parcel of one's sense of self, it is nevertheless simply a construct in the mind.

Isn't this perception, that the experience of being an individual person is the feeling of identifying with a self-image, exactly what the various spiritual teachings have stressed throughout the ages? We discussed above the teachings which state that the separate individual does not exist, that it is only an illusion. They have observed that the separate individual is a construction in the mind, that is, it is only thoughts. And although object relations theory makes exactly the same observation, it is interpreted very differently. From this point of view the self-image is (or at least determines) who we are, and that is that. The individual is an intrapsychic development which determines and structures our minds, our perception and our world, and that is how we experience ourselves, period.

Otto Kernberg, one of the main contemporary theorists of object relations theory, uses the term "ego identity" to refer to the concept of the self plus the world that it relates to. He states that the world the ego perceives is a "representational world," which is not exactly the real world, and that it is constructed, just like the ego, by the integration of mental representations (images) of objects:

> It has to be stressed, however, that this internal world of object representations as seen in conscious, preconscious, and unconscious fantasies never reproduces the actual world of real people with whom the individual has established relationships in the past and in the present; it is at most an approximation, always strongly influenced by the very early object-images of introjections and identifications. [Otto F. Kernberg, *Object Relations Theory and Clinical Psychoanalysis*, p. 33]

The general attitude of psychologists is to accept this ultimate lack of objectivity of the ego's perception as inevitable, although of course much of psychotherapy consists of a learning process in the patient which results in a more "realistic" perception of himself and his world. The spiritual teachings, however, claim that it is not necessary to let the ego's identification define ourselves, but that we can know ourselves more directly, in a much more real way. They claim in fact that identification with the construct of the self-image in the mind cuts us off from our true nature and from seeing the true nature of reality.

We must understand that developmental psychology has not been concerned with whether human beings have a more real nature, a nature beyond the mind. The spiritual teachings, on the other hand, are concerned with human nature beyond ideas, images or concepts in the mind. For them, a mental construct such as the self-image is fundamentally nonexistent, is illusory. For them, the fact that the mind contains a concept of a person does not mean that there is truly a person, any more than the concept of an apple is an apple. If we take the mental construct away, there is no separate individual; these teachings say that when the mind is still, then we see that there is no such thing as a separate individual.

Enlightenment does not involve simply the perception that the person is only a concept. It means that all conceptualization is ended, all images and representations in the mind, whether conscious, preconscious or unconscious, are eliminated, or at least not identified with. When this profound stillness of the mind is achieved, it is asserted, true reality is perceived, not by an entity which is a separate individual. The experience is one of unqualified Being, wordless existence, infinite and eternal.

The claim of these teachings is that while the individual has no true existence because it is an idea in the mind, Being is a true existence; it is what is actually there, whether we are aware of it or not. And it is this existence, this presence of Being, independent of any inner image, that is what we are.

We are not using the term "being" in its everyday sense. Usually, "being" means mere existence, and that "existence" is, like everything else, experienced conceptually. The spiritual traditions, on the other hand, use this term to refer to the actual presence of true nature which can be directly experienced. We are using the term in this latter sense. As human beings we are presence, we are being, we are actuality; we are not simply mental constructs.

The sense of oneself as a separate individual, which as we have seen depends upon the development of a cohesive self-image, can be seen as composed of memories, and in fact cannot exist without its connection to memories, to personal history. But the memory of a person is not the same as a person. The memory is of something that supposedly existed at some point in the past. This is another reason traditional teachings say that the individual or ego does not exist. A

28   memory exists as an idea, but not as a presence independent of the
mind. In other words, the separate individual has no beingness, no
substance and no true existence. Our true nature is an existence
which is not based on memory or on time at all. Being is eternal and
timeless. We are not referring here to what people call "being in the
present," but are pointing out that we are timeless presence, that our
nature is not time bound, as ego is. "Timeless" means that the sense
of time is irrelevant to our true nature. "Eternal" means that there is
no sense of memory or future in it. There is no concept of time, so
there is no sense of present time. When the mind is still, there is just
presence, just Being, unqualified by ideas or concepts of time or individuality. Thus when we cease to construct entities in the mind, we
see that the ego does not exist. We then simply are.

So, to believe that we are the separate individuality is to take ourselves to be something that does not truly exist, and to fail to see who
we are, to fail to realize our true essence. No wonder, then, that we
are dissatisfied and suffering, just as the Buddha observed.

We can note here that this suffering is not a problem that can be
solved therapeutically; it is not a matter of emotional conflict.
Psychologists and psychotherapists deal usefully with human suffering
by working on the conflicts of the personality, but from the perspective of spiritual teachings this approach clearly cannot deal with the
basic problem, the root of all emotional conflicts.

When the Buddha said that life is suffering, he did not mean only
neurotic suffering. He was referring to the more fundamental understanding that there is bound to be suffering in the life of the ego, because one is not seeing reality correctly; one is taking oneself to be
something that actually does not exist. It is a problem of mistaken
identity.

This perspective of the man of spirit, which contrasts ego with Being
and sees the latter as fundamentally real and the former as illusory, is incomprehensible from the perspective of ego, which cannot conceive of
experience that is not related to a separate individuality. For ego, each
experience is personal, related to oneself. The man of the world will
understandably ask: "How can there be experience if I am not there?"

The fact is that the experience of impersonal universality, the
boundless presence with no hint of personality, the unfathomable
Void, are not the only ways to experience Being, our true essence and

existence. Most teachers who have this perspective of absolute Being talk as if one can experience either the separate individuality of ego or the universal impersonality of the ultimate nonconceptual reality. But this view neglects the richness of the human essence and the ever-abundant realm of Being, and thus fails to communicate to the man of the world, who feels misunderstood and cannot see the truth or even relevance of the spiritual viewpoint.

To make matters worse, the man of the world might then hear the man of spirit speak of the fact that from the perspective of unfathomable nonconceptual reality, there is no such thing as a person or personal life, and furthermore there is no such thing as a body, or humanity, or life, or a world, or anything like that. From the perspective of the ultimate reality there is only absolute oneness, not single, without any differentiation or discrimination. Every thing, all objects, all occurrences, are merely concepts, not truly existent. At this point the man of the world might well dismiss this view as utter nonsense.

This book, however, will develop an understanding which shows that the two perspectives are not actually incompatible, and which further shows how they are related. Clearly, looking at things simply from the spiritual perspective does not do justice to the question of human living. The perception that life itself is a conceptual occurrence, which might be ultimately true, does not help us much to understand what human life is all about.

As we will see at the end of this book, this perception is needed, ultimately, for a true human life. The absolute reality of which we have been speaking is the source of the human being, and the spring of all life. But human life is lived in the manifest world, with all its differentiations, colors and richness. To truly understand human life is to know the nonconceptual reality and still live a personal life of love, work and knowledge. It is to know directly that we are the unfathomable reality, that all differentiations are conceptual, and still live in this differentiated world, appreciating its richness, variety and beauty. For human life to be complete and balanced, it must consist of the harmony of all dimensions of reality, from the ultimate nonconceptual source to the various dimensions of manifest existence. It must integrate in a harmonious whole the universe of the man of spirit and the universe of the man of the world. Otherwise there is either no life or a fake life.

30   A certain understanding will unfold in this book, which here we
state in summary: In several different traditional systems and
philosophies, human beings, along with the rest of creation, are seen
to "come out of" or to be manifestations of "higher" realms of Being.
In the actual experience of these realms there is not any sense of
"higher," but there are definite perceptions of the phenomenal realm
arising from something that can be called "nonphenomenal." And this
coming out is not a random appearance of the various physical, organic and mental phenomena, discontinuous with the other realms,
but rather more a structured "unfolding." There is a pattern to this unfolding, and it reflects the structuring of Being on the level that is
called in some traditions the Divine Names, and in others qualities of
Essence; in Tantric Buddhism as well as in Taoism there is an appreciation of this structuring of the qualities of creation, and in certain
Indian traditions this also may be found. In his book on Sufism and
Taoism, T. Izutsu states:

> The Perfect Man is the one whom the Absolute penetrates
> and whose faculties and bodily members are all perme-
> ated by the Absolute in such a way that he thereby mani-
> fests all the Perfections of the Divine Attributes and Names.
> [T. Izutsu, *Sufism and Taoism*, p. 232]

In the West it was Plato who spoke of this level of being, referring
to "Platonic forms," as what we might think of as abstract "blueprints"
for what is created in the phenomenal realm. Some traditions call this
"permanent archetypes." In this book we will sometimes use the
language most common in the Sufi tradition, speaking of the different
qualities of Essence (although much of the language is also unique to
our work). This is partly because the Sufi tradition has worked most
closely with the personal level of the essential aspects, identifying the
manifestations of them in the person, even locating the centers of the
different aspects in certain places in the body. (Tantric Buddhism and
some aspects of Taoism, and probably others, also work on this
level.) Our experience with many students over the years has shown
that this model, used in conjunction with more Western ways of
modelling human reality, is extremely useful for guiding students
toward realms of experience beyond ego, since at the level the Sufis
call the "latifa," the essential aspects manifest to some extent in all
human beings. Most people certainly don't experience this level as

such, being identified with the mental, emotional and physical content of experience, but it is relatively easy to learn to perceive this realm. In conjunction with learning to perceive one's ego from the "outside," so to speak, this level of experience can lead one directly to the more profound levels of Being. In addition, the essential aspects as we describe them in this book are closely related to normally experienced human qualities, such as love, will, compassion, strength and peace, and in fact the ego individuality itself is a reflection of the Personal Essence. Thus our choice of this language for our teaching is designed to make these qualities more comprehensible and accessible. (Our understanding of the essential aspects is discussed in much more detail in two other books by the author: *Essence—The Diamond Approach to Inner Realization* (Samuel Weiser, 1986) and *The Diamond Heart—Book One: Elements of the Real in Man* (Diamond Books, 1987).)

Although as we will show in some detail in this book, an identification with ego is incompatible with the complete experience of Being, and thus the apparent dichotomy between the reality of the man of spirit and the experience of the man of the world has a very real basis, it is also true that it is possible for human beings, even in the process of moving towards identification with ego as children, to be open to the realm of Essence. In fact, the arising of the different aspects of Essence is part and parcel of normal human development. Our understanding of how essence arises in children and then is put aside in favor of ego identifications is a new and rather surprising set of observations, which at first glance fits neither into the object relations understanding of human development nor into the world of impersonal being.

Human beings are born into the realm of Being, and from the beginning manifest the true differentiated aspects of Being. This Being is never totally lost, and actually manifests in the child in predictable and supportable ways. It is true that awareness of this Being is lost in the process of the structuring of and identification with ego, but by understanding in detail this structuring, and the patterns of identification, we can actually remember in detail the process of our "forgetting." We can remember, understand and undo this forgetting, retrieving what has been suppressed and opening the way for growing into true maturity and realization.

32   Thus it is possible to experience egoless beingness, to be, as a substantial presence that is not a mental construct, and still live a human, personal life, in which love, work, knowledge, creativity and accomplishment make sense, a human sense.

This true existence, this presence, this being beyond time that makes sense of human and personal life, is the Personal Essence. It is the reality of which ego is only a reflection. It is the truly integrated and developed human being. This is the beautiful presence that the traditional literature of work schools calls the "pearl beyond price."

The experience of universal impersonality of ultimate reality occurs when the separate individuality is transcended, when the separate individuality is seen not to be our true self. But this is the result of transcending the personality in its totality. Something different happens when we investigate the personality's manifestations in more detail, exploring the hidden essential truth within it.

The ego is a reflection of this true element of Being, the Personal Essence, and exploring the characteristics of the reflection can lead us to the reality being reflected. By isolating and understanding the elements of the false, we can begin to approach the elements of the real.

PART II

THE DISCOVERY
OF THE
PERSONAL ESSENCE

I n this section we will begin our exploration of the Personal
Essence through reports and discussions of material from
students who have been involved in a process of self-discovery
and inner transformation. Since we will be using these accounts throughout the book, here we will note briefly the context in which they arise. Many of these students are involved in an
ongoing set of practices, including meditation; they see the author or
other teachers for private interviews in which Reichian breathing and
analytic work is often used, and belong to a group of students meeting regularly and working with the author on issues having to do with
their process. Some students have been working for a number of
years and have dealt very deeply with issues involving many aspects
of the ego identity; some reports are from relative beginners who are
experiencing certain things for the first time.

In most of these reports, then, the student has written a description
of his work with the author in a group setting. The material that arises

34 is always part of a much larger process going on with the students, and often represents the culmination of months or even years of exploring certain areas. The accounts are similar to what are called clinical vignettes in psychological literature, but it is important to remember that the work reported is part of a process which is not primarily therapeutic, but rather has to do with self-discovery and inner transformation.

The work that is being done in the group setting is primarily verbal, directing the attention of the student to his feelings, thoughts, body sensations and more subtle states. Sometimes emotional catharsis of one sort or another occurs as the conflicts that are blocking the student's experience of himself are brought to consciousness. Unconscious material arises and is investigated, and this generally allows an expansion, or spaciousness, in the student which in turn allows the more subtle qualities to manifest. The fundamental attitude which governs how we work with students is what we call "allowing." That is, the teacher refrains from judgment and pushing the student, instead using skillful questioning and compassionate presence to allow the student to investigate what is happening. Also the student is encouraged to experience his emotions, thoughts, sensations and conflicts without rejecting them, but rather gently investigating them. When this attitude of allowing is learned, the student can then confront amazingly deep and terrifying material. And the process of learning this "allowing" attitude is in itself a loosening of the ego's constraints, since as we have discussed, it is in the nature of ego to reject present reality and focus on its fears or desires.

The case histories we will be presenting should be understood to be occurring, then, in a very much larger context than is clear from the description of one working session. Many of the students have been working for years, integrating their understanding and essential development into their lives, and working through issues at various levels. The experiences of the Personal Essence and other aspects of Being which are reported, as well as the experiences of extremely deep defenses and perceptions of the ego states, are the result of long and difficult work. Once these experiences begin, the student must deal with the consequences of the process of his transformation over and over in his life, learning from his experience as new defenses and illusions are uncovered by his process of realization. Sometimes these cases will seem from the reports as if some "magical" process is taking place, both in terms of what the student is able to experience and also the apparent ease of the resolution of his conflict. Our noting the following facts will make these reports more comprehensible:

- As we have stated, the sessions we report, in order to illustrate certain facts about the process of inner realization and certain connections between aspects of Being and ego issues, are often culminations of months or even years of work.

- Although the sessions reported might be culminations of work in one sense, they are always also beginnings of a new level of integration and exploration. When a new essential aspect is experienced, for instance, the student will face all the defenses in his mind and in the situations of his external life which have denied the absence of, or faked the presence of, this aspect. Also, the process of the work, which in our perspective we call the Diamond Approach, consists of many interdependent facets which sort themselves out both in the psychological and essential processes the student undergoes as well as in his "external" life.

- The experiences of Being and subtle perceptions of one's state are much more accessible than it would seem in just reading the cases. Even beginning students often learn quickly to perceive and appreciate their subtler states, as well as to become more clear about what is happening on the physical and emotional levels.

Another factor in the ongoing process of realization is the resistance to the process, caused by many kinds of fears and illusions. Students must learn to experience their fears and attachments without acting them out in their lives; for instance, if a student is working on a level which involves a greater sense of autonomy and is feeling a desire for essential autonomy, he might suddenly decide that he should divorce his wife or quit his job; these inclinations must be explored and objectively understood if the student is to find the real autonomy he desires rather than acting out his desire on an inappropriate level. So we will see in many of the case histories references to issues that are coming up in the life of the student, which are then connected with the issues which are surfacing in the work itself. This reflects the understanding that the life of ego is a reflection of the deeper life of the essential Being, and allows for an elegant, grounded and personally compassionate way of transforming the personality.

36   This is only a sketch of the context of the Diamond Approach work, which involves a whole complex of psychological and essential factors; it should, however, suffice for putting the case histories in context. With this understanding of context established, we can proceed to our exploration of the nature of the Personal Essence.

The Personal Essence has four primary characteristics: autonomy, beingness, personalness and contact. Investigating these characteristics will allow us to contrast the Personal Essence with the personality of the ego and also with the impersonal essence or Being. In the process of essential development, exploring these four characteristics can precipitate the experience of personal Being. As our case histories will show (and as is discussed at length in our book *The Void*), these characteristics usually announce themselves to one's consciousness through an acute feeling of their absence or lack in one's sense of self or in one's personal life. By following the thread of the quality that one feels is missing, given the right circumstances and the right guidance, one comes to experience the missing element, and then to recognize it as a characteristic of one's sense of Being.

Encountering this experience of personal Being, we have a precious, peaceful sense of self-recognition, sometimes of "coming home." However, the experience is not generally permanent, and students usually must repeatedly experience this sense of Being, each time exploring a different characteristic, until the sense of Being is a permanent attainment. The work involved in this process will be discussed in later chapters; here we focus on the discovery and initial experiences of the Personal Essence.

We will investigate, then, one at a time, the qualities of autonomy, beingness, personalness and contact, as manifest in experiences of the Personal Essence.

Chapter Three

Autonomy

S andy is a married woman in her thirties who has been working with the author in a group situation. Her explicit reason for being in the group is to understand herself, to grow, and to learn to be more herself. She was sick for some time, and has been back in the group for only a couple of months. She begins speaking, obviously with some guilt about what she is feeling. She relates hesitatingly that she almost did not come to the group meeting this particular evening, and has been feeling increasingly unwilling to come to the sessions. When I inquire whether she knows the reasons behind her feelings she says that because she was sick for a long time and did not have fun, now she feels she would rather go out and have fun rather than sitting in group sessions and scrutinizing herself. When I ask what she means by having fun, she grins and says it is doing what she wants to do, and relates that she resents coming to the group because she must abide by a certain schedule and accommodate herself to a structure imposed on her from the outside. So in the group sessions she has been feeling frustrated, hemmed in and resentful.

I indicate that I agree that it is good for her to have fun and enjoy herself, and that I understand how her illness has curtailed her life. I then inquire about why she feels imposed upon and restricted by coming to the group, when it is her choice to be in the group and benefit from the work done in it. She responds by affirming that it is her choice, that she understands the benefits of

37

38   participating in the group, and that she does not understand why she feels so frustrated.

As we inquire further into her emotional states, she sees that she feels she is losing something by adhering to a certain structure and schedule: she feels she loses her freedom, and this makes her feel frustrated. She relates then that this pattern is not new for her. She has had the same conflict in almost every job she has had, and actually lost some jobs because of it. Even jobs she has liked, she could not completely enjoy because of this conflict. So she leaves what she is doing, even though it is useful to her, in order to avoid feeling this overwhelming sense of frustration and heaviness.

We see here that Sandy is recognizing the present situation as part of a pattern that she has repeated many times in her life, which has brought her much discontent and frustration. As she becomes aware that her reactions to the group structure are repeating this pattern, she becomes more motivated to explore her state. As she continues, she tells me that she knows that this pattern has to do with her relationship to her mother, that she always felt restricted by her, not allowed to live her life as she wants. But she is frustrated, she says, because she has seen this pattern many times, and has understood its genesis for a long time, but there has been no change.

I point out to her that it seems she does not know how to have the freedom she wants except by saying "no" to a situation she feels is restricting. It becomes clear to her that she believes that freedom is gained only by doing what she chooses to do, and many times this means not doing what others want her to do. I point out to her that "freedom" acquired in this way is nothing but a reaction to the situation, and that a reaction is not a free choice, since it is determined by the other and is not a spontaneous response. It is simply a compulsive, automatic reaction.

Here she admits that she does not usually enjoy the freedom she believes she is gaining, but continues feeling frustrated, and, in addition, leaves activities and situations that are actually useful to her. She acknowledges also that even when she believes she is gaining autonomy by removing herself from some situation, she still feels the lack of the true freedom she wants.

At this point I ask her what it is exactly that she wants to experience by having her freedom. She says she just wants to be herself, to be free to be herself. She believes that if she does what she chooses, she will be herself as herself, the way she really is, and not the way others want her to be.

I ask her to tell me more specifically what it means to be herself. In her past work she had often felt that "I don't know what I want," and now she realizes that she has never looked at the situation from the perspective of what it really means to her to be herself. She was wanting something, which she somewhat vaguely associated with autonomy. Now she finds it hard to describe more specifically what she means, and the very asking of the question puts her into deeper contact with herself. Here, I ask what she is feeling now. She says she is much less frustrated, and that she feels okay. I ask her what kind of okay, what does she really feel in her body? She says she feels calm and peaceful, and the issue of autonomy no longer feels significant.

I express surprise that she feels so peaceful, and not concerned about what was such a bothersome issue. I ask her to tell me more about the calm feeling. She says she feels the calmness especially in her belly, and that the calmness also feels strong. The strength somewhat surprises her, because when she was sick she was feeling mostly weak. I keep asking her to pay more attention to the calmness, to describe it more specifically. She feels the strength and calmness growing in her, filling her chest.

I ask her what she means by the feeling filling her. Here she realizes she is not only feeling an emotional state, but that the calmness and strength are effects of a sense of fullness in her body, which was in her belly but now increasingly pervades her body. The more she senses this fullness, the more it expands. The effect is that she feels a fullness of presence that is calm, peaceful, and collected. This makes her happy and contented.

I ask her to recall her desire for autonomy and freedom. Here, she realizes that now she feels she is being herself. The presence of the calm fullness makes her feel present as herself. The more the fullness, strength and calmness expand, the more she feels present, present as herself. She experiences herself as a being, a presence, a fullness. She is not an action or a reaction. She is not a feeling or a thought or an image, but a firm, strong, full and exquisitely alive presence.

Sandy had been taking autonomy to mean engaging only in activities of her choice, but acting out this belief failed to give her the

40   autonomy which she wanted and felt she lacked. The actions or reactions that she thought would give her freedom and personal autonomy served only to temporarily cover up the sense of lack. Her work in this session allowed her to see the futility of her habitual attempts to cover up the lack of autonomy, and by allowing herself to feel the lack instead of running away from it, she was able to see more clearly what it was she really wanted, the sense of being herself which she thought autonomy would bring. This understanding precipitated the sought-after state of autonomy, which turned out to be simply the presence of who she is, the fullness of her Personal Essence. Autonomy, it became clear, is simply the freedom to be. When there is personal presence of Being, then there is autonomy.

We should note here that an important factor in the ease with which she arrived at the experience of the Personal Essence has to do with the fact that the teacher's state of Being, which responds to her need, will support her by manifesting in the state she feels is lacking. We will discuss this point later.

However, as we have just seen in Sandy's initial attitudes, autonomy is rarely understood in terms of Being. In Western culture (especially in the United States) independence and autonomy are generally understood to mean being able to "do one's own thing." This means, usually, to be successful, to have made it, to be self-reliant physically, psychologically, socially and, most important, financially. In terms of development, autonomy means to be able to live independently from one's parents, to support oneself financially, to not be dependent on anyone. These are clearly all signs of autonomy on the ego level of development, but hardly constitute autonomy on the level of Being.

Independence, autonomy, making it on one's own, are strong ideals in the United States, but these qualities are also coveted in most human societies. Autonomy is one of the great hallmarks of a strong ego; the stronger the ego, the more independent is its individuality. Autonomy is considered a manifestation of mature human development. Object relations theory sees autonomy as an expression of individuation, of achieving a separate individuality and a sense of self. In fact, individuation is seen as the result of—or even equivalent to—psychical independence and autonomy. Mahler takes autonomy to be the aim of the separation-individuation process, which arises in the second subphase, the practicing period, and becomes more of an intrapsychic reality in the fourth subphase of the process. Writing about this intra-psychic accomplishment of individuality, she states: "We see a lot of active resistance to the demands of adults, a great need and a wish (often still unrealistic) for autonomy (independence)." [Margaret S. Mahler et al., *The Psychological Birth of the Human Infant*, p. 116]

As we discussed in Chapter Two, the accomplishment of separation-individuation is understood to be the acquiring of independence from the mothering person in the process of forming a stable self-image and sense of self. Its final outcome is indeed the achievement of individuality, the capacity to be a person in one's own right and to function autonomously. Thus, in terms of ego development, acquiring autonomy is the same as the achievement of the intrapsychic task of the separation-individuation process, the attainment of identity, separateness and individuality. We can see then that society's idealization of autonomy points to the deeper significance of the desire of the man of the world for autonomy: it means to him becoming "his own person." It means individuation, growth and maturity. Independence and autonomy within society, "making it," achieving the capacity to support oneself and one's family, the ability to make free choices about one's life, are the adult's expression of individuation, signs of the maturity of his ego development, and the fruition of the solidification of his individuality.

The findings of object relations theory, however, show that these phenomena which are taken by society to indicate autonomy may only be skin deep. These findings identified a more basic level of autonomy, that of emotional independence, as the core of actual autonomy. Thus some individuals who may appear autonomous, because they are successful, productive people, may lack the intrapsychic achievement of independence and therefore lack a true inner core of autonomy. In these cases, it is well known, the individual lives a life of emptiness and emotional desolation. This situation of apparent autonomy without its real emotional support is regarded as characteristic of certain character pathologies, especially those of the narcissistic personality and the borderline conditions, and sometimes even the schizoid character. These personalities have not accomplished the tasks of the separation-individuation process, and thus the sense of self is not formed cohesively. It is fragile and vulnerable, very dependent on external achievements and praise, and largely defensive.

42   Object relations theory might say that Sandy's conflict in our presentation above is a manifestation either of incomplete individuation or of some conflicts about it. While this is a good general diagnosis, it fails to explain the final result in the work session. Sandy finally saw that autonomy means being who she is, experiencing a full, strong presence of Being. She did not end up feeling an emotional sense of autonomy, nor did she gain a clearer concept or image of herself. According to object relations theory, Sandy will be autonomous when she finally has a separate individuality and a stable sense of self, which allow her to pursue and enjoy her endeavors with minimal frustration. As we have seen, this would involve her establishing a well-rounded, secure self-image and also object constancy. While we agree that these developments may give her a sense of emotional autonomy, we note that the final outcome in the session involves a far deeper level of autonomy than that dealt with by object relations theory. In fact, it raises the question of whether ego autonomy is autonomy at all.

Here we return to our dialogue between the man of the world and the man of spirit. In developmental psychology, emotional independence and ego autonomy are seen as the culmination of ego development. While this perspective explains one of the deepest aspirations of the man of the world, the desire for autonomy, it does not take into consideration the values of the man of spirit, and the deepest insights of man's most profound teaching. Object relations theory, at least as it is understood in the United States, does not take Being into consideration, but rather takes the self-image as the core of human realization. And as we saw in Chapter Two, from the perspective of the man of spirit, the self-image is not real, it is only a conceptual construct. Thus the accomplishment of the tasks of separation-individuation, however necessary, cannot be the acme of human realization, since it is based on an illusory identification. Of course in object relations theory much more than establishing the self-image is involved in ego development; it involves an integration of the various developmental achievements and the various so-called ego functions such as perception, memory, thinking, synthesis, defense and so on. But the basic "accomplishment" is experiencing oneself as a separate individual, based on a self-image composed of memories. From the perspective of the man of spirit, however, one is actually a Being independent from mind, existing outside the field of memory. From this perspective, the accomplishment of ego autonomy is ultimately a prison. In identifying with the self-image constructed through the process of ego development, we cage ourselves. How can this be autonomy, this bondage which is the primary source of human suffering?

Only when developmental psychology takes into consideration the fact that the nature of man is Being will a true understanding of autonomy emerge. Again we note that its perspective is not incorrect, only limited. (A similar limitation is seen sometimes on the side of the man of spirit. Some people actually seek out the impersonal levels of Being in order to avoid dealing with the issues of autonomy which must be faced in ordinary ego development as well as in the development of the Personal Essence.)

When one does have the experience of ceasing to identify with the self-image and simply being, it is clear that the autonomy of ego is a sham, since the ego personality is perceived not only as ephemeral, a kind of surface phenomenon which is in the nature of an idea, but also as reactive, responding automatically to the world. From Being, which is felt as the true and solid reality, ego's individuality is seen as simply a dark network composed of beliefs in the mind and patterns of tension in the body.

Thus the supposed autonomy of ego is, from this perspective, nothing but the feeling that accompanies an image in its relation to another image. It is striking that this is exactly what object relations theory states: that autonomy is based on the establishment of a self-image. We wonder how one can know that what he believes he is, is simply an image, and stop at that, without feeling that something is not right?

The answer, of course, is that as long as one identifies with the self-image, the implications of the theory are not suspected, or if they are suspected they cannot be clearly seen without an experience of Being. One must go through a very deep process of inner transformation to see the profound implications of this apparently simple understanding of ego identity. Another reason most people cognizant of object relations theory do not see its deeper, shocking implications is the fact that they are usually focused on mental disorders, and that normality and health are generally viewed in relation to pathology. Since the pathologies are in general ultimately due to the absence of

44   complete ego autonomy, ego autonomy has come to represent health or normality.

We can see here, however, that object relations theory does, by its very defining of ego as mental structure and image which achieve some sort of autonomy, point to some other reality which is *not* image. We believe that object relations theory will in fact some day expand to include consideration of Being; this has already been hinted at in the work of D.W. Winnicott and Harry Guntrip. Winnicott, a British psycho-analyst, relates Being to the inherited potential of the human infant in his discussion of the infant in his human environment:

> In this place which is characterized by the essential exis-tence of a holding environment, the "inherited potential" is becoming itself a "continuity of being." The alternative to being is reacting, and reacting interrupts being and an-nihilates. Being and annihilation are the two alternatives. [D. W. Winnicott, *The Maturational Processes and the Faci-litating Environment*, p. 47]

Clearly, Winnicott holds Being as central for human development, and is quite definite that Being is the opposite of reacting. As we will elaborate later this accords with our point of view. It is unfortunate that many of the concepts of this eminent psychologist have been incor-porated into the mainstream of object relations theory, while his em-phasis on Being has been completely ignored. We know of only one exception, Guntrip, who saw its implications, and included it in his theory and practice. He writes clearly about the importance of Being:

> An absence, non-realization or dissociation of the experi-ence of "being," and of the possibility of it, and along with that, incapacity for healthy natural spontaneous "doing" is the most radical clinical phenomenon in analysis. [Harry Guntrip, *Schizoid Phenomena, Object Relations and the Self*, p. 254]

He writes further about the importance of the experience of Being for all human development:

> The experience of "being" is the beginning and basis for the realization of the potentialities in our raw human nature for developing as a "person" in personal relation-ships. [*Ibid.*, p. 254]

Although they made Being a central concept in their theories, Winnicott and Guntrip did not pursue the implications of the contrast between Being and ego, nor did they conduct a direct exploration of Being itself. The concept of Being is, of course, present in other psychologies, such as existential psychology; however, we do not discuss them here because our approach is quite different, and in particular because our approach is psychodynamic, while these psychologies are generally not.

In our work on the realization of Being, we have found a consistent pattern that dealing with the issue of autonomy always leads to the experience of the Personal Essence. This is true for all students who have undergone an appreciable segment of the process. The case of Sandy above was a good example of this pattern. In work based only on object relations theory, the guide or therapist might work on the issues around autonomy, the feelings involved, the life situations affected, and perhaps then deal with the genesis of these in terms of the patient's relations with the primary love objects in early childhood. The focus there is on supporting the ego structure so that the individuality will gain more autonomy. Gertrude and Rubin Blanck, for instance, consider the function of the psychotherapist to be, in part, the guardianship of autonomy:

> By guardianship we mean that, even at the point when the patient telephones for his first appointment, the therapist has in mind that this person is to be helped to leave in a state of independence some day. That he is not independent at the outset is one of the factors that brings him into therapy. That he becomes dependent upon the therapist need not be feared. That he grows increasingly independent as therapy proceeds is the result of the therapist's professional use of himself to promote growth. [Gertrude and Rubin Blanck, *Ego Psychology*, p. 357]

In our work on self-realization, we do much the same thing, but rather than looking only at the cognitive and emotional aspects of the situation, we focus on the actual existential presence or absence of the state of autonomy. We consistently find that when the student experiences a state of autonomy, it is related to a sense of Being that arises just at that moment. The student then experiences a palpable presence, a state of fullness, strength, and wholeness, which makes him feel autonomous and authentically himself. The presence of fullness is usually identified as who one is, as opposed to identification with an image or emotional state.

46   From this we see that true autonomy is simply the capacity to be the Personal Essence, one's fullness of Being. The sense of freedom, independence, autonomy and individuation is experienced at such times as a very clear, precise and certain fact. There is no vagueness or uncertainty about autonomy when one recognizes the Personal Essence as one's true being.

The issue of continuing to do the work in the group, as opposed to going off on one's own, frequently arises when this issue of autonomy develops in the student's process. As we have noted, the essential states which are coming up in the student's development usually manifest at first as a sense of their absence. The student will then tend to resort to his habitual ways of dealing with the lack, which in the case of autonomy might be asserting his independence, which will often involve acting out or at least strongly desiring to act out by leaving the group or leaving some other situation. In the case of Sandy it manifested as conflicts about being in the group.

Dealing with this issue requires careful perception on the part of the teacher, who must see the situation for what it is in order to deal properly with the student's desire for autonomy and thus allow him to experience the Personal Essence. There is always some negative behavior or attitude on the part of the student, similar to the behaviors Mahler observed in the subphases of practicing and rapprochement. Even when the teacher understands the situation, the student might still terminate the process before completion, surrendering to the lure of "autonomy."

When this process is broken off prematurely, the individual goes off, doing things in his life which he believes are autonomous, while in reality he is only covering up a big hole, a state of deficiency which is the absence of the Personal Essence. Even when the student has experienced this state, he might terminate prematurely if he has not fully recognized the Personal Essence for what it is, or not fully dealt with the areas of lack connected with this aspect, which are many and deep. Thus the student might experience the Personal Essence but not recognize or accept it as his true being, but rather take it to be an effect of some physiological or psychological state.

This usually indicates the presence of strong defenses against real autonomy. One such case is a business woman who did private work with the author for about a year and a half. Toward the end of this period she was dealing with issues of separation and autonomy, with her boyfriend and also with her job. In most of her life situations, especially with men, she acted out a dependent and submissive role. As a result of her work with me, she was becoming stronger in her relationship with her boyfriend, asserting herself and making independent moves. She was promoted in her job, with more responsibility and autonomy. At some point she began to experience the fullness of the Personal Essence in her belly, which she liked, but was still full of anger and resentment about how she had been treated in her more dependent days. A few weeks after this development she decided to terminate, feeling that she was now strong enough to go her own separate way. She was then much stronger than when she started, but was not even close to integrating the Personal Essence in any permanent way. Clearly, she was acting out her need for autonomy rather than working through the issues surrounding it. It is likely that she was afraid that if she really attained her autonomy, she would lose her relationship with her boyfriend. She left believing she was gaining her freedom, when the fact was that she had had a taste of freedom, a taste that frightened her and made her leave, and thus fail to integrate fully the state of autonomy.

In our experience, students who had in their childhoods strong disruptions and conflicts in the process of separation and individuation, are the ones who tend to abort the process of development around the time when Personal Essence is arising in consciousness. This is another pattern that illustrates the connection between Personal Essence and autonomy.

Another student, Anna, had a very long struggle with this issue of independence. Every time there was a movement towards autonomy, which manifested as a success in her life such as a better job or a good opportunity, she would become physically ill. Finally she was able to recognize her Personal Essence as her true Being and identity. However, she reacted with the usual negative, separation-seeking feelings and behavior. She missed several group sessions. However, because she worked on the issue hard and long, and was truly desperate about needing her autonomy, she managed to work out some of the issues herself and return to complete her work. Here is a report of a part of her process:

The last session I had with you I was feeling as if I wanted to quit the group. I felt that there was no place that I fit in, and that whenever I was asked to do anything at all I felt as if I did not want to do it. I felt that if I did do it, it was losing a part of myself. While talking to you about this, I realized that it was all connected to my feeling of independence, and that I needed to cling to my new-found independence, and that anything that I did that others asked me to do made me feel it is an impingement on that freedom.

The growth that I have made in gaining that freedom and independence has seemed a long and hard struggle for me. I do not want to lose this feeling of power and independence. You helped me see how this part of me cannot be lost because it is a part of what I am, my Essence.

I feel very powerful and strong, except when I get close to someone giving me love, and then I become frightened. My fear of the group and the feelings I have of not belonging are also tied to the feeling of losing a part of myself if I give in, if I stop fighting. I feel as if I have to fight in order to preserve what I am. And I feel the fight as a loss of something that I want even more than myself, sometimes.

For the first time in my life I can remember, I am functioning out of what I really am, from the place where I truly come from.

There are a few points that we want to single out from this account:

1. There are other reasons behind the desire to terminate, besides acting out resistance. We see in Anna's case that independence brings about a conflict of feeling she doesn't fit in, and also the fear that she will give up independence for the sake of a love object. This conflict between having one's independence and having the love object or its love is a very common one, connected with issues of the rapprochement crisis which we will discuss in detail in later chapters.

2. The definiteness and certainty of the state of autonomy accompanying the experience of the Personal Essence.

3. The value, the preciousness of the Personal Essence and its attendant feelings of autonomy. People go to great lengths doing what they think will preserve this autonomy of Being. The value of the Personal Essence is experienced both in the ways it feels and in what it implies for one's life. The fullness, completeness, strength,

feel very pleasurable, even smooth and sensuous. There is a burst of joy when we realize this personal sense of Being, and when we see the implications of this freedom and autonomy for our lives.

Ironically, however, when we realize the Personal Essence, that is, when it is a permanent attainment rather than simply an experience, we no longer feel the desire for that coveted autonomy. It simply ceases to be an issue, and falls away, leaving us with no need or desire for autonomy, nor any conflicts around autonomy. We are, and in our Being we are absolutely autonomous. We are ourselves, our own person. Our qualities are completely our own, our capacities are simply part of us. We are able to act freely and autonomously, appropriate to the situation, without feeling or thinking we are autonomous. Our autonomy is now second nature, and is not qualified by our situation. We might be practically restricted from doing what we want, but nothing can stop us from being who we are. We might be literally in prison, but as our Personal Essence we are free and autonomous. We need do nothing to be autonomous; our sense of Being is our autonomy.

Thus when our actions or expressions are controlled by external circumstances, we experience no loss of autonomy, no loss of self-esteem; the restrictions are felt as just external and superficial restrictions. Our bodies, even our minds, can be restricted, but who we are cannot be touched.

We seek autonomy, have all kinds of issues and conflicts about autonomy, only when our autonomy is not completely established. And ego autonomy is never complete autonomy. Only the realization of Being can bring complete, absolute autonomy.

Chapter Four

Beingness

To appreciate the autonomy of Being, and to see that ego autonomy is no more than a pale shadow of this autonomy, one must know Being. But one can know Being only by being. Short of, or in addition to, this *gnosis,* we can illuminate the contrast by looking more closely at ego structure and its development.

In this section we will investigate in more detail how the development of identifications with ego structure removes the child's experience from the realm of Being, looking at this issue from the perspective of the perception of the "external" world and one's relations with other people, and also from the perspective of the experience of self. Then we can describe how in the work of the Diamond Approach towards inner realization, the understanding of psychic structure made possible by object relations theory can help us pierce through the identification with ego and thus experience the Personal Essence as Being.

According to object relations theory, the development of ego structure through the process of separation-individuation happens primarily by means of the internalization of object relations through the formation of inner images of self and other. The "object" is generally the human love object, and an object relation is simply the relation between self and object, usually an emotional relation. "Object relations" then generally refer to the mental representation of this relation, which consists of three parts: a self-image, usually called a "self-representation"; an object-image, usually called an "object-representation"; and the emotional relation or affect between the two, such as love, anger, fear or desire.

Thus ego formation occurs in the context of a relationship to a primary love object, the mothering person. This is the source of the English analyst W. Ronald D. Fairbairn's naming this approach "object relations theory."

Every situation or interaction between infant and mother is an object relation. Except in the very earliest phases, in which there is no differentiation at all, the infant always sees himself in relation to the mother, not in isolation. The memories of such interactions are mental representations of the object relations. The infant remembers not only himself (that is the image of himself) but always also the image of the mother in the interaction. The fixation of these representations in the mind is called "internalization." As more of these representations accumulate, which means as more memories are retained and fixed, there begins a process of organization of these representations. This organization of internalized object relations is the task of the separation-individuation process, which ordinarily culminates in the development of self and object constancy.

According to Kernberg, the process of internalization and organization of object relations occurs through different mechanisms, depending on the stage of development. He groups them in three categories: introjection, identification and ego identity:

> *Introjection* is the earliest, most primitive, and basic level in the organization of internalization processes. It is the reproduction and fixation of an interaction with the environment by means of an organized cluster of memory traces implying at least three components: (i) the image of an object, (ii) the image of the self in interaction with that object, and (iii) the affective coloring of both the object-image and the self-image under the influence of the drive representative present at the time of the interaction. This process is a mechanism of growth of the psychic apparatus. . . [Otto F. Kernberg, *Object Relations Theory and Clinical Psychoanalysis*, p. 29]

Then he relates this definition of introjection to the mechanism of identification:

> *Identification* is a higher-level form of introjection which can only take place when the perceptive and cognitive abilities of the child have increased to the point that it can

recognize the role aspects of interpersonal interaction. [*Ibid.*, p. 30]

Thus identification is like introjection, except that the object relations internalized are on a more developed level. The object is seen as a person with a specific role, for example, the role of protecting or mothering, rather than just as a vague object that is needed. These internalized roles are expressed later in development as traits of character and personality. In other words, this internalized repertoire of roles becomes organized into a cohesive self-image through which the child at the end of development is interacting with his environment. Kernberg puts it this way:

> Since identifications imply the internalization of roles as defined above, behavioral manifestations of the individual, which express one or both of the reciprocal roles of the respective interaction, become a predominant result of identification; the behavioral manifestations of introjections are less apparent in interpersonal interactions. [*Ibid.*, p. 31]

Kernberg calls this final organization of internalized object relations the "ego-identity." It refers to the overall organization of identifications and introjections under the guiding principles of the synthetic function of the ego, which constitutes the final integration of the ego into a self that is continuous in space and time, plus the representational world of all object images.

Thus the sense of self, based on the cohesive self-image, is the result of an integration of the very earliest object relations. This ego organization is modified constantly as more object relations are internalized, but later identifications, after the age of approximately three years, add little in terms of the basic structure.

This contradicts the popular belief that people change as they grow in years. The fact is that the passage of time only solidifies the already established structure. This is one reason why change in psychotherapy is not easy. Whether he is in psychotherapy or not, an individual merely lives out an already established structure, expressing an already formed individuality, with its previously established roles. New situations may appear to bring changes, but these changes are rarely fundamental, in general merely bringing out in behavioral manifestation other roles from the unconscious repertoire of the self. These roles or identifications are what the person takes to be the content of who he is. The more harmony these roles have with each other and with the environment, the more normal and healthy the individual is. Failure of the process of integration to create such harmony results in mental disorder.

The recognition that the continuity of the personality is not a complete unity, that the individual is not actually a cohesive entity, but a relative harmony between many roles, was made long ago by the ancient and traditional psychologies. The teacher G. I. Gurdjieff, speaking about the illusion of a unitary "I" said:

> There is no such "I," or rather there are hundreds, thousands of little "I"s in every one of us. We are divided in ourselves but we cannot recognize the plurality of our being except by observation and study. [G. I. Gurdjieff, *Views from the Real World*, p. 75]

Usually, there is a general sense of being a person, an individual with a sense of self or identity. However, this is only the surface phenomenon. At deeper levels of the personality, there are many self-images, with definite traits, organized in a particular structure that gives the feeling of an overall self-image.

Different life situations bring to the surface different self-images and their corresponding object relations. This determines the changing of moods, emotions, states of mind and actions throughout a person's life, and even throughout a day. This activation of past object relations is called "transference" by psychologists. Kernberg relates how in the process of psychoanalysis, as the patient goes deeper in understanding his mind, there first manifests the general overall self-images and their corresponding object relations, but that as the process deepens, the more specific constituent sub-self-images become expressed in the analytic situation. He writes in a paper about psychoanalytic technique:

> Here, in the course of the psychoanalytic process, the development of a regressive transference neurosis will gradually activate in the transference the constituent units of internalized object relations that form part of ego and superego structures, and of the repressed units of internalized object relations that have become part of the id. [Harold P. Blum, Editor, *Psychoanalytic Explorations of Technique*, p. 211]

Thus transference occurs, in object relations terms, when past object relations are activated. However, it is not only in analysis or

54 psychotherapy that these small units of object relations are activated. It happens for all egos at all times, and simply becomes apparent under scrutiny. As Freud first emphasized in *The Psychopathology of Everyday Life,* such transference is a normal everyday occurrence, not an isolated instance in analysis. Thus no interaction is ever absolutely in the present. The individual identifies with one image and projects the other image on the other person in the interaction. (Of course, all this occurs in the context of the overall sense of self constituted by the sum of the integrated images.) The past is always present in the form of the object relation activated. In fact, the present is always perceived through whatever object relation— whether it is an overall ego-identity or a more specific subject-object relation—is active at the time.

Some of the most interesting implications of this fact are not generally considered by the very people who are most aware of it. Both psychologists and laymen who are aware of the fact of transference rarely appreciate the fact that their interactions with the environment are actually being filtered through past object and self-images. They are not, in other words, seeing reality for what it really is. The present cannot be known by ego, for it is always overlaid with the past. In the words of Kernberg:

> The world of object representations, then, gradually changes and comes closer to the "external" perceptions of the reality of significant objects throughout childhood and later life without ever becoming an actual copy of the environmental world. [Otto F. Kernberg, *Object Relations Theory and Clinical Psychoanalysis,* p. 34]

We recall also that the ego structure organizes the apparatuses of primary autonomy, the functions of perception, cognition, synthesis, memory and so on, again making a filter through which the world is perceived.

Some people, of course, do not believe that the sense of self is based on mental structure. In fact, some object relations theorists, such as Guntrip, think of the ego as a whole personal self, which is not a structure. However, neither Winnicott nor Guntrip clearly differentiate between Being and mental structure. Their inclusion of a realm of experience that is not just self-image is accurate from our perspective in that it corresponds more closely to normal experience—most individuals do experience the sense of presence and Being in some circumstances—they simply do not clearly see or understand the experience. Normal experience is a mixture of categories of experience, including that of presence, but conscious experience remains almost exclusively in the realm of emotions, thoughts, images, etc. So although the British psychologists are again formulating object relations in a way closer to actual experience than their American counterparts do, their lack of clarity and specificity in regard to the concept of Being, and their failure to distinguish it from other categories of experience, limits the usefulness of their formulations for those who want to learn about the experience of Being.

Also, the British psychologists' understanding of normal experience from the perspective of psychic structure is not as refined or developed as that of the American theorists such as Jacobson, Mahler and Kernberg, whose precise and detailed descriptions of the psychic structure have so powerfully facilitated our journey beyond that psychic structure toward the realm of Being. Furthermore, this precise understanding of psychic structure is useful for unravelling the vicissitudes of ego because it is this very structure, and not the realm of Being, with which most normal people identify. Guntrip and Winnicott's confusion of these realms makes their theories problematical. In our work we make a very definite demarcation between the experience of Being and that of ego, since as we will see in subsequent chapters, the confusion of these two categories can lead to a lot of trouble for the student of inner realization.

We have noted Kernberg's statement that the world of inner representations gradually approximates the real world, but never completely matches it. The fact is that we cannot know how close the approximation is until we know the real world directly. And the real world is the world of Being, the world of the Now. One must see from the perspective of Being to have an idea of how far away from reality the perception of ego actually is. It comes as a shock to those who have this privilege. There is some relationship between ego perception and that of Being, but as we will see, there are fundamental differences that cannot be anticipated. Perceived from Being, forms might retain their shapes, but their inner reality is very different from what one has thought, and the relationships between "objects" is seen to be drastically different from what one has believed. Seeing reality

56   without the filter of the past is a cataclysmic experience, which un-
covers forces and energies which are not even conceived of by ego.

So even though ego perception does become closer to actual reality
in the course of normal development and maturation, the approximation stops far short of an ability to perceive what is actually there,
which latter perception requires the cessation of identifying with the
ego structure. As we will see later, one might view the movement
toward Being as a continuation of normal development, as some
transpersonal psychologies are beginning to do, but it would be a
mistake to assume that the perception of Being is on the same order
of reality as ego perception. The realizations involved are not those
typical of the therapeutic process, for instance, the realization that a
certain man is not actually your father, although you had been seeing
him as such through your transference. The direct perception of Being
actually challenges your conviction of what a man is, what a human
being is, what actually makes up the world.

Other psychologies besides object relations theory, for example,
cognitive psychology, note that perceptions depend upon personal
history (one's experience in the past), through the operation of one's
perceptual schema. Ulric Neisser defines a schema as follows:

> A schema is that portion of the entire perceptual cycle
> which is internal to the perceiver, modifiable by experi-
> ence, and somehow specific to what is being perceived.
> The schema accepts information as it becomes available at
> sensory surfaces and is changed by that information; it
> directs movements and exploratory activities that make
> more information available, by which it is further modified.
> [Ulric Neisser, *Cognition and Reality*, p. 54]

Not only one's perception but of course one's emotional responses
and behavior as well are determined by the self-image a person is
identifying with. For instance, to the same situation one individual
might respond with fear, another with anger, another with apathy,
with corresponding behaviors. Very often the behaviors are stylized
and obviously automatic; in any case one never has a choice about
emotional states that arise, whether they are appropriate or not. This
automaticity of response is much greater than either normal subjective
experience or modern psychological theory acknowledges.

It is in the nature of mind to be in a constant state of reactivity; and
here we do not simply mean what is implied in the usual sense of the

word. We mean something more fundamental: that the individual is always reacting with certain very limited patterns of emotion and behavior which reflect the self-image he is identifying with, and that this self-image is itself a reaction, in two senses: first, that the specific self-image that is operating is automatically elicited by the situation, and second, that the self-image is itself a construction made up of reactions to past events from early childhood. This self-image is thus never a spontaneous response or a free choice, but is always a compulsive reaction. We will explore later what a free and spontaneous response can be, when we explore the issue of functioning from the perspective of Being.

We can see that this activity of personality—which consists of reacting to situations by dredging up memories of certain childhood object relations that are somehow associated with the situation, identifying with one or another of the images in the object relation and then manifesting certain automatic emotions and behaviors—completely lacks freshness, newness. It is a reaction of the past to the present. Being, on the other hand, is the absence of such reactions. Being means no reaction, no mental activity that defines who or what one is. In fact, Being is not an activity at all; it is an existence, a suchness, a thereness, a presence that is not doing anything to be there. Since Being is itself existence, it does not need the mind to be there. It is like a physical object, which does not need the activity of mind to exist.

The ego structure, on the other hand, is maintained, must be maintained, by the constant activity and reactivity of the mind. And as Winnicott seems to have understood in the passage quoted earlier, this reactivity is incompatible with Being; he says it "annihilates being."

To identify with the reaction that is the ego is to be cut off from Being, one's true nature and identity. This is what the man of spirit means when he says the ego "is not," it has no true existence.

Now, we can understand in a deeper way the autonomy of Being. From the perspective of Being, what we are is not determined by either the past or the present situation. We are not a reaction; we simply are, an essential existence, totally free from the past. Our nature, our identity, cannot be influenced by situations. The main difference between Being and ego—which is that Being is just being-as-such and ego a

58 reaction from the past—makes Being the true autonomy, and ego autonomy a delusion.

It is ironic that object relations theory first describes so competently the way in which ego is structured from past object relations between inner images and, therefore, is compulsively reacting to situations in conditioned patterns, and then goes on to describe this same entity as autonomous! How can this set of reactions from the past be said to be autonomous, when true autonomy can be recognized to be the fullness of the presence of Being in the present? Again this understanding will be difficult for those who have no direct experience of what Being is; but actually almost everyone has had some experience of some deeper aspects of experience which are not completely dominated by ego activity. Here it is a matter of seeing these experiences for what they are, for their great significance.

The Personal Essence is the personal experience of Being, and is therefore the true individual autonomy, undetermined by anything except one's true and essential nature. Another way to contrast this experience with ego is to look at ego as constructed of a series of "identifications." Blanck and Blanck, discussing the contributions of Heinz Hartmann and his collaborators, write:

> They further discuss identification as a varying process, depending upon the level of development at which it takes place. . . Identification proper is a process of internalization, whereas imitation is not. Therefore, identification makes for a greater degree of independence from the object. This is the road to autonomy. [Gertrude and Rubin Blanck, *Ego Psychology: Theory and Practice*, p. 36]

Perhaps identification is the "road to autonomy" in that it leads to more autonomy from the mother, but from our perspective it is actually the road to bondage, ensnaring the individual in concepts about who he is that become his greatest misfortune. In a later chapter we will discuss the ideal fate of these identifications in a person who is undergoing a development of the Personal Essence.

Not only does this process of developing "ego autonomy" put one in bondage to one's past in the form of self-images, it also leaves one relating to the object images of one's early primary caretakers, and therefore under their coercive influence, which functions as what the analytic model calls the "superego." Thus even though the ego might be relatively independent emotionally from the love object, its sense of identity is definitely not. The sense of self of the ego, and its individuality, are fundamentally dependent on the traits of the objects in the inner world, and on the particulars of the childhood interactions with it. We will discuss in some detail later how the development of the Personal Essence is related to the ego development which occurs through identification. When one is the Personal Essence, one does become free of these identifications and of the influence of the early caretakers which has lived on in the ego's object images. The Personal Essence is an ongoing sense of Beingness, completely independent of mind and memory, and hence completely free. It is the true autonomous individuation. Not being based on the past, the inner state and the external behavior that functions in the manifestation of the Personal Essence are completely objective and appropriate responses to the present situation.

Just as we saw in the last section that following the thread of autonomy can lead to the experience of the Personal Essence, we will examine in this section our finding that following the thread of who one truly is can also lead us to the Personal Essence. This process involves becoming aware of the identifications used by the mind for identity. One also becomes aware that these identifications function to give one a sense of a continuous identity. Usually, one is so identified with the self-representations that it is difficult to achieve an objective awareness of them. One needs some distance, some disidentification from the self-images, for there to be clarity about their nature. Disidentification involves the awareness of both the identifications and the process of identifying with them. This is possible when one is not totally identified with a particular self-image, when one is already sensing that these images are just images, and they are not who one truly is. Thus the process of seeing through identifications is one of becoming aware of them and then disidentifying from them. Most self-representations which make up the ego-identity are unconscious, so one must deal with both the absence of direct awareness of the self-representations, and with the presence of active unconscious identification with them. When a previously unconscious self-representation becomes conscious, one might still identify with it, but it does become possible to disidentify.

Such awareness is seen by most traditional teaching schools to be of fundamental importance for liberation and inner realization. Some

60 of these schools have emphasized the need for disidentification. Gurdjieff, for example, speaks in the following excerpt from a talk about identification and self-remembering:

> Identifying is the chief obstacle to self-remembering. A man who identifies with anything is unable to remember himself. In order to remember oneself it is necessary first of all *not to identify*. [P. D. Ouspensky, *In Search of the Miraculous*, p. 151]

Here we can contrast the process of psychotherapy with that of inner realization in light of our understanding of identification. Most forms of psychotherapy involve a gradual process of disidentification from pathological self-representations and their corresponding object relations. However since the aim of psychotherapy is not self-realization but a "healthy" ego, not all self-representations are exposed and worked through.

The work on inner realization, however, requires that one bring to consciousness all the ego identifications which are used for identity, and that one then gradually (or sometimes abruptly) disidentify from this mental content. At the beginning, the more superficial identifications are seen through. These are the chronologically later identifications which were internalized after the development of a relatively stable sense of identity. They generally involve some content connected with modeling oneself after one or both of the parents. At this level one deals especially with object representations established in the development of the superego. Working through these identifications usually removes the repression against some of the deep feelings about the parent with which one identifies. The letting go of the identification then brings to light the actual personal relationship to the parent, revealing the real emotions of the relationship. An example is the working through of the identifications that function to repress the castration and Oedipus complexes. The girl, for instance, typically manages her oedipal feelings by finally identifying with the mother, so that she becomes like her rather than a rival to her for the father's affections. When this identification is exposed, the oedipal feelings of rivalry with the mother will emerge and must be dealt with.

This process of becoming aware of and disidentifying from ego identifications begins to shed light on the nature of the personality as

a substitute for true Being. For instance, a typical development in 61
students going through this process is a tendency towards increased
selfishness and self-centeredness. Self-centeredness is a basic quality
of the ego self, which becomes increasingly obvious as the ego identifications, which are the building blocks of the self, begin to dissolve.
But this dissolution threatens the stability of the ego self, and hence
there results the reaction of holding on more tightly to this self. The
desperate clinging to this identity exposes the basic quality of self-
centeredness, the attitude of perceiving and relating to everything and
everyone in the world from the perspective of oneself, considering
what is for me and what is against me. What will I get from this and
what will I lose from that? As the ego identifications dissolve, one can
see more clearly how pervasive, invisible, deceptive and convincing is
this attitude, pervading almost everything in one's life. Everything is
considered from the perspective of whether it will support one's ego
or not, without much regard for others or for the truth.

Even when the other is considered, he is generally considered only
from the perspective of one's ego. This is a consequence of one's identity being always at one pole of an object relation, with the other person simply being the object at the other pole of the relation. Who the
other truly is cannot be perceived, let alone considered. This omnipresent self-centeredness of ego is generally not seen, because of the
identifications with the ego self. Only when the identification is
loosened can one begin to see the blinders that ego's self-centeredness
puts on perception and experience.

But when we do become aware of this basic stance of ego, we can
begin to understand the psychodynamic causes of our self-centeredness. We gradually become aware of how thoroughly we are enslaved
to security in all its forms, physical, emotional, and financial. We become aware of the deep insecurity that is basic to ego, both to its
sense of self and to its sense of individuality. This insecurity results
from the fact that ego is not Being; how could a structure of images,
concepts, memories, and feelings be secure? And the insecurity might
for a while seem to become even more pronounced as we learn how
readily these images evaporate as a result of our simply seeing them
for what they are. Actually, the basic insecurity that has always been
there in the unconscious is simply being exposed by the process of
dissolving ego identifications.

62   How is the individual to gain the courage to engage in this process of disidentification, given the deep and sometimes terrifying insecurity that is thereby exposed? It is made much easier if there is some support to take the place of the usual ego supports which come through the object relations, such as approval, recognition, social acceptance and success, love and admiration from friends and family for one's individuality, financial security, and the like. Clearly one's attachment to these things is very strong. In fact, our observation is that we are willing to perceive these phenomena without using them for ego support or self esteem only when we have a sense of a more basic, more real support and value. In the process of inner realization this support can be provided by some of the essential aspects.

Letting go of ego identifications on a profound level is possible only after the activation of certain essential aspects, primarily those of the five *lataif* (subtle energy centers in the body) and the aspect of true value. The lataif aspects—strength, will, compassion, enjoyment and intuition—provide the true support of essence which makes it possible to see through ego supports and not compulsively pursue them. The emergence of the aspect of value, for instance, which is the true existential value of Being, makes it possible to see through the ego mechanisms of seeking self-esteem and to become less dependent on them.

These preliminary experiences of essential aspects are very helpful in seeing through and abandoning ego identification, but they are not absolutely necessary. Some students seem to be able to see through their ego identifications without all the aspects mentioned above; yet the presence of these aspects makes the process much easier and smoother, and makes the arising anxieties and insecurities more tolerable.

One way to describe this ego, which we have discovered is extremely self-centered, and which fails to consider the reality of others, is to call it "narcissistic." If we consider narcissism to be alienation from what one truly is, taking oneself to be something that is not truly oneself, then it is clear that ego is in its very nature narcissistic. This again is readily apparent when one is present as the Personal Essence, and sees ego from this perspective. Ego is not a presence, and has no beingness; when we take ourselves to be any self-image from the past, we are automatically distant from what we truly are. We will deal with the subject of narcissism in relation to Being in greater detail in

Chapter Twenty-Two. We are mentioning it here in connection with discovering the contrast between ego and Personal Essence.

Of course all the myriad manifestations of narcissistic insecurity arise as certain ego identifications are dropped in the process of inner realization. Our unlimited hunger for love, money, admiration, power, insight, even inner development and enlightenment, come to the fore, and we see that they are continually generating fear and anxiety. Seeing these desires for what they are, and disidentifying with the structures they support, generally precipitates the experience of Being in the aspect of the Personal Essence.

So we have seen several threads we can follow through the labyrinths of ego identification in order to disidentify with them and come to an experience of our true Beingness. Here a case history will illustrate this process.

David is a professional man in his thirties, grappling with his self-image and his identifications. He has been working with the author, both in a group and in private teaching sessions, for about four years. He has lately been concerned with his relationship to me. I keep pointing out his attempts to get my approval, recognition and acceptance, as if I were withholding them from him. This work has been uncovering his identifications with one self-image after another, along with the corresponding object relations. He has been becoming angry and frustrated, because he sees over and over again that his feelings towards me are not really about me, that they are transferences; they repeat his childhood feelings about his father. He is becoming aware that he is not seeing me, and that he is nothing but an identification with how he experienced himself at some point in the far past.

David is a successful young man, pleasant to relate to. He is intelligent and educated. If we were to make a psychological diagnosis of him, we would say that he is primarily a normal personality, with some predominance of narcissistic traits.

Finally, in a private session, David becomes fed up with his patterns. When he is confronted with his identification he sees with a lot of pain that he is only a reaction, that everything he feels is a reaction based on transference. Seeing this brings to the surface a deep sadness, a profound hurt and an overwhelming disappointment. He sobs uncontrollably, hurt and disappointed that he is not himself, that he has no idea what it means to be himself, that he is a mere reaction.

64   The sadness, the hurt and the crying open his heart to a feeling of tenderness, and compassion for his personal situation. He is now not angry or rejecting himself. Seeing his hurt and disappointment allows him to be compassionate, soft, accepting of himself. He gives up trying, and reacting to his trying. He just lies quietly, sad and tender at the same time.

Here I ask him what he really wants. He responds, amidst another explosion of sobs that shake his entire body: "I just want to feel me. I just want to relax, let go and experience myself. I want just to stop reacting and thinking, and just be here in the present, in the room with you." I can see his pain, his sincerity, his love for me and the truth that he doesn't yet understand. I tell him that I see and understand his state and his feelings, and suggest to him that he not try to be himself, to just relax and see what happens. After a few minutes of tender silence, he turns to me and says: "I feel okay. I feel I am here." I ask him to say more. He continues: "I just feel present in a new way. I do not feel anything dramatic, but I feel quite clear and relaxed."

He continues talking, reporting his observations of his state:

> I feel I am here, present with you, I don't have any specific emotions about anything in particular. But I experience a kind of peacefulness and a sense of being settled and not so concerned with who I am. I don't have all the usual feelings about you. You are just the person sitting there talking with me.

He seems relaxed, settled and still. I ask him to sense himself more, and to tell me what specifically he feels. He reports that he is not feeling that he is reacting to the situation. He is aware of some reactions, but they feel insignificant and he feels separate from them. The more he focuses on the specifics of his state, the more the sense of presence increases and deepens. He feels still within himself; his mind is empty and clear, but he still feels present.

I ask him to describe what he feels when he experiences the sense of presence. He reports feeling a fullness that has the sensation of smoothness, and that this fullness is coexistent with his body. He feels this fullness to be himself. Recognizing his personal Being brings gentle and quiet tears to his eyes, a sense of silent gratitude.

To experience the Personal Essence through the process of disidentification makes clear its sense of beingness. One feels oneself as a presence. One feels oneself as a fullness, as a Beingness, in contradistinction to reactivity or activity. One feels oneself because one is oneself. Being is recognized by being it. The perception is most direct. The contact with oneself is complete. There is no subject separate from the Being.

This is an important point about the nature of Being. One knows Being by being it, because Being is self-aware. It is self-aware because it is pure consciousness. This consciousness is not an activity, it is a presence.

Since Being is pure consciousness capable of direct awareness of itself, it does not require thinking and deduction for it to know itself. This is what most distinguishes it from the personality of ego, which knows itself through reference to the past. One reason it is not easy to have a clear experience of Being is that the habit of ego is to know itself through reference to other perceptions, as in Descartes' "I think, therefore I am."

But Being's perception of itself is immediate and direct. The experience is more like "I exist," felt with immediate, definite certainty. It is the feeling "I am." "I am because I am." The experience of Being is like being a certain medium or substance in which each point or atom is exquisitely and clearly aware of itself as pure sensation or consciousness. There is pure sensation, exquisite aliveness.

The Personal Essence fullness is the presence of consciousness in a unique sensation of firmness, strength, smoothness, dense fluidity and flexibility. One experiences oneself as a full and rounded presence, like a firm, strong and well-developed muscle, vibrant with robust life and sensuous pleasure. One is truly full for one is the consciousness of fullness itself. There is no deficiency or lack. One is the sensuousness, the smoothness, the firmness, the robustness, the aliveness, which are not characteristics of some object, but are the actual constituents of the beingness and substance of the Personal Essence itself.

These characteristics of the consciousness of the Personal Essence are not described here in a metaphorical or allegorical way. Certain aspects are described in some of the more esoteric areas of the traditional spiritual literature, Taoist and Sufi for example, and these descriptions are very like much of the experience of many of our students, who show a remarkable consistency in their reports in this regard.

66   Our reports from students on their experiences during or related to work sessions are good illustrations of the property of fullness in the experience of the Personal Essence. Natalie has been in a group situation for slightly more than three years, and has had some clear experiences of her self as the Personal Essence, but has not worked through all the issues around it nor seen all its implications. She is reporting on her work with the author in a group session:

> Last Sunday I worked with you on my having an abortion, and on the emptiness in my belly. The memory of the abortion remains in my uterus, genitals and in my mind. There is a strong sense of protecting this area, a holding. Sensing my belly and genitals I feel grief, loss, fear and sadness that they won't feel as pleasurable as they did when I was pregnant. As I feel these feelings, I arrive at the emptiness. It is difficult to remain with the emptiness, wanting to fill myself. The emptiness scares me. I have all kinds of beliefs about it, but when I allow the emptiness, my pelvis expands and there is fullness. It is fluffy and kind of soft and gentle. It feels the way it did when I was pregnant. Sensing this area allows for a greater awareness of presence and beingness.
>
> Since this meeting I have been observing how much my beliefs get in the way of my experiencing what is.

The relative ease with which Natalie experienced and recognized her Personal Essence is due to the fact that she is not in the initial stages of discovery, but in the process of working through the issues connected with establishing her Essence permanently.

We notice that the fullness, softness, aliveness are palpable, almost physical. Natalie relates to it as pleasure, like physical pleasure.

This case also demonstrates the common association between pregnancy and the Personal Essence. Natalie's abortion had left her with a sense of loss and emptiness. Physically, she had lost an embryo, along with the physiological processes that accompany a pregnancy. Emotionally, she felt it as a loss of fullness, softness and pleasure. The emergence of the Personal Essence filling the emptiness indicates that she had unconsciously taken the loss of the pregnancy to be the loss of her personal sense of Being; she was equating pregnancy with being her Personal Essence.

Many women make this association, and in fact many women have come to me anxious and wondering whether they are pregnant, when the Personal Essence is arising. A woman will feel a warmth, a full-ness and an aliveness in the lower belly. Her belly feels as if it is full, extended and bulging. Only when she focuses on her experience of fullness and it expands to fill the whole body does a woman lose the feeling that she is pregnant. We could say that she was pregnant, but with herself.

Some women begin to feel a desire to become pregnant when they are working on the issues of the Personal Essence, and the presence is coming closer to consciousness. They usually feel an emptiness in the belly, just as Natalie did, and the emptiness manifests emotionally as a deep longing to feel a warm fullness in the belly. The longing is actually for the Personal Essence; the emptiness is nothing but the condition of absence of this sense of Being. But since the fullness feels something like pregnancy, it becomes unconsciously associated with it. The longing is actually, then, to have the feeling of a being in her belly.

We know that the longing for pregnancy at such times is actually for one's own Being and not really for a child, because the longing often arises when the woman is certain on a conscious level that she does not want to be pregnant and that her practical life situation does not allow it. Of course, a woman can have an unconscious desire for pregnancy or for a child even then, but our observation is that when the woman does become aware of the fullness of her Personal Essence, the desire for pregnancy very often disappears just as sud-denly as it appeared.

We are of course not implying that all desires for pregnancy are really for the Personal Essence. The two desires might be there together, and the desire for pregnancy might remain after the realiza-tion of the Personal Essence. It is our experience, though, that this displaced desire for pregnancy is very common, a true desire for pregnancy being much rarer than is commonly thought. Sometimes, also, this longing for pregnancy can arise in connection with some es-sential aspect other than the Personal Essence. In general our observa-tion is that it is very common in women to desire pregnancy which they believe would fill the painful emptiness which results from the lack of the Personal Essence or of other aspects. For many reasons, pregnancy and babies are unconsciously associated with lacking aspects of Being.

68   Men, too, experience the presence of the fullness of the Personal Essence, when it is manifesting in the belly, as a bulging kind of warmth and presence that brings to mind images of pregnancy. They do not, of course, come to believe that they are pregnant, but they do sometimes jokingly report that they feel as if they were pregnant. This is probably the closest a man can come to feeling what it is like to be pregnant. Again the man is in a sense pregnant, with his own Beingness.

This brings us to the concept of rebirth in relation to the Personal Essence. Rebirth is a recurrent theme in the literature of inner transformation. Inner transformation is primarily a death and rebirth, the death of an old identity and the birth of a new one, on a deeper level of reality. While we can see the realization of each essential aspect as a process of death and rebirth, it is the discovery of the Personal Essence which is actually felt by many students as the birth of who they are. It is the true birth of the Human Being, and is recognized as such by the experiencer himself. If the development of the separate individuality of ego is the psychological birth of the individual, then the realization of the Personal Essence is his essential birth.

The death, of course, in this process of rebirth, is the abandoning of ego identifications. In this sense the "birth" of the Personal Essence is fundamentally different from the birth of the ego, which is not preceded by a death but arises out of a state of nondifferentiation. There is no conscious identity preceding ego identity which needs to be dissolved to allow the birth of the ego. However, the birth of ego does mean the loss of contact with Being, as we will see later.

This is a significant fact which is relevant to the relationship between the birth of ego and the birth of the Personal Essence. Many work systems and their teachings consider ego a preliminary stage that precedes the conscious existence of Being. Ego existence is considered the childhood of humanity. When a human being truly grows up and becomes an essential adult, he lives the life of Being. This is one reason the Sufis call the man of Being the "complete" man, and the man of ego the "unregenerate" or "undeveloped" man.

The source of this point of view is the fact that the man of Being is almost always one who has experienced a new birth and development, which was preceded by identification with the ego. It is rare that a human being is from the beginning essential; if such a person appears, he is what the Sufis call a prophet.

In this book we will develop a different point of view. We will view the Personal Essence as what is meant to be developed through the separation-individuation process (or any model of ego development). We see ego development, as it usually manifests in the birth of a separate individuality, as an incomplete or arrested development. We will explore this theme fully later. For now we continue with our discussion of the characteristics of the Personal Essence.

Chapter Five

The
Personal Element

O
ne of the main reasons the life of the man of spirit does not
attract the man of the world is that it appears to lack the personal element. The man of the world misunderstands and rejects the impersonality of the man of spirit. The man of the world values
his personal characteristics, as they are expressed in living his life. He is
not willing to sacrifice his sense of himself as a person, and does not
understand why the man of spirit exhorts him to do so. He does not see
what is objectionable about being personal and living a life dedicated to
the pursuit of personal fulfillment and personal excellence.

When the individuality of ego develops harmoniously and without
much distortion, it has a personal sense to it. One is not only a self,
but feels oneself as an individual, a person. The man of the world experiences this sense of being a person as a sign of and an expression
of his humanity. So he quite naturally considers impersonality to be a
nonhuman quality. He is not willing to give up personhood to
embrace the universal impersonality of Being, because he believes
this would involve losing his humanness. He is confounded when
spiritual teachers and gurus speak of a supposedly desirable enlightened state as impersonal.

He feels insulted, not considered, when he is not treated as a person. He takes it as a sign of lack of respect. He expects, and feels it is
his right, to be treated by others as a person in his own right.

An adult human being considers it an expression of mature human
love that he relates to others as persons, and sees this capacity as an

70

expression of his human nature. He enjoys, values and loves the personal element in him. To be personal means to him to be a human being, capable of enjoying intimate personal contact. It means respecting oneself and the other, loving oneself and the other, and valuing oneself and the other. The personal element is actually considered the essence of what it is to be a human being. It is what differentiates a human being from machines, inanimate objects, impersonal forces, and other forms of life.

Thus it is not surprising that most of us respond to the impersonality of the man of spirit with awe, noncomprehension or even revulsion. The personal element is the point of divergence between the man of the world and the man of spirit; the first pursues it and cherishes it, and the second rejects it and shuns it. Most of the profound spiritual teachings of the world, speak of the personal element as an expression of ego, and hence of falsehood. Thus the man of spirit mostly equates the personal element with the personality.

It is intriguing that the man of spirit looks at the personal element as the barrier against the true life, while the man of the world regards it as the prize of his human maturity. Object relations theory considers the capacity to be personal the final achievement of ego development. It is one of the results of the attainment of object constancy, which can be seen as the capacity to experience oneself as a whole person and to relate to the other as a whole person. This is understood to develop through the integration of the various, so far split, representations of self and object. The other is now a human object, a person, because he is now whole. Kernberg writes:

> Jacobson, Mahler, and I agree that this stage of development consists in a gradual and more realistic integration of "good" and "bad" self-representations and the parallel integration of "good" and "bad" object representations; in this process, partial aspects of self- and object representation become integrated or, respectively, total self- and object representations. [Otto F. Kernberg, *Internal World and External Reality*, p. 112]

The British school of object relations focuses more explicitly on the personal element. To become a person is considered the most important aspect of ego development. Guntrip considers that the primary field of dynamic psychology is the study of the person. He writes:

72

> In the late nineteenth century the concept of the person did not exist philosophically in the way it does today, as the concept of an irreducible reality, and individuality *per se.* . . . Person is the essence of the truly human being at every level of development. [Harry Guntrip, *Psychoanalytic Theory, Therapy, and the Self,* p. 93]

In another part of the same book he writes:

> The problem of having an unquestioned possession or else a lack of a sense of personal reality and selfhood, the identity problem, is the biggest single issue that can be raised about human existence. [*Ibid.,* p. 119]

However, there is no specific definition or study, as far as we can tell, of what it means to be personal with another. There is a definition of the person or the separate individuality, but there is no specific focus on the personal element itself. Fairbairn comes close to defining the personal element by the concept of ego relating, which is meaningful emotional contact with an object (person).

When we speak of the personal element, we do not mean only the knowledge that one is a person interacting with another person; we are referring to the actual state and feeling of being personal in an interaction. One can have object constancy, and know one is a person interacting with another person, but still interact impersonally.

It is not only object relations theory that (with the slight exceptions described above) does not specifically study this personal element; we are not aware of any psychological school or scientific field that does so. It seems surprising that a phenomenon so central to human life psychologically and emotionally, and so prized by mature human beings, escapes psychological or even spiritual study and investigation.

But again, this neglect becomes understandable when we realize that the personal element, the capacity to feel and be personal, is a characteristic of the Personal Essence, which is an aspect of Being. It cannot be truly understood, or even specifically conceptualized, until one experiences and understands the Personal Essence. In fact, to be personal is the unique quality of the Personal Essence, one that distinguishes it from other aspects of Essence and from the unqualified Essence, the impersonal aspect of Being.

What does this mean about the personal element that is characteristic of the individuality of ego? We did mention in a previous chapter that ego is a reflection of the Personal Essence. As we will see shortly, the capacity of the ego to be personal is a reflection of the personal quality of the Personal Essence, and it is really a pale shadow of that quality. It is this pale reflection that evokes for the man of the world his potential, and motivates him to pursue the personal life. It is the shadow that reminds him of who he truly is. It is the false gold that tells him of the preciousness of true gold.

We find that pursuing the thread of the personal element is the most certain way to discover the Personal Essence. We need only to genuinely investigate what it means in our experience to be personal, for the Personal Essence to emerge.

In the section on beingness we discussed some of the perceptions that become possible when we see through ego identifications. We described the self-centeredness, the basic insecurity and the sense of separateness that characterize the individuality of ego. We saw how the identification with past object relations makes it almost impossible to see another person for who he is, but causes us to see instead a projected image, or to see things through a veil of images.

How can one be truly personal in an interaction when the other is not seen for who he is? How can an image be personal? If one's experience is restricted to the level of object constancy, which according to object relations theory is the culmination of ego development, then it is not possible to be personal in any way that is not purely mental. A self-image relating to an object image is not a true personal experience.

The true capacity to be personal does in fact arise around the time object constancy is achieved, and even when there is ego present, it is possible to be personal. But the capacity to be personal cannot be the capacity of an individuality based on ego identifications. To be truly personal one must have achieved a development beyond that of a coherent self-image.

In other words, one has to be a real person, and perceive the other as a real person, as who he actually is, for there to be a real personal interaction. Otherwise, the interaction, although it feels personal and even intimate, is but an approximation of real personal interaction. And when one sees through one's identifications with past object relations one becomes acutely conscious that this approximation is fake. One is shocked into the realization that his personal contact and consideration

74   have always been vacuous, constituting nothing but the replay of past object relations, or the replay of an organization of those object relations. One was not making contact with the other person, and was not really considering the other person. He was considering somebody else, in fact, only an image of a person, an image which is not even an accurate image of the person he is interacting with.

When we no longer need to identify with the images of past object relations, the collapse of the false consideration of the other, which is now seen as transference, brings about a sense of impersonality. We now painfully feel the absence of the personal element, and our incapacity to be personal. We feel unable to see the other as a person, but see him only as an object, a screen upon which we can project an image. We feel impersonal, and our interactions feel impersonal, as if the other does not count, the other is not even a person.

This is a very interesting condition. It does not imply that we are uncaring, unloving, hateful, angry or emotionally detached. In fact, we might be experiencing love and compassion, and still feel impersonal. This in fact occasionally happens in the process of inner realization. A student might realize the aspects of love, compassion, kindness and selflessness, and still be unable to be personal. Among all the aspects of essence and Being, it is only the Personal Essence that has the personal element. One can be realized on a very deep dimension, but without the Personal Essence.

At such times the student is usually baffled and chagrined. He thinks, "How can I be so full of love and kindness and still I cannot be personal?" The perception at such times is that one is full of love and kindness, and is quite willing to help but can see the other only as one who needs help. The other cannot be seen in his uniqueness, but is simply an object to be helped, to be acted upon. The other becomes an object of one's universal and impersonal love, compassion and helpfulness.

Some spiritual teachers are in this condition, and are trying to help their students out of an abundance of love and selfless kindness. The love is universal, it is for everybody and everything. The problem is that the student does not figure as a real, unique person. He is seen only as a student, a seeker, an ego that longs for release. The student does not truly feel loved and valued unless the love and value are personal, for him personally, for his uniqueness. He does not respond, at a deep place within him, if the love of the teacher is limited to the universal. He feels: "My teacher does not love me for who I am uniquely. He just loves everybody and everything. I am not truly important for my teacher."

It is difficult for the student to respond fully to universal love alone because the student still identifies with personality, and believes in and cherishes the personal element. When the teacher makes his contact with the student personal, a deep place in the student stirs. The core of his ego begins to relax. He is seen; his uniqueness is valued.

However, when we are confronted with impersonality in the course of letting go of ego identifications, if we neither posit it as the ultimate reality, nor reject it, but genuinely investigate the truth, we will ultimately come upon the personal element. The absence of the personal element, which is felt as an impersonality, can be seen at such times either as an emptiness in the chest, or the presence of a hard impersonal shield over it. The emptiness is felt as almost physical, as an empty hole or cavity in the chest. The emptiness affects the individual by making him feel that he doesn't have what it takes for him to relate in a personal way. He is impersonal because he lacks the personal element. He feels the emptiness as a deficiency, a lack in who he is. This deficient emptiness is simply the state of the absence of the Personal Essence. The rigid shield is a defense against this deficiency, which gives the individual a sense of being a person that is not personal. In fact, it is what is usually referred to in depth psychology as a schizoid defense. It is a defense against personal contact, because of the vulnerability that it might expose. So the individual employs this impersonal defense of isolation and emotional detachment so that he does not feel either the vulnerability of personal involvement, or the sadness about the lack of it. This condition is much more common than is normally acknowledged, for it is usually hidden by the ego's fake sense of being personal.

The dissolution of this defense can bring into consciousness a deep emotional hurt, which is felt as a wound of being cut off from one's own Being. If it is seen with compassion, this deep wound will lead to the emptiness in the chest, which feels as if something is lacking, that a precious part of oneself is missing. We give the report of a student, Natalie, whom we discussed earlier in this section, in another

76 experience of the Personal Essence. Here, we find her grappling with the painful feeling of impersonality:

> On Friday night I talked with you about feelings I have that I am impersonal, cold, dry, monotonous and holding back. I feel this way with my friends and with my clients. My communications with my clients lack a personal touch. The holding back is experienced in my chest, with contractions in my solar plexus. Behind the holding is softness with vulnerability. There is fear of exposure and rejection, as well as of being liked by others. And yet this soft vulnerability is sweet and pleasant. I feel closer to myself—personal—and from this source my energy feels open to make contact and to be real. When I am isolated from myself I feel distant from others.
>
> It was interesting to me that as soon as I started talking with you I felt very warm, alive and personal. At the moment I expressed and exposed the feeling of lack, my Personal Essence was felt, disproving my belief that I am not capable of personal contact.

Here we see that the experience of the Personal Essence was precipitated by the dissolution of the defense against the lack of it. The feeling of lack surfaced first, and when she accepted it, she started feeling the fullness of the Personal Essence. (This is a very common pattern in our work; when one ceases defending against the sense of lack of some quality, and simply feels the emptiness, the quality then appears in the experience.) We call this aspect of Essence the Personal Essence because the personal element is its distinguishing characteristic. The name is descriptive; it is Essence (Being) and it is personal. The traditional name for it is the "pearl beyond price" or the "incomparable pearl." The aptness of this terminology is readily grasped when we directly perceive the Personal Essence.

We also see a greater depth of the meaning of personal in the experience of Natalie in the previous chapter. She says: "I feel closer to myself—personal—and from this source my energy feels open to make contact and to be real." So the sense of feeling personal is a sense of feeling close to, and intimate with, oneself in a personal way. One feels very close to oneself as a person, as a being, as a human being. One feels involved with oneself, immersed in one's unique beingness. One is intimately touching one's own depth, one's own substance, one's own soul. One is touching the atoms of one's being, in intimate contact, in an embrace where one is embracing one's own being. He who embraces and he who is embraced are the same being, the Personal Essence. The subject is the object. The perceiver is the perceived. The intimacy is so complete that there is no duality.

The personal feeling in this experience is the constituent consciousness of the Personal Essence, the intimate feeling tone of this personal being. Just as water is composed of two parts hydrogen to one part oxygen, so the Personal Essence is composed of consciousness that feels personal. So being personal does not exactly mean that one is aware of oneself as a person, and because of this one feels personal. Not exactly. The feeling of being personal is its own feeling, independent of what one takes oneself to be. This point is difficult to communicate, because on the ego level, being personal is habitually associated with being a person.

When one is deeply absorbed in the state of being of the Personal Essence one might not be aware of oneself as a person, but one will still feel this state to have a personal sense. The personal element is a state of Being or a state of consciousness on its own. It is not a quality of something else.

The personal element is a specific and absolute aspect of Essence. Like other aspects of Essence, it is a Platonic form. When one experiences the personal aspect one is certain that one feels a personal consciousness, or a personal state of Being. Just as love, will or joy are readily recognized when they are experienced in the pure form of the essential aspect, so is the personal aspect readily recognized. There is always recognition of one's true nature when it is experienced. As Socrates said, one does not learn from anybody or from experience about the Platonic forms. One remembers them from one's own deep resources. One merely remembers oneself.

The interesting thing about the essential aspects, including the personal aspect, is that they are amenable to the most precise descriptions and discriminations by the one having the experience, but the words will not communicate the essence of the experience to another who never had the experience. However, if someone has had the experience then it is easy for him to understand what is being described. Because of this, descriptions of essential aspects are useful mainly to those who have had a specific experience or are on the verge of having it. It is also true, however, that these descriptions, like literary

78   and poetic ones, can evoke those deeper and truer experiences of reality and of one's nature; in some artistic or spiritual contexts, the ego can become slightly more "transparent" and one will intuit some new level of truth.

On the ego level, we usually feel most personal when feeling deep emotions or being in emotional situations with others. This is in marked contrast to the personal element of Being. Being is not on the emotional level. Being is a much deeper and more profound level than emotions. Emotions are responses of the nervous system, very much linked with the organization of past object relations. Being personal on the Being level can mean some kind of sharing and communication, but not necessarily. One can be personal and completely alone. It is a way of being, a way of experiencing oneself and a way of living. One is personally involved in, is intimately in contact with whatever one is doing or experiencing.

In fact, this expression "to be involved" used on the level of the personality of ego comes close to the quality of being personal on the Being level. To be personally involved means that we are more wholehearted about, more in contact with, more intimate with, whatever situation or activity we are in. It means we are more present in the activity. And when we are really present, we are present as the Personal Essence, for it is our personal Being.

So on the level of Being, to be personal means to be the Personal Essence. Contact, communication or interaction is personal when one is personally present as the Personal Essence. One can be personal with another without saying or doing anything. It is a way of being with the other. One is actually being there, oneself. From the perspective of Being, the content of the communication is not what determines whether an interaction is personal or not. There might be emotional communication or even physical contact, but if one is not present as the Personal Essence then one is not personal. One can be interacting with a total stranger, discussing abstract ideas and still be personal.

So to be personal is to be present in the interaction, to be present as who one really is, the Personal Essence. There is both presence and reality. There is genuineness. There is truth. There is immediate contact.

The emotional genuineness most people feel as their most personal state is a far cry from the genuineness of Being. Emotional genuineness, in its very nature, expresses the past. The genuineness of Being

expresses reality, for it is in the present. There are no defenses, no
roles, no manipulations. One is, and one's communications are real.

The practice of being genuine in one's communication is a good way to reach the Personal Essence. When one is genuine about oneself, expressing an authentic concern, then one is personal. This is why Natalie, in the report above, experienced the Personal Essence with relative ease. She was genuine in her concern about her state. She felt personally hurt, and made a genuine personal plea to me for help. She was not trying to defend herself or to manipulate me, but was direct, genuine and personal. It was this attitude which made her open to the arising of the Personal Essence. Her hurt and concern were not a reenacting of past object relations; she was genuinely responding to an actual state, the absence of her Being. That by itself was disidentification from past object relations. Her emotions were genuine because they were a response arising from disidentification and not from identification.

Sometimes, even for someone who is not engaged in spiritual work, an acute or unexpected personal situation can precipitate such genuineness in feeling and perception. At these times the individual becomes present in a clear and definite way unusual for him or her. Psychotherapists probably notice this phenomenon in deep or intense sessions. The patient becomes more present when he or she is genuine in a personal way. It is likely that the Personal Essence is present at such times but not recognized directly as what is responsible for the unusual state of presence.

Not only intense or dramatic emotional states can lead us toward being genuine in a personal way. One might recognize or express a deep desire, or experience a true concern for oneself or another human being. One can make a simple but genuine personal contact; a look, a touch, or a word are sometimes sufficient. Any of these simple but personal acts can precipitate the presence of the Personal Essence.

In a private teaching session, Jackson, a professional man in his forties, is talking to me about his difficulties in making contact with other people. I ask him how he feels with me at the moment, whether he feels there is contact or not. He feels isolated. Exploring this state of isolation, he realizes he always feels that others are demanding something from him, and that this feeling originated with his early

80   relationship with his mother, in which he felt she was not there for him, but was always demanding and intrusive. His response to the situation was to withdraw, which pattern he retained in all his adult relationships, especially those with women. I comment that although he believes he is withdrawing from relationship he is, in fact, relating to me and others within the object relation he had with his mother. Seeing this, he begins to feel alone and vulnerable. He feels he does not have what it takes to make contact with me, although he feels I am present for him. As he manages to tolerate the vulnerability, he starts to feel more present. After a short while, he feels in contact with me in a real and simple way. When I inquire about his state, he reports that he feels the fullness and realness of the Personal Essence. He feels present, full and in immediate contact with me, a contact beyond the content of his mind. He feels personal with me in a simple way, with no feelings about demand. He is surprised at the simplicity and ease of the whole session. We must not forget here that Jackson has been working on understanding himself for a long time, with a dedicated effort towards finding the truth. Yet it was a simple insight that led him to feel a genuine wish for real contact.

All truly personal acts can precipitate the presence of the Personal Essence. It is experienced as a personal human presence. It is what can experience a personal concern for another human being. It is what can bridge the separateness of ego. It is what can make personal contact.

Chapter Six

Contact

The personal element is most palpably discerned in human contact. The ability to make contact with another person is the hallmark of the Personal Essence. Only the Personal Essence has the capacity to make such contact; in fact it *is* the capacity for personal contact. Neither the ego with its intrapsychic structures, nor the non-conceptual state of Being with its impersonality, has this capacity, a distinguishing characteristic of being human. The ego cannot truly make contact, because of these characteristics which we have noted:

1. *It is based on identity with self-image or images.* How can a structure in the mind make contact? It is nothing that is truly present; it is only a conceptual structure, a structure of ideas. This structure is devoid of presence and consciousness, and thus cannot make contact.

2. *Interactions of the ego are basically the reenactments of past object relations.* When the overall individuality of ego interacts with something, that interaction is an approximation of the actual situation that is dependent on the integrations of past interactions. So it is not present-centered. How can an interaction which is a replay of the past be called a genuine human contact?

3. *The other person is seen either as an image, one pole of a past object relation, or through a structure of images.* The other person is not truly seen or related to. The fact that ego cannot make real contact is lamentable, and indicates a terrible waste of human potential. We cannot see each other when we are identifying with self-images from the past. We are strangers to each other, merely relating to projected

81

82   images, to parts of our own minds. This is the normal, everyday life of most us, not only the emotionally disturbed.

We are confronted occasionally by a student who reports with astonishment and disappointment how his husband, wife, friend or lover is really a stranger. When a student achieves some distance from ego identifications he realizes suddenly that he does not really know who the other is. The other feels like a stranger when stripped of the projected images. This usually can be very frightening, for it leaves the individual in a state of utter aloneness.

4. *The individuality of ego has a sense of separateness that is based on the building of self-boundaries.* These boundaries contribute to the sense of being an individual. However, these boundaries become walls separating the individual from other human beings, and from the universe in general.

Even if we take psychological individuation to be more than the development of the psychic structure, for instance if we take it to be the emotional experience of oneself resulting from such mental structure, the boundaries still function as walls, which are not permeable to real contact. Ego boundaries create a much more profound separateness than is usually recognized. Object relations theory regards ego boundaries as necessary for the sense of being a separate and unique individual, the fruit of the process of ego development; but it does not appreciate how much such boundaries separate human beings from each other, or how they make true contact impossible. We will explore this point more fully.

This might not be clear for an individual identifying with ego, but it becomes acutely obvious when one knows oneself as a being, and not as a self-image. One then experiences the structure of ego giving rise to the sense of separateness as thick and rigid shields around oneself, restricting him from truly touching another human being or being touched by another in any deep way. There is also a profound isolation from the rest of reality, which becomes the most important barrier against the experience of oneness with the universe.

To state the case succinctly: there is no genuine contact when there is transference. True contact happens when one is free from transference. This is not an either-or case; the most accurate statement is that the less identification there is with past object relations, the more genuine personal contact is possible.

Laura has been a member of a work group with the author for
about two years. Her relationship to me has always been superficial,
emotionally conflicted and quite difficult for her. She would relate to
me always as a little girl, coy and embarrassed, scared or angry. She
sees me as the powerful, desirable but unloving and unavailable
father. Whenever she talks to me she is unable to have a distance
from this object relation. She is nervous, giggly and ends up reacting
with anger, fear or sadness. For a long time she saw that she was not
seeing me, but was merely reacting to an image of her father. This did
not help her to be real with me, but she continued seeing and understanding the vicissitudes of her father transference onto me. She always wanted just to talk to me, just to make a simple human contact.
But she was shut off from this simplicity by her identification and
projection. Finally, in one group meeting, she was able to break
through this barrier. She did it on her own initiative, going through
the emotional difficulties and succeeding in making the contact. This
is her report of her work in the session:

> My experience working with you yesterday began with
> my saying your name when you were still working with
> somebody else. While I waited and listened I felt a lot of
> energy—exhilaration—that continued while I worked with
> you.
> Then we talked about contact which I wanted to have
> with you before the summer vacation. I talked about your
> work with another group member last week. It brought up
> some sadness for me when you said that sadness is the
> gap between what we are or experience and what we
> want, or something like that. I felt some sadness, and you
> asked about that. It had to do with wanting more contact
> with you. I mentioned that I have been observing myself
> judge myself and that I was having a judgment about want-
> ing you to see the state I have been experiencing lately.
> The judgment was that wanting recognition from you is an
> ego reaction.
> You said something about the state I was experiencing;
> present, clear, peaceful, solid, powerful, etc. I felt scared
> because I was afraid you or I would deny my experience
> or that by experiencing this state I will be alone. You as-
> ked me about the aloneness and I saw it is not myself but
> my superego that would be gone. I noticed that the fear
> makes it difficult to get my breath into my abdomen and
> that there is something forced about it. I noticed my eyes

start to get unfocused. You appeared smaller or farther away. You had me do something to relax my eyes. While I did that you talked about contact, presence and fullness. At one point it seemed humorous to me.

This contact with you was quite nice. It seemed like I had huge, wide-open eyes, no barriers, and a lot of presence, aliveness, and not much separateness. There continued to be some sort of fear, but it seemed more like a lot of energy.

We see here that some transference remains in the interaction, but she did manage to make the contact. We also see that the contact went along with two specific phenomena: disidentification from past object relations, and a sense of alive presence. I did not try to guide her to a more specific recognition of this presence because I thought she was already having a breakthrough, and that greater depth might merely bring in deeper defenses.

This report illustrates how the transition from identity with past object relations to the presence of the Personal Essence is a prerequisite for true personal contact. Her issue with being real and making contact is not completely resolved; this is only an initial breakthrough, which will have to be repeated many more times, as more unconscious object relations are brought to the surface, seen through and abandoned. Establishing the Personal Essence as a permanent presence requires much more work, as we will see as we go on.

It is always the case that when someone is working with the issue of contact, he is working on the realization of the Personal Essence. Contact is the most specifically personal act, and when it is real it is the act of the real Being. Students normally come to the issue by feeling a certain deficiency about it. One might feel unable to make contact, as in the case of Laura above. One might feel desire for contact, for instance wanting me to contact them personally. Here, the individual believes she cannot initiate the contact, and needs me to do so.

Another case is that of Leslie, a young single woman who has moved recently to a different town, and now has virtually no close friends. She has been feeling acutely lonely and self-denigrating. In a private teaching session she is hating herself and feeling very frustrated, believing that she is alone because nobody wants her company. Understanding the situation, seeing how her self-rejection and hatred have nothing to do with the present situation, and looking at things objectively, does nothing to change her state. She cries and feels more frustrated. This is unusual for her, because it is usually relatively easy for her to be objective and disidentify from her emotional states. Finally I ask her to look me in the eyes and make the contact directly. This instantly changes her state. She quickly begins feeling warm, full and present. She feels herself as a sense of Being that is personal. And from this vantage point she sees the dramatic unreality of her emotional state. This becomes a starting point for her making contacts in her new environment, and engaging in useful and meaningful work. Of course, the change is not attributable only to this single session. She had been involved in the work of realization for some time, and she did need to work on the issue more in subsequent sessions.

We observe here the typical pattern of taking contact to be an expression of personal love and caring. This fact will help us in understanding the nature of contact. The following report points to this fact and the fact that contact is also taken to be a recognition of our own experience of Being. When we feel truly contacted we feel that our true beingness is being seen and recognized. The need for recognition, which is taken by the mind as a support for who one is, often manifests before or after a long separation. Here, Donna, a woman in her thirties, in one of the helping professions, and a member of a work group for several years, reports about her first session after my absence of a month:

> I had been experiencing a deep pain which burned and felt knife-like in my solar plexus and chest. It spread into my whole diaphragm. It started about thirty minutes prior to the meeting. A sense of weakness and frustration accompanied the pain. I was afraid to talk but wanted to talk to you. While I worked the pain went away and I was left with a sense of peacefulness throughout my body. I felt the fullness of the Personal Essence in my chest after the pain went away. I felt embarrassed and silly when I realized I just wanted contact, and it being related to you being gone for four weeks.

The pain here is the hurt of missing the Personal Essence, the precious aspect of one's Being. The longing for her personal beingness manifested as a longing for one of its main qualities, contact. She was not aware that she wanted to feel herself but felt it as a painful

86   longing for personal contact. The pain disappeared when her Personal Essence manifested in her chest. When she made the contact with me she simultaneously made the contact with herself.

The fact is that the presence of the Personal Essence is the presence of the capacity for contact. So contact with oneself and contact with another are felt as the same. It is the presence of the Personal Essence in the interaction. The following case presentation demonstrates one student's experience of the Personal Essence through a route different from that of contact, but she comes to see contact as connected with the experience.

Rachel is a young mother who is in a group and also does private work with the author. She has been having difficulty for some time as her one-year old child starts taking steps towards emotional separation from her. She sometimes feels hard and rigid, which makes her feel strong and masculine like her father, or she wants me to support her when she sees me as the strong father. Her need for support sometimes manifests as powerful oedipal longing for her father, usually transferred onto me. Finally this investigation revealed a deep attachment to her mother, which manifests mostly as identification with some of her traits. Seeing through these identifications in a private teaching session, she starts feeling that she has no sense of structure. She feels jelly-like in her body. She has a strong judgment about this state, feeling it as a weakness, which explained her usual identification with the hardness of her father as a defense against this jelly-like state of no structure. As she understands the judgment she relaxes, but feels the need for a sense of structure. Staying with the state of no structure without reacting to it, she starts feeling firm and full. She feels present as a presence that is strong without being hard. It is a firm fullness that is alive and feels like her, not like her mother or father. Feeling her Personal Essence, she becomes aware that she feels in direct contact with me without the usual oedipal or negative feelings.

The manifestations of the issue of contact described so far imply the feeling, conscious or unconscious, of the lack of the Personal Essence. The issue can manifest in various other ways. It could appear as a difficulty in reciprocation of contact. One feels unable to be present when the other is making contact. One feels that one does not have what it takes to be present for such contact. This was the situation in Jackson's case.

In such situations the individual is not aware of a longing for contact, but is aware of a difficulty with it. Individuals with marked schizoid or narcissistic tendencies tend to exhibit this difficulty. It takes much sincerity for the individual to admit to himself such a deficiency; in general he denies the reality of the situation, explaining it away by blaming the other or by rationalization.

Now we turn our attention to the nature of contact. What is it? Why is the Personal Essence the only aspect of Being capable of it?

We saw in Laura's report that when the Personal Essence is present there is openness and no defensiveness. She was not doing anything to defend or protect herself emotionally. This is one reason why true contact is not easy; one is open to whatever is there in the interaction. Without the Personal Essence, true contact is blocked by the usual defenses of the schizoid type—psychological isolation, withdrawal, intellectualization and so on.

The other characteristic of the Personal Essence we can see from the reports above is the absence of barriers, which indicates the absence of the boundaries of the individuality. The individual lets go of the need to protect his sense of separateness, thus ceasing to identify with or project images from the past.

All this indicates that there is an actual vulnerability. This vulnerability is reported especially by individuals in their first encounters with personal contact. The question arises, why is there vulnerability when there are no defenses or separating barriers? There can be openness and absence of barriers without the experience of vulnerability, as happens in the experiences of space or emptiness, for example, in which one feels an expansive openness, a spaciousness, a lightness, without any hint of vulnerability. [See *The Void*, A. H. Almaas, 1986]

Vulnerability in openness indicates the presence of beingness. When there is no presence then there is no expectation of danger, even with openness, and hence no feeling of vulnerability. This was clear in the case of a young woman student who always had some good reason why being personal was not desirable. Whenever she worked on being personal or on making personal contact she entered a state of impersonal expansion. The state was a very deep one of no self and no boundaries. She felt light, open, happy and boundless. But she sensed no particular presence or fullness. It was a long time

88   before she realized she was using this state, which she developed
through extensive Buddhist meditation, to avoid feeling present in a
personal way, because she found it difficult to tolerate the feelings of
vulnerability.

So contact involves not only openness and vulnerability, but, also,
the presence of a sense of Being. One is open, vulnerable and
present. However, the reader might object that this is the condition of
the presence of any aspect of Essence. Whenever Being is felt as
presence there is necessarily some openness, and a measure of disidentification from ego and its defenses. This is true, but this does not
yet make for contact. The presence of a state of Being means the
presence of pure consciousness, in any of its absolute forms. This
means there is awareness, sensitivity and openness. There is a sensitive consciousness of the other, an empathy and an appreciation of
the other's existence. In these states, one might be very accurate in
one's perception of the other, and observant of his state. There might
be tender love, warm kindness or even joyful interaction. But this is
not necessarily contact. Consciousness is not necessarily contact, although it can make possible sensitivity and empathy with the other.

Although Being is necessary for contact it is certainly not sufficient
for contact in its unqualified form. For there to be contact, the Personal Essence has to be present. Contact implies personal contact. It
implies a being in contact with another being.

This is difficult to imagine without the experience of the Personal
Essence. But when the Personal Essence is present, then one cannot
help but exclaim: "Aha, of course, how else can it be! I have to be
present, as who I am, for me to make contact." The contact of the
Personal Essence feels so direct, so immediate, so complete, so full,
that when it is known it becomes impossible to call any other state of
consciousness contact. One is making contact because one is personally present in the interaction. One is actually there, as one's own
substance, filling the interaction with immediacy and significance.

The personal contact then is as actual, as concrete, as immediate as
physical contact. In such contact one is touching the other's Being
with one's own Being. The substance of one's unique personal beingness touches the substance of the other's unique personal beingness.
It is a touching of each other without the presence of ego boundaries,
and without the loss of one's unique individuation of Being. One is

present, as oneself, as one's unique individuation. One is not being anything from the past, so one is totally genuine. One is personal. One is present as an individuated Being, a unique human being. And contact is this presence being with another presence.

To make contact on the Being level is to be, with another being. There is no need for words or any other kind of communication for there to be contact. But words and actions of communication do not necessarily negate it. To make contact with someone is to be personal in a real way with that person. It is that simple.

Even in the experience of one who lives in the undifferentiated realm of Being, the personal element must be present for there to be contact with other human beings. One might not be experiencing oneself as a person, but as an unbounded and impersonal reality, but there must be the manifestation of the personal element of consciousness for there to be contact. This is not an easy condition to imagine; it is not easy to imagine how one can be not a person, and it is even more difficult to imagine how one can then be personal. This is one reason we differentiated in the last section between the personal element and the sense of being a person.

To summarize our explorations in this Part we conclude that the Personal Essence is characterized by the following primary qualities:

- It is a presence of Being.
- It is true autonomy.
- It is personal.
- It alone can make direct contact.

PART III

THE ESSENTIAL PERSON

All aspects of Essence, both differentiated and nondifferentiated states of Being, are generally experienced as one's true nature; this is because they are all recognized as the intrinsic existence and presence of one's Being. The Personal Essence is experienced as such, as one's own nature and Being, but it is also experienced as a person. One experiences oneself as a Human Being.

The sense or perception of being a person, here, is not a feeling about oneself, nor a thought or idea about oneself. It is not an inference from looking at one's body or one's behavior. It is not a reference from past perceptions, taken as a continuity in time. It is not an image in the mind. It is not a conclusion, mental or emotional, that results from an image in one's mind. It is not a feeling, thought or concept about oneself that results from memory or from interaction with the environment.

The experience of the Personal Essence is independent from memories. This is because the Personal Essence, with its sense of

92   being a person, is neither an image nor a feeling dependent on an image. It is independent from the mind and its structures, and hence it is independent from the memories of one's personal history. It is direct perceptual recognition of a state of Being, in the here and now. It is direct and immediate knowing of one's true personhood, that is inseparable from being the person.

This kind of knowing is characteristic of Being in general. The usual kind of knowing is through inference. The knowing of Being is by identity. One knows oneself because one is oneself. It is knowing by being what is known. So it is an immediate, direct, and existential knowing, in which there is no duality of subject and object.

So the recognition that Personal Essence is oneself as a person is a definite, clear, profound and unassailable knowingness. There is confidence and certainty. One experiences oneself as a human being, as an ongoing-personal-beingness. One is real for one exists absolutely, irrespective of the past and of the environment. One is an ongoing-sense-of-beingness that is made out of alive consciousness, consciousness that is a palpable presence and not merely the capacity to be conscious.

To be is not just to know in one's mind that one is. To be is to be Being, as existence, and as a substantial presence that is experienced as concretely as physical reality. So to be the Personal Essence is to be a substantial presence, a fullness, a compact consciousness that feels personal.

We must remark again that this attempt to describe the sense of being a person on the Being level is not an attempt to communicate the experience to the reader. That would be a futile effort. However, the individual who has already had some experience of it might gain a greater recognition and understanding from this discussion; or the individual who is close to the experience might get closer to it. Even those who have perhaps done no explicit work on these states have probably had some experiences in their lives which give a flavor of the Personal Essence, and looking at these experiences from the perspective introduced here might enable them to see these experiences in a new light. Beyond that, our words will probably sound like abstractions. These descriptions, however, are useful for continuing with our exploration.

In this Part we will explore the qualities of the Personal Essence   93
from several perspectives: that of the man of the world, that of
legends and fairy tales, that of the perspective of the man of spirit,
and that of the Personal Essence in spiritual traditions.

Chapter Seven

Personal Essence and the Man of the World

T he man of the world experiences being a person as a mental-emotional-physical phenomenon. He conceives himself as a person via his body image. His sense of himself is inferred from his perception of his body, his mind and his behavior. His sense of being a person cannot be separated from, and cannot exist without, his memories of himself in past interactions. He sees himself as a person who was born as an infant to a certain set of parents, and who has grown and developed and had many experiences throughout the years. His sense of who he is as a person cannot be separated in his experience from his personal history, from all that has happened to him. He cannot separate his sense of who he is from his relationship to his environment, and the people in it. He cannot separate who he is from what he thinks, and what other people think of him. In other words, he cannot just be who he is, independent of his mind. Who he is and who he thinks (consciously or unconsciously) he is are inseparable for him.

This is in great contrast to the experience of the Personal Essence, where personal history is irrelevant to being oneself. The person of Being has no sense of age; number of years cannot apply to him. Time to him is conceptual, and only the present is real. The person of Being is independent, in terms of being himself, from his physical parents. He does not need to refer himself to parents or to anybody or anything.

It is clear from the findings of object relations theory, why the sense of being a person of the man of the world cannot be independent from mind, memory, past experiences, age, sex, parents, environment, body and so on. As we have seen, the man of the world's sense of being a person is explained by object relations theory as a psychical developmental achievement: the achievement of a separate individuality with a sense of self, or as Mahler would describe it, the establishment of a unified self-image. This individuation is primarily a development in the mind, and thus is seen from the perspective of Being as ephemeral and undeserving of the label of reality.

We asked in a previous chapter, why do all people, if they are astray as the man of spirit asserts, follow the same path of illusion: that of adopting an individuality and pursuing a personal life? A possible answer comes from the understanding of the nature of the Personal Essence. The man of the world, in pursuing a personal life, is trying to reach his true human individuation. His values and aspirations reflect a truth, the truth of the possibility of being a real person, an essential person with a fulfilled personal life. The truth of the Personal Essence resides at his human core; it is the unconscious archetype of what he can be. He is not completely astray, but rather dimly senses his potential as a human being and goes about trying to realize it. However, he falls short of the reality, because there is inadequate guidance, knowledge or modeling in his formative years. His development in this direction is greatly influenced by the development of the people who take care of him as a child, and who educate him later. He ends up developing into an image, a reflection of the reality of what he can be.

The man of the world values and pursues personhood for it is his human potential, his real individuation. It is this personal quality that he values and identifies with, which makes him often not listen to the impersonality of the man of spirit. He believes in the personal life not merely because he is trapped in the illusions of his ego, but also because it evokes his true human nature and potential. To abandon the sense of being personal would feel like the loss of the Personal Essence. The Personal Essence is his valued and cherished human core. It is his unique human form in this universe. He might not be aware of it consciously, but he cannot help being drawn towards it.

Our understanding that the personality of ego is an imitation of the essential person, the person of Being, can be made more clear by what we call our "theory of holes." This perspective, which was developed in detail in our books *Essence* and *The Void*, states that whenever an essential aspect is missing or cut off from one's consciousness there results a deficiency, or hole, in its place. This hole is then filled by a part of the psychic structure that resembles the lost essential aspect. One fills or covers up the deficiency with a false aspect in its place.

An example of this theory is the issue of Will. Will is one of the aspects of Essence, an element of the true human potential. In childhood it can be cut off and lost from one's sense of who one is. The absence of this aspect will be felt as a sense of castration, of a lack of inner support and a lack of personal confidence. This deficiency is then usually defended against by creating a false will. The false will is a willfulness, a hard and rigid kind of determination, a stubbornness. This false will is an imitation of the real Will which has been cut off. It is a psychic structure constructed out of self-images and object relations from the past. The essential Will, on the other hand, is an aspect of Being, an existential presence, an actuality in the present. It is flexible and realistic, and does not have the rigidity and hardness of the ego will. It manifests as a natural, spontaneous and implicit sense of inner support and confidence.

The same pattern applies to the aspect of the Personal Essence. For some reason in childhood it is not allowed in consciousness, or is cut off from one's awareness. There results a deficiency that is then covered up by the development of the separate individuality of ego. Although it is false, it is still a reflection of the essential person. The loss of this reflection will be resisted because it is experienced unconsciously as the loss of the Personal Essence. This is because the loss of the reflection will expose the hole, the lack of the Personal Essence.

We saw this in our earlier descriptions of the emergence of the Personal Essence resulting from seeing through ego identifications. Achieving some distance from ego identifications means abandoning the reflection, the false gold. And as we have seen in the various case reports, the deficiency appears first, followed by fullness of the essential person.

We will explore shortly, in more technical detail, this understanding of the personality of ego as an imitation of and substitute for the Personal Essence. For now we present a case which shows how the individuality of ego is an imitation of the real thing, the

Personal Essence. (The case of David in Chapter Four, shows much
the same thing.)

Jordan is a professional man in his thirties, married, and a member of a work group with the author. For a long time he dealt with the narcissistic issues of continually wanting recognition for and value from achievements, finally becoming aware of the lack of the sense of true self. This led to the experience of the aspect of the Essential Self, which precipitated many painful and joyful deep feelings. Then the dominant issue became his compulsive busyness; he could not stop working or worrying about work. He saw his personality as always busy, always working, always endeavoring to find more work. He could not just relax and be. In time this led to states of feeling small and alone, deficient and unable to take care of himself. He recalled how in early childhood he did not receive the nourishment and supportive contact to just be himself. He dealt with the issues relating to the essential aspects of Strength, Will and Nourishment.

At this point in his process, during a group session he becomes aware that part of the motivation for his compulsive attitude towards work is to avoid a very deep depression. Confronting this depression he starts to feel lighter and more relaxed. He starts having times where he feels slow and mellow. This then readily leads to the fullness and beingness of the Personal Essence, which makes him feel intimate with himself. He feels the fullness pervading his body. This starts a whole segment of his work, in which he realizes that he is always busy because if he is relaxed and slow then he will be the fullness of his Being, and this brings all kinds of issues and conflicts. So he has adopted a personality that is busy, active and productive, which is an imitation of the efficiency and maturity of the Personal Essence, so that he will feel that he is a mature and grown-up man who is capable of taking care of himself and his family. He feels he is a capable person, efficient and not deficient. In seeing that this false functioning is incompatible with the presence of the Personal Essence, Jordan is motivated and able to learn to tolerate the fullness of his being.

From the above discussion we see that the man of the world has a truth, a spiritual truth, a truth related to Being. This deep truth of Being patterns his life; it is the archetype for his life. However, this truth is hidden, is known only through a reflection, which is the ego. Hence it is distorted and imprecise. It is no wonder that complete and

98   permanent personal fulfillment is rarely attained. The life of the reflection cannot be truly fulfilling, even though it is a reflection of reality. Its fulfillment and satisfaction, which are always dependent upon external circumstances, are bound to be only a reflection and imitation of the real fulfillment and satisfaction of essence. However, the reflection can lead to the reality reflected. The reflection of the Personal Essence in the ego is seen in the personal quality, in the value of autonomy and in the capacity to make personal contact. We have already seen how the pursuit of understanding these characteristics can lead directly to the experience of the Personal Essence.

Chapter Eight

Personal Essence in Legends and Fairy Tales

T he process of the realization of the essential person is one of the main themes in ancient mythologies, folklore, legends and fairy tales. It is the story of the hero, the puer aeternus, the young man in his lonely quest. This theme appears in many forms, but it involves the hero proving himself to be mature and worthy by finding a precious object of a special quality. One example of such a "seeking and finding" story is that of the quest for the Grail. One well-known author of many such stories, Mary Stewart, writes:

> The stories of the Holy Grail, identifying it with the cup from the Last Supper, are twelfth-century tales modeled in their main element on some early Celtic "quest" stories; in fact they have elements even older. These Grail stories show certain points in common, changing in detail, but fairly constant in form and idea. There is usually an unknown youth, the *bel incannu*, who is brought up in the wilds, ignorant of his name or parentage. He leaves his home and rides out in search of his identity. He comes across a Waste Land, ruled by a maimed (impotent) king; there is a castle, usually on an island, on which the youth comes by chance. He reaches it in a boat belonging to a royal fisherman, the Fisher King of the Grail legends. The Fisher King is sometimes identified with the impotent king of the Waste Land. The castle on the island is owned by a king of the Otherworld, and there the youth finds the object of his quest, sometimes a cup or a lance, sometimes a sword, broken or whole. At the quest's end he wakes by the side of the water with his horse tethered near him, and

the island once again invisible. On his return from the Otherworld, fertility and peace are restored to the Waste Land. Some tales figure a white stag collared with gold, who leads the youth to his destination. [Mary Stewart, *The Hollow Hills*, p. 444]

In the Grail legends, and in some other stories, the hero starts from the visible world, the world of ego and personality and goes to the invisible world, the world of spirit and Essence, to find what he is seeking. As Mary Stewart says, the hero, by finding the object of his seeking, finds his true identity. This brings peace and fertility to the Waste Land, the land of the false, implying its transformation.

In other stories, the hero comes from the invisible world, or is a descendent from royalty, who goes to the visible world, the land of lies and false identity. It is there, through trial and effort that he finds the object he is seeking. Proving his maturity in this way, he goes back to his original land, ready to assume responsibility. Heinrich Zimmer, commenting about one such tale, writes about the exiled hero:

> The fairy prince desires deliverance from this exile, and his kingdom awaits his return; yet he is permitted to make the necessary journey only when bearing the human rider on his back. Only by assisting the mortal hero to immortal life can the superhuman prince effect his own salvation. The human being attains also thereby salvation, completeness, and the power to overcome distress, while the fairy realm, receiving back its prince, reintegrating the lost one into its system, is healed of its affliction, restored to perfection, and flooded with joy. [Heinrich Zimmer, *The King and the Corpse*, p. 50]

The two kinds of legends point to the truth from two perspectives. The first points to the truth that the object sought is of the nature of the invisible world of spirit, and hence is more real and precious than the ego structures (to put it in the language of our previous discussion) found in the Waste Land. The second kind of legend points to the equally important truth that the sought-after object (which in our context is the Personal Essence), although it is of a special nature, must be found in the land of ego, the land of suffering, effort and illusion. One finds his true identity and maturity by wrestling with difficulties of the world. The comment of Zimmer, above, includes both meanings. The human rider indicates that the Personal Essence is the real human being, who is the fullness and completeness of the human potential.

A similar story is that of the hero who frees an imprisoned princess, whom he eventually marries. The hero comes to his manhood, indicating his assumption of human maturity, and marries the woman he saves. This indicates the living of a personal life, of marriage, family, pleasure, creativity and so on. Often the personal life is a royal life, indicating it is not the life of the personality of ego, but the life of the essential person, of the Personal Essence. Royalty in legends and fairy tales, like godhood in mythologies, indicates that there is a spiritual quality, an elevated and noble human element. And this noble human element is his own Being, which is real, true and hence most precious. Zimmer comments about the abundance of the reign of a king and queen, in one of the mythical stories:

> Such descriptions of natural abundance are not unusual in the legends of beneficent reigns; for when two faultless rulers conform to the divine law of the universe and guide their people by their own model conduct, they bring into operation the quickening power of perfection. The consummate king and queen make manifest together what the Chinese term *Tao*: the virtue of the universal order. They make *Tao* manifest as *Teh*: the virtue of their own proper nature. And this virtue is self-effulgent. Its influence penetrates like magic into the vital centers of everything around them, so that even the spirit of the land appears to be affected. Harmony and beatitude go out from it. The fields produce, the herds multiply, and the cities thrive, as in a Golden Age. [*Ibid.*, p. 26]

The sense of nobility and royalty is not only an association with the richness and abundance of essential experience, the manifestation of what Zimmer referred to as Teh; it is an actual feeling of royalty and nobility, a state where one feels of royal origin. Once in a while, a student reports the experience of the Personal Essence as accompanied by a feeling of royalty or regalness. One feels not only present as a real person, but because of the purity and preciousness of this reality, one attains a sense of being noble and royal. One feels oneself to be relaxed, settled, accepting of one's nature, and secure. One is not only carefree and absolutely secure, but lives a life of value, preciousness, fulfillment and abundance. One feels like a prince or princess, a king or queen, master of one's life, which is one's dominion. The inner experience of Essence, with its richness, abundance, fullness and beauty is not envisioned by the ego, except in the

102   stories of ancient royalty. However, it is an actual reality, a living experience, when the Personal Essence is realized. Idries Shah, in the
beginning of the quest story of the King's Son, writes:

> Once in a country where all men were like kings, there
> lived a family, who were in every way content, and whose
> surroundings were such that the human tongue cannot
> describe them in terms of anything which is known to man
> today. [Idries Shah, *Tales of the Dervishes*, p. 217]

Idries Shah is a Sufi; he does not write just for entertainment. His
books of stories are instructional material. The images given in the
stories beckon one's consciousness to an actual reality, the reality of
Essence. Man is of royal origin, because his origin is Being. And the
one who knows the realm of Being knows that there is no preciousness, no abundance, no nobility and no royalty that approximates that
of Essence and Being. The values and archetypes of nobility and royalty have their origins in the experience of Essence. The roles of king
and queen, prince and princess are universal, in almost all human
civilizations. Royalty are always dressed in gold and silver, precious
gems, silk and velvet, with abundant color and ornament. Why is
royalty associated with gold, gems, and abundant ornament?

These images of kings and queens, princes and princesses, and
other nobility, must be archetypal, for they are almost universal. These
images symbolize to man his royal origin, that of the magnificence
and abundance of Being. They also symbolize to him, and beckon
him to, his potential, his possibility of attaining true royalty; the individuation of his Being. In ancient mythologies and fairy tales,
royalty were not only rich and powerful; they were also the embodiment of wisdom and sagacity, justice and benevolence, which are
characteristics of Essence.

We can say each man aspires to be a king, and each woman aspires
to be a queen. Their aspirations are really for the true individuation,
the human maturity that is the actualization of one's true potential.
The images of a king or a queen, a prince or a princess, appear occasionally in the experiences of some students in the process of inner
realization. They usually indicate certain breakthroughs in the integration of the Personal Essence. Youthfulness of actualization is sometimes experienced in the feeling of being a prince or a princess, while
maturity of actualization can be experienced in the feeling or state of

being a king or a queen. There is then a sense of being more grown up, of truly being a master of oneself, one's mind, and one's life. The state of prince or princess means realization of Being; the experience of oneself as made out of precious and noble consciousness, but one is still young. One is not a master yet of one's mind and life.

In the stories, the realization of the Personal Essence is not symbolized only by the quest, but specifically by freeing the imprisoned princess and marrying her. In fact, some stories make the princess herself the Personal Essence. She is then called, as in some Sufi stories, the "Princess Precious Pearl." As we have remarked before, the traditional name for the Personal Essence is the pearl beyond price or the incomparable pearl. So marrying the princess is the process of integrating the Personal Essence. This brings about a fulfilled and true personal life, a royal life of Being.

In one such story, the story of the magic horse, related by Shah in his book *Caravan of Dreams,* the hero, Tambal, is a youth who is introspective and more interested in the simple values of life, and who has the curiosity of a child, in contrast to concern with practical things. He finds a magic horse, a wooden horse that can read his heart's desire and carry him to it. When he inquires about his real heart's desire the magic horse carries him on a long journey to a land of a magician king, with a daughter, Princess Precious Pearl, who is constrained in a whirling palace. After many adventures and misfortunes, which are beautiful poetic descriptions of parts of the path of inner realization, the prince is united with his beloved princess and eventually rules the kingdom.

The quest sometimes takes the form of looking for a precious gem, guarded by a monster, such as a serpent or a dragon, as in the example of the King's Son story. The hero must subdue the guardian monster, which here symbolizes the fake personality of ego, to acquire the precious gem and return to his origins. The gem is frequently a precious pearl, representing the Personal Essence. The following story is one version, which appears in the Acts of Thomas, titled the "Hymn of the Soul":

> When I was an infant child in a palace of my Father and resting in the wealth and luxury of my nurturers, out of the East, our native country, my parents provisioned me and sent me, and of the wealth of those their treasures they put

together a load, both great and light, that I might carry it alone. . .

And they armed me with adamant, which breaketh iron, and they took off from me the garment set with gems, spangled with gold, which they had made for me because they loved me, and the robe was yellow in hue, made for my stature.

And they made a covenant with me and inscribed it on mine understanding, that I should not forget it, and said: If thou go down into Egypt and bring back thence the one pearl which is there in the midst of the sea girt about by the devouring serpent, thou shalt again put on the garment set with gems and the robe whereupon it resteth and become with thy brother that is next unto us an heir in our kingdom.

And I came out of the East by a road difficult and fearful with two guides and I was untried in travelling by it. . .

But when I entered into Egypt, the guides left me which had journeyed with me.

And I set forth by the quickest way to the serpent and by his hole I abode, watching for him to slumber and sleep that I might take my pearl from him. . .

And I put on the raiment of the Egyptians, lest I should seem strange, as one that had come from without to recover the pearl; and lest they should awake the serpent against me.

But I know not by what occasion they learned that I was not of their country, and with guile they mingled for me a deceit and I tasted of their food, and I knew no more that I was a king's son and I became a servant unto their king.

And I forgat also the pearl, for which my fathers had sent me, and by means of the heaviness of their food I fell into a deep sleep.

But when this befell me, my fathers also were aware of it and grieved for me, and a proclamation was published in our kingdom, that all should meet at our doors.

And then the kings of Parthia and they that bare office and the great ones of the East made a resolve concerning me, that I should not be left in Egypt, and the princes wrote unto me signifying thus:

From thy Father the King of kings, and thy mother that ruleth the East, and thy brother that is second unto us; unto our son that is in Egypt, peace. Rise up and awake out of sleep and hearken unto the words of the letter and remember that thou art a son of kings; lo, thou hast come under the yoke of bondage. Remember the pearl for which thou wast sent into Egypt. Remember thy garment spangled with gold and the glorious mantle which thou shouldest wear and wherewith thou shouldest deck thyself. Thy name is in the book of life, and with thy brother thou shalt be in our kingdom. . .

The letter flew and lighted down by me and became all speech, and I at the voice of it and the feeling of it started up out of sleep and I took it up and kissed and read it.

And it was written concerning that which was recorded in my heart, and I remembered forthwith that I was a son of kings, and my freedom yearned after its kind.

I remembered also the pearl, for the which I was sent down into Egypt, and I began with charms against the terrible serpent and I overcame him by naming the name of my Father upon him. . .

And I caught away the pearl and turned back to bear it unto my fathers, and I stripped off the filthy garment and left it in their land, and directed my way forthwith to the light of my fatherland in the East.

And on the way I found my letter that had awakened me and it, like as it had taken a voice and raised me when I slept, so also guided me with the light that came from it.

For at times the royal garment of silk shone before my eyes and with its voice and guidance it also encouraged me to speed and with love leading me and drawing me onward. . .

And I stretched forth and received it and adorned myself with the beauty of the colours thereof and in my royal robe excelling in beauty I arrayed myself wholly.

And when I had put it on, I was lifted up unto the place of peace and homage and I bowed my head and worshipped the brightness of the Father which had sent it unto me, for I had performed his commandments and he likewise that which he had promised.

And at the doors of his palace which was from the beginning I mingled among his nobles, and he rejoiced over me and received me with him into his palace, and all his servants do praise him with sweet voices. . . [Compiled by Robert Cecil et al, *The King's Son*, p. 5]

Many interpreters take the gem or the pearl to symbolize Being in general, or sometimes to refer to individuation. The fact remains that, as in the story above, the pearl represents a particular aspect of Being, the Personal Essence, and not just Being. The fact that the implication

106   of the story is more than just the realization of Being in general is indicated by the presence in the story of other symbols and precious artifacts, symbolizing other aspects of Essence. These are the garment, the robe, the letter, the gems, the King of kings, the queen of the East, the brother and others.

Carl G. Jung and his followers seem to include the Personal Essence in the archetype of the Self, as we see in the following words of Ira Progoff, discussing Jung's contribution to depth psychology:

> The archetype of the Self is expressed in the form of many historical symbols that represent various phases of the individuation process in the life history of nations. A particularly frequent symbol of the Self is the "Divine Child," which often appears also as a savior-messiah. In alchemical types of symbolism the Self as the ultimate achievement of psychological work is represented as the "pearl of great worth," the "philosopher's stone," or other symbols that convey the emergence of a small precious jewel as the result of the integration of the psyche. [Ira Progoff, *The Death and Rebirth of Psychology*, p. 182]

Jung used the term individuation to refer to the completion of the quest, which is similar to our usage, but not identical to it. We must also point out that the essential aspects are not the same as the archetypes as defined by Jung. Jung sometimes defined archetypes as images in the collective unconscious, but sometimes made a distinction between archetypes and archetypal images. Sometimes he seemed to use archetypes as universal tendencies, at other times as motifs in the human psyche. At one point he gave the following suggestive description:

> Archetypes resemble the beds of rivers: dried up because the water has deserted them, though it may return at any time. An archetype is something like an old watercourse along which the water of life flowed for a time, digging a deep channel for itself. The longer it flowed the deeper the channel, and the more likely it is that sooner or later the water will return. [Carl G. Jung, *Psychological Reflections*, p. 36]

He also defined them as Platonic forms, which might cause some readers to confuse them with essential aspects as we have defined them. Whatever the Jungian archetypes are, it is clear that Jung did not specifically see them the way we conceive of essential aspects, as

states of Being: the presence of Essence in specific and quite concretely experienceable and recognizable qualities. If archetypes are
like riverbeds, then Essence is like the water of life itself; in fact, it is
the water of life.

The way Jung defined archetypes—as universal processes and
patterns in the psyche—makes them a much wider and more
general category than the essential aspects. If we define an archetype as any universal form in the soul then obviously essential
aspects can be considered archetypes, but in that case, so are
fatherhood and motherhood. An aspect of Essence, however, is always an ontological presence, which can be experienced in time,
but is eternal. This cannot be said about Jungian archetypes in
general. That is why, for instance, images can obscure the experience of essential aspects, but tend to illuminate the understanding
and recognition of the archetypes.

We are focusing on this point because it is our experience that
some individuals who are familiar with Jung's theory of archetypes
jump to the conclusion that they know what an essential aspect is because they know the concept of archetype. This can lead to the common illusion that one knows Essence when one is actually thinking of
quite a different dimension of experience. Essence is a much less
known category of experience than the Jungian archetype. To know
Essence is to experience directly the eternal truth of Being.

To categorize the essential aspects as a subset of the Jungian archetypes because they are universal forms that are part of the potential of
the soul is reasonable in principle, but in doing so one runs the risk,
again, of confusing Essence with the usual categories of experience of
the psyche, when Essence is simply Being. One also might assume
that the Jungian process of individuation as it occurs in analytic psychology is equivalent to the process of essential realization. However,
the former is based on the general idea of archetypes as defined by
Jung while the latter is not.

While Jung's individuation concept, guided by the archetypes
towards self-realization is not necessarily incompatible with our conception of the process of essential realization and the subprocess of
essential individuation, the differences are significant. This is clear
from the various accounts of the Jungian individuation process in Jungian analysis. Essential realization is the actualization of Being and its

108   various aspects; essential individuation is the realization and development of the aspect of the Personal Essence. These are not guided by images, archetypal or otherwise.

More specifically, the myths and fairy tales which are widely used in Jungian psychology, like any conceptual framework, can cloud the consciousness when a state of being is actually manifesting. They can, on the other hand, illuminate various processes in the psyche, even processes involving essential aspects, as we have seen in this chapter. So they can help us to understand the aspects. They can tell us, for example, that the Pearl Beyond Price is the product of individual realization, and can point to some of the barriers, but they cannot inform us about what the actual experience of the Pearl is like. Only the presence of the aspect of the Pearl in one's consciousness can do that. The fact is that the realization of Essence necessitates the experience of Being beyond all images. Jung and some of his followers would most likely agree with this last statement, but it is also true that the Jungian literature does not emphasize the realization of Essence as an ontological presence. Thus the Jungian process, even when it deals with spiritual realities, is more emotional and psychological in nature than the process of the realization of Being we are discussing here.

We are not saying that Jung's way of seeing things never elicits the experience of Being. We simply want to distinguish between the archetypes as Jung defined them, and the aspects of Essence or Being. This difference implies a divergence in methodology and a different emphasis in terms of experience.

Chapter Nine

Personal Essence and the Man of Spirit

A s we saw in Chapter One, most spiritual teachings, especially those of the Far East, take the view that Being is not personal. A Tibetan Buddhist, Karma Phrin-las-pa, says:

All sentient beings possess the nature of Buddhahood, continuously present since its beginningless beginning. What is this nature of Buddhahood? . . . (it is) the beginningless time-encompassing dimension of Being (Dharmadhatu) unbroken, impartial, radiant in itself, as the pristine existential experience of Being (Dharmakaya). [Herbert V. Guenther, *The Tantric View of Life*, p. 124]

Lao Tzu, the founder of Taoism in China, says:

Perhaps you may call it the Form of the Formless, the Image of the Imageless. Yet the elusive, subtle Oneness remains nameless. [Translated by Ni Hua-Ching, *The Complete Works of Lao Tzu*, p. 10]

To be free from ego means to the man of spirit the realization of Being, and Being is almost always taken to be impersonal. For them it is not possible to experience oneself as a person without identifying with ego. Being a person is for them a clear indication that one is not free. It is also an indication that one is not experiencing Being, but only identifying with a self-image.

The personal quality is usually relegated to ego. To be personal and to care about the personal life is taken to indicate the self-centeredness

109

110   of ego. This is not surprising in view of the fact that wherever we look we encounter only the personality of ego. The experience of the true individuation of Essence is so very unusual that the Personal Essence is called by some Sufis the "rare Mohammedan pearl."

The main reason for this attitude is the absence of the experience of the incomparable pearl in such teachings, or the lack of understanding of such experience, or perhaps sometimes only a matter of emphasis and preference. For such teachings, to feel personal, to value the personal life, to experience oneself as a person, are all seen to be a manifestation of ego. They are taken to be false, and seen as the seeds of suffering.

This perspective denies, in effect, the existence of the Personal Essence. It denies the possibility of being a person and being real. It does not see that it is possible to have a personal experience that has a spiritual value, in terms of Being. It is this attitude that is most responsible for making such teachings incomprehensible to the man of the world.

This attitude comes from real experience: the experience of Being in its impersonal aspect. However, although this experience is real, it is incomplete. It does not take the Personal Essence into consideration.

It is possible to see the Personal Essence as a concept, as not having a final reality. This is the perception of the nonconceptual aspect of Being, the supreme unknowable ground of reality. It is the experience of absolute oneness in which there are no discriminations, as Lao Tzu says above. All forms are seen to exist only as concepts, and hence are taken not to have a separate existence. All duality is absent in this realization.

However, from this perspective, not only the Personal Essence is seen to be a concept, but so are love, compassion, consciousness, awareness and so on. In other words, from the perspective of the supreme reality of the undifferentiated aspect of Being, all aspects of Essence are seen to be conceptual (as well as, for that matter, the entirety of the physical world, including the body). Only the unqualified Being exists, and differentiation and discrimination are only appearance, ultimately unreal.

This is the nature of the experience of the nonconceptual reality of Being, of Being-as-such. This experience also feels so real, so

profound and so comprehensive that it has a flavor of finality to it. It   111
is experienced as an objective fact. In the theistic traditions it is
usually equated with God, the Supreme Being. One of the most well-
known Sufi shaikhs, Ibn 'Arabi, writes about the Supreme Being:

> And when it is allowed that the existence of the beggar
> and the existence of the sick are His existence, it is al-
> lowed that thy existence is His existence, and that the exis-
> tence of all created things, both accidents and substances,
> is His existence. [Ibn 'Arabi, *"Whoso Knoweth Himself. . .",*
> p. 10]

Also from this perspective, it is not only that there is no person;
there is also no life and no humanity. All are concepts, appearance,
the dance of Maya or the dream of God.

This is a very profound dimension, which shows us our ultimate
nature. This level of realization is required for complete freedom from
ego identifications. It is, nevertheless, only a part of the true potential
of the human being. In a sense it is the ultimate dimension, but it is
not the only dimension. There are other dimensions of Being, the
dimensions of Essence, those of differentiated Being.

From the vantage point of each dimension of Being, the more differentiated dimensions appear to be less real. Each dimension both includes the more differentiated dimensions and transcends them. This is
experienced from the first dimension of Essence, going through its various levels, to the dimension of the Supreme Reality, and then to that
of the Transcendent Absolute. However, all these dimensions make up
the true potential of the human being. The human being is incomplete
if he identifies with one dimension, regardless of how "high," to the
exclusion of others. The complete man is the integration of all dimensions of reality. We will see in subsequent chapters that this integration
is possible only with the Personal Essence. We will see that the Personal Essence undergoes a development which is equivalent to the
integration of all dimensions of reality. It is still not the highest experience; nevertheless, it is the highest development. One who has integrated the Personal Essence completely is able to experience any
dimension of reality, depending on the requirement of the moment.
One who is identified with a particular dimension may be realized on
the Being level, but is still not complete in his development, for he is
unable to move to different dimensions.

112   The Personal Essence, although it is not as universal or final an experience as the Supreme or the Absolute, is actually a greater miracle.
The Supreme is an unknowable reality because it is nonconceptual.
However, it is easily recognized when experienced. It is easily understood, though not by the mind. The Personal Essence, on the other
hand, is a much more mysterious experience. It is much more difficult
to understand or grasp. It is quite a mystery, a miraculous mystery,
that Being can feel personal. None of the aspects of Essence, not even
the Supreme and the Absolute aspects, feel personal, except for this
one aspect.

It is true that it is easier, for most people, to precipitate the experience of the Personal Essence than the experience of the nonconceptual aspect of Being. However, this is different from the full
integration of the Personal Essence. One can have some, or even
many, experiences of the Personal Essence and still identify with ego.
But this is a far cry from its full development and integration. It seems
that the full integration of the Personal Essence is a much more
difficult realization than that of the Supreme Reality. The realization of
the oneness of the nonconceptual Being is, in fact, one of the requirements for the integration of the Personal Essence. We find Lao
Tzu himself hinting at this truth, in the *Hua Hu Ching,* when he gives
a list of the various ancient holistic sciences: "14. The holistic science
of embracing absolute transcendental Oneness in order to nourish
one's 'mystical pearl' and accomplish the mystical conception."
[Translated by Ni Hua-Ching, *The Complete Works of Lao Tzu,* p. 145]

We will discuss the relationship between the Personal Essence and
the state of oneness of Being in greater detail in a later chapter; but we
can say here that the state of absolute Being is needed to completely
establish that the individuality of ego is mental, and hence nonexistent.

This might be the reason why there are more human beings
realized on the impersonal dimension than ones with full integration
of the Personal Essence. This full integration is what is called by the
Sufis, for instance, the Complete Man.

The Personal Essence is the true integration of the ideals of both
the man of spirit and the man of the world. It is Being, but it is also a
person. It is a person that is completely spiritual, made out of spiritual
substance, but at the same time living in the world a personal life. He
is Being, and he is a human being. He is both the man of spirit and

the man of the world. For the one who has integrated the Personal Essence there is no separation between the world and spirit. There is no separation or difference for him between the life of the spirit and the life of the world. He is spirit in the world, living the personal life of a human being.

This is clearly a greater development than either living the life of the man of spirit or the life of the man of the world. The complete man lives both, as one integrated life. He can be impersonal spirit and he can be an embodied person. He is the integration of both. He is both as one.

Usually, the man of spirit, because of his experience of personality, is unable to conceive the possibility of a person who is real, who is a person of Being. But this is exactly the experience of the Personal Essence. One is a person, who is Being and not a mental structure. One is not self-centered, although one is unique. One is completely self-less, loving, compassionate, real, generous and human. How else can one be? His nature is Being. He is pure consciousness. He is an integration of love, kindness, joy and all aspects of Being. And he is fully aware of all these aspects and dimensions, without much preoccupation with them. He is fulfilled but is concerned with the fulfillment of others. He is satisfied and contented, and he is concerned with the satisfaction and contentment of others. He is personally fulfilled, satisfied, contented and happy, living a personal life that is completely and unselfconsciously devoted to the service of humanity.

He does not think of helping. He does not plan to serve. He does not feel a desire to help, serve or enlighten. He just does what is personally fulfilling to him. And this spontaneously, and completely unintentionally, always happens to be the best he can do to help, serve, and enlighten others. He is himself. He just needs to be himself, does what comes naturally and spontaneously to him, and this is always what is most fulfilling to him and most useful for others.

There is no self-sacrifice, not a hint of personal renunciation, but he is not selfish, not self-centered and not preoccupied with himself. His service is the expression of love, compassion, and truth. But he does not necessarily feel that is why he serves. He does not even think that he is serving. Love, compassion and truth are the constituents of his personal beingness. He is all of Essence, and so does not need to think of it or of acting according to its values. That is what it means to

114   be a person of Being, the essential person. He is a precious pearl, rare and incomparable.

Knowing this, can we blame the man of the world in his pursuit of the personal element, in defiance of the exhortations of the man of spirit? It is true he pursues a reflection, an image of what he can be; but this brings out our compassion, understanding and love for him, not rejection or condemnation.

From the perspective of Essence, the person is a Platonic form, a pure aspect of Being. It is as much a definite reality as love, compassion, will, consciousness and awareness. These aspects of Essence are universal, in the sense that all human beings have the capacity to experience and know them. They are like the Jungian archetypes, except that they are states of presence and Being. They are independent of one's personal mind and its creations. They are experienced the same by all human beings. Love is love, whether one is American or Chinese, man or woman, old or young. This universality is also true of the aspect of the person, the Personal Essence.

And the Personal Essence is the personal element in the human form, as a person. How this relates to the person of ego, and how it relates to the body, will be discussed later.

Chapter Ten

Personal Essence in Spiritual Traditions

T he knowledge of the Incomparable Pearl and the process of
its development is rare even in the most complete spiritual
teachings, and the traditions that know it do not speak much
about it. This is why the overwhelming impression one gets from
most spiritual teachings is that the goal of spiritual work is the realization of impersonal Being or the realization of the Soul's relationship to
it (as in the Christian tradition.) The literature regarding the Pearl is
sparse, and when it can be found, it is usually couched in metaphorical and symbolic language. Sometimes the language is more direct
and descriptive, but it appears metaphorical to most people, because
they lack the direct experience. The story, "The Hymn of the Soul," in
Chapter Eight, is an example. There are very few direct references to
the Personal Essence in the literature, and these are found mainly in
old books not in circulation. In this chapter we will describe some of
those references; although they are rare, they tend to confirm and
support our own understanding of the importance of the development
of the Pearl.

Generally speaking, the Far Eastern spiritual traditions, those of
Vedanta, Buddhism, Taoism and Zen, tend to be more impersonal
than the prophetic traditions, such as Judaism, Christianity and Sufism.
Once in a while, though, we find an Eastern teacher or book that
refers to the Personal Essence, the Pearl Beyond Price. The following
passage from a Taoist text describes an alchemical process leading to
the experience of the Incomparable Pearl:

115

116   When the practiser first achieves the state of stillness he realises only minor serenity which lasts one day in which dullness and confusion cause him to be unconscious, like a dying man who is breathless. Then he will experience medium serenity lasting three successive days, and major serenity lasting seven successive days. This third stage should not be mistaken for death (by transformation) for it only reveals the return of spirit and vitality to the source, the revival of (eternal) life and the sublimation of the alchemical agent into a bright pearl. [Lu K'uan Yü, *Taoist Yoga*, p. 95]

We find that the more complex and complete the spiritual teaching, the more it includes the personal element. In Buddhism, for instance, we can contrast the Theravada school with the Mahayana school. The first is a monastic, austere, and simple discipline and teaching for arriving at enlightenment. The ideal is called the Arhat.

> There is no better way of understanding the spirit of the Old Wisdom School than by considering the type of man which it wished to produce, and the idea of perfection which it set up for the emulation of its disciples. The ideal man, the saint or sage at the highest stage of development is called an "Arhat." [Edward Conze, *Buddhism: Its Essence and Development*, p. 93]

The aim is the realization of Sunyata, the ground and nature of all reality. Mahayana, on the other hand, is more complex. It includes in its aim, in addition to the realization of Sunyata, the realization of Bodhicitta, which is taken to be compassion and altruistic helpfulness. The ideal is the Bodhisattva, who is interested not only in enlightening himself, but is also dedicated to the enlightenment of all other beings. The Diamond Sutra says:

> Here, O Subhuti, a Bodhisattva should think thus: "As many beings as there are in the universe of beings. . . all these should be led by me into Nirvana, into that realm of Nirvana which leaves nothing behind." [*Ibid.*, p. 130]

So,

> the Bodhisattva would be a man who does not only set himself free, but who is also skillful in devising means for bringing out and maturing the latent seeds of enlightenment in others. [*Ibid.*, p. 128]

For the Mahayana (from which Zen is a development) there is more concern and human consideration about other people. One's own enlightenment is not divorced from helping other beings. It is interesting that usually the Hinayanists (Theravadists) are referred to as more interested in personal enlightenment than the Mahayanists. We see here, the usual meaning of the word personal, referring to one's individual person. According to our understanding of the personal element, we see the Theravadists as more impersonal and the Mahayanists as more personal, for the latter seem to be concerned with other persons. Of course, this is the difference between the ego quality of personal and the Being quality of personal.

When we look at the more complex Buddhist schools of Vajrayana, in Tibet, we find more inclusion of the personal element. They themselves consider Mahayana to be more inclusive than Theravada, and Vajrayana to be more inclusive than Mahayana. In Tibet the Buddhists have more personal life, and are more involved in the life of the world. Their rituals and disciplines have more color, variety, and richness. Many of the lamas are married and have families, and live a worldly life, side by side with the monastic one. Even the head of the Sakya sect, in which the lamas are celibate, is involved in the worldly life to some extent: he is the Dalai Lama, the secular head of old Tibet. In the following passage he describes how compassion adds another element to the impersonality of Sunyata:

> In the Perfection Vehicle there is a description of wisdom and method conjoined. For example, before entering into meditative equipoise on emptiness, one generates an altruistic mind directed toward becoming enlightened. Then the meditative equipoise is conjoined with the force of that altruistic motivation. Also, when one is practicing altruistic acts-giving, ethics, and so forth these should be conjoined with the force of the mind realizing emptiness. [John Avedon, *An Interview with the Dalai Lama*, p. 74]

The clearest expression of the reality of the essential person in the Buddhist teachings is found in the concept of Nirmanakaya. This is distinguished from the Dharmakaya, which is the experience of Being-as-such, the nonconceptual reality, and from the Sambhogakaya, which is the Body of Spiritual Enjoyment. These three; Dharmakaya, Sambhogakaya and Nirmanakaya, are the three bodies of the Buddha, indicating three kinds of realization. Lama Govinda describes them thus:

> Thus we discern in the figure of the Buddha three "bodies" or principles:

1. that, in which all Enlightened Ones are the same: the experience of completeness, of universality, of the deepest super-individual reality of the Dharma, the primordial law and cause of all things, from which emanates all physical, oral and metaphysical order;
2. that which constitutes the spiritual or ideal character of a Buddha, the creative expression or formulation of this universal principle in the realm of inner vision: the Sambhogakaya, the "Body of Bliss" (rapture or spiritual enjoyment), from which all true inspiration is born;
3. that, in which this inspiration is transformed into visible form and becomes action: the Nirmanakaya: the "Body of Transformation," the human embodiment or individuality of an Enlightened One. [Lama Angarika Govinda, *Foundations of Tibetan Mysticism*, p. 213]

So enlightenment is equated with Dharmakaya. However, the life in the world after enlightenment is seen in the concept of the Nirmanakaya. So Nirmanakaya is the presence of Being in the world. Although Dharmakaya is seen to be the ultimate reality, Nirmanakaya is still regarded as a further development. It is embodying the realization of Dharmakaya in a human life in the world. This is seen in the famous Zen ten ox-herding pictures that illustrate Zen enlightenment. Although the Dharmakaya is the ultimate reality, which is symbolized by an empty circle, it's only the eighth picture. The last picture, the tenth one, which symbolizes Nirmanakaya, is usually referred to as "in the world"; it's a picture of a man in the marketplace, that is, a person in the world.

Nevertheless, Buddhism does not emphasize the personal element. Enlightenment is seen ultimately to lead out of the world. The idea is that when one reaches the ultimate state of enlightenment, that of Buddhahood, the cycle of human birth and death is ended, and one does not come back to earth after death. This notion, which involves the idea of reincarnation, is shared by most Far Eastern religions, and is probably of Indian origin. So in Buddhism, enlightenment is seen not as what is needed for the complete human life, but rather as what will end the cycle of birth and death.

There are many schools, sects and teachings within Hinduism. They range from the most impersonal, as in Vedanta, to the most personal, in the sects based on Krishna's teachings. Many of their Gods are personal, but the one that stands for the Personal Essence more than any of the others, is Krishna, the amorous God.

Krishna is considered to be God himself in a personal form; he is an incarnation of God on earth. There are many legends about him and his adventures, his love affairs and pranks. But there is a very definite personal flavor to the whole thing. The well-known Bhagavad Gita is the teaching of Krishna, which is the yoga of action. The whole teaching is given by the Lord Krishna to his disciple, Arjuna, a military leader, just before battle.

It is interesting that the pictures depicting Krishna almost universally show him with a full body ornamented with many pearls. It is more interesting that his body is always painted with a pearly sheen to it, indicating the relation to the Incomparable Pearl.

Some of the texts actually speak of the personal element as a personal God. They speak of spiritual realization in the realization of Being as a person. Some go as far as to say that this realization is higher or more final than the impersonal realization.

The late Indian guru Baba Muktananda, who represented the Siddha path in the West, describes in his spiritual autobiography some experiences of a personal God. He speaks of his central realization as that of the blue pearl. He describes in detail the experience and some of the qualities of the essential person:

> Lo! The gloriously shining Blue Pearl, as it moved closer to me, began to expand with its innumerable lustrous, inner rays. It became an oval and continued to grow into a human shape. I was beholding its expansion with amazement. The oval finally assumed a human form. . .
>
> The Blue Pearl, that had enlarged into a human form through an oval shape, stood before me. Its radiance began to wane. Then I discerned a blue human figure within it. How enchantingly beautiful! His blue form shimmered and sparkled! . . . He was a mass of pure Awareness, the Life of Muktananda's inner life. [Swami Muktananda, *Guru*, pp. 152-153]

Clearly, he is describing here his inner nature as a person of consciousness, a real person who is not an identity with ego structure. He is experiencing his beingness, which he recognizes as the blue consciousness, both as a universal impersonal consciousness, and as a personal form of the same consciousness. This personal form he usually sees as the "blue pearl," but sometimes as the blue person of consciousness, as in the above passage.

120   Another Indian teacher says in his book about esoteric psychology
that spiritual development goes through seven stages. He describes
the fifth stage as the spiritual level, characterized by the development
of a spiritual personality or ego. However, he does not see this
spiritual personality as completely Being, but views it as still on the
level of ego, while capable of spiritual experience and perception.
Describing the stages in terms of "bodies of realization," he says about
the fifth:

> The fifth body is the richest. It is the culmination of all that
> is possible for a human being. The fifth is the peak of in-
> dividuality, the peak of love, of compassion, of everything
> that is worthwhile. The thorns have been lost. Now, the
> flower too must be lost. Then there will simply be per-
> fume, no flower. [Bhagwan Shree Rajneesh, *The Psychology
> of the Esoteric*, p. 86]

He says that one has to let go and go beyond the spiritual individuality for the next dimension to unfold, that of the universal consciousness or Cosmic Being:

> The sixth body is cosmic. The tension is between you—
> your feelings of individuality, of limitation—and the un-
> limited cosmos. Even in the fifth stage you will be em-
> bodied in your spiritual body. You will be a person. That
> "person" will be the tension for the sixth. So to achieve a
> non-tense existence with the cosmos, to be in tune with
> the cosmos, you must cease to be an individual. [*Ibid.*,
> pp. 106-107]

This is actually a subtle understanding, implying some knowledge
of the Personal Essence. However, our understanding is that it is not
the person which is the tension, but the attachment to it. According to
our understanding, the point he makes is true before the Personal
Essence is completely integrated. One experiences the Personal
Essence but is still identified with ego. So there is love, compassion,
joy and so on; but there is still self-centeredness. The identity and
boundaries of the ego are still present. This, however, does not mean
that the Personal Essence itself has the self-centeredness and
boundaries of ego. We will discuss, in a future chapter, the relationship between the Personal Essence and ego boundaries. For now we
can note that we find that it is very difficult for most individuals to let
go of the separateness of their individuality, a condition necessary for

the realization of the unbounded aspects of Being. However, the presence of the Personal Essence makes this transition much easier and more natural. We must remember that the Personal Essence is a state of Being. The impersonal reality is a state of Being. The transition is much easier from one state of Being to another, than from ego to a state of Being, especially that of unqualified and unbounded Being.

The experience of the Personal Essence is that of "I am," and allowing this sense to expand is a very efficient way for the transition to the impersonal reality. Nisargadatta Maharaj, the Vedanta teacher, uses this as his main teaching to his students:

> Go deep into the sense of "I am" and you will find. How do you find a thing you have mislaid or forgotten? You keep it in your mind until you recall it. The sense of being, of "I am" is the first to emerge. Ask yourself whence it comes, or just watch it quietly. When the mind stays in the "I am," without moving, you enter a state which cannot be verbalized but can be experienced. [Sri Nisargadatta Maharaj, *I Am That*, p. 2]

This is reminiscent of the hero in The Hymn of the Soul, who returns to the King of kings (impersonal supreme Being) after he acquires the pearl (the Personal Essence).

Another Indian teacher and voluminous writer, Sri Aurobindo, saw the reality and value of the personal element. His universal, impersonal realization came first, but he was left with the feeling that "this cannot be it," that if oneness and universality were truly the summit of human experience, what about the person? He writes:

> The individual therefore exists though he exceeds the little separative ego; the universal exists and is embraced by him but it does not absorb and abolish all individual differentiation, even though by his universalizing himself the limitation which we call the ego is overcome.
>
> Now we may get rid of this differentiation by plunging into the absorption of an exclusive unity, but to what end? For perfect union? But we do not forfeit that by accepting the differentiation any more than the Divine forfeits His oneness by accepting it. We have the perfect union in His being and can absorb ourselves in it at any time, but we have also this other differentiated unity and can emerge into it and act freely in it at any time without losing oneness: for we have merged the ego and are absolved from

the exclusive stresses of our mentality. [Sri Aurobindo, *The Life Divine*, p. 370]

Of all the modern Indian teachers, Aurobindo was most knowledgeable about the varieties and riches of Being. He did not take one state to be the only real and final one, but built a system that takes into consideration many aspects of Being.

Examining the Middle Eastern traditions, we find the personal element becoming more important, and sometimes central. The Judeo-Christian-Islamic tradition is much more personal than Buddhism or Taoism. Although the absolute reality (or God) is seen as a universal and impersonal power, He is related to personally. Moses argues with Him, Christ calls Him father, and Mohammed receives personal communications from Him.

In Christianity Christ is considered to be the son of God, and hence he is both personal and divine. He is a human being, but both man and God, the son of a human and of a deity. This is precisely the experience of the Personal Essence. It is of Being, hence divine; and it is a person, hence human. The way Jesus saw himself as both the son of Man and the son of God, is a religious way of understanding the Personal Essence. The experience of being the son of Man is normal for the Personal Essence. Most individuals experience themselves then as purely human, the essence of being human. The experience of being the son of God usually occurs at an advanced stage of the development of the Personal Essence, after the entry into the universal, divine and impersonal realms. When one understands the relationship between the Personal Essence and these realms, the image of son and father is seen to be very apt.

Most Christians take Christ to be divine in a special way, a way not accessible to themselves, even though Christ showed clearly what it is like to be the Personal Essence, and thus through his example showed man his true potential. He showed that man is both human and divine; he is a person but his nature is of the divinity of Being.

Orthodox Christianity looks at Christ as a saviour because he is a special being: the son of God come to earth to save humanity. The assumption is that this is the greatest boon. But is it not a greater boon, and a more loving message, that Christ shows that all humans can be like him? Is it not a more optimistic and more useful teaching that any human can know himself not only as the son of Man, but

also as the son of God? The story of Christ in the West is very similar
to the story of Krishna in the East. Both tell of how God becomes a
person, a human being.

We are not saying that Jesus was not truly divine. But what was
special about Jesus was his individuation, and his understanding of his
relationship to higher realms; he was definitely a rare, precious pearl,
and extraordinary in the way Buddha was extraordinary. Buddha was
the examplar of impersonal enlightenment, and Jesus was the examplar
of "personal" enlightenment.

In Islam, the Sufis place great emphasis on the Personal Essence.
They define the Sufi as one who is "in the world but not of it." This is
exactly the feeling, experience and understanding of the Personal
Essence. One is in the world, lives in the world, is a person, but one
is of the nature of Being, which is not of the world.

The Sufi tradition is the clearest in terms of giving the personal life its
due importance and value. Some Sufis, in fact, consider their work a
further advance beyond the teachings of Lao Tzu and Buddha. The inclusion of the personal element is part of their reason for this claim.
Their ideal is the perfect man or the complete man, and they consider
the prophet Mohammed as the clearest exemplar of the complete man.
He was not only integrated in the spiritual realms but also lived a complete human life. He was a prophet, and hence a religious leader and
founder, and a statesman, the secular head of state. He lived a personal
life, was married several times, enjoyed women, fathered children, and
had friends. He was reputed to have said: "Three things are close to my
heart: prayer, women and perfume." So he saw prayer, indicating the
connection to Being, and pleasures of the world as compatible. And
they were compatible in his life. He was completely integrated; some
of his passages in the Koran constitute the purest and most beautiful
utterances about the realm of Being, and at the same time he could
fight in battle. He shunned the monastic life, and asserted that the religious life is the normal life of man in the world.

Some Sufis equate the consciousness of Mohammed with that of the
Personal Essence, "the rare Mohammedan pearl." In the following
passage, Henry Corbin writes about the view of a well-known Sufi
from the 14th century, Alaoddawleh Semnani, concerning the birth of
the Personal Essence, the pearl beyond price, which he connects with
the latifa (subtle center) at the left side of the body:

124   The third subtle organ is that of the heart (*latifa qalbiya*) in
        which the embryo of mystical progeny is formed, as a
        pearl is formed in a shell. This pearl or offspring is none
        other than the subtle organ which will be the True Ego, the
        real, personal individuality (*latifa ana'iya*). . . .This subtle
        divine center conceals the "rare Mohammadan pearl," that
        is to say, the subtle organ which is the True Ego. . . .
        [Henry Corbin, *The Man of Light in Iranian Sufism*,
        pp. 124–125]

We rarely find such a direct reference to the Personal Essence.
Semnani not only knows of the Personal Essence, but he understands
its nature and significance. He recognizes its central position, its relationship to the Lataif, and its significance as the real individuality of
Essence. He terms it the true ego or the spiritual ego. He shows here
his knowledge that the ego is an imitator, a reflection of the true ego,
the incomparable pearl, which finally emerges in the divine center,
the latifa at the center of the chest. The pearl is formed (conceived) in
the latifa at the left side of the chest, but is born (manifests) in the
latifa at the center of the chest.

No wonder, then, that Sufis, like Mohammed and his close com-
panions, live a life of work, family and creativity which is not divorced, and in fact is inseparable, from their spiritual life. Though all
Sufis value and live the personal life of Being, some of their schools
manifest the personal element more than others. Some of the Sufi
orders are more religious, and their leaders have a spiritual image, as
we see in the guru tradition of India. But other schools, like those of
Central Asia, completely eliminate the differences between the
worldly and the spiritual. The teacher does not have the image, or
life of the "holy" man, as the Indian gurus do. The teacher is more of
an integrated individual, who lives a normal personal life, and
teaches students in ways that change according to time and culture.
There is no particular image visible to outsiders that indicates
spirituality. The image is assumed according to the needs of the
teachings, and not according to any tradition. The objective is an
efficient and practical way of imparting knowledge to individuals so
that they develop to the station of essential or complete man, and
can be their own persons. The work is not seen as spiritual or worldly; it is rather taken to be the work of developing completely integrated human beings. Shah writes:

This inner unification of personality, expressed through a diversity of ways, means that the Sufi teacher does not resemble the outer, idealized personality of the literalist. The calm, never-changing personality, the aloof master, or the personality which inspires awe alone, the "man who never varies" cannot be a Sufi master. [Idries Shah, *The Sufis*, p. 349]

We can see the difference between the more impersonal guru tradition and the Sufi tradition of being in the world but not of it, by listening to the words of the Indian teacher Ramana Maharshi and contrasting our experience with that of listening to Idries Shah. From Maharshi one gets the impression of the expansion, richness and beauty of the universal realm of Being. From the Sufi one gets the impression of a highly individuated person, very practical, very much in the world and knowledgeable about its ways, but one cannot separate these characteristics in his person from those of integrity, dignity, reality, truth and other aspects of Being. One gets the impression of great spiritual attainment from gurus like Maharshi, Muktananda or Nisargadatta, but the impression one is left with from Sufis, like Shah, is of a spiritual attainment integrated into the world.

Gurdjieff was an excellent example of a teacher with a highly integrated Personal Essence. He had no "holy man" image. He was practical, down to earth and very personal. The personal element is central to his teaching, which is his synthesis of what he learned in both the Sufi and Tibetan traditions. He recognized that the man of ego lacked a true individuality, the personality of Essence. He says of the integrated man in his system:

Instead of the discordant and often contradictory activity of different desires, there is *one single I*, whole, indivisible, and permanent; there is *individuality*, dominating the physical body and its desires and able to overcome both its reluctance and its resistance. Instead of the mechanical process of thinking there is *consciousness*. And there is *will*, that is, a power, not merely composed of various often contradictory desires belonging to different "I"s, but issuing from consciousness and governed by individuality or a single and permanent I. [P. D. Ouspensky, *In Search of the Miraculous*, pp. 42-43]

When Buddhist and Indian teachers do integrate the Personal Essence, their style becomes more personal, more tailored to the student

126   and more intimate. The personal interaction with the student becomes more important, or sometimes the autonomy and freedom of the student is taken into more consideration. The fact that the student lives his own personal life, integrating the teaching in his own personal way, instead of using the teacher as a model or the school as a family substitute, becomes of greater value. For this personal life allows the development of the "pearl beyond price."

PART IV

PERSONAL ESSENCE
AND
EGO DEVELOPMENT

We have so far established our understanding that the Personal Essence is the "true person," as opposed to the ego individuality experienced by most people and seen by psychology as a structure in the mind. We have also seen some connections between functions of the ego and qualities of the Personal Essence, for instance, issues of autonomy and personalness, and pointed out that the ego can be seen as a "reflection" of the true Beingness of the Personal Essence. In this Part we will investigate several questions which will enable us to understand in a very detailed way the relationship between ego and Personal Essence. These questions are:

1. If the Personal Essence is the true person, then what is its relation to ego with its separate individuality?
2. Why is it that in almost every case, as a child matures it is the ego structure and not the Personal Essence that develops?

127

128   3. Assuming this way of seeing things makes sense, what are the factors that lead to the development of the ego instead of the Personal Essence?

4. What is the relation of the Personal Essence to what are called the inborn apparatuses of primary autonomy, or the ego functions?

In order to answer these questions, we must consider also the following question:

5. Is individuation merely the result of building the ego structures that organize and integrate the innate capacities, as object relations theory claims, or does it include other elements not considered by object relations theory as we have discussed it?

Mahler writes: "... individuation consists of those achievements marking the child's assumption of his own individual characteristics." [Margaret S. Mahler et al., *The Psychological Birth of the Human Infant*, p. 4] This development also functions to integrate and organize the various ego functions for the purposes of defense, adaptation and growth.

The ego functions, described by Hartmann as the inborn apparatuses of autonomy in the beginning of life, are those of synthesis, integration, regulation, organization, anticipation, attention, decision making, delay, drive taming, identification, intelligence, intention, judgment, language, memory, motility, neutralization, object comprehension, object relations, perception, productivity, reality testing, self-preservation, speech, symbolization, thinking and volition. The ego functions also include defense. Hartmann's idea was that these functions of ego are part of the potential of every human being. He writes:

> Mental development is not simply the outcome of the struggle with instinctual drives, with love-objects, with the super ego, and so on. For instance we have reason to assume that this development is served by apparatuses which function from the beginning of life. [Heinz Hartmann, *Ego Psychology and the Problem of Adaptation*, p. 24]

These apparatuses are inborn as potentials but develop and are organized during the first few years of life. Their development, organization and integration is part of the structuralization of ego and the development of the self (image). In other words, "the self-representation also comes to include access to the autonomous functions and the sense of mastery that they provide." [Althea Horner, *Object Relations and the Developing Ego in Therapy*, p. 158]

Our question is, can one truly assume one's own individual characteristics and move towards maturity by merely developing a unified
self-image and the structures supporting it? Our exploration, so far, of
the Personal Essence indicates that a far deeper development, in the
realm of Being, constitutes the true maturity.

One might argue that there is not much difference experientially
between the experience of the individuality of ego and that of the
Personal Essence, and that the latter is the result of ego development. However, the case presentations and reports in this book strongly
establish that the sense of individuation of the Personal Essence is quite
different from that of normal ego development. The depth, profundity,
definiteness and sense of reality are always experienced as unusual.
Our students are relatively well-integrated. Psychologists would be
likely to regard them as dealing with neuroses and some structural
issues. The students are always astonished by the depth and reality of
individuation in the experience of the Personal Essence. The sense of
Being is very clearly not within the experience of ego.

Following is a report from a young woman, Pamela, with a relatively
well-developed and integrated ego structure and a normal life history.
She is describing her work with the author in one group session:

> At first I experienced fear, helplessness and anger at the
> fear and helplessness. Talking to you the feeling of fear in-
> creased and I started feeling weak in my shoulders and
> arms. I could also feel tingling sensations in other parts of
> my body.
>
> When the fear increased I felt defenseless and weak in
> my arms and legs. My shoulders started to hurt, and I felt
> hollow and burning. My lower arms felt limp and my
> hands very cold. When you asked me how I felt in my
> belly, at first, it just felt full. Then I started feeling full and
> solid there. It felt round in my belly, like a watermelon. My
> arms and legs felt very weak like I could not even pick
> them up to move. When I became aware of the water-
> melon-like fullness in the belly I felt safe, not afraid of
> being weak. My belly felt very much like an actual round
> watermelon; full, with no seeds. I also felt present then,
> more than I have in the last few weeks.
>
> Then I felt a full, slow flow into my shoulders and down
> my arms and legs. When they felt full I did not feel weak
> anymore. I felt light and full. I felt myself glowing. I ended
> up feeling very full, present and calm, very peaceful. I also

felt very different towards you and everyone, including myself. I felt connected and without boundaries and very much myself, not my image of myself or my emotion or thoughts.

I also felt surprised and happy when I found the round fullness in my belly, as everything changed and grew from there. Whenever I find something inside so different from what I usually think of as me I am awed, thunderstruck, and amazed. I really enjoy discovering, although it is still hard to believe it is me.

This account leaves no doubt that the sense of individuation, of being oneself, characteristic of the Personal Essence, is quite different from that of the usual identity of ego. We find Pamela, here, first dealing with a state of weakness, as a result of abandoning some ego structures. Most object relations therapists would be surprised that she moved so quickly to a state of strength, fullness and integration. She could not have felt such presence of individuation by building more ego structures in the session. As most psychotherapists know, this would be a long and arduous process. The definiteness of the presence of the Personal Essence, that it felt almost like a watermelon, cannot be a structure of ego, or a result of such structure. And it is very clear that although she felt more herself and present as herself, she recognized in a definite way that it is not her usual sense of herself. Her surprise was obvious, and so was her delight. We should note here that the strength and clarity of this experience, and the ability to recognize it, are a result of years of previous work.

One might postulate that individuation on the level of Being is different and more profound than that of ego, but that it is probably a natural development from ego individuation. This is the understanding of many of the spiritual teaching schools. It implies that the life of ego is the childhood of humanity, and the life of Being is its maturity. Even if this is the case, it is not correct to assume that it is a spontaneous and automatic development, for this would lead us to expect most of humanity to achieve the development of Being, which is clearly not the case. Normal ego development can be seen as a subphase of the development of Being, but since spiritual development beyond or instead of the ego level is very rare, we can see that it is not simply a naturally occurring continuation of ego development.

Chapter Eleven

Maturity, Ego and Personal Essence

Individuation and the development and integration of the inborn apparatuses of autonomy are clearly related to maturity. However, maturity is not an either-or phenomenon; one can be more or less mature. An interesting question arises: How is it that two individuals can each have normal ego development and individuation, but greatly differing degrees of maturity?

Normal development of ego is necessary but not sufficient for mental health, according to object relations theory. Neurosis is usually thought to be a mental pathology of someone with normal ego development. Blanck and Blanck establish this principle in the following quote, which occurs in a discussion of Kernberg's classification of mental disorder according to the stages of ego development:

> At the fourth stage in the development of internalized object relations, pathological development is represented by the neuroses. These patients have identity, a well-integrated ego, and a stable self and object representations. [Gertrude and Rubin Blanck, *Ego Psychology: Theory and Practice*, p. 78]

In object relations theory individuation is understood to be a lifelong process. Mahler says:

> Like any intrapsychic process, this one reverberates throughout the life cycle. It is never finished; it remains always active; new phases of the life cycle see new derivatives of the earliest processes still at work. [Margaret S. Mahler et al., *The Psychological Birth of the Human Infant*, p. 3]

132   Since the last phase of the separation-individuation process is understood as open-ended, it is termed "on the way to object constancy." Thus the theory does allow room for variation in kind and degree of individuation and maturity. But does it allow room for the maturity of Being? Otto Kernberg writes of individuation and maturity:

> Individuation includes the gradual replacement of primitive introjections and identifications with partial, sublimatory identifications fitting into the overall concept of the self. Emotional maturity is reflected in the capacity for discriminating subtle aspects of one's own self and of other people in an increasing selectivity in accepting and internalizing the qualities of other people. [Otto F. Kernberg, *Object Relations Theory and Clinical Psychoanalysis*, p. 74]

This means that maturity is based on the overall concept of the self, established by the end of the third year of life. It also means it is still a process of internalization and identification. Thus it is a matter of modification of the already existing psychic structure. So according to Kernberg, continuing individuation and maturity still do not include the element of Being.

If we think of maturity in the way Kernberg defines it (taking his to be typical of the object relations perspective), we would expect to see that maturity involves the solidification, strengthening and expansion of the ego and its structures. But this does not correspond to experience. True, some individuals become more rigid, more stereotyped and less alive with age, but it is also the case that some individuals do show signs of greater flexibility and aliveness. The latter development is considered by object relations theory to be the result of greater ego strength, more well-rounded development and more harmony between the parts of ego. The individuality becomes more pliable and more sensitive to others as it becomes stronger and more harmonious within. Kernberg continues in his description of emotional maturity: "Mature friendships are based on such selectivity and the capacity to combine love with independence and emotional objectivity." [*Ibid.*, p. 74]

The fact is that as an individual matures, he manifests qualities reminiscent of the various aspects of Essence, although the sense of self is still based on ego identification. Two questions suggest themselves at this juncture:

1. Why do only a few individuals show such signs of maturity, although the majority of human beings do achieve a well-formed ego?

2. What factors allow the maturity of ego to result in the experience 133
   of oneself in ways reminiscent of Being, although there is still identity with past object relations?

Maturity and The Secondary Autonomy of Ego

In the course of answering these two questions, we can present several observations related to maturity and individuation. The first is that some individuals occasionally do come upon the experience of the Personal Essence. It is most often the individuals who show signs of relative maturity who seem to have such occasional experiences. Usually there is no direct and clear recognition and appreciation such as we have seen in the cases we have reported. But there is in those experiences a sense of intimacy with oneself, a sense of greater presence and clarity, and a sense of strength. This manifests in spurts of initiative, creativity and expansion within oneself and one's personal life. One feels suddenly confident of oneself and one's capacities, and there is more courage in actualizing one's goals. This condition can last from a few minutes to months, even years. Usually it does not last very long, for there is no understanding of or support for this transformation.

The second observation is that we find in our work with students that those with more rounded ego development find an easier time with the experience of the Personal Essence. It is, generally speaking, easy for these individuals to experience the Personal Essence, and their process of developing and integrating it runs smoothly. Individuals with neurotic fixations or with more structural deficiencies have a much harder time in experiencing and realizing the Personal Essence. It takes them longer to get to the initial experiences, and they usually deal with a great deal of conflict in the process of integration.

The third observation is that individuals with structural problems of the ego and those with neurotic conflicts undergo different processes while integrating the Personal Essence. Students with structural difficulties seem to be able to reach the experience of the Personal Essence faster than those with neurotic conflicts, but they usually cannot retain the experience. The more neurotic individuals, although it is more difficult for them to have the initial experiences, are usually

134   more able to integrate the Personal Essence with the passage of time and the increase in understanding.

The fourth observation is that some students, after an initial experience of the Personal Essence, begin to recall similar experiences in early childhood, as early as the beginning of the second year. Sometimes, the process of working through the issues around the integration of the Personal Essence involves these early memories.

The fifth and last observation is in regard to the direct observation of children of various ages, in normal life situations. The author and some of his associates have observed that the Personal Essence is occasionally present in children. The experience often seems to begin as early as one year of age, but most often in the second year. Its frequency seems to depend on age and on the character of the child. When the Personal Essence seems to be present the child behaves in a confident, strong, expansive and more grown-up way. It is amazing to see how a child who is behaving in a dependent and clinging manner, and who shows no signs of capacity for greater individuation, can suddenly, when the Personal Essence is present in him or her, begin acting more independent and grown up. At such times the functions of autonomy are greater and more integrated. The physical coordination is better, language is suddenly easier, and interactions with others seem to make more sense. There is also a clear expression of joy in the child's individuation.

All these observations indicate a direct relationship between individuation and the presence of the Personal Essence. More important for our investigation, there seems to be a relation between the experience of the Personal Essence and ego development, although this relation does not seem to be direct and is certainly not an identity or equivalence. We need to understand this relationship in a way that explains in a satisfactory manner the above observations, and is able to answer the two previous questions.

We can get a hint of this relationship by analyzing the processes through which students come upon the experience of the Personal Essence. As we have seen in our case histories, disidentifying with an ego structure often exposes a sense of deficiency, lack or weakness, which is sometimes experienced as an emptiness, or more specifically, an empty hole. Allowing and understanding the deficient emptiness precipitates the emergence of the Personal Essence in consciousness.

The most important step for our discussion here, and in fact the
most crucial in the whole process, is that of moving from identification with part of the ego structure to the state of deficiency. It is clear in all the cases we have given, as well as in the rest of our experience with students, that this identification, although it gives a sense of identity, is also used for a defensive purpose. It functions partially, in fact primarily, to ward off or cover up the deficiency and its painful affects. When the student abandons the defensive posture, the deficiency is revealed.

Freud was the first to observe that identification is used for ego defense; thus this is the original understanding of identification in psychoanalysis. Freud also discussed its role in ego and superego building. It was Hartmann and his collaborators who emphasized the dual function of identification. They "describe the concept of identification as a process which may serve two purposes, the already-known defensive one, and one serving normal development." [Gertrude and Rubin Blanck, *Ego Psychology: Theory and Practice*, p. 36]

The implication for our discussion is quite clear: As long as an ego structure is used for defense it acts as a barrier against the experience of the Personal Essence. This point brings us closer to understanding what might be the factor contributing to maturity. It has to do with the fact that when ego becomes more developed and rounded it becomes also less defensive. This process was seen by Hartmann, which led him to coin the concept of secondary autonomy. Blanck and Blanck describe the process as follows:

> As thought processes develop, involving delay of drive discharge, intelligence serves the ego by aiding the organization of percepts and memory traces, making meaningful action possible. This organization of the inner world—the world of internalizations—is the very process of structuralization. As this proceeds, certain forms of behavior change in function. A process which had originated as a defense—for example, the essential mechanism of reaction formation in toilet training—acquires adaptive autonomy when the purpose changes to maintenance of hygienic habits and orderliness. With change in function, the activity becomes pleasurable in its own right, whereas when it is still in its archaic defensive form it counteracts pleasure. The end result of change in function is attainment of secondary autonomy. [*Ibid.*, p. 32]

136   In fact, it is possible to see the process of psychotherapy as partially that of attaining secondary autonomy. Processes and structures that started as defense, which created emotional conflicts, can change functions toward adaptation, through the process of therapy. This contributes to ego strength and development, which leads to maturity.

We can give now a partial answer to the two questions at the beginning of this chapter:

Most people do not show signs of real maturity with the passage of time partly because the secondary autonomy does not develop well. Increasing rigidity and stereotyped behavior patterns indicate an entrenchment in the defensive position.

We can say then that a possible factor that allows the mature ego to more closely approach the qualities of Being is that the ego becomes less defensive as it grows and develops, acquiring more flexibility, pliability and hence openness to essential perceptions.

That the process of secondary autonomy is possibly an explanation of the first and second observations mentioned above is self-evident. The explanation of the third observation is less evident. But it is easy to see that the degree of defensiveness is a primary factor. The neurotic individual has strong and well-established defensive structures, stronger than one with structural difficulties. So it takes longer and requires more work for him to have the initial experiences of Being. It is then easier for him to integrate the experiences because his defenses are already loosened and relaxed, and he already has a developed capacity for integration and synthesis. An individual with structural deficiencies has less well developed defensive structures and thus is more open to the initial experiences. However, he is not able to integrate the experiences smoothly because his defensive structures are more chaotic; also his weak ego has a diminished capacity for synthesis and integration.

It is, however, not yet clear how we might further explain the last two observations.

Identification and Defense

The development of secondary autonomy may partially account for the questions and observations above, but it does not explain the emergence of Being. When a process or behavior changes from defensive to adaptive there is no apparent opposition to the emergence of

Being; here, however, we are discussing something specific and not just any process or behavior. We are discussing identifications and identification systems. Identification has both defensive and adaptive functions, according to Hartmann. So the secondary autonomy of identifications (or identification systems of ego) involves such identifications decreasing their defensive functions and increasingly serving adaptation and growth. There is an assumption, however, that the identification systems of the ego will continue to exist. The individual will continue, at least unconsciously, to take such identifications (which are composed of internalized object relations) to define who he is. This means he is still identified with a self-image, although the self-image is now purged of its defensive properties. This is in line with the definition of self or object constancy, as the cathexis of a constant mental representation regardless of the state of need.

As we can see in our case presentations, this differs from the process that leads to the realization of Being. The student not only relinquishes his defensive posture; he also stops identifying with a particular self-image or ego structure. We discussed in some detail in Chapters Two and Three that one must disidentify from ego structures, object relations and self-image, in order to move to the realm of Being. In our case presentations so far there is a pattern of the student experiencing first some self-image and its respective object relations, and then when there is disidentification from this system it disappears to reveal a state of deficient emptiness. The implication of the concept of secondary autonomy, in contrast, is that one stops defending but continues to identify with the particular ego structure.

Our understanding is that to continue identifying with the particular ego structure is to continue the defense. In all the cases of an individual going from an ego state to a Being state, the main defensive maneuver is the identification with an ego structure, a self-image or an object relation. While it is true that one must deal with other defense mechanisms, like repression, reaction formation, projection and so on, ultimately one comes to face the identification systems themselves as the ultimate and most subtle defense.

It is true that the identifications give the individual a sense of self or individuality, which is taken by object relations theory to be needed for adaptation and development, but they are exactly what constitute

138   the defense against the particular state of deficiency related to the Personal Essence.

In relation to the Personal Essence, the experience is always as follows: One is cut off from the Personal Essence. There results a sense of lack and deficiency. Since the Personal Essence is the feeling of being a real and rounded individual, the deficiency is experienced as an affect of a lack of this sense of oneself. One feels weak, lacking his own sense of beingness. One feels one is really not a person, cannot be personal and cannot make contact.

Now, what is the best defense against such a painful state? Clearly, the best defense is the belief and feeling that one is a person who is strong and able to make contact. This is exactly what is provided by identifying with the ego structure or with part of it. We can call this function adaptive, but even if we admit this possibility, we cannot deny that it is also defensive. It is, in fact, a reaction formation to the state of deficiency.

It is possible for an object relations theorist to believe that such identification serves only an adaptive function, which is in this case the building of ego and its structures, because he does not consider the existence of Being, and hence is not aware of the painful deficiency that such identification serves to defend against. He takes the attitude that identification systems can exist in the psyche independently, and hence they do not need to be seen as defenses against anything.

From our perspective, however, just as it is known in psychoanalysis that some identification systems are defenses against other systems, or against id impulses, they (all identification systems) are usually defenses against the various aspects of Being. Being is always there; it is what we are in the most fundamental way. That it is not in conscious experience indicates the presence of defenses against it; it becomes part of the content of the unconscious. And any identification system taken to give the individual a sense of self or individuality is bound to function as a defense against Being because Being is who one is, is the true self. The identification systems are, at the least, in rivalry with Being and its aspects, and will always function defensively to ward off the deficiency resulting from loss of contact with Being. This defensiveness becomes apparent in the early stages of work on inner realization.

If object relations theory includes the concept of Being in its formulations, it will end up acknowledging the defensive nature of these identifications at the deepest level. In all our experience, with hundreds of students, identification systems always turn out to have a defensive function. This is also the understanding of the profound spiritual teachings of mankind. This passage from Gurdjieff gives the flavor of this understanding:

> "Identifying" is one of our most terrible foes because it penetrates everywhere and deceives a man at the moment when it seems to him that he is struggling with it. It is especially difficult to free oneself from identifying because a man naturally becomes more easily identified with the things that interest him most, to which he gives his time, his work, and his attention. In order to free himself from identifying a man must be constantly on guard and be merciless with himself, that is, he must not be afraid of seeing all the subtle and hidden forms which identifying takes. [P. D. Ouspensky, *In Search of the Miraculous*, p. 150]

This implies that in the secondary autonomy of identification systems, the change of function is only relative, never complete. Identification becomes less defensive, but never loses its defensive function completely. Kernberg points to this fact in a discussion of the secondary autonomy of thought processes:

> We might say that secondary autonomy of thought processes presupposes such emancipation of thought processes from their connection with early identification systems. . . . The emancipation of cognitive functions is, of course, always a relative one, but rather severe failure of such an independent development occurs in the borderline personality organization. [Otto F. Kernberg, *Object Relations Theory and Clinical Psychoanalysis*, p. 51]

Our conclusion here is that identification can never be completely divorced from defense. This implies that the ego structure, including the sense of self, of separateness, and of individuality, all have a defensive function by their very nature.

The defensive nature of ego has always been recognized since the time of Freud. Some object relations theorists have seen, in fact, that ego as a differentiated structure starts as a defensive process. This is the point of view of Kernberg:

> It is suggested that the ego as a differentiated psychic structure, in the sense of Freud's (1923) description, comes about at the point when introjections are used for defensive purposes, specifically in an early defensive organization against overwhelming anxiety. [*Ibid.*, p. 35]

Developmental psychologies usually attribute such overwhelming anxiety in early childhood to physical or psychological traumata. Kernberg, for instance, believes that the anxiety is primarily due to negative introjections; and that is why defenses, especially splitting, are needed:

> This serves the purpose of preventing the anxiety arising at the foci of negative introjections from being generalized throughout the ego and protects the integration of positive introjections into a primitive ego core. [*Ibid.*, p. 36]

There is clearly truth in this theory, but it does not take into consideration that overwhelming anxiety can be generated from the loss of contact with Being, or that it can lead to the loss of Being. In the latter case the result is that the early defensive nature of the ego is understood to serve not only the defense against the overwhelming anxiety, but to also ward off the experience of loss of Being that generates the anxiety. This in effect leads to the building of identification systems that eventually become barriers against the experience of Being. This point will be explored in detail in subsequent chapters; here we present a case report, to illustrate our discussion. The report is from James, a businessman in his thirties, who has been in the group for about three years. He has been dealing with some narcissistic issues and the painful affects related to them. He writes of his work in a group setting:

> Working with you, I felt a desire to understand, and yet I felt scared of talking in group and especially about my dream. The fear of talking lessened as I talked. The experience of disintegration and falling apart and space was frightening initially. Feeling the space with the pieces in it, instead of just the pieces was rather unifying and made me feel present.
>
> I still felt incomplete in my presence and felt that I was lacking some important part of me, like only having one eye instead of two. I wanted something of mine back.
>
> As much as I have felt space and falling apart and the resulting peace I still have resistance. The dream seems to

be the tip of an iceberg. I have resisted looking at it. Working with you I got a sense of a layer of crust being
removed to find a feeling of a crustier one underneath, of
more feelings; hurt and wanting in order to gain something, to be complete, from mommy.

Driving home, the feelings of annihilation came up for
me as I sense the pieces falling apart. Then I felt calmer,
my belly felt warm, round, and full.

One could argue whether the overwhelming anxiety was the result
of the disintegration of part of the psychic structure or that the disintegration of a defensive structure exposed an anxiety related to the loss
of Being: the warm, round and full sense of presence. We discuss in
much greater detail the second point of view in our book, *The Void*;
the reader can refer to it for more discussion. Experientially the two alternatives are felt the same. Of course, we do accept that disintegration
itself causes anxiety. But it is also known that anxiety causes disintegration, and that is what Kernberg was saying in the passage above. However, he does not see, as we have already pointed out, that anxiety can
be caused by loss of Being, or even that it is related to it in any way. In
the report above the disintegration, annihilation, and so on, finally
resulted in the emergence of the Personal Essence, with its rounded
and warm fullness. The longing for completeness is a longing for this;
one feels complete when one is experiencing the Personal Essence.

The relationship of anxiety to Being was recognized by some object
relations theorists. The British analyst, Winnicott, writes in a passage
quoted earlier:

Anxiety in these early stages of the parent-infant relationship relates to the threat of annihilation, and it is
necessary to explain what is meant by this term.

In this place which is characterized by the essential existence of a holding environment, the "inherited potential" is
becoming itself a "continuity of being." The alternative to
being is reacting, and reacting interrupts being and annihilates. Being and annihilation are the two alternatives.
[D. W. Winnicott, *The Maturational Processes and the Facilitating Environment*, p. 47]

So for Winnicott early overwhelming anxiety is directly related to
annihilation, which is due to the loss of the "continuity of being."

It is interesting that, with few exceptions, this point of view is completely overlooked by other object relations theorists. It is possible

142 that this is due to the fact that he did not explain how he was using the concept of Being, so it is easy to misunderstand him, and believe, for instance, that by Being he meant the presence of the feeling of self due to the psychic structure or even the body sensations. But it is clear that he did not mean that, for he was writing about early infancy prior to the establishment of a feeling of self.

We have noted that object relations theorists are aware that the identification systems of ego always have a defensive function. This is due to the belief that defense is something that is always needed by any individual. The ego begins as a differentiated structure with a defensive purpose out of necessity, and it is out of necessity that it retains some of its defensive nature. Defense is even seen as appropriate, especially in early childhood, for adaptive purposes. It is not envisioned that a human being could ever be beyond the need for psychological defense.

As we have noted, however, secondary autonomy does reduce the defensive function of ego, making it more harmonious within, more sensitive to external reality, more emotionally objective and more open to profound states.

This makes sense from the perspective of Being in that the personality based on identification is like a surface membrane over the reality of Being. The more normal is the structure, the more consistent and homogeneous the ego membrane. Greater integration and maturity allows this membrane to become thinner and more permeable to the reality of Being, which accounts for the depth and objectivity of mature behavior.

Some spiritual work schools, in fact, do not accept students unless they approximate such ideal ego development. For it is understood that it is easier for such individuals to cross over to the realm of Being, and that the crossover will be the next natural developmental step, which these individuals will spontaneously desire.

This does not mean that this crossover is a matter of the ego membrane becoming thinner and thinner until it directly, concretely allows the reality of Being. A more accurate way of seeing it is that there is an abyss separating Being from the ego membrane. This abyss is the experience of the absence of Being. To cross it means completely and finally abandoning the identifications of ego.

We must remember that the personality of ego is of a different nature than that of Being. It cannot move to the realm of Being

through successive approximation. Fake gold cannot become real 143
gold, regardless how good the forgery.

Returning to the assumption found in most of the literature of psychology that the human being always needs defensive structures, we wonder: Why does an adult human being need to defend himself against his inner experience? It is understandable for an immature and dependent child. For an adult without gross structural distortions, defense merely implies the unwillingness to confront inner anxieties that have already lost any realistic grounds. Confronting these anxieties will bring an understanding of their groundlessness, and make it possible to abandon the defensive posture.

Since this would mean abandoning ego identifications, our conclusion must be that true maturity is not possible within the realm of ego states, but requires a movement into the realm of Being.

Chapter Twelve

Being
and
Functioning

F rom the kinds of observations and experiences of Being we have described, some people have come to the conclusion that ego development is not needed at all, or that it is a temporary mechanism that must be dropped at some point to allow the experience of Being. This might seem to answer our questions and explain the five observations listed in Chapter Eleven.

In fact, many individuals who claim sudden enlightenment report that the personality with all of its identifications and roles simply drops away and one ends up in the realm of Being. One such report conveys this experience:

> I became non-existential and became existence. That night I died and was reborn. But the one that was reborn has nothing to do with that which died, it is a discontinuous thing. . . . The one who died, died totally; . . . utterly. . . . That day of March twenty-first, the person who had lived for many, many lives, for millennia, simply died. Another being, absolutely new, not connected at all with the old, started to exist. [Vasant Joshi, *The Awakened One, The Life and Work of Bhagwan Shree Rajneesh*, p. 66]

This kind of experience has been reported by many individuals throughout history, and in some of these cases there does appear to be a permanent change of identity. However, the phenomenon raises several considerations:

1. The sudden dropping away of personality structures usually leads, as in the case above, to the universal and impersonal aspects of

144

Being. It does not result in the experiences of the Personal 145
Essence.

2. It does not account for what happens then to what are called the ego functions, such as memory, thinking, motility and so on, which are thought to be inseparable from the development of object relations. This would seem to mean that the dropping of such structures involves abandoning a life-long integration and organization of functions necessary for life, survival and everyday functioning, but clearly this does not generally happen to those who undergo the sort of change described above.

3. If ego development were not needed then how would these functions develop and become organized and integrated? How would an individual manage to survive physically, and learn to function?

4. The point of view that ego structure can be summarily, suddenly dropped, seems to contradict the already established fact that the lack of ego structure results in mental disorder.

These considerations are probably some of the reasons why most psychologists do not listen to the teachings of the man of spirit about the impersonality of Being.

It does seem that ego development is necessary for learning to function. Hartmann sees the development of ego as primarily involved with adaptation. The ego functions develop out of the innate endowment of the organism, the apparatuses of primary autonomy, which are necessary for adaptation, and hence for survival and growth. These functions, including that of defense, contribute to the maturation of the organism. These functions, in their turn, are developed and integrated as part of the development of object relations in the context of interacting with the primary caretakers, mostly the mother. The final outcome of the process of adaptation is the organization of the ego functions in an overall integrated ego structure, at the center of which is a unified self-image that functions as a self or identity. The capacities of autonomy become part of the developed individuality, available for the autonomous functioning of the total personality, under the direction of the self.

The implication here, which is the implicit core of ego psychology, is that the development of ego, which involves the establishment of a self, separateness and individuality, is the way a human being learns

146   to adapt, survive and grow. So the adaptive functioning of the organism is inextricably linked to ego development.

In the situation we are exploring, we need an understanding that can account for the following two facts: First, the development of the integrated capacity of the organism to function autonomously, which according to object relations theory requires ego identifications; and second, the occurrence of experiences of Being, which implies the abandonment of ego identifications, without the loss of the autonomous functional capacity.

Integration and Absorption of Experience

The second fact above points out the possibility of functioning in the absence of ego structures. We can look at this phenomenon from the perspective of everyday experience, and also of psychological theory. The capacity for functioning can develop in such a way that the individual is able to function skillfully with complete absorption in the activity, without consciousness of self. Mahler writes about the individuated person:

> Consciousness of self and absorption without awareness of self are two polarities between which he moves with varying ease and with varying degrees of alternation or simultaneity. But this, too, is the result of a slowly unfolding process. [Margaret S. Mahler et al., *The Psychological Birth of the Human Infant*, p. 3]

We ask: How can functioning happen in such moments of absorption, when there is no consciousness of self, if the self is at the center of the functioning ego? Also, does an individual need to establish a psychic structure in his mind in order to learn a new skill? In other words, does he need his memories of learning to swim to be able to swim? To consciously remember will certainly hinder his skill. The more skillful he becomes, the less he needs these memories. When he is so skillful and proficient that he can be absorbed to the degree of forgetting himself there will be no memories at all. Does this mean these memories must have become part of an unconscious structure of his ego?

Of course, object relations theorists would not necessarily say that one needs to establish new mental representations to learn such skill.

But they do apparently assume that the capacity for learning is the
result of already existing individuation, and hence is dependent on already existing psychic structures. This is in fact what is meant by the
ego functions being organized within the structure of ego.

We need an understanding that includes a process of integration of
functioning that is not contrary to the nature of experience of Being.
This understanding is made possible by certain experiences and perceptions encountered in the process of the inner realization of Being,
which can be stated in the form of an hypothesis that explains how it
is possible to learn new skills and functions without needing ego
structures. The hypothesis is that one can absorb a skill so well that
all memory, conscious and unconscious, becomes unnecessary. It becomes, so to speak, part of one's being. The body and mind can become so adapted to the skill, that it resembles instinctual capacity.

Our suggestion is that this capacity of integration and learning must
be included as one of the apparatuses of primary autonomy, that it is
an inborn human capacity. The implication is that this capacity, although it needs ego development to begin functioning under normal
circumstances, is already part of the potential of the human organism
and is not the product of ego development.

So our hypothesis is that there is a certain human capacity, one of
the apparatuses of primary autonomy, that we will call "absorption,"
and define as follows:

*Absorption is the innate ability of the human organism to completely
assimilate learning from experience, to absorb it to the degree of not
needing the memory of the learning process, either consciously or unconsciously.*

Absorption, then, is a process beyond identification, but does
depend on identification. Thus learning happens in three general
stages: conscious memory, identification, and absorption.

For example, when one is learning a skill he needs to remember his
learning experiences at the beginning. His learning is more integrated
when he reaches the level of identification. This means that the
memory traces are internalized and integrated into the already-existing
psychic structure. This is the process of internalization as defined by
object relations theory. The learning becomes completely integrated
when it reaches the level of absorption. What is absorbed is part of
the ego structure, the part related to the acquired function or skill. At

148 this point the skill or learning becomes so much part of oneself that there is no need for mental representations involving it, consciously or unconsciously. This capacity for absorption can function the moment an identification system becomes established.

This hypothesis regarding ego development has profound consequences. The first and most obvious is that this hypothesis provides us with the understanding of how it is possible to function autonomously without identifying with ego structures. Also it explains how it is possible to experience Being without losing autonomous functioning. So our hypothesis makes it possible for us to account for the two facts at the beginning of this chapter. It also explains the two unexplained observations stated in Chapter Eleven regarding the presence of the Personal Essence in children; children can experience Being without the loss of functioning because they sometimes integrate their learning to the point of absorbing the corresponding ego identifications.

The relation of our concept of absorption to the experience of Being must now be explored. Our hypothesis is still somewhat vague. To make it more definite, we turn now to our basis for this suggestion, which arises out of certain experiences in the process of inner transformation that show the relationship between ego structures and Being. The process of essential realization itself can be seen as a process of "metabolizing" identification systems. Every time a system of identifications, a self-image or an object relation, is understood objectively, it seems to dissolve and an aspect of Essence is born. We will explore this further as we discuss understanding in the next chapter.

But now we will focus on certain experiences and perceptions that do not arise until the more advanced stages of the process of inner essential realization. These are experiences in which the student is becoming increasingly aware of a part of his personality, and as a result this part begins to lose its defensive property. At some point this part of the personality will not merely dissolve, allowing an essential aspect to be born, but one observes the simultaneous existence of both realities, side by side, so to speak. One is aware of Being, in one or more of its aspects, but is still aware of identifying with a certain self-image or object relation.

One of several resolutions occurs at this point, depending on the particular issue. Sometimes the sector of the personality becomes transformed by the action of Essence into some essential aspect. This happens particularly with the identification systems that give one the sense of being separate from the rest of existence. Usually, an aspect of love acts on the boundary structure and transforms it into the Personal Essence. This generally happens only in the most advanced stages of inner realization, in which personality structures are speedily disappearing. At some juncture of this process one comes upon schizoid-like defenses, that seem to operate at the very core structures of the personality. These schizoid-like defenses, isolation and schizoid withdrawal, usually occur after one has seen through the major narcissistic and borderline-like defenses. Finally, and usually after the entry into the realm of undifferentiated Being, one comes upon an ego state of "purified" personality. This is usually a very subtle perception, and to be aware of it one needs to be in a profound state of stillness and attentiveness. One becomes aware of identifying with a kind of personal feeling, which feels very familiar and quite intimate to oneself.

This is a state of experiencing one's personal identity (an ego state) devoid of any defensiveness, which happens after the process of secondary autonomy has gone through its full course with regard to this ego structure. One feels intimate with oneself, soft and cozy. But the most important distinguishing quality of this feeling of self is the recognition that this is what one usually feels *is* oneself. It is the emotional tone that characterizes one's personality. One feels, "This is me." However, one is at the same time aware it is only a feeling, an emotional tone that goes along with some image. This is because one is also aware of the presence of undifferentiated Being, which feels like an impersonal presence without any recognizable characteristics. One is in fact going back and forth, identifying with one and then the other.

The personality aspect is an identification that is completely devoid of defense; it is just a familiar sense of oneself, completely undefended and unprotected. That is why the schizoid defense of isolation, which is the most basic defense, must have been dropped before this experience.

By staying with this experience one becomes slowly and subtly aware that although this aspect of ego has no defensive structure, it nevertheless has a potential or virtual defense. Whenever there is the possibility of it being touched by any strong sensation it contracts, just

150   as an amoeba will do if touched by a strong stimuli. It will withdraw within itself. It will harden parts of itself whenever there is a possibility of an intense experience. Its attitude is that intense experiences would be overwhelming or even shattering.

This sense of personal identity is experienced as the most distilled, inner aspect of the personality, which is usually protected by the defensive structures of the ego. It is this which withdraws in the schizoid withdrawal, avoiding contact, interaction and any strong emotional experience, because it is felt to be too much for one's structure. Guntrip writes about the schizoid defense:

> We have seen how too early and too intense fear and anxiety in an infant who is faced with an environment that he cannot cope with and does not feel nourished by, sets up a retreat from outer reality, and distorts ego-growth by a powerful drive to withdrawal and passivity.
> The infant cannot take literal flight, and can only take flight in a mental sense, into an attempt to create and possess an hallucinated or fantasied safety in a purely psychic world which is part of his own experience, an inner world split off from the realities of everyday living. [Harry Guntrip, *Schizoid Phenomena, Object-Relations, and the Self,* p. 87]

This happens in the process of inner realization as the individual works through the various defenses against this withdrawn part of the ego, this sheltered part of the personality. Usually, when this happens, the individual feels lazy, lethargic and uninterested in anything. He feels like just staying in bed, doing nothing and feeling nothing, just being cozy and safe in a warm place. Contact with Being is felt as dangerous because it is very intense and will cause too intense a sensation. However, Being is present in the experience.

Observing this, one becomes aware that there must be some way that this part of the personality is keeping itself from contact with Being. When identified with this ego part one feels separate from Being, without a feeling of interest or curiosity about it.

One becomes slowly aware of a very subtle resistance in this personality aspect, against the presence of Being, which makes it feel separate from it. One becomes aware that the structure of this part, its very fabric, is pervaded by an extremely subtle posture of resistance; this resistance is part of its familiar sense of identity. To understand the difference between this subtle resistance and the usual resistances of ego defenses, one can visualize the usual resistance as a block of rubber. If you push against it, it pushes back, it resists you. In comparison to this thick block of rubber, the subtle resistance is like a very thin cloud of rubber. Whenever there is a strong feeling, one part of this cloud condenses and becomes a full-fledged resistance. However, at all times the thin cloud of rubber pervades, so to speak, the withdrawn personality segment.

It is in such deep and subtle perception that one can perceive directly that an identification cannot be absolutely devoid of defense or resistance. There are many aspects of this experience, but we will focus on what happens next. As usual, when the resistance is seen and understood it begins to dissolve. This resistance is understood to be an attempt to avoid contact with Being, to stay separate from it, untouched by it.

As this subtle resistance starts dissolving, one starts feeling oneself becoming absorbed in the undifferentiated Being. The experience of being absorbed by something bigger and unknown is quite definite and clear. There is no fear by now, because there is understanding, but sometimes there is some sadness, as if one is losing an old acquaintance. One feels one is being absorbed, as if one is a liquid being absorbed by a sponge. As the absorption proceeds one becomes less the personality and more the impersonal Being.

One has to forget about the experience and not pay attention to it, or the process will not proceed. Paying attention at this juncture means that one is taking himself to be an individual who can direct his attention, and hence means identification with the personality. One sort of forgets, gets busy with something else, but once in a while feels this sense of being absorbed.

At some point, one is suddenly the impersonal Being. One experiences a sense of absolute oneness. One is not the separate individual, but one is the oneness of all that exists. And after this perception, one experiences oneself emerging again as a personal presence. However, one is no more the withdrawn part of the personality. What emerges is the Personal Essence, with its fullness and preciousness.

This is an experience of the complete integration of personality into Being. The personality, as an ego structure with its sense of self, becomes actually and experientially absorbed into Being; and the

152 integration results in a new synthesis, the emergence of the Personal Essence.

This is one of the ways that the Personal Essence can be born. The Sufis call this process the "remaining after extinction." One is absorbed into the Supreme Being (the Sufis call it God), but then one is reborn, as an essential person.

In this experience, the process of absorption is clear, definite and undeniable. One feels taken in, assimilated, completely absorbed into Being. We can summarize the process thus:

1. It is the personality of ego, and its identification systems, that is absorbed.
2. It is absorbed into Being.
3. The result of the process of absorption is a new integration, the Personal Essence.

In the advanced stages of the journey of inner realization, many experiences involve this process of absorption. Such experiences, as far as we can tell, do not occur at the initial stages; if they do, the steps are not so clear and definite. They require the capacity to drop all defenses of ego, the capacity to recognize Being and the capacity to distinguish it from ego states.

To actually experience absorption, one must be aware of Being directly, so it is understandable that the process of absorption has not been conceptualized by object relations theory, which has set its task as the study of mental processes and representations that are normally accessible to everybody.

The five observations we listed in Chapter Eleven point to the possibility of this process of absorption, and the direct experiences of it show the reality of it. Our conclusion is that the process of integration of ego, which Kernberg says begins with introjections and ends with the formation of ego-identity, does not necessarily have to stop at the fixation of an organized structure of identifications in the psyche. In other words, psychic metabolism of experience does not have to end in the mind. For such metabolism to be complete, it must end in Being. This is what explains the process of true inner transformation, which now can be seen as the completion of ego development, to the level of the essential person.

Chapter Thirteen

Personal Essence and Object Relations Theory

We are presenting here a perspective that is supported by a wealth of experience—in fact, by all the spiritual experience of mankind—that inner integration can go beyond the mind, and into the realm of Being. Our goal here is not to demonstrate the truth of this spiritual experience, for this is humanity's common knowledge, but to demonstrate in detail the relationship between this experience and ego development. The connecting factor is the development of the Personal Essence, which is both personal and within the realm of Being.

In contrast, object relations theory utilizes the concept of psychic metabolism, but with a few partial exceptions (such as the work of Michael Balint and Fairbairn) restricts its application to the content of the mind. Most writings indicate that when early experience is metabolized it becomes integrated into the structure of the ego.

Since this field does not include the concept of Being, it does not take into consideration what we consider to be the ultimate goal of ego development. Thus ego development is seen as occurring in a completely different realm from spiritual transformation, which is not addressed at all. These assumptions are what underly the mistaken belief in the gulf between the man of spirit and the man of the world.

The Personal Essence can be seen as the integration or absorption of personality into Being, as the synthesis of the man of the world and the man of spirit. However, it is more accurate to see it as the ultimate

154   product of ego development. In other words, ego development and spiritual enlightenment are not two disjoint processes but parts of the same process. The understanding of the Personal Essence shows how they are linked. This point is a radical departure from the understanding of both traditional spiritual teachings and modern psychology. It unifies these two fields into one field, that of human nature and development.

To explore further the consequences of our perspective, we will look more closely at the process of absorption, expanding our investigation beyond the adult ego states we have so far mainly considered. Our question here will be, what are the conditions needed for the absorption of ego into Being?

We have identified secondary autonomy as one such condition, showing that the relinquishing of the defensive aspect of any ego identity is always only partial.

We have also explored how it is possible to go farther, seeing that just before the process of absorption begins, the remaining general but subtle defensive posture of an identification system can dissolve. This indicates that for absorption to occur the process of secondary autonomy must be complete and not only relative. Absorption occurs only when personality completely surrenders its defenses. When personality (any identification system of ego) ceases all resistance, it is readily absorbed, and a transformation occurs that ends in the emergence of the Personal Essence. So the transition from ego to Being hinges on the abandonment of defense. This mirrors the age-old spiritual understanding that surrender leads to enlightenment and realization.

We have observed that abandonment of defense can happen at any age, not only in adulthood. This means that the experience of the Personal Essence can occur in childhood, which we earlier reported having observed. It also explains why some individuals begin to have memories of it after they recognize it in adulthood.

If we look at the question of absorption from the beginning of ego development, recalling that identification systems arise out of internal representations of early interactions with the environment, we see two alternatives: any given identification system has a defensive function, or it does not. If it has a defensive function it cannot be absorbed. If it does not have a defensive function then it is absorbed and this results in the experience of the Personal Essence. If it has a defensive function it will continue to be a content of the mind unless at some point it loses its defensive function and is absorbed into Being. If it does not lose its defensive function it becomes integrated with other identification systems (which also have a defensive function) into the overall structure of ego.

This understanding connects with a view held by the early English object relations theorist, Fairbairn, who believed that ego identifications were built only from object relations with negative affects, i.e., only negative object relations are internalized. Our understanding lends a partial support to this view. We see that the identification systems of the ego persist as mental structures only if they have a defensive function. This implies that many of the object relations internalized are negative in affect, but not necessarily all of them. One sees from closer study of internalized object relations that some of them are positive, or more accurately, considered by the individual as positive. A positive object relation can be used, for example, as a defense against another object relation that is considered negative. The first one is positive in that it defends against greater negativity, even if it is somewhat negative. The other case is that an object relation which is positive, for example a loving interaction with mother, can be used in a defensive way if there is a need to defend against a loss of an aspect of Being, such as Will.

So our understanding is that the personality is not made up only of negative identifications, but that it is made up only of identifications that have defense as at least one of their functions.

The most important consequence of this understanding for the field of ego psychology is that the development of self and object constancy is not the most complete individuation possible, even in childhood. Taking into consideration the discussion in Part II, we must conclude that the goal of ego development is not the individuality based on self-image, but rather it is the realization of the Personal Essence. We described in detail the following characteristics of the Personal Essence:

- It is a sense of real autonomy and independence.
- It is a sense of being oneself, as a full and strong presence.
- It is a personal sense of oneself. It is the person of Essence.
- It can make direct personal contact.

156   These four characteristics include but are not limited to the characteristics of object constancy and the establishment of individuality which object relations theory states are the outcome of ego development. To restate Mahler's capsulization of the tasks of the last subphase of the separation-individuation process: "(1) the achievement of a definite, in certain aspects lifelong, individuality, and (2) the attainment of a certain degree of object constancy." [Margaret S. Mahler et al., *The Psychological Birth of the Human Infant*, p. 109]

Object constancy is usually defined as the capacity to see and relate to the other as a person in his or her own right. This capacity is part of the quality of the Personal Essence, of being personal and able to make direct personal contact. The sense of individuality is the normal feeling of the experience of the Personal Essence, as we discussed in Part Three. Thus the Personal Essence satisfies the conditions of individuation as defined by object relations theory. Moreover, it satisfies them on a much more real and profound level of experience, that of Being.

It is interesting that when someone is regarded as mature he is often referred to as having a "well-rounded" ego or personality. This sense of being a well-rounded person is exactly what students report when they experience the Personal Essence. The sense of roundedness becomes even more tangible, as in Pamela's report in Part IV. One feels rounded, full, integrated. The presence of the Personal Essence makes one feel a sense of integration, togetherness, definiteness, almost a sense of structure. All these qualities which are attributed to the integrated ego are experienced in a very definite and palpable manner in the experience of the Personal Essence. The following report demonstrates the sense of structure and definiteness.

Marian is a professional woman in her forties, who has been in a group led by the author for a few years. She has always had difficulty being definite in her communications, and is usually vague about her feelings. It is hard for her to pinpoint exactly what she feels, or what to say to communicate her feelings. This has frustrated her a great deal and sometimes filled her with a feeling of emptiness. She has been working for some time on her relationship with her mother. She reports her work in one group session:

> I wanted to talk about three things today: separation, conflict and my nausea and other physical symptoms. I do not

know what I wanted to know about separation, only that, for sure, I have separated in some way from my closest female friend. I feel frustrated when I cannot make sense. I feel a separation from my job, my friends, even my pets. I cannot remember what words I said to you about that. I was aware again that I speak all around a subject, but not about the subject itself. It is as if I cannot get there. I am too busy trying to make myself understood or making the words pleasing to the listener. You told me that a good aim for me to take would be to be more definite, when it feels like I am going to be vague, and to sense and see what else comes up when I am vague. I felt something similar to going blank, like time standing still. Blood rushes inside me and I feel panicky. You suggest that I relax my eyes, and when I do I feel a deep sadness and sobs in my belly. I feel frustrated about not knowing why I am sad. I feel a thickness in my chest which goes all the way to my throat. I feel sexual around my pelvis. The thickness fills my entire chest. I am aware of how it touches my sides. I feel calm now. I feel aware of my body. I seem compact. I feel small and I feel big. I feel full around my diaphragm as this feeling seems to puff me out in front. Yet the fullness seems weightless. My body feels compact. The feeling is not unpleasant. I like how I feel definite.

Marian does not describe the process she underwent going from the state of vagueness to that of fullness and definiteness, but it is clear that there was some sadness, frustration and even emptiness. Her state would most likely be understood by object relations theory as a difficulty in ego integration, a difficulty in experiencing herself as a real person with a definite sense of self. We recognize all that in her state, but the state also tells us that she was experiencing the absence of the Personal Essence. So her problem appears to be the state of deficiency resulting from not experiencing the Personal Essence. We see also that she experienced the fullness as giving her structure, compactness and definiteness. She became definite about how she felt—she felt definite and she liked it.

We could give many more case presentations to demonstrate that the presence of the Personal Essence is associated with the sense of integration, roundedness, wholeness, completeness and individuation. However, we have thoroughly made our point that a great deal of evidence shows that the qualities of individuation are present in the experience of the Personal Essence.

158   These qualities and manifestations of individuation are sometimes seen in children, as has been noted by Mahler and her collaborators in their famous studies. They are not usually so clear and definite as we see them in our case presentations, but occasionally they are. It is not an unusual sight to see a child of two walking, playing or interacting with a sense of confidence, independence, definiteness and a clear sense of personal presence.

One could read these phenomena as resulting from the development of a separate individuality with a unified self-image. However, this development is not established until later in the process of separation-individuation, later in the third year of life, so this does not explain the occurrence of these manifestations of individuation much earlier, around age one or one and a half years of age. If a unified self-image is needed for such manifestations of individuation, and this happens only by the end of the third year, then how can we account for such manifestations, when they can happen two years earlier?

In our perception it is very clear at such times that the Personal Essence is present in the experience of the child, and that is why the individuation seems so complete. This is partly because sometimes the integration of a certain segment of ego goes as far as absorption, and thus precipitates the presence of the Personal Essence.

It is also our observation that the more stable development observable around age three lacks the fullness and the definiteness of individuation that is expressed sporadically earlier in the child's development. It is true that by this time the child behaves as if he has a separate individuality, but we cannot fail to notice that the sense of fullness, definiteness and presence is somewhat vague. In our perception this is because the stable individuality that becomes established is that of the ego, and hence lacks the richness and reality of the Personal Essence.

A developmental psychologist might be more willing to believe that the earlier sporadic expressions were so clear and definite because they were unrealistic, perhaps the expression of grandiosity, characteristic of the practicing period at eighteen months. This is sometimes true, but we are referring to instances in which the child behaves in a more realistic way than usual. At such times, he seems better able to judge his capacities, and his performance, physical, mental or emotional, is actually more competent than usual. The most telling

manifestation is the capacity to relate to others, and to express himself
in a real and personal manner.

Of course, it is understood in object relations theory that ego development is not a linear process; there are regressions of varying degrees and duration all throughout the process. However, the early
manifestations of such clear signs of individuation cannot be thus explained since regressions are to less individuated states and not to
more developed ones.

Our psychologist might postulate that the ego has the capacity to
act in an individuated way before final integration, which capacity can
manifest sporadically under favorable conditions but cannot last. This
would mean that ego can act in an individuated way before it is individuated. But what is it then that acts this way at such times, if the
structure is not there? What is this capacity?

We know that the Personal Essence always has such a capacity,
regardless of the age at which it manifests. This is a characteristic of
the Personal Essence that the ego and its individuality do not have. It
does not develop in terms of its capacity for personal contact. This
capacity is part of it; it is its mode of consciousness. Of course, the
capacity for autonomous functioning does develop, but this has to do
with the integration of the functions of primary autonomy into it, as
we will see in a subsequent section.

Regardless of how early it appears, the Personal Essence always
manifests as a personal presence, with the capacity for direct personal
contact. Of course it manifests more often as the child grows in years,
because it needs the child's capacity for perception, cognition and object comprehension. Emotional capacity for relating cannot function if
there is still no capacity for discrimination, cognition and so on.

Unlike ego structure, aspects of Essence do not develop. They always
exist as part of the potential of the human being. When the child
reaches a certain maturity in his physical and cognitive functions it becomes possible for him to contact these aspects of his Being. As his maturation increases he becomes able to contact and experience more of them.

This is somewhat similar to emotions. Rage and sadness are part of
the potential of being a human being. They do not develop, although
they do become involved in the internalized object relations. At certain stages of development the human organism becomes able to feel
and express different emotions.

160   Although emotional states change, essential states are there from the beginning. The child is not aware of them, but as his capacities of perception and cognition develop he becomes capable of awareness of them. It is difficult to communicate how these essential aspects are independent of ego. One has to experience them to see the implication.

The Personal Essence not only has the capacity for individuated contact, it is the state of contact itself. It is a state of integration and wholeness. It is already there, integrated, definite and together. The human organism becomes able to contact and embody it as it matures and develops in its physical, mental and emotional capacities. The capacities involved in ego development, the processes of internalization, identification, and ego organization and integration, are required for it, as is clear from our discussion of absorption. That is why it generally manifests sporadically around age one, because by then there is already the capacity to organize and integrate internalizations. The Personal Essence is actually what makes this capacity grow and mature. It is the "archetype" of the capacity. We will explore this more fully when we study the ego functions in their relation to the Personal Essence.

So as the capacities of organization, integration and synthesis develop, it becomes possible to experience the Personal Essence early in life. The less need there is for the defensive function of the ego, the more it is possible to experience it, and the more frequent and profound are the experiences. So depending on the situation in childhood one can grow to be completely identified with the self-image, or the identification can be loose and relaxed due to frequent and prolonged experiences of the Personal Essence.

The early contact with the Personal Essence gives the child an innate sense of confidence and individuation beyond that of his ego. His sense of who he is partly influenced by these experiences. Like other experiences of childhood, the experience of Being does become internalized, and influences one's personality. Such experience does not necessarily make one identify with Being, because any image, even an image gained from experience with Being, is a mental content and not Being. However, it is bound to influence the personality toward more openness and less resistance to similar future experiences, and also contribute to greater capacity for individuation and maturity.

The Personal Essence is the real person, the true individuality. It is 161 the true ego, just as the fourteenth century Sufi, Semnani, stated, when referring to the left latifa: "This subtle divine center conceals the 'rare Mohammadan pearl,' that is to say, the subtle organ which is the True Ego. . ." [Henry Corbin, *The Man of Light in Iranian Sufism*, p. 125] It is what is meant to be realized in ego development. It is the actual goal and completion of this development. It is the real individuation. It is not on the ego level or the spiritual level; for it is neither and both. There is only one human individuation, and that is the realization of the Personal Essence.

In contrast, object relations theory, and developmental psychology in general, consider ego development a complete process on its own, and spiritual teachings consider ego development either as a wrong development, or as a development that should be superceded by spiritual development.

In our understanding it is more accurate and certainly much more useful, to see ego development as an incomplete development. It is more correct, from our point of view, to consider ego development and spiritual transformation as forming one unified process of human evolution. A human being grows and develops by learning from experience. Difficulties can occur at any stage of this process, including getting "stuck" on the ego level.

We have so far discussed personal inner evolution, from birth, through ego development, to the realization of the Personal Essence. We will develop this understanding further in subsequent chapters, and show that the realization of the Personal Essence is the step that leads to the realization of the more advanced spiritual states, such as those of oneness or the Absolute. So it is one process of evolution from the beginning of ego development to the final stages of spiritual enlightenment. We will explore this evolution as the process of the personalization of Being. It is how Being, impersonal and eternal, becomes a person, a human being on earth. So the process is a matter of Being, which is spirit, learning to live in physical embodiment.

Chapter Fourteen

The Metabolism of Experience

We saw in the last section that for metabolism of experience to be complete, identification systems must be absorbed into Being. This hypothesis raises a few questions, such as this one: Can the totality of the personality, with all its identification systems, be absorbed into Being? The answer is that all identification systems can be metabolized (integrated into the psychic structure), but only some can be absorbed.

There are two types of identification systems that cannot be absorbed: the first are any identification systems which serve only a defensive function. Clearly these cannot be absorbed because absorption, as we have noted, requires the absence of all defense. A purely defensive identification simply dissolves as defenses are dropped. When a defense stops being defensive, it is no more. On the other hand, if identification systems began as defensive but through the process of secondary autonomy lost their defensive function while remaining part of the ego identity, they can be absorbed.

The second type of identification system that cannot be absorbed is one composed solely of fabrications of the mind, such as fantasies of what was supposed to happen but did not, or a dream of what one wants to happen, which are used for the purpose of building the ego identity. Such identification systems are common, and become apparent at certain stages of inner realization. One may discover fantasies about what happened in one's childhood, or dreams for the future, which are experienced as part of one's sense of self.

These systems are clearly defensive, although they are not usually experienced as such. Sometimes they are defenses against specific memories, such as a very painful disappointment, but when they are of global significance to the personality they should not be regarded as purely defensive.

These fantasies, beliefs and misinformation actually accompany almost all internalized object relations to some extent. Internalized object relations are rarely true representations of actual events or relationships. One's memory traces include all kinds of ideas, fantasies and images that never had an objective reality. Another source of extraneous material comes from the psychic processes of organization and integration themselves. These processes modify the original object relations as more impressions are internalized. This is necessary for the integration of object relations units of various affect and content.

This extra material, whether it is attached to actual memories of object relations or consists of pure fabrications, cannot be absorbed into Being. This is an important difference between the mind and Being. The mind can absorb and identify with any psychic material it believes to be true. It does not have the capacity, on its own, to discern what is objective truth and what is not. In other words, the mind can be deceived, even by itself.

Being, on the other hand, is pure reality. It is the actual stuff and consciousness of truth, and cannot be deceived. It does not try not to be deceived; it is simply truth by its nature, a self-conscious medium made of pure sensitivity.

Any falsehood, that is, anything which is not the objective truth of what actually happened in past interactions which produced a particular object relation, is felt in comparison to Being to be dull, gross and distasteful. When one is in contact with Being, these falsehoods are felt to be lifeless, thick and heavy veils in comparison to the luminosity of Being.

In order to discover why Being will not absorb certain materials, we must ask, what is it that Being actually absorbs? We have stated that it absorbs identifications which are devoid of resistance; but these are merely memories of experiences, and elaborations of such memories. What is it in these memories that Being will absorb?

Being is like an individual who is aware, intelligent, discriminating, truth-loving and undeceivable. If you present a story to this individual,

164   what will he take within himself, and what will he leave untouched? He will take in the truth and leave the false without touching it. So identifications will not be absorbed into Being unless they are absolutely empty of falsehood. Only when an identification contains exactly what objectively occurred in the original interaction will it be readily absorbed. Identifications that are pure fabrications will not be absorbed at all; and identifications which contained an original truth of experience will be absorbed only when they are completely purged of falsehood. Being does not, of course, reject or judge the falsehood; it simply takes into itself what is of its own nature, that is truth and reality, and leaves the false alone.

   Thus, defensive identifications cannot be absorbed because they constitute a resistance against some truth. Also, in maturity the presence of defenses against the truth of past experience is in itself a falsehood, for it is normally no longer needed.

   We come then to the understanding of what is required for inner transformation: impressions will be completely metabolized, to the point of absorption into Being, only when completely purged of falsehood. Ego is absorbed into Being only after it is completely purified.

   This is the original sense of spiritual purification, which has nothing to do with morality but involves separating the true from the false. This understanding is one reason the Sufis call the process of inner transformation the "purification" of the ego. We see here, too, the role of truth in this process: since human development is constituted by the metabolism of personal experience, and for this metabolism to be complete the true must be separated from the false—the former to be absorbed and the latter to be discarded—we can see that the specific requirement for growth, maturation and development is truth, the truth garnered from personal experience.

   In general, the process of eliminating falsehood is spontaneous; the mind generally lets go of an impression when it recognizes it to be false. Since it can no longer be used for purposes of identification, and cannot be absorbed, the false impression simply dissolves. An exception to this pattern is when a clearly false belief is part of a larger system, most likely unconscious, which the mind still takes to be true; then the mind will hold on to the falsehood until the larger belief system is revealed.

   The permanent presence of identification systems in the mind can now be seen as a kind of indigestion or constipation. Any such system is a mental contraction, which is accompanied by physical contractions in the body. When the inner sensitivity is refined, the tensions in the body which accompany identification can be seen. These tensions are what Wilhelm Reich called "body armor"; he further recognized that any character structure has a defensive pattern, which he called "character armor," which was revealed in the tension patterns of the body armor. [Wilhelm Reich, *The Function of the Orgasm*] Identifying these tension patterns can be very useful in the process of becoming aware of one's identifications.

The work of inner transformation, then, becomes partly that of correcting the indigestion, so that metabolism can occur naturally, on its own. The presence of ego structures indicate that there is unmetabolized psychological food in the identification system, both useful "nutrients" which can be usefully absorbed, and "waste products" that must be eliminated.

(Many students who are well on their way in the process of inner transformation and are working on metabolism, report tensions and various other sensations in the area of the spleen and pancreas. The spleen has the function of eliminating dead white blood corpuscles, which are part of the immune system and have the function of defending the body. The process of metabolism has the analogous function of eliminating no longer needed defensive ego identifications. We can see a connection between these two levels of functioning; this sort of connection has been reported by many researchers studying psychosomatic phenomena. [Franz Alexander, *Psychosomatic Medicine*])

The perception of parts of the personality as waste products which are retained in the mind because it still believes they are needed, is sometimes reflected in dreams. One student reported a dream in which he finds himself walking near slime. He sees a colorful peacock in the distance. The peacock then becomes "infected" with the slime, which was directed at it by a gun. The colors of the peacock dim, and fade to brown. This is done to the peacock for its own good. When the student explores the dream, he realizes that the "good" of the peacock is its protection.

This sense of being "infected" by the personality occurs frequently when one is working on the ego identifications stemming from the early stages of development. One feels as if one absorbed the

166   personality from the environment, sometimes in the form of unclear
air or some kind of dull and dirty substance.

This brings us to another question raised by our model of metabolism: Why is complete metabolism so rare in human experience? The conditioning theory of learning and the findings of the various depth psychologies reveal that in early childhood defenses are necessary, partly due to environmental inadequacies and partly due to the incapacity of the yet immature human organism. The necessity for defense and the internalization of a lot of falsehood have another cause which is rarely noted in psychology: it is the omnipresent ignorance of Being in most human societies. This ignorance is taken in by the developing infant and becomes part of its ego structure. The identity of the personality develops in the absence of the awareness of Being. The presence of love helps in the process of metabolism, but it does not have much power when understanding is lacking. A great deal of knowledge of a specialized nature is needed for children to be raised in a way that will steer them towards complete human development. The psychological and spiritual knowledge now available to most human societies is insufficient for this task, because Being is almost completely ignored in the normal social perspective.

It seems that a few spiritual traditions still possess fragments of this specialized knowledge, largely those traditions which have a long history of transmitting essential experience through the generations. We have in mind some of the Tibetan Buddhist schools and some of the Sufi schools of central Asia.

Even when favorable circumstances allow one to remain connected to Being while growing up, one will still develop a self-image, but the identification with self-image would be more flexible and transparent. In the early stages of mental development, the infant's capacity for perception and especially for understanding do not develop fast enough for him to recognize his identity as Being. The first perceptions that can become memory traces are those of forms and images. Also, the need to learn how to function dictates a certain attachment to such images.

When one is familiar with nonconceptual Being, it becomes clear that the development of the mind cannot be divorced from the creation of images, since mind deals with images. There is no knowledge without images, for knowledge is composed of concepts, which are

various sorts of images; the creation of these images is indispensable
for discrimination in the mind.

To know that one is Being, which is not within the realm of images, is such a subtle understanding that it seems impossible for a child to have this knowledge. Enlightenment must wait for the maturity of perception, discrimination and understanding, since it depends on self knowledge. These capacities depend upon concepts. We can say then that ego is needed for enlightenment, since the beginning of conceptualization in childhood is inextricably linked with the development of the ego.

So first the ego, which is needed for knowledge and functioning, develops; then the capacity for discriminating knowledge, among other things, leads to the dissolution of the ego. The final result is the life of Being, including the development of functioning within the realm of Being.

This interdependence between ego and Being can also be seen in the process of inner metabolism. Ego on its own cannot complete the metabolism of experience and hence cannot bring about complete human development; Being is needed for this process to take place. On the other hand, Being cannot accomplish on its own the whole process of metabolism; it cannot dislodge ego when ego is defensive. From the perspective of the mind, Being can be resisted easily with a slight movement of ego; thus ego must first cooperate by relinquishing its defensive posture.

It is up to ego to cease resisting. When it ceases its defensive posture completely, then Being acts. This is an important understanding for methods of inner realization. The work on purifying or understanding ego will not lead, by itself, to transformation. Being by itself cannot do it either. The work must be done from both directions—the letting go of ego defenses and the development of Essence.

The understanding we develop in this book, which will further detail the process of inner transformation, depends in like manner on the two different facets of human understanding: psychological knowledge, especially object relations theory, and traditional spiritual knowledge. Object relations theory contains extremely useful, detailed information about the beginning stages of the metabolism of experience, and its concepts about ego development make it useful even up to the point of realization of the Absolute Truth. The principles of

168   spiritual practice provide the overall understanding of Being as well as the understanding needed for the later stages of metabolism. The teacher Gurdjieff understood the importance of acquiring and digesting impressions, as one of the three basic foods:

> Impressions, air, and physical food enable the organism to live to the end of its normal term of life and to produce the substances necessary not only for the maintainence of life, but also for the creation and growth of higher bodies. [P. D. Ouspensky, *In Search of the Miraculous*, pp. 181–182]

Spiritual practice is primarily the cultivation of presence, understanding, awareness and surrender. These are the capacities needed for the later stages of psychic metabolism. Awareness and understanding are needed for the purification of ego identification. Presence and surrender are needed for the process of absorption itself. One learns to be open, vulnerable and present to one's experience, in order to allow effective metabolism. This means that one learns to be in direct contact with one's experience, which in turn requires the presence of the Personal Essence, which is the aspect which can make such direct contact without defensiveness. Thus, when one is realized as the Personal Essence, metabolism becomes a natural, spontaneously occurring process. Effective metabolism leads to the realization of the Personal Essence, and the Personal Essence, in its turn, makes metabolism a natural process of living. The life of the Personal Essence is a continuing, ever-expanding process of integration and individuation.

Chapter Fifteen

Personal Essence and Ego Functions

S ince the Personal Essence is the true individuality, it is closely related to the capacities of primary autonomy, which are usually referred to as the ego functions. We have seen that the development and integration of these capacities is intertwined with the development of object relations. Thus we might wonder what happens to these capacities when the object relations are finally metabolized.

The answer is that they finally come into their own. They become more developed, more integrated and more synthesized into a harmonious whole, not dependent on a mental structure. Their true origin, the extent of their function and their real meaning become clear.

In general, the presence of the Personal Essence brings about a radical expansion and individuation of autonomous functioning, indicating the greater development and integration of the apparatuses of autonomy. Its realization brings about an increasingly radical movement towards autonomy and individuation, leading to greater actualization of one's potential. One becomes more creative, more productive, more original and more fulfilled in personal involvements.

Accomplishments and developments manifest externally in one's work and in personal relationships. One begins to become clear about one's place in the scheme of things, more definite about roles and functions.

The meaning and purpose of one's life become clear, definite and actualized. One's potentials develop and expand in a meaningful way, in accordance with one's real aims. A sense of confidence in one's capacities develops speedily, along with a certainty about who or

169

170   what one is. One increasingly values one's real presence, and the capacities and manifestations of this presence. The confidence, certainty, and value are not mental or emotional, but are more in the nature of a recognition of facts. We will discuss some of these developments in more detail when we discuss the development of the Personal Essence; now we will focus on its relationship to some specific capacities of autonomy: *integration, synthesis, object relating, regulation* and *intention*. This will shed more light on the Personal Essence as the true individuation, on how the capacities are perceived from the perspective of Being, on what it means that they are integrated into it, and on many more important questions.

1. *Integration:* The feeling of the Personal Essence is a sense of being integrated, together, whole and complete. So its presence is itself experienced as an integration. From the understanding we have developed so far, it is clear it is the integration of all that the individual has experienced and learned.

At the beginning, as we have described, it is a definite sense of a personal presence that feels whole, balanced and able to make contact. Then this personal presence is seen to integrate into itself the other aspects of Essence. At the beginning these aspects of Essence, such as love, compassion, clarity, understanding, intelligence, will, joy, pleasure, empathy, truth, intuition, strength and many others, exist as Platonic forms, as absolute aspects of true existence. After the Personal Essence is realized, they become integrated into it through a process of absorption, in which they become personalized. They continue to exist in their original forms, but now they also exist in another form, as a part of the very substance of the Personal Essence. We will discuss this process in more detail in the section on the development of Essence.

The Personal Essence, then, becomes the integration of all aspects and dimensions of Being, and is clearly experienced as the integration of one's experience and learning. It is not only an integration, but it is also a capacity for integration. The fact that it is an integration gives it this capacity. This is like the function of crystals. If one drops a small crystalline structure in an appropriate chemical solution it acts as a kind of seed, starting a process of crystallization, replicating itself. The Personal Essence is the presence of an integrating consciousness which brings about more integration like itself, and into itself.

It also affects the organism in a more general way by exerting an activating and developing influence on the integrative functions at all dimensions of the organism. For instance, the effect of the Personal Essence on the mind is that it brings out its integrative capacity. One's mind becomes spontaneously better able to integrate, and more inclined towards integration. Integrative ideas and insights become a matter of course, whatever field or situation one puts one's mind to.

We can see the Personal Essence as the prototype, on the Being level, of an integrated and integrating capacity. So when it is present its integrative function is felt not only on its own dimension, that of Being, but on all other dimensions. It tends to enhance the integrative capacity of the body, the nervous system, the intellect, the intuition, the energy system, the emotional tendencies and so on. Even the tendency of ego structure to move towards greater integration, under optimal conditions, is greatly enhanced by the presence of the Personal Essence. So we believe that when it makes its appearance in childhood it facilitates the integration of ego identifications.

The capacity for integration exists on all levels of organismic functioning: physical, mental, emotional, and on the Being level. But since the Being level is the deepest, when it is present it enhances all dimensions of integrative capacity. It also integrates all these dimensions into a whole, individuated presence, the essential person. One feels *one*, and not composed of parts. The Being, the body and the mind are all experienced as one presence.

2. *Synthesis:* One can see from the perspective of the nondifferentiated Being, the Supreme reality of the oneness of existence, that all aspects of Essence are differentiations proceeding from this original nondifferentiated source. The Personal Essence is the synthesis of all differentiated aspects of Essence. This is similar to Hartmann's concept of differentiation from the undifferentiated matrix, and his notion that the final ego development is the integration that follows such differentiation. So individuation is the integration of the results of differentiation.

The incomparable pearl is the individuation on the Being level. It is a new synthesis, which in a sense creates a personal Being from the impersonality of the nondifferentiated Being.

The capacity for synthesis on the Being level belongs to another aspect of Essence—objective understanding. This aspect has the

172   capacity for both analysis and synthesis on all levels of perception and knowledge. It is closely related to the Personal Essence; it is the inner guidance needed for its realization and development. But, like all other aspects, it becomes integrated into the Personal Essence at some point in the process of inner realization. The synthetic capacity is then experienced as a quality of one's own Being.

Synthesis is not experienced as putting things together in a unified whole: this is the quality of the synthetic capacity of the mind. The Being capacity for synthesis manifests in the ability to see the unity before differentiation. One does not bring two things together; one simply does not see them as two.

Our understanding that ego development and spiritual realization form one process of human evolution is an example of such a synthesis. This conception was not arrived at by integrating the two processes, but resulted from perceiving the one process of human evolution.

3. *Object relating:* Ego is considered to have the innate capacity for object relations, which enables it to relate to another as a person. We discussed in detail, in Chapter Three, the capacity of the Personal Essence to relate in a personal way. It is the true personal element, the real capacity for personal contact and relating.

We can see the ego's capacity for object relations as only a step towards the true capacity. The pearl beyond price can relate in a personal way without the need to activate past object relations. So its capacity is not only innate, but also natural and spontaneous.

4. *Regulation:* The ego is considered to be able to regulate its inner states and its behavior. The Personal Essence is an integration and synthesis of all aspects of Essence in a unified presence of consciousness; it manifests, in its own presence, whatever aspect or aspects of Essence are needed at any moment for the regulation of both inner states and object relations. When there is emotional hurt, compassion manifests; when there is a feeling of weakness, strength manifests; and so on. Whatever the situation requires in terms of capacity is spontaneously and instantly manifested by Being. When the situation requires understanding, the aspect of objective understanding dominates the consciousness. When the situation requires firmness, will dominates the consciousness.

This capacity for regulation depends on the degree of integration that one has attained in terms of essential realization. When it is present it is seen to be a capacity beyond the wildest wishes of ego; the regulation is spontaneous, exact, specific, coordinated and to the point. This is somewhat similar to the capacity for regulation of the well-integrated ego, but on the Being level.

The regulation of ego is largely determined by internalized object relations, so is influenced by defense and falsehood, which makes the regulation somewhat inexact and inefficient. The regulation of Being, on the other hand, is determined only by completely metabolized true experience and by the present situation, and thus cannot be distorted by defense or falsehood.

5. *Intention:* Ego can intend, and can act according to intention. However, because of the presence of unmetabolized experience, ego's intention is separate from natural forces. The intention of ego is a sign of its separateness from the realm of Being. Realizing the will aspect of Essence makes this rather subtle point clear; one sees that when ego intends and acts real will is usually blocked.

For the Personal Essence, on the other hand, intention has a different meaning. It is related to the integration of essential will. When this happens one realizes that one's actions must be in harmony with all natural forces, even on the level of Being; otherwise there is a splitting from Being, and an incorrect action will result. So instead of intention one experiences a spontaneous flow of intelligent and purposeful action, realizing that Being flows through one, as one, and it is the flow that determines one's life, action, interests, creativity and so on. Students who have only partially integrated the Personal Essence become aware of this reality.

So there is nothing in Being that is similar to the function of intention of ego. One is so integrated into reality that it is reality that is the source of one's actions. As the Personal Essence, one becomes the spearhead of reality. Reality acts through one by one being the individual manifestation of it. In religious language this is called surrender to God's will, or flowing with the Tao.

The popular understanding of what it is to be spiritually realized conceives such realization as divorced from personal functioning. A common image is of the holy man not interested in the world and its ways, but also inefficient and unskillful in these ways. These days another idea of the spiritually realized person is the guru surrounded by his disciples and sheltered from the world and its concerns.

174   But this is not the life of the Personal Essence. It might be the manifestation of some universal aspects, but then it is not the full realization of the human potential. The presence of the Personal Essence is equivalent to the presence of efficient, intelligent, integrated and mature functioning that is not split off from Being, but manifests and embodies it.

The
REALIZATION
of the
PEARL
BEYOND PRICE

BOOK TWO

Table of Contents

PART I

INNER EVOLUTION

O ur discussion of psychic metabolism might lead one to assume that the process of inner realization consists of a development, rather than a discovery, and that the development is determined by the vagaries of one's experiences, rather than by an immutable reality.

This assumption has some truth to it; certainly, experience is a determining factor, for it is the nutrient specifically needed for essential realization, especially for the realization of the Personal Essence. Nevertheless, the Personal Essence is an essential aspect, meaning it is a Platonic form. This means that although it appears as if it is a development from something else, its realization is actually a matter of discovery. Many of the case reports we have presented illustrate this fact.

The realization of the Personal Essence is the aspect of inner realization which can be particularly clearly seen as both development and discovery. For other aspects of Being, like love or will, the experience is more definitely a discovery. And for the nonpersonal aspects, such as Cosmic Consciousness, undifferentiated Being and the Absolute, it is certainly a discovery. However, seeing inner realization as

180   either development or discovery is not a matter of objective truth; it depends on one's frame of reference. It is also a question of how one comes upon this realization, and what methods or disciplines have led to it.

We can see the situation more clearly by looking at the experience of the Personal Essence. The development of ego identifications involves processes which are equivalent to the process of metabolism of experience. When this development reaches a certain stage it becomes possible for the metabolism to be completed, and hence, for the Personal Essence to appear. This manifestation appears to be the final stage of a developmental process.

However, the whole process can be seen from a different perspective. One can take the point of view that the Personal Essence is not the final stage of a development, but that it is a Platonic form that is always present in its usually experienced form, remaining part of one's potential until certain conditions are satisfied and it can emerge into consciousness. These conditions are satisfied when the metabolic process reaches the stage of absorption. At this time it becomes possible for the consciousness to become aware of the Personal Essence. From this point of view the process is clearly a matter of discovery.

This resembles the process of uncovering unconscious material in psychodynamic psychotherapy. The finally emerging emotional state (for instance anger that has been repressed) is not a development, but can be experienced when certain conditions are satisfied. From this point of view, the Personal Essence, and all other aspects of Being, are already present in final form, but repressed in the unconscious. This point of view is developed in our book *Essence*.

So it is possible to conceive of the process of inner realization as either a development or a discovery. Some spiritual teachings say that it is a predetermined process, that Being is already there, in our depths, and it is always influencing us, in one way or another, as if it is beckoning to us to pay attention to it. The fact that it is the very depths of us makes us see its influence on us as messages from it, and if we follow such messages we will come upon its reality. Although this description sounds rather mystical, it is exactly how psychologists view the nature and influence of unconscious material.

The Personal Essence itself can be usefully seen from this perspective: it is the prototype of an integrated and integrating reality, which is present in the depths of our being. It influences us through this quality of integration, affecting the mind by exerting an integrating influence on its content. This content becomes increasingly integrated as it is affected by the Personal Essence, or as it gets closer to it. In other words, as the integration becomes more complete it approximates the state of integration of the Personal Essence, and hence the consciousness becomes more able to reach the latter. When the process of integration reaches a certain stage it arrives at the Personal Essence itself, at which point one becomes conscious of its presence.

One can see the whole process of ego development as determined and guided by the Personal Essence, or even as the unfolding of an already existing topography or design. We cannot, however, say the same thing about ego. Ego does not exist in its final form in the potential of human beings. It exists, at birth, only in its functions, which we have already discussed as reflecting more the Personal Essence itself. Seeing realization from different, but equally valid points of view, is a reflection of the truth of Being: it is the original, eternally existing reality. Being is where we come from, and how we go back to it can be understood from many perspectives, because perspectives are conceptual constructs, while Being precedes concepts.

Chapter Sixteen

Enlightenment

One development in the process of inner realization is what is sometimes called "enlightenment." The concept of enlightenment is used, overused and abused. Many traditions and many teachings say that the goal of human evolution is enlightenment. Many people claim they are seeking enlightenment, and some others claim to have attained it. From all this one might get the impression that enlightenment is a well-defined concept, that those who use the term are certain of what it means, and that all people who use it mean the same thing.

Actually, there is no universal or agreed upon definition, or even understanding, of the concept of enlightenment. Different traditions use the word differently. Different teachers refer to different realities when they use it. And most people have not the vaguest idea what they are talking about when referring to enlightenment.

Sometimes enlightenment means the attainment of a certain state of Being. Sometimes it refers to a certain insight, perception or understanding. Sometimes it refers to a certain stage of inner development, usually the final stage, which becomes problematic since different traditions take different conditions to be the final stage. Sometimes it signifies the transcendence of ego, other times the death of ego, still other times the transformation of ego.

Even when enlightenment is defined in terms of ego or its absence, we still need to find out what ego is exactly, which brings us back to where we started. In fact, we can find a supposedly "enlightened"

master who defines his "enlightenment" as the death of his ego in
some experience, while another master can observe the operation of
ego in the state of the first master. This is the subject of many famous
Zen stories. Ego states can become so subtle that one can embody the
state of Cosmic Consciousness, for example, and still have some unseen identification with ego. Can we say this individual is enlightened?
And how can we understand an individual who does not embody the
state of Cosmic Consciousness, but can experience states not available
to the first individual, such as that of the Absolute?

However we define enlightenment, can we claim it is the final development? Buddhism, which uses the concept of enlightenment, does
not consider it the final development. In Buddhism enlightenment is
usually seen as the realization of Dharmakaya, Being-as-such, nonconceptual and transcendent. However, spiritual realization is then
considered to proceed to further stages, that of Sambhogakaya, and
then Nirmanakaya. So enlightenment is not the end of development,
even though it can be the highest realization. And if the realization of
Dharmakaya is equated with the complete surrender of ego, then why
is there need for further inner work to go to the other stages? Spiritual
work always involves seeing through ignorance, and it would seem
that if there is ignorance about who one is remaining, then there must
be some ego identifications left.

Some teachings and some teachers consider enlightenment to be a
definitive experience or insight. But even the Buddha went through a
long process of transformation, which he called a gradual process,
before he had the various insights under the Bodhi tree.

So it appears that the term "enlightenment" has no universal meaning. The concept can be useful only in a teaching that defines it very
specifically. But we cannot use the concept assuming it means the
same thing in all teachings or traditions.

The term "enlightenment" is primarily of Indian origin. Buddhism,
Taoism and various Hindu teachings employ the concept to signify
some sort of ultimate realization or liberation. However, the Buddha is
known to have established his teaching because he was not satisfied
with the Hindu teachings of his time. Buddhism, Hinduism and
Taoism all use the concept of enlightenment, but there are basic differences among their traditions, and thus differences in their concepts
of enlightenment.

184   In the prophetic traditions, which dominate as we move west from the Far East, the concept of enlightenment is less central, if indeed it is referred to at all. The concept of spiritual development is emphasized without reference to a definitive experience, insight or state. The Hebraic tradition, as reflected in the teachings of the Kabbalah, employs the concept of progressive enlightenment or development. The Sufi tradition employs many distinctions describing the various processes and realizations. It speaks of evolution, development, refinement, purification and enlightenment. All these are taken to be progressive processes of realization, which can include various experiences and insights.

The perspective we follow in this book is that the human being is born with many and various potentials. The more he actualizes these potentials the more he develops and matures. This process of maturation is the realization of his potentials. Most important of these potentials is Being, with all its aspects and dimensions. Each aspect, even those of the Nonconceptual Reality and the Absolute Truth, is integrated through successive steps: the discovery of the aspect of Being, the permanent realization of this aspect, and the actualization of the aspect, meaning the complete integration of it in one's human life. Any of these steps can be termed enlightenment. However, each one of them involves the working through of some segment of ego, i.e., complete metabolism of it. This working through can appear as a process or as a sudden realization.

Furthermore, the human potential cannot be encompassed by the imagination, for it is ultimately beyond conceptualization. Hence it is not possible to imagine something like the realization and actualization of all human potentials.

The Process of Inner Transformation

Because there are many and various potentials in the human being, there are naturally wide variations in the perception of how the process of maturation proceeds. Different teachings emphasize different parts of the human potential. There are also differences in the value attached to the various potentials, and in the ways these potentials are conceptualized. Two major views of how the process proceeds stand out:

(a) *The progressive or sudden abandonment of ego identifications to* *the point of realizing the nonpersonal aspects of Being.* The work or practice is centered around ego and not Being. The attitudes emphasized are those of impersonality, detachment and objectivity. There follows a process of realizing the personal aspects, seen sometimes as the process of bringing Being into the world.

The most representative tradition of this perspective is Buddhism. In legends and fairy tales, this perspective is reflected by the seeking stories where the hero must go to an invisible land to find the object of his seeking, and bring it back to his original homeland, with peace and prosperity.

(b) *The gradual and progressive realization of the differentiated aspects of Being, the essential aspects, by the working through of segments of ego identifications.* The emphasis is on developing the Personal Essence. The work or practice is centered more around Essence, and is less focused on ego. The attitudes emphasized are those of loving the truth and serving God. This process is seen to continue till the entry into the nonpersonal realms.

The most representative tradition of this perspective is the Sufi one. In legends and fairy tales, this perspective is reflected by the theme of seeking and finding, where the hero comes from a sublime homeland and goes into a world of illusion and lies, where he finds the object of his seeking, and then goes back to his origin, more mature and developed.

A perspective, of course, determines methodology, philosophy, style of life and ideal of evolution. The religions based on the first perspective tend to be nontheistic, while those based on the second tend to be monotheistic.

There are, of course, many other perspectives. Some of these perspectives are more psychological. Jung's analytic psychology is an example. Ego psychology is a completely psychological perspective.

There are perspectives that are Being oriented, but emphasize or acknowledge only one step of the two in the above two perspectives. The Vedanta of India, for instance, acknowledges only the first step of perspective (a), the realization of the nonpersonal aspects only. The Gurdjieff system, on the other hand, emphasizes the first step of perspective (b), the realization is pursued mainly on the personal dimension.

Chapter Seventeen

The
Diamond Approach

The understanding of human development we have been evolv-
ing in this book, related to the realization of the Personal
Essence, is the core of a whole perspective which we refer to
as the Diamond Approach. We use the term "diamond" for many
reasons. The approach has some of the characteristics of a clear and
cut diamond. It has an exactness and precision that becomes extremely sharp at critical points of understanding. There is a clarity and
objectivity to it that can cut through emotional barriers and biases. It
is multi-faceted; it is an integration of many perspectives that make up
a larger overall perspective without losing the specificity of the various smaller ones. Each perspective is a reflection or an expression of
a certain aspect of Essence, and is complete on its own. The realization and understanding of any aspect allows one to see reality from a
certain angle. We can look at everything, for instance, from the perspective expressing the aspect of Love. The perspective is always the
expression of an experiential reality, and not an intellectual system.

The Diamond Approach is an integration and synthesis of all these
perspectives in a comprehensive view of man. Since the Personal
Essence is a central aspect, our discussion will benefit from some
general understanding of the overall Diamond Approach. A systematic
development of another central aspect is presented in our book *The
Void—A Psychodynamic Investigation of the Relationship between
Mind and Space*. In that book we discuss human development from
the perspective of the aspect of Space, which is the spacious and

empty nature of mind. An overall, general presentation of the Diamond Approach can be found in our book *Essence—The Diamond Approach to Inner Realization*.

Just as the sense of a separate individuality is the main outcome of the separation-individuation process, integrating into itself other parts of the ego, so the Personal Essence is the main development in essential realization, which integrates the other aspects of Essence into itself as it develops, as well as integrating the functional capacities of the various aspects. The Personal Essence is a central aspect because it is the real person, the essential person, which we have seen is the product of the complete metabolism of identification systems. Identifications, however, involve not only ego. There are superego identifications, for instance, that make up that structure of the mind. The metabolism of all identification systems leads not only to the realization of the Personal Essence, but also to the realization of all aspects of Essence. Each segment of identifications is connected to a certain essential aspect.

The identifications responsible for the sense of individuality are the ones specifically connected to the Personal Essence. Other identifications are associated with other aspects. For instance, the identifications responsible for the sense of self or identity lead to the aspect of the true self, which is not the same as the Personal Essence. It is a sense of identity and not of individuality.

A more fundamental reason for our use of the term "diamond" is related to the aspect of Essence that we have mentioned which functions as inner guidance. This aspect is that of objective understanding, the understanding necessary for the realization and development of the Personal Essence. This aspect affects the consciousness in a very specific and unmistakable manner. One feels clear and objective. One's consciousness becomes sharp, precise and luminous. There is an immediate sense of a brilliant and precise intelligence. One's consciousness becomes crystal clear, exquisitely objective but alive. This objective consciousness, which has the function of understanding, we refer to sometimes as the Diamond Consciousness, because its experiential qualities resemble those of a clear and sharply-cut diamond.

This Diamond Consciousness is a certain integration of all essential aspects, which can exist in a dimension that is more refined and more

188   objective than the usual, most recognizable one. This dimension is that of the existence of all aspects of Essence as aspects of understanding. All aspects of Essence function in this dimension in the service of understanding. For instance, the aspect of compassion does not exist in this dimension only as the presence of the state of compassion, but also as the precise understanding of compassion and its relation to objective understanding. Compassion is experienced as a warmth and an empathic desire to help. At the beginning it is experienced as a desire or movement to relieve an individual of his suffering. When compassion reaches the dimension of objective understanding, it will emerge with the precise understanding that it is the quality that allows the individual to experience the pain without rejection, and hence will make it possible to perceive the truth in the situation. So Compassion becomes an aspect in the service of truth, and not simply a way to eliminate suffering, in the narrow sense of the word. In some sense, the Diamond Consciousness is the integration of the mental faculties—intelligence, discrimination, synthesis, understanding and so on—into Being, just as the Personal Essence is the integration of another level of qualities.

This aspect of Essence is the source of true insight, intuition, knowledge and understanding. It functions through a capacity of simultaneous analysis and synthesis. Its capacity for analysis is stupendous; it can move in closer and closer, its perception becoming sharper and sharper, and its understanding more and more precise, as one contemplates any subject. It synthesizes all that is available to the consciousness of the individual, making its analysis ever more precise. And it can reverse the whole process, using the insights and perceptions arising from the analysis for greater synthesis. Unlike all other aspects of Being, it has the capacity to use knowledge from memory and synthesize it with immediate knowledge in the moment, thus utilizing both mind and Being. This capacity is functioning to some extent in the normal experience of insight, but can operate as Diamond Consciousness only when it is recognized and integrated.

The Diamond Consciousness is the prototype, on the level of Being, of the faculty of understanding. The ordinary capacity for understanding is only a reflection of this capacity. When an individual manifests an unusual or brilliant capacity for analysis and synthesis in his or her understanding, it is usually an indication of some degree of realization 189 of the Diamond Consciousness. We can see the functioning of this capacity in the work of the great original synthesizers of mankind, such as Gautama Buddha or Sigmund Freud.

The Diamond Approach is the result of the perception and understanding, by the Diamond Consciousness, of the realization and development of the human potential. This aspect is experienced in the work of inner realization as a guidance, specifically a guidance for the realization and development of the Personal Essence. It is the inner guide, on the Being level, for the essential person. The Jungian archetype of the wise old man, the guide for the journey of individuation, is an image that symbolizes some of the functions of the Diamond Consciousness. This aspect of Essence, however, is not an image and not merely an archetype; it is an actual state of Being.

The methodology of the Diamond Approach is based largely on the presence and functioning of the Diamond Consciousness. The qualities of the Diamond Consciousness can be seen in the attitudes of individuals who have some integration of it, such as Buddha and Freud as we have noted, or additionally, the Sufi Sheikh Ibn Arabi and the Greek philosopher Socrates. All these individuals, on different levels and to varying degrees, embodied a thirst for understanding reality, especially the reality of man. They all showed a great love for truth and objectivity. Buddha left the comfort and ease of a royal life to lead a life of wandering and search. His overriding concern was to understand completely the precise truth of human existence and reality. He went from one teacher to another, learning all they could teach him. He learned much, but was not satisfied. His knowledge was not complete, his understanding was not completely objective. So he turned completely to himself, in a supreme expression of individuation and autonomy. He used his own objective consciousness to finally gain the understanding he was seeking. He expressed his teaching in precise and specific terms which embody both analysis and synthesis. Not only was he realized, but he had a specific, detailed and comprehensive understanding of the process of realization, which became the momentous teachings of Buddhism. Only rarely do realized persons understand their process of realization. This understanding requires the integration of the capacities of the Diamond Consciousness, which does not always occur in the process of realization.

190   In the Far East Buddha is referred to as the Omniscient One, indicating the full realization of the Diamond Consciousness. Omniscience here does not mean that one knows everything; it rather signifies the more useful ability to know and understand what is objectively needed to be known and understood. This is exactly the function of the Diamond Consciousness, which is why its guidance is objective, precise and efficient.

Buddha applied his understanding to spiritual realization; Freud, on the other hand, applied it to understanding the psychological functioning of the mind. Freud's books are a pleasure to read because of the aesthetic beauty of his capacity for precise analysis and comprehensive synthesis. His love for, and joy in, understanding the truth can also be felt in his life. He broke with both the medical orthodoxy and the psychology of his time, and risked alienation and rejection in the service of the truth. He was not interested only in therapy; he wanted to understand the mind. In the Diamond Consciousness, love of truth for its own sake, and compassion for others' suffering are completely integrated, and actually experienced as the same thing.

Freud revolutionized the understanding of the mind and its functioning; his concepts are inseparable from our modern way of understanding human phenomena. He exposed himself to ridicule, contempt and rejection by his community by asserting that neurosis has a sexual etiology, and especially by introducing the concept of childhood sexuality. In his case, as in Buddha's case, we perceive the expression of autonomous functioning, coupled with an exquisite capacity for understanding. This is the reflection of the coupling of the Personal Essence and the Diamond Consciousness.

To see this coupling, to understand how the Diamond Consciousness is a guidance, and to understand the methodology of the Diamond Approach, we return to the process of psychic metabolism. We have seen that metabolism is complete and can lead to the Personal Essence only when it reaches the stage of absorption. We also noted that an identification system can become ready for absorption only when it is completely purged of falsehood. For an identification system which is an aspect or expression of one's personality to be completely purged or purified, the following is required:

• To see psychological defenses, to understand them and to recognize that they are false and unnecessary.

- To separate the true, in this segment of the ego, from the false. This means to exactly see, and understand, what actually happened in the past, and to separate this from those things which one still feels and believes but which did not really occur.

For this one must experience the segment of the personality, and look at the memories of the original object relations, without defenses and with complete objectivity. One cannot look at oneself with any prejudice, opinion, attitude, expectation or assumptions without losing objectivity. One must approach the experience wanting nothing and expecting nothing. The only motivation that can work is the innate and spontaneous love of truth for its own sake. If one wants truth because it feels good or is going to lead to a good result, or if one wants the truth because it will relieve one's suffering, then one is already prejudiced and cannot be objective. So for there to be absorption, absolute objectivity is required.

What we are seeing here is that the love and appreciation of truth for its own sake is an absolute requirement for objectivity, which in turn is required for complete metabolism. If one is not interested in the truth, or is interested in it for other purposes, which amounts to the same thing, then one might get what one wants, but not the truth. Even if one wants complete metabolism, development, or enlightenment, then one is looking for a certain result or end, not for truth.

Thus, in the Diamond Approach, the age-old spiritual dictum that desire leads away from truth and towards suffering, becomes a specific understanding of the requirement for objectivity, and hence for metabolism and transformation. This objectivity is not easy to attain, or even to understand. Love of truth for its own sake is actually the expression of essential heart. When one perceives the heart on the Being level, one can recognize that love is the expression of truth.

Seeing that a necessary requirement for objectivity, which is usually considered a mental quality, is pure love of truth, which is a heart quality, we observe the organic interrelation between the various aspects of Essence. It is interesting to remember that the beginning of ego has a defensive character, and defense is nothing but hiding a certain truth of experience. So the requirement for inner realization is the converse of the most basic characteristic of the ego; defense and resistance are the enemies of truth, and love is its ally.

192   The love for truth, which reverses the attitude of defense, leads
directly to the truth of experience, the truth that was defended
against. And, as we already know, it is this truth that is the nutrient for
the development of the Personal Essence. This indicates that when the
heart loves truth it is approaching the specific nutrition needed for the
essential person. So we can say, although it is only a conceptualization, that the heart loves the Personal Essence and its development.
This again shows the organic interrelation between the aspects of
Essence. These perceptions can go on forever, the understanding becoming more precise and more specific, reflecting the functioning of
the Diamond Consciousness.

We have shown how objectivity is needed for psychic metabolism,
and we have explored the love of truth, for its own sake, as a necessary requirement for such objectivity. Objectivity is the function of the
diamond guidance, and hence, love of truth is a necessary requirement for the presence and operation of this indispensable guidance.

Another quality, which usually accompanies the love of truth, that of
curiosity, is required for purification of the ego. One can have the
capacity to be objective, but if one is not curious then one will not
have the opportunity to apply it. One must pay attention and be involved in the experience in order to see the truth, and this requires
curiosity. Curiosity does not necessarily mean searching for truth. The
seeking for truth, realization or enlightenment is a pale reflection of the
true quality needed for them. Searching implies desire, it implies an
end in mind, it implies preconceptions and assumptions, and hence it
is counter to the attitude of love of truth, and counter to objectivity.

On the other hand, curiosity involves love for truth, and joy in the
truth. True curiosity is a rare quality. It is a quality of Being, and ego
usually kills curiosity to avoid exposure of ego's falsehood. We can often see true curiosity in the play of children. Often when a child finds
a new object, he will be so curious and so involved in investigating it,
that he becomes completely absorbed in the activity, pulling the object apart or putting it back together, or whatever. He is not seeking a
result, or trying to gain something. In fact, after a while, when his
curiosity is satisfied, he will probably throw the object away, as if it is
of no more interest to him. But during the investigation, which has
the character of play, he is totally absorbed, completely enraptured,
fully enjoying and loving the investigation.

This is just the attitude necessary for inner transformation. Although we 193 call it work, it is more like play. When there is love for truth and curiosity about it, then there is a serious kind of play, profound but light. Curiosity can be seen as the expression of the essential aspect of Joy. And Joy, like love, is a heart quality, which again is an expression of truth.

Curiosity, love of truth for its own sake, opens the Joy aspect. This can manifest as curiosity about truth, curiosity motivated by love, and not by gain. When there is love of truth and true curiosity about it, it becomes possible to see the objective truth in the particular experience. Seeing the objective truth is the function of the Diamond Guidance. Thus, the sincere desire for truth for its own sake—love and curiosity about truth—is what precipitates the presence and functioning of the Diamond Guidance. This understanding of the way to truth is told beautifully by the following Sufi story, in which the Diamond Guidance is called "Khidr," the green guide:

The Land of Truth

A certain man believed that the ordinary waking life, as people know it, could not possibly be complete.

He sought the real Teacher of the Age. He read many books and joined many circles, and he heard the words and witnessed the deeds of one master after another. He carried out the commands and spiritual exercises which seemed to him to be most attractive.

He became elated with some of his experiences. At other times he was confused; and he had no idea at all of what his stage was, or where and when his search might end.

This man was reviewing his behaviour one day when he suddenly found himself near the house of a certain sage of high repute. In the garden of that house he encountered Khidr, the secret guide who shows the way to Truth.

Khidr took him to a place where he saw people in great distress and woe, and he asked who they were. "We are those who did not follow real teachings, who were not true to our undertakings, who revered self-appointed teachers," they said.

Then the man was taken by Khidr to a place where everyone was attractive and full of joy. He asked who they were. "We are those who did not follow the real Signs of the Way," they said.

"But if you have ignored the Signs, how can you be happy?" asked the traveler.

"Because we chose happiness instead of Truth," said the people, "just as those who chose the self-appointed chose also misery."

"But is happiness not the ideal of man?" asked the man.

"The goal of man is Truth. Truth is more than happiness. The man who has Truth can have whatever mood he wishes, or none," they told him. "We have pretended that Truth is happiness, and happiness Truth, and people have believed us, therefore you, too, have until now imagined that happiness must be the same as Truth. But happiness makes you its prisoner, as does woe."

Then the man found himself back in the garden, with Khidr beside him.

"I will grant you one desire," said Khidr.

"I wish to know why I have failed in my search and how I can succeed in it," said the man.

"You have all but wasted your life," said Khidr, "because you have been a liar. Your lie has been in seeking personal gratification when you could have been seeking Truth."

"And yet I came to the point where I found you," said the man, "and that is something which happens to hardly anyone at all."

"And you met me," said Khidr, "because you had sufficient sincerity to desire Truth for its own sake, just for an instant. It was that sincerity, in that single instant, which made me answer your call."

Now the man felt an overwhelming desire to find Truth, even if he lost himself.

Khidr, however, was starting to walk away, and the man began to run after him.

"You may not follow me," said Khidr, "because I am returning to the ordinary world, the world of lies, for that is where I have to be, if I am to do my work."

And when the man looked around him again, he realized that he was no longer in the garden of the sage, but standing in the Land of Truth. [Idries Shah, *Thinkers of the East*, pp. 66–67]

There are other requirements besides curiosity for the full operation of the Diamond Guidance, but we have discussed the central ones. Discussing the rest of the requirements would entail going into the understanding of all other aspects of Essence in their relation to the dimension of objective consciousness, which is beyond the scope of this book.

As we have described, the complete purification of ego needed for absorption requires the separation of the false from the true: the false

to be eliminated, and the truth to be absorbed. It is not possible to 195
separate the truth from the false if there is the slightest imprecision.
And for there to be precision, specific perceptions and insights are required. Thus the exactness, precision and specificity of the Diamond
Guidance are required for the process of psychic metabolism, and
thus for the realization of the Personal Essence.

For a teacher to be able to guide a student towards inner realization,
especially the realization of the Personal Essence, he must have at least
some realization of the Diamond Guidance. The more this aspect is
realized and integrated the more the teacher can be objective, exact
and precise in his guidance, and hence more effective. The realization
of the Diamond Guidance is a possibility only for one who has
realized, or is in the process of realizing, the Personal Essence; because
the Personal Essence brings a sense of specificity and particularity.

The Diamond Approach is based on, and is the expression of, a
certain integration of the Diamond Guidance. It is not based on, or
taken from, any tradition, psychological or spiritual, although it draws
on modern depth psychology. It is the expression of the author's particular realization of the Diamond Guidance. There is no claim here
that the Diamond Guidance can be expressed only in this particular
manner, nor is this method the only possible path to the Personal
Essence. It is a precise and specific body of knowledge about inner
realization, and a methodology for actualizing it. The approach is a
highly objective method for the metabolism of experience, including
the metabolism of segments of the personality. The beginning of the
process is focused on metabolizing personality, since the metabolism
occurs on whatever is in present experience, and personality is what
the student mostly experiences at the beginning. This leads to the
emergence of the various aspects of Essence, but primarily to the
realization of the Personal Essence.

The presence of the Personal Essence makes it possible to have
direct contact with present-centered experience, to be present, open
and vulnerable to experience. This capacity, aided by the operation of
the objective understanding of the Diamond Guidance, makes it possible to absorb present experience readily. One's life becomes the
metabolism of the interaction of the essential aspects with the environment. This continuing and ever-expanding integration is the process of development of the Personal Essence. This ever-deepening

196   and expanding individuation and maturity leads ultimately to the nonpersonal realms of Being, like those of Cosmic Consciousness, Nonconceptual Reality and Absolute Truth; this is the natural and spontaneous outcome of the development of the Personal Essence. It is part of the human potential, and if the process of maturation is proceeding in its correct path, then it is bound to occur.

The presence of the Personal Essence is a sense of Being, of experiencing "I am." There is presence without resistance. So it is bound to go deeper into more expanded realms of Being. This understanding that the experience of "I am" can lead directly to the nonpersonal realms is not an uncommon one among teachers of Being. One such teacher, the late Sri Nisargadatta Maharaj, an embodiment of the Supreme and Absolute aspects, considers the experience of "I am" the easiest and most direct way to the experience of the supreme reality. He advises his students to just stay with this sense of themselves. He says:

> All I can say truly is: "I am," all else is inference. But the inference has become a habit. Destroy all habits of thinking and seeing. The sense "I am" is the manifestation of a deeper cause, which you may call self, God, Reality or by any other name. The "I am" is in the world; but it is the key which can open the door out of the world. [Sri Nisargadatta Maharaj, *I Am That*, p. 199]

It is interesting to note that Nisargadatta Maharaj advises his students to merely stay with the sense of "I am," without telling them what this implies. He talks about the "I am" experience as if it is the normal everyday perception of everybody. This is significant because it gives a clue about how he himself attained his realization. His history shows that he attained it by staying with the sense of "I am." He said it took him about three years, which is a surprisingly short time for such an accomplishment. But our surprise diminishes when we see the implication of his story. He talks to everyone as if the sense of "I am" is an easy everyday perception, because that was probably the way it was for him, before his realization of the Supreme and Absolute aspects. He was able, in a natural way, to be, simply. Allowing oneself to be can easily lead to the Supreme aspect.

This indicates the possibility that Nisargadatta Maharaj had the good fortune of a great deal of maturation in his early life. His Personal Essence must have developed in a natural and smooth way, possibly due to favorable life experience. The Personal Essence must have

been so much a part of his experience that he took it for granted that 197
it is normal for everybody. This is not uncommon; when one grows
from childhood with some essential presence intact, he might not observe it in himself or other people because it was never lost. Some
traditions refer to such people as "natural saints."

It is likely that some individuals who come to a radical spiritual
realization in early adulthood were already realized on the personal
level. Any aspect of Essence becomes less obvious and is taken for
granted the longer one experiences it. It is also understandable that
such individuals will experience their realization as letting go of being
a person, because for them it is a movement from the Personal
Essence to the nonpersonal aspects. The realization of the essential
person will develop naturally into the experience of the nonpersonal
realm, but not if one holds on to personal realization. We will discuss
this further when we come to exploring the relation between the Personal Essence and the nonpersonal aspects of Being.

The discussion of the Diamond Approach so far might lead one to
assume that it is an example of the perspective on inner realization
which says that realization is a gradual process, and emphasizes the
development of the Personal Essence. The approach is not intentionally
aimed in that direction, but since it is based on the metabolism of personal experience, and personal experience is usually not very advanced, the progression of experiences and insights does tend to take
the more gradual route. Nevertheless, in rare cases, and for varying
reasons, the more sudden jump to the impersonal realms does occur.

The understanding of the psychic metabolism of experience seems
to imply that human realization goes from the development of ego, to
the realization of the essential aspects with the Personal Essence as
the central aspect, to the enlightenment on the nonpersonal levels of
Being; however, the realization of the nonpersonal aspects does not
involve abandonment of the personal and other aspects of Essence. In
fact, the Personal Essence goes through another stage of development
as its relation to the nonpersonal aspects is understood and
metabolized. It becomes the personal actualization of the nonpersonal
aspects of Being. We will discuss these nonpersonal realms in detail in
Part III of Book Three. For now we will examine further the development of the Personal Essence.

PART II

PERSONAL ESSENCE AND THE PROCESS OF SEPARATION-INDIVIDUATION

H aving presented a brief overall view of the Diamond Approach, we will in this part go into a detailed description of how we work with the concepts of object relations in this method, as well as the cultivation of the various essential aspects.

We have seen that there is a close connection between the separation-individuation process and the realization and development of the Personal Essence; in this part we will explore that connection in depth. Our case presentations show that all students associate with the Personal Essence the sense of autonomy, independence, individuation and individuality. Although they are going through a development in the realm of Being, most students who experience the Personal Essence react to it in the way they would react to an expansion of their sense of

200   ego individuality. In fact, during most of the process of the realization of the Personal Essence, the personality reacts as if the Personal Essence is the separate individuality of ego. So the issues that arise, and must be resolved, are the usual psychodynamic and structural conflicts and difficulties characterizing the various stages of ego development. Those conflicts related to the symbiotic stage and the various sub-phases of the separation-individuation process are dominant here.

However, since the Personal Essence is an aspect of Being, the issues have a different character and meaning than the purely emotional ones. The stages of ego development function in another dimension in addition to that of developmental psychology, or, more accurately, there are parallel stages in this deeper dimension, exposing issues of a different kind. These are issues and difficulties not of a structural or psychodynamic nature, but of an existential, phenomenological and epistemological nature. We will see that all these dimensions—structural, psychodynamic, existential, phenomenological and epistemological—are all involved in the issues, conflicts and perceptions relating to the Personal Essence.

Most psychotherapeutic systems attempt to isolate the emotional dimension from that of Being. We will see, however, that all the dimensions of human experience are interrelated, and cannot be separated without the loss of objectivity. Of course, those who are not aware of the dimension of Being will be satisfied with the approximations they make in understanding the situation, believing they are looking at the whole picture, while they are in fact perceiving only the surface. Even for purposes of therapy, however, looking at the deeper dimension of experience is useful.

The issues, conflicts and perceptions which are related to the Personal Essence that are characteristic of the phases of symbiosis and separation-individuation mainly involve separation and separation anxiety, fear of annihilation and abandonment, the question of aloneness, rapprochement conflicts, issues of cohesion and integration, conflicts around self and self-esteem, questions of ego strength and ego inadequacy, and the like. We will examine them now in some depth.

Chapter Eighteen

Separation

T he Personal Essence often manifests when one is dealing with the question of separation, that is when one arrives at a state in which he feels separate from others, or when he is asserting his separateness or desire for it.

Lara is a professional woman in her mid-thirties, married and a mother for some time. She has been dealing with a deep conflict in her mind, which sometimes manifests as a conflict between family and profession, and sometimes between who she is and what she has to be. She has been working with the author for a number of years, both privately and in a group. She has experienced the Personal Essence frequently and dealt with some of her issues about it. She still finds it difficult to just be herself, or express who she is. We find her grappling with this conflict in a private session, in which both analytic and energetic methods are used. She is feeling angry, which she sees is a way for her to assert her separateness. It is a rebellious anger; she is saying "no" to the other. Exploring the anger further, she finds out that it is difficult for her just to feel separate, without having to be angry. The sense of separation by itself leaves her feeling guilty and alone. She is also afraid that if she does not feel angry she will feel loving, and this makes her insecure in her sense of separateness. She believes that her love will make her be like others rather than herself. This brings a desire to protect her chest and heart. She protects herself by controlling herself and her feelings. She feels very frustrated, and starts getting angry. As she explores the frustration, it mounts and her

202   anger increases. Finally she explodes, furiously kicking the mattress she is lying on. She kicks, yells and screams, first in frustration and then in mounting rage, which she expresses loudly and strongly. Her words express self-assertion, wanting to be separate from her mother. Her voice becomes stronger and more booming as she tells her mother that she is tired of being confused, a part of her, or a reaction to her. She wants to be separate and to be herself. The more she asserts her separateness, the more her voice becomes full and strong, and the more the movements of her body become coordinated, integrated and powerful. Her body looks red and vibrant.

She reports that she feels heat throughout her body, and that the more she asserts her sense of separation the more she sees images of red hot fire. When she is through expressing her anger and separateness, I ask her what she experiences. She answers with a happy smile, and with an assertive voice, that she feels strong and her body is full of energy and heat. As she is leaving at the end of the session, she tells me in an astonished tone that she feels big, expanded, but also full and grounded. I can see her fullness and presence. She looks me in the eye as she speaks, making direct contact. With this presence and fullness she expresses some of her personal feelings and appreciation for my patience and caring. She tells me how she feels present, as herself, full of her self the way she always wanted. Her sense of autonomy and individuation is palpable in the interaction.

This is a typical example of an experience of separation leading naturally and directly to the individuated state of the Personal Essence. It is in accord with Mahler's formulation that the process of separation is distinct from that of individuation, but that it proceeds alongside it, and is indispensable for it. She writes:

> Separation and individuation are conceived of as two complementary developments: separation consists of the child's emergence from a symbiotic fusion with the mother (Mahler, 1952), and individuation consists of those achievements marking the child's assumption of his individual characteristics. [Margaret S. Mahler et al., *The Psychological Birth of the Human Infant*, p. 4]

Mahler conceives of the separation track as starting at the first subphase of the separation-individuation process, that of differentiation, and culminating in the establishment of the self-image:

It is at the end of the first year and in the early months of the second year that one can see with particular clarity that the intrapsychic process of separation-individuation has two intertwined, but not always commensurate or proportionately progressing, developmental tracks. One is the track of individuation, the evolution of intrapsychic autonomy, perception, memory, cognition, reality testing; the other is the intrapsychic developmental track of separation that runs along differentiation, distancing, boundary formation, and disengagement from mother. All of these structuralization processes will eventually culminate in internalized self-representations, as distinct from internal object representations. [*Ibid.*, p. 63]

In the case given above, Lara was confused about herself because she was dealing with a representation that involved both her mother and herself; in other words, she was dealing with a nondifferentiated self-object representation, in which self and object (mother) are still not seen as separate. These nondifferentiated representations are, according to object relations theory, the identifications acquired in the symbiotic stage, when the child still cannot conceive of itself as separate from mother. Psychological "hatching," according to Mahler, occurs in the differentiation subphase, which starts at the end of the symbiotic stage. Due to locomotion and the development of the perceptual and cognitive functions the child becomes able to see itself as separate from the mother and to behave accordingly. This indicates the beginning of differentiation of the nondifferentiated representations in the mind into a self-representation and an object-representation, which is needed for the later establishment of a self-image and a separate object-image. According to Kernberg:

The differentiation of self and object components determines, jointly with the general development of cognitive processes, the establishment of stable ego boundaries. . .
[Otto F. Kernberg, *Object Relations Theory and Clinical Psychoanalysis*, p. 64]

Lara had first to become aware of the nondifferentiation—the sense of not being able to be separate from her family, and especially her sense that feeling a certain kind of love would make her unable to be herself but cause her to be like someone else—before she could separate. It is significant that her process of separation went through several phases in the session. She began with confusion and conflicts,

204   moved to feelings of frustration, and then to furious anger, and then to assertive strength, to separation, and finally to the autonomy and fullness of the Personal Essence. These are the typical phases of this process, which we have observed with many individuals. It will be useful to explore each phase in some detail, so that we understand this process as fully as possible, noting that these phases can take some time and, typically, several sessions to unfold.

1. *Confusion and conflicts about separation and individuation.* The confusion is due to not being able to see herself as a separate person. This usually leads to vagueness about identity or self. It is difficult for the ego to have a sense of self when there are no clear and stable boundaries that separate it from the object. The boundaries in Lara's case are not clear because of a remaining identification with a nondifferentiated self-object representation. The conflicts are also due to her unconscious attachment to this identification, whose existence is incompatible with the full development of the Personal Essence. Also, as we saw in the above passages from Mahler and Kernberg, differentiation of representations is needed for both boundaries and self representations.

2. *Feelings of frustration and negativity.* The feeling of frustration is the specific affect that characterizes the negativity in the nondifferentiated representations resulting from negative experiences during the symbiotic stage. This frustration, according to Mahler, becomes one of the main motivations behind the desire for, and movement towards, separation. This frustration, resulting from negative experiences, plus the pleasure in autonomy, motivates the child to create more distance from its mother, in part to disengage from the frustration.

In Lara's case, this affect coloring the nondifferentiated representations seems to be also the result of the confusion about who she is and what she wants, i.e., it is also a result of the condition of nondifferentiation. We will later discuss this confusion and the related affect of frustration itself in more detail. The frustration, then, is associated with a negative nondifferentiated representation, which Lara tries to move away from with anger and separation.

3. *Besides the fact that it is a natural response to, or development from, frustration, anger seems to be one of the main ways that individuals attempt to separate.* Anger gives the individual both a sense of strength and the energy needed for the movement of separation. In

anger, one rejects the mother, or at least the negative interaction with her, and thus creates a distance from her. However, our careful and repeated observations reveal that anger on its own does not lead to real separation. The anger is part of the affect of frustration that characterizes the painful nondifferentiated state. So the continuation of anger means the continuation of this nondifferentiated state, which defeats the purpose of separation. This points to, and explains, the next phase of the process.

4. *Assertive strength is what actually makes it possible to separate.* What is needed is strength and energy that allow one to feel that he can exist on his own, without the mothering support of the object. Anger must give way to the assertion of one's strength and expansive energy, and is often the way to it. Although the process often starts with anger, in the cases where separation actually succeeds, it always ends with the sense of expansive and assertive strength. This strength indicates the dissolution of the affect of frustration, and always ushers in the sense of separation.

5. *The state of separation:* object relations theory indicates that this happens when there is finally a separate self-representation in the mind, distinct from an object representation. So it is seen as a mental achievement. In Lara's case, however, and in our observations of the state of separation with many individuals, we notice that besides the presence of a separate representation, there is also a state of Being, with clear characteristics. Lara felt strong, powerful, expanded, full, but also hot and fiery, in this state of separation. The fullness and strength are definitely not the same as those of the experience of the Personal Essence, but more energetic, more active, more assertive, and less rounded and still. There is no specific or clear feeling of integration, togetherness and structure, but also no issues or conflicts about such feelings. The fact that this state of separation does not always lead to the experience of the Personal Essence (though it usually does) indicates again that it is a different state.

6. *The Personal Essence.* This is definitely felt as a presence, which is not only full, but also peaceful and rounded, and gives the individual a sense of individuality, reality, structure and integration. At this stage the feeling of separateness is in the background, and is felt as a support for the individuation of the Personal Essence. The sense of heat and strength feels available but not necessarily asserted or directed.

206   Separation is needed for the realization of the Personal Essence, just
as it is needed for the separate individuality of ego. We will see, as we
go on, that the process of the realization of the Personal Essence is in
many respects parallel to the process of development of the ego sense
of individuality. Thus the momentous understanding of the separation-
individuation process, contributed by Mahler, can be extremely useful
for guiding the process of essential realization.

The Personal Essence is a sense of being a person, unique and distinct from other persons. This sense does not exist at the symbiotic
stage or before it, even at the Being level. The organism must develop
and mature to a certain degree before it can embody this presence. Part
of this process of development is separation, which clearly includes
separation on the ego level of identifications as described by Mahler.

So we can see Lara's process as the differentiation of the self-
representation from the object representation, which then allowed
absorption to take place. The nondifferentiated representation could
not be completely metabolized, until it was seen as it is, a result of
past interactions, and not a true representation of the present situation. Seeing this truth brings about differentiation and the state of
separation. Now the identification system can be absorbed, for its
truth has been recognized. It seems that this is exactly what happened in Lara's case, because she became aware of herself as the
Personal Essence and not as an image (self-representation).

The state of separation itself, as well as that of individuation, is a
state of Being, and not merely a mental process or representation.
What is this state of Being? According to Lara's experience, and many
others like it, it is a state of fullness that is characterized by the following properties:

- It is a presence, a beingness.
- It has a sense of strength and power. The strength is not felt as
  characterizing one's body or sense of self, but is the presence itself.
  This state of Essence is the presence of Strength. One does not exactly feel strong, but feels more like, "I exist, as the very substance
  of Strength," or "I am Strength."
- The sense of Strength has a feeling of energy in it. It is an energetic
  sense of power, a sense of compact excitation and aliveness. This
  gives it a feeling of being active, although it is actually a presence,
  and not an activity.

- The Strength, as a result, feels assertive or aggressive in a positive
  way. It feels like the energetic presence needed for dynamic, assertive and aggressive action.
- It has a sense of largeness and expansion. One feels energetically
  big, as if one's energy and presence is much larger than the dimensions of one's body.
- Capacity: when this aspect of Essence is present one feels able. If
  the characteristic state of the Personal Essence is "I am," then that
  of this aspect is "I can." One feels a sense of expanded capacity.
  One particularly feels the capacity to be oneself. This sense of
  capacity is the main factor which associates Strength with separation. This feeling of capacity to be allows the differentiation, and
  precipitates the "I am"-ness of the Personal Essence.
- The actual affect of this state usually has a feeling of heat. One
  feels hot all the way through, with a sense of fire and redness. This
  again indicates its energetic quality. The heat does not come from
  physical activity, as one might assume in the case of Lara above.
  The heat is similar to how one feels hot when angry, except it has
  a sense of positive and calm presence. This sense of heat, energy
  and activity is connected with the function of the sympathetic
  branch of the autonomous nervous system. To illustrate further the
  factor of heat, as well as other characteristics of the Strength aspect,
  we present another case report.

This is a report from Andrew, whom we mentioned in connection
with his dream about the peacock. He is a married man in his middle
years, a business man, a father and has been a member of the group
for over four years. A recurring personality conflict is the issue of separation from his mother. This subject arises in one group meeting, and
as he feels more separate from his mother's representation he begins to
feel strong and hot. He writes in a letter describing his experience:

> The burning I experienced was like an intense consum-
> ing fire. I saw the problems associated with my mother as
> a pile on the floor, and I burned them all up with the fire. I
> felt a very warm feeling in my solar plexus and in my
> back. I have been able to experience the heat many times
> before. I also remember that at first I thought I had some
> sort of fever, my whole body became hot.
> As I discussed with you on Friday, I felt I had a blackish
> kind of lump or ball in my solar plexus, as big as a basket

ball. I felt this blackness peeling or dissolving to reveal some kind of beautifully translucent presence in the belly. As I talked with you this presence grew very quickly and filled me up enough to give a sense of a full belly. When it went into my chest it strengthened my shoulders. I felt very pleased with myself, very happy, just as if something good had taken place.

I am feeling stronger, more accepting of myself and more aware of liking me. As I write this I feel happy and also as if I have a secret. Partly I want to share this feeling but at the same time I want to keep it for myself.

In this case we can see clearly the progression from the dominance of the Strength Essence to that of the Personal Essence. We notice the strengthening he feels in his body and structure. Object relations theory would call it ego strength, which is correct if we think of ego as the Personal Essence.

The Strength aspect of Essence typically emerges initially connected with issues other than separation. The issue of weakness often precipitates it; the absence of Strength is felt as an emptiness or deficiency with the affect of weakness. The weakness is felt on all levels: the physical, energetic and ego levels. One might feel so weak that one feels unable to even lift a finger. And at such times it is obvious that the weakness is not caused by physical factors, because the moment the issues are worked through and the Strength Essence emerges, one feels miraculously restored, invigorated and strong.

One of the main causes of the sense of weakness is resistance against the state of separation. For one reason or another the individual defends against the state of separation, and for this he must block the presence of the Strength aspect because it will make him feel separate. But blocking it will feel as loss or absence of Strength. This feeling or state of weakness, resulting from repressing the Strength Essence, makes it impossible for the individual to feel the individuated state of the Personal Essence. In fact, many individuals resist the Strength aspect because they feel unable or unwilling to feel autonomous and individuated. That separation can lead to individuation is very clear in these cases. However, if the conflicts around autonomy are worked through the individual will then allow the Strength Essence. The result will be both strength and autonomy. The following case illustrates this sequence.

Hank is a young man in his early thirties, married, but still having problems in establishing a career of his own. He held a job in the past, but now we find him living mostly on his savings and with the help of his parents. His wife finally had to work, to bring in some income. He does some work, but he keeps feeling that he wants something that is really his own. He has been working with the author for about five years, both in private and in group situation. He tends to be passive and lazy, although he is well-educated and talented. He feels weak frequently, lacking active energy. He comes to one of his private teaching sessions feeling very good and strong. He feels quite optimistic about establishing work in a different city. After a while he starts feeling blocked in his feeling. It turns out he was feeling afraid to go out and really put himself out in the world. This brings the feeling of weakness. He feels weak all over, with an emptiness in his belly. Discussing this feeling of weakness in relation to his work it turns out he feels if he is strong he has to leave the house and that means he will miss his wife and child. At a deeper level it means separation from his parents, which brings about fear of death. He believes that if he is strong then he is separate from his parents, and this means the loss of their support, which he takes unconsciously to mean that he is going to die. Realizing the unconscious reasons for his weakness, he starts to feel warm all over his body and especially in his chest. This brings about the sense of Strength, and then of fullness and autonomy that he associates with having his own career. This one session does not resolve his conflict completely, of course, and he later must deal with the various facets of it, which for him is a central part of his ego structure. This case is a good illustration of how the sense of weakness can be the result of resisting the sense of separation and autonomy.

In therapeutic circles employing object relations theory, therapists often use what they call "ego strengthening" techniques, especially with individuals with weak or badly-integrated ego structures. The goal is to strengthen the integration and cohesion of ego identifications. In our understanding, such an approach will eventually bring about more of a sense of weakness, although it might seem to be working for a while. The strengthening of ego structure without regard to the presence of Being, will most likely increase the person's separation from his Being. And since Strength is an aspect of Being, one will be even more

210   estranged from one's true source of strength. One might appear to be more integrated, but this is only on the surface, while there is even a bigger weakness and deficiency at the core.

In the Diamond Approach, dealing with these issues often results in what could be seen as a strengthening of ego structures, but this is more or less a side effect of the workings of objectivity and compassion which are involved in the work. As we discussed in the section on metabolism, as the ego structure is purified it becomes less defensive and more open to the realm of Being. Our method is not to strengthen ego structures, but to confront the state of weakness itself, regardless of how painful or undesirable it feels. This confrontation will reveal the deficient emptiness that will then lead to the aspect of Strength. One then integrates part of one's true potential, which is already there and cannot be developed through identifications of any sort. The results we have attained through this direct approach sometimes seem almost miraculous when compared with the results of ego-strengthening techniques. The changes are fast and definite, and have far-reaching consequences in terms of the students' experience of themselves.

We must note, however, that the population of students we have experience with are not those with severe pathological problems, like those with true borderline or narcissistic structures. Our work is not psychotherapy, and we are not making the claim that our approach would be effective with individuals needing psychiatric attention. For such individuals, ego strengthening might be necessary, although the strength gained is superficial compared with the Strength aspect of Being.

Nevertheless, at least theoretically, it seems that since Strength is an aspect of Being, meaning that it is a potential every human being has, which can be liberated, it is possible that such a direct approach—or a variation on it—will be of use even for individuals lacking ego strength. Liberating this true Strength might even have an integrating effect on ego structures, since they are involved in the process of psychic metabolism. We leave further investigation of this vital subject to those with the necessary qualifications and interests.

We turn our attention now to exploring the Strength aspect as it relates to ego development, returning to our earlier observation that the process of separation frequently begins with anger. We saw that

anger does not really lead to separation, and hence does not power
the process of development. Only when anger is replaced by the
assertive energy of the Strength aspect does separation become possible. Object relations theory has identified a similar process:

> A major theoretical proposition put forth by Hartmann is
> that of neutralization, that process which moves both
> libidinal and aggressive energies from the instinctual to the
> noninstinctual mode, thereby rendering them available to
> the ego. [Gertrude and Rubin Blanck, *Ego Psychology:
> Theory and Practice*, p. 33]

The idea is that the human organism is equipped with two instinctual energies, which initially operate in the service of instinctual
gratification. The process Hartmann calls neutralization (which is
similar to Freud's idea of sublimation) causes these energies to lose
their instinctual character and attain more a purely energetic form.
Hartmann and others had the idea that this neutralized energy is what
powers the process of ego development. In other words, neutralized
aggression, in particular, is the energy needed for the process of
separation-individuation.

> At the twenty-seventh International Congress of Psycho-
> Analysis, the theme of which was *aggression*, R. Blanck said:
>> Even though it awaits validation from biology, it has
>> been postulated that the aggressive drive serves the aim
>> of identity formation by providing the impetus for
>> separation-individuation. This view extends our thinking
>> about the aggressive drive into the area of study of its
>> role in ego development. Thus, aggression may no
>> longer be regarded as stimulating solely hostile, pain-
>> inflicting wishes, but as having the more positive aim of
>> serving ego development as well. . .
> In that same discussion, E. H. Erikson proposed the term
> *aggressivity* to connote those aspects of the aggressive
> drive which are growth promoting and self-assertive rather
> than hostile and destructive. [*Ibid.*, pp. 350-351]

It seems to us that the concepts of neutralized aggression and ag-
gressivity are closely related to the Strength aspect of Essence. It is
seen as the energy powering the process of separation-individuation.
We are not aware of any energy having this function besides that of
the Strength Essence. It is our understanding, also, that the Strength
Essence is the force behind what is often called the instinct for

212   self-preservation. This idea is developed in our article "Essence and Sexuality" [*Energy and Character*, Volume 14]. So we do not really have to look to biology to find the true aggressive energy for the organism; it is one of the aspects of Essence. It is interesting, however, that psychoanalysis considers the aggressive energy, or drive, as negative in nature, or at least instinctual; and that it needs to go through the process of neutralization to be utilizable for developmental purposes. Our perception is the opposite. The aggressive energy is, from the beginning, and, in fact, innately and always, "neutralized." It is the Strength of Being, and hence it is the prototype or archetype of all capacities of strength at all levels. When present it infuses the organism with an innate strength that affects all levels of functioning. It gives the organism the sense of capacity, of the ability to exercise any of its functions. Its effect is to expand the capacity of the organism so that all its functions, at all levels, the physical, emotional and Being—are strengthened. Thus it aids the processes of separation and of essential development. It is the fire for it, the fuel that keeps it going. It is energetic, like fire. It is expansive, so it naturally leads to greater expansion of the organism, which is fundamentally what development is. Above all, it is an innate potential of the human being, an aspect of Essence, indestructible and inexhaustible.

Before the differentiation subphase this energy operates as strength, vitality, expansion, and so on, in close coordination with the sympathetic branch of the autonomic nervous system. At the differentiation subphase it becomes more dominant, for its strength is needed to propel the organism towards greater development and autonomy. And because it is what powers the process of separation, it becomes associated in the mind with separation.

From the beginning it functions as the energetic strength of the organism, as the force behind its life energy, and hence has no negative or destructive sense. It is purely a life giving and life supporting strength and energy. The negative connotations and the destructive tendencies that are normally seen in the aggressive energy are not innate to the Strength Essence. They are, rather, the emotional reactions resulting from the blockage of the Strength Essence. When it is impeded from functioning, for one reason or another, there results a frustration in the organism. This frustration is then experienced, coupled with the energetic quality of the aspect, as aggression, anger, rage, destructiveness and so on, qualities which are usually seen as manifestations of the aggressive drive. It is the organism's attempt to eliminate the blockage and the resulting frustration. However, the energy is no longer the Strength Essence, it is no longer an aspect of Being. Being cannot be aggressive in a destructive way. The destructive tendencies are on the emotional and drive level, but not on the Being level.

One could call this distorted and blocked Strength Essence the real energy of aggression, as does the mainstream of psychoanalysis, and then consider the Strength aspect the neutralized form of it. But then we would be taking a reaction to be the real thing, and the real thing to be a result of changing a reaction. Psychoanalysis considers the neutralized form as an outcome probably because it was conceptualized later in theory building.

In our perception and understanding, the force that powers all processes of maturation and development is the Strength aspect of Essence. We see it manifesting when the destructive tendencies are understood, and we see these tendencies manifesting when the Strength Essence is blocked.

In psychoanalysis the processes of neutralization presumably occur in the therapeutic process through verbalization, as opposed to acting out. In our work we observe the same thing. However, we see that anger turns into strength not because of verbalization itself, but because one feels the energetic aspect of the emotion instead of its conceptual part. The conceptual part can be eliminated through understanding, as in verbalization. However, the fact that anger can turn into strength by merely staying with the energetic aspect of the emotional state without acting out, indicates that this energetic aspect is already that of the Strength Essence.

In other words, the process of metabolism related to this aspect occurs by purifying the associated object relations from the negative affects, which are due to reactions not appropriate for the individual anymore. When this occurs the metabolism results in the Strength aspect. To illustrate this with a case we give another report from Andrew, whom we mentioned in relation to the heat quality of the aspect. We find him here, two months later, dealing with the issue of separation in the presence of anger. In the beginning of his report of

214   a certain group session we find him projecting the image of his mother on people in general. He writes:

> On Friday I discussed with you my feelings that the world is peopled with stupid people, and my anger at them. As I have been experiencing more of Essence I become more aware of the ignorance of people in general. You talked to me about my wanting to be me without false personality, and how my anger is at feeling pressured to adapt when I am not prepared to, and how that goes back to having to be nice to get what I want.
>
> You suggested that I just feel the energy of the anger, without having to do anything with it. As I allowed anger to flow I experienced a fullness in my belly area. The fullness increased when I said out loud that I wanted to be myself.
>
> You asked me what I felt at the base of my spine. I felt a burning sensation. When I let this burning move into the rest of my body I felt very strong. The sensation of fullness and strength produced an exhilaration and I felt especially good about me and my work in the group.
>
> On Saturday night I was feeling very good about the work I did, but suddenly flipped into a state of acute fear and doubt. I stayed with the feeling without trying to intellectualize it, and it passed after an hour. It was most acute just before it went away.

In his work in the group, Andrew was angry because he could not be himself, and he attributed that to people wanting him to be that way. His projection of his mother on people is obvious. I did not try to analyze his relation to his mother then because, partly, I have done that before in other occasions, and partly because I wanted to show him how he can turn his anger to strength by merely feeling its energetic quality. He first experienced the fullness of the Personal Essence, which is what he wanted and felt he could not have. He then felt the manifestation of the Strength Essence.

He did not want really to feel the sense of separation although he wanted to be himself, because separation would have brought out much anxiety. This separation anxiety is what surfaced the next day, and it is probably the reason why he preferred to feel angry instead of strong in the first place. Anger still bound him to his mother, while strength separated him from her.

Separation anxiety is one of the main reasons the Strength Essence is blocked or repressed. There is a cul-de-sac that frequently occurs in relation to separation. One resists separation, due to anxiety or other causes, and thus blocks the Strength Essence. One then feels weak, and unable to separate. This weakness is then taken as the reason behind not being able to be separate, while in fact it is the result of resisting separation. It is really the state of the absence of the Strength Essence, and hence it is the state of lack of separation. This difficulty can be surmounted by confronting the weakness itself. This will then expose the anxiety that led to the weakness. Understanding the source of the anxiety then precipitates the experience of the Strength Essence, as we saw in the case of Hank, above.

We will not go into further detail about this aspect of Essence. We are doing a short discussion here only to show its relation to the process of separation, and hence to the process of realization of the Personal Essence. It is, however, an aspect of Essence, on its own. It has its own issues, questions and conflicts that need to be resolved for its realization. It has its own detailed perspective of the process of development. This development can be seen, in fact, from beginning to end, as a process of gradual separation and expansion, with separation taking subtler meanings as the process progresses.

We need only add a few points, relevant for the discussion in this book. First, this essential aspect must be realized in a permanent way if the Personal Essence itself is going to be realized and developed. It is the motivating force and fuel for the process of individuation, and hence is indispensable for it.

Second, the issues and the conflicts around the Strength aspect include all the usual issues and conflicts related to the ego process of separation. However, there is a level of issues and questions not encountered when dealing only with the emotional ego level. For instance, true separation is not really between self and mother representations; that would merely be the separation of one image from another, and this is not enough for essential development. Ultimately, separation is from ego, from representations of past object relations, from identifications. This separation is what we have called before disidentification, a condition needed to look at identification systems in an objective manner necessary for the process of psychic metabolism. This condition is connected with the understanding of this aspect in its relation to the Diamond Guidance. This

216   separation is obviously the ultimate one leading to the experience of the Personal Essence.

The last point, which is related to the example above, will be put in the form of a question: If the Personal Essence is a state of Being, and not the separate individuality of ego, why is it then that one reacts to it with issues of separation that reflect the ego level?

Answering this means understanding what separation means for Being, which is bound to be different and more profound than it is for ego. We have discussed separation so far from the perspective of ego, as defined by object relations theory, and looked at the issues of separation relating to the Personal Essence from this perspective. We have discussed separation in Lara's case as differentiation of representations. However, this is the beginning of the process of separation. As Mahler has said, the separation track runs along differentiation, distancing, boundary formation and disengagement from mother. Some of the cases we have presented reflected the more advanced stages of separation, those of distancing and disengagement from mother. The child is more separate when he or she is able to be away from the mother for longer periods of time. Separation is understood to be more complete when the child can function autonomously for long periods of time. The attainment of a separate individuality is the final outcome of separation. It goes through the differentiation of representations, then the integration of all self representations into the unified self-image, and integration of all object representations into the unified image of the mother.

The child's capacity to be separate is understood to reflect the greater internalization and integration of the mother's image, which is consolidated in the last subphase of the separation-individuation process. So the achievement of separateness is dependent on the attainment of object constancy, as Mahler says:

> The establishment of affective (emotional) object constancy (Hartmann, 1952) depends upon the gradual internalization of a constant, positively cathected, inner image of the mother. This, to begin with, permits the child to function separately (in familiar surroundings, for example, in our toddler room) despite moderate degrees of tension (longing) and discomfort. [Margaret S. Mahler et al., *The Psychological Birth of the Human Infant*, p. 104]

So, according to object relations theory, the process of ego separation leads basically to two related attainments:

- The capacity to function autonomously, away from mother.
- The sense of being a separate person, an individual in one's own right, separate and distinct from all others, but specifically from the mother.

Also these attainments are dependent on the internalization of a good image of the mother.

The obvious implication is that physical and emotional separation become possible because—besides the maturation of body and mind—mentally and emotionally one remains close to mother. The sense of self does not feel abandoned by the mother, does not feel completely alone, because mother is still around, as a cathected image. So one can feel independent and can function in a separate and autonomous manner because there is a constant (although mostly unconscious) feeling of the mother's nearness. This is such a deep insight about the development of ego, to the credit of object relations theory, that it cannot be adequately appreciated until one goes very deep in the process of inner freedom from dependence. The deeper the freedom, and the finer the realized consciousness, the more one becomes aware of this background feeling of mother's nearness, as some kind of omnipresent reminder of her.

Since the sense of self and individuality of ego are based on the self-image, one always unconsciously feels the mother's presence nearby, although one can feel separate from her. This is because her image is firmly established in one's mental structure, as part of one's mind. So one can leave mother by taking her with him, in his mind.

Now we can use this understanding to see what happens when one experiences Being, as in the state of the Personal Essence. The experience of the Personal Essence feels like a sense of autonomy, independence, individuation and so on. However, since one still identifies with ego, or reverts to this identification, one believes that such autonomy is more separation than one can handle. One feels that his distance from mother, emotionally, is becoming bigger, and this is felt as a threat to his sense of identity, as a pressure on his level of integration. And if the individual still has unresolved conflicts about separation, dating back to the first few years of life, then these will be activated by the pressure of the essential experience.

218   This is normal for any experience of greater separation or individuation. Normally each individual has established a certain degree of separation as part of his ego structure. Experiences of more separation become a pressure and demand on his capacity to be separate. This will bring up old unresolved conflicts about separation, or simply exert a new but greater demand on his already existing capacity. Simply put, it will stretch his capacity for separation. The greater the demand or the more difficult the activated unresolved past conflicts, the greater the hardship in adapting to the new situation. One will have to attain a new and more mature individuation.

All these difficulties, the normal issues of ego separation, arise naturally after the experience of autonomy on the Being level, because the ego responds to such autonomy as a demand on it for greater separation, since the individual still identifies with ego. However, the experience of Being, in any of its aspects, implies a separation of a more profound and fundamental nature. When one experiences himself as Being, the internalized image of mother becomes of no use for support or soothing.

When one feels more separate as the individuality of ego one is still the self-image, and the self-image always feels the mother's image nearby. This self-image is formed from past object relations. So each constituent self-representation is really one part of a pair, the other part is that of the object-representation. So regardless how separate this self-representation is from the object-representation, it is always related to it, always in relation to it. This is the core implication of object constancy. Self-image cannot be seen in vacuum. It is always one end of an object relation. So the self-image, and the individuality based on it, are never completely free of the mother's image. Separation indicates more distance and more boundaries, and more disengagement, but never complete aloneness.

However, when one experiences oneself as Being, one is no longer the self-image. One's sense of being a human individual is now based not on the internalized self-image, but on pure beingness, beyond all images of mind.

This means that this new sense of oneself is not in relation to mother's image. It is not dependent on past object relations, and is not a reliving of them. This is the autonomy of Being, that we discussed in detail in a previous chapter. The mother's image is completely irrelevant to this sense of being oneself. It is in fact in a completely different dimension of experience. One is living on the Being level, while mother's image and all mental representations are on the mind level. These representations are experienced as mere thoughts, concepts, images and of no fundamental reality.

The disengagement from the mother in this experience is complete, utter. One feels no relation to the memories of mother or her image, in the sense that one's sense of identity is completely independent from both. The experience of the mental representation of the mother is seen as completely alien to one's experience of Being, as if from two different universes of experience.

So the separation involved in the experience of Being is complete, total, and profound. Ego never feels such separation, regardless how separate and autonomous it is on the mental sphere. It is a different order of separation. Ego separation is like a distance on the surface of the earth; while Being separation is like going to another star system. In fact, it is more like dying. And many individuals respond to it as a kind of death.

So now, either due to a remaining partial identification with ego or a late reversion to such identification, the ego reacts to this perception of such radical separation. This will naturally activate the already existing unresolved old conflicts about separation. However, even if ego development has been smooth and very successful, with little conflict around separation, there is bound to be a much greater pressure on one's capacity for separation. The ego has never experienced such a measure of separation, and this naturally scares the hell out of it. The fear of death or disintegration is one of the usual reactions among others, as we have seen in Hank's case given earlier.

Individuals vary in their reactions to such radical experience of separation. The more integrated and rounded the ego development, and the fewer remaining old separation conflicts, the more tolerable is the realization, and the less distorted is the reaction to it. But it is obvious that repeated or continuous experience of Being is bound to bring to consciousness all the conflicts and difficulties around separation still remaining in one's unconscious. Even small and insignificant conflicts or misunderstandings, felt by ego usually as minor irritations, become exaggerated and magnified in light of the new but radical pressure of the separation of Being.

220   It is conceivable, of course, that one will not revert back to ego identity. Then, of course, there is no fear reaction. But this would involve complete, instantaneous transformation, which is very rare. The process of essential realization is more likely to involve a gradual process of separation. One becomes more and more able to be radically separate. This also implies less and less identification with ego.

The student reacting to increasing separation often tries to resist it by clinging to old object relations, sometimes activating very painful old object relations, just so that he does not feel this separation and aloneness. We find Paula, a young professional, dealing with this resistance to separation. Here is her report of working in a group meeting:

> I was feeling my fear of death, of not existing. I talked about my fears of vulnerability, aloneness, and my physical death. I talked about my recent experience of myself as pushing away Essence, and saying "no" to Essence. I also talked about observing myself deliberately bringing up issues and getting stuck in them and in negative merging; to avoid the loss of myself, my personality, and my identity.
>
> As I talked, the fear grew and I felt myself becoming dissolved and disintegrated, dying. The feeling of death made me tremble, but as I stayed present I experienced tremendous relief and peace in the expansion. Then I experienced a growing intense warmth in my chest, where I have been feeling very hurt. I felt warmth and fullness. I felt personal, objective, and separate. I had no thoughts, feelings, or memories at the time. I was personal, objective, and separate; separate from my usual negative self or personality, an amazing but simple beautiful existence. I felt sweet, and I was loving towards myself and everyone and everything.

This is an example of the advanced stage of separation. Going through the separation anxiety, which meant death and loss of herself, led Paula to a space of peace. It is this sense of peace that students first experience as death, because it is a profound stillness. It is actually the dissolution of the self-image. (See our book, *The Void—A Psychodynamic Investigation of the Relationship between Mind and Space*, for more discussion of death and peace.) But then there is a rebirth. She ends up experiencing both the Strength Essence (warmth)

and the Personal Essence (personal fullness). Love replaces fear in her 221
experience.

Paula's reactions to the separation would probably be understood by object relations theory to indicate the presence of a pathological development of the ego. However, Paula's ego is very well-integrated. Her reactions indicate a pressure of separation seldom encountered by ego. It was the integrity of her ego, in fact, that allowed her to easily move through the fears, and to emerge on the level of Being, with greater integration. In the process of essential realization experiences of disintegration, dissolution and death are frequent. They indicate the dissolution of identification systems. We can see from our reports that essential realization requires much preparation and maturity.

As we see, the process of separation which leads to ego development is only partial. The separation of self-representations from object representations is necessary for the realization of the Personal Essence. If there were no separation of representations then there would be no development of the person, ego or Being. However, the development of the Personal Essence involves even more separation: it requires complete abandonment of past object relations.

Thus the separation of ego anticipates the separation of Being, which leads to the Personal Essence. To use Winnicott's terminology, the mother's image functions as a transitional object, needed before realization of the Personal Essence. He saw that the child in its continuing separation from the mother employs transitional objects, like a blanket or a doll, to soften such separation. The transitional object reminds the child of his mother. So it is useful until the mother's image is finally internalized. The mother's image within the dyadic object relation is then the transitional object which must be given up for Being.

Just as true individuation is the realization of the Personal Essence, and not the separate individuality of ego, so is true separation the realization of the Strength Essence, and not the separation of ego boundaries.

It is amazing when, time after time, a student will be having all kinds of emotional conflicts about separation, but the moment the Strength Essence is present in the experience the conflicts will evaporate, leaving a sense of strength and separation. There is a sense

222   of separation, and a capacity to separate, without a sense of boundaries, or a need for them. One is the Personal Essence, which is
Being, and one can see clearly that boundaries are only mental constructs. The issue of boundaries as it relates to separation and individuation is a very deep and subtle one, which is not resolved till
later in the process of essential development. We will leave discussion
of this issue to another chapter.

Chapter Nineteen

Merging

O n the psychodynamic and structural levels, the main resistance against the radical separation perceived in the experience of Being is due to the unwillingness or inability of ego to be completely separate from the mother. The individual feels he is losing his mother, and his connection to her, because now he is not an individual based on past object relations to her. The remaining identification with ego reveals his unconscious attachment to her image. So the profound autonomy in the experience of the Personal Essence, and the sense of separation of the Strength Essence, both uncover the deep need for, and attachment to, the mother's good image. The loss of contact with the mother's image is often felt as a sense of loss and emptiness. At the beginning stages one does not necessarily feel the loss, but the possibility of this loss brings to the forefront of consciousness not only the attachment to the mother, but also the conflicts and deprivations in one's relationship to her in early childhood.

In Chapter Three we presented a report by a woman, Anna, who was experiencing her Personal Essence and dealing with issues of wanting not to be in the group because she felt that being in it meant loss of her autonomy. We give now the rest of her report, to complete the picture regarding her feelings in relation to the group:

> As I have been experiencing more and more of my independence I have been getting closer to my need to have someone to love and to love me, to my need for a love relationship with someone. And the closer I get to these feelings the more frightened I become, because I am afraid

that I have to give up my independence and a part of myself in order to have someone to love me.

I am and have been feeling the need for my mother's love, in a deeper way than I have for a long time. I have also felt that she is incapable of loving me in the way that I want to be loved.

I am afraid that a part of me is gong to die, that I will do what I did in the past and change myself in order to have this illusionary love that my mother never gave me.

I feel powerful and strong except when I get close to someone giving me love and then I become frightened. My fear of the group and the feelings I have of not belonging are also tied to the feeling of losing a part of myself if I give in. I feel as if I have to fight in order to preserve what I am, and I feel that the fight is a loss of something that I want even more than myself, sometimes.

We see in Anna's experience that the autonomy of the Personal Essence exposed a deep need for her mother, and her love. Object relations theory would interpret this reaction in terms of difficulty in separation due to insufficient gratification in the beginning stages of ego development. The more the mother is attuned, and provides what the child needs, the more the child is able and willing to separate and become more individuated. This good mother is then internalized, which supports the child's developmental thrusts. But when the mother is not able to provide all the child needs, it becomes more difficult for the child to separate; partly because the child does not feel ready, and partly because separation means the loss of whatever (inadequate) mothering there is.

In Anna's case, it is clear that the more she becomes separate and individuated, the more the sense of deficiency resulting from what she experienced as inadequate mothering is revealed. Her need for the love and the nourishment, which she did not receive enough of in childhood, makes her afraid that she will give up her autonomy for it. In fact that is exactly what she did in her childhood and during most of her adult years. She became what her mother wanted her to be. She gave up her autonomy in the hope of getting the motherly love.

The realization of the Personal Essence, which makes her feel the possibility of losing her image of her mother, exposed the deficiency in her early mothering. This resulted in feelings of longing to be in a love relationship, and to be more a part of the group. This longing made her afraid of losing her autonomy. It was not that the group would take her autonomy away; she was afraid of her own feelings of need. She was afraid of giving up her autonomy in order to belong.

To summarize Anna's case, the experience of autonomy brought up these reactions in her for three reasons. Autonomy meant for her loss of her mother, because that was her experience in childhood when she tried to be independent. It also exposed a deficiency in her early mothering, which made her feel unable to be separate and autonomous. It also meant loss of the mother's image, because she felt the autonomy on the Being level where there are no images.

The development of greater autonomy always exposes deficiency in one's early relationship to the mother. The most important phase for later differentiation and separation, in terms of positive mothering, is that of the symbiotic stage, in the early months of life. The quality of mothering, or the quality of the relation to mother in this phase, makes separation either more or less difficult. Mahler states this clearly:

> We found that those infants whose mothers enjoyed the symbiotic phase without too much conflict, those infants who were saturated, but not oversaturated, during this period of important oneness with the mother, seemed to start at the average time to show signs of active differentiation by distancing slightly from the mother's body. On the other hand, in cases in which there was ambivalence or parasitism, intrusiveness, "smothering," on the mother's part, differentiation showed disturbances of various degrees and forms. [Margaret S. Mahler et al., *The Psychological Birth of the Human Infant*, p. 60]

The inner image of mother can actually be felt to be lost or to dissolve in some of the experiences involved in essential development. Like any identification system, when it dissolves it reveals a sense of emptiness and lack. Object relations theory explains this emptiness as due to the loss of part of the ego structure, in this case, mother's image. We consider this explanation true but incomplete; it overlooks the fact of Being, and the fact that ego structures are usually built partly to cover up and fill deficiencies that result from the loss of some aspects of Essence. We will illustrate this point with a case presentation.

Penny is a professional woman in her early thirties, successful and generally cheerful and considerate. However, her main complaint is

226   that she is never able to maintain a deep loving relationship with a man, for any considerable length of time. At the point we find her here she is dealing with deep feelings of loss due to a recent breakup of a relationship she had been having with a man. She starts talking to me in a group session about these feelings of loss and hurt. I listen to her as she talks and cries. When she is finally quiet, and looks downcast I ask her what she is experiencing at the moment. She says she feels emptied out and sad. I ask her what she means by being emptied out. Now she becomes aware of a very distinct sense of emptiness in her chest. She reports that she feels empty in the lower part of her chest. When I ask her to describe her experience of emptiness, she says she feels the emptiness like a deep and dark well that goes backward in her chest, and seems bottomless. I suggest that she feel herself to be as deep in the empty well as possible. She becomes very quiet and introspective. Then tears well up in her eyes. She says she feels a sense of a wound at the bottom of the well. She feels as if she is wounded, hurt, at a great depth in her, at her core. I ask her what the hurt is about. She cries and says she feels she wants her mother. She reports that the hurt and the longing are very deep and difficult to stay with, and she wants to shut off the experience. I recommend that she merely feel the wound and the longing without doing anything, or hoping for anything. I ask: "Is it possible to experience all these feelings without rejecting them?"

When she just allows the feelings she reports that the wound opens up to a deeper place in her. And in this deeper place she starts feeling something new, soft and luminous. She reports, in a flash of insight, that this is the exact feeling she wants when she feels she wants her mother. And that this is exactly what she wants to feel when she thinks of having a relationship with a man. I ask her to stay with the experience, to feel what it feels like, and to tell me specific details about it.

She feels a softness deep in her chest, as if there is a very soft and delicate flow in her heart. She describes it as a kind of delicate presence, that feels sweet, warm and melty. The more she describes it the more it fills her. She now feels her chest full of this exquisitely melted kind of sensation. She feels her chest like a pool of very sweet, soft, delicate and transparent presence that fills her with a golden glow. The more this sweet presence fills her the more she feels her boundaries melting away. She feels the presence as a sweet love that melts her sense of boundaries, and makes her feel not separate from her environment. She feels now the golden sweet love filling the whole room, making her feel merged with everything. She feels that the love is her own presence, her own Being. However, at the same time, she has the curious feeling that now she has the mother that she always wanted. She feels happy and contented; a joyous smile lights up her face.

This case presentation, and others like it, do not signify the complete and final dissolution of the inner image of mother. The image of the mother is as deep and firmly established as the sense of one's individuality. It takes a tremendous amount of work and understanding to be completely independent from it. Penny's case indicates an experience of loss of this image. The image comes back, and Penny would have to deal with her attachment to it for a long time. We are presenting this case, and others like it, to show one important issue that arises as a result of experiencing the Personal Essence. This is the issue of the relation to mother in childhood, which is reflected in the personality in the relation to her internalized image. It is interesting that in these experiences students do not distinguish between the mother and her inner image. When one feels the loss, or the possibility of it, it can be seen to be only a psychic structure, an image, but one feels and behaves as if it were a real loss of the real mother, or the real relation to her. One might be on good terms at the time with one's mother, but the emotional states do not take this fact into consideration. This shows us that the whole process is intrapsychic, expressing internalized past object relations. The above case presentation, and many cases like it, point to the following facts:

- When the identification system that is equivalent to the inner image of mother is experienced as lost or absent, there is revealed underneath it a large, deficient emptiness.
- This deficient emptiness, when looked at objectively rather than trying to avoid it or fill it with a new structure, will reveal underneath it an aspect of Essence, a presence of consciousness in a specific Platonic form.
- This essential aspect is experienced both as part of oneself, and as the good mother that one always wanted.

This aspect, which we call the Merging Essence, is not a result of experiencing the mother's image, but rather the result of losing it. Our

228   observations, and the reports of thousands of experiences from hundreds of students, all indicate this fact, which cannot be accounted for by object relations theory, or any branch of developmental psychology at the present time. However, it is not incompatible with developmental psychology, and in fact we can use the findings of object relations theory to gain some understanding of it.

The Merging Essence is not revealed exactly by the loss of the mother's inner image, but more specifically by the loss of the deeper layers of the psychic structures. The unified mother image is a composite of images of mother remembered from all phases of ego development. The earliest, and hence the deepest, layers of it were formed in the symbiotic phase of ego development. This phase, which starts sometime in the second month of life and lasts until about the tenth month, is characterized by the infant behaving as though he and his mother were a unified functioning system, as though they formed a dual unity with a common boundary. Mahler called such behavior symbiosis, not implying the biological concept of symbiosis, but describing

> that state of undifferentiation, of fusion with mother, in which the "I" is not yet differentiated from the "not-I" and in which inside and outside are only gradually coming to be sensed as different. [*Ibid.*, p.44]

This means that the infant's first object relation, the first time it becomes aware of relating to another, is in a form that cannot be strictly called a relation. There is still no separation or differentiation, in its mind, between self and other. There is still no concept of self or object, no concept of inside or outside. There is only a sense of a unity that has two vaguely perceived objects in it, what Mahler called a "dual unity."

Symbiosis is considered in object relations theory to be a development from the normal autistic phase in the first month, in which there is no differentiation whatsoever. Also, it is considered that the ego has its inception in this symbiotic phase, meaning that the first memory traces internalized are of experiences, pleasurable or painful, when self and mother are still undifferentiated. This means that the first inner representations are undifferentiated; they are called "undifferentiated self-object representations." Kernberg, writing about the second stage of development of object relations, states:

> The consolidation of the pleasurable or rewarding "good" self-object image signals the beginning of this stage, which extends from the second month of life to somewhere between the sixth and eighth months of age. This is the basic "good" self-object constellation, which will become the nucleus of the self system of the ego and the basic organizer of integrative functions of the early ego. [Otto F. Kernberg, *Object Relations Theory and Clinical Psychoanalysis*, p. 60]

This indicates that the deepest layers in both self and object images are composed of undifferentiated self-object representations. So the deepest and most basic layers of the "good" mother image are primarily those of the "good" undifferentiated self-object representations. So when an individual feels the loss, or possibility of loss, of the mother's image, he might be feeling the loss of these deep layers. The deepest experiences of losing mother must be those of the loss of these undifferentiated representations.

Object relations theory indicates that these undifferentiated representations become differentiated at some point in the process of ego development. Our observations indicate that either the process of differentiation does not happen completely or all individuals tend to regress to such undifferentiated representations when there is a possibility of a complete loss of the mother's image. The evidence suggests that the ego is never devoid of unconscious undifferentiated representations.

Our view is that the loss of the "good" undifferentiated representation leads to the activation of the Merging Essence. We give a report of one student, a professional woman in business, in her thirties. Ruth has been working with issues of identification, mainly her masculine identifications; she has become increasingly aware of these but is finding it hard to let go of them. She works with the author in a group setting and at the same time has private teaching sessions with another teacher, an associate of the author. She writes after a weekend in which there were several group meetings:

> This has been a good weekend for me. I am beginning to see how much I identify with my mother. We discussed my dream of not being able to breathe, and how it is men (you, my private sessions teacher, my husband) who come to me in my dream, and tell me I can breathe. I was afraid to show I could breathe for fear of dying. I see men as

> able to breathe and get away from mother. That is one of the reasons I had the hard masculine defense, trying to get away from her. Now I am embracing my womanhood and giving up my masculine hardness. I enjoy being a woman and that means I am like my mother, and I become afraid to breathe. My aim the last three weeks was to ask myself why I sell myself short. This aim has done a lot to bring up my feelings about myself and my ties to my mother. Part of the reason I sell myself short is to try desperately to get her love; she did not want me to be me and do well. Another is the terror of losing her and really seeing that she never loved me; she hated me.
>
> I felt a large gaping hole around my heart and lungs as you spoke. I kept trying to fill it in various ways, one of which is trying to be my mom. When she is sick and upset I get sick. I worked on the hole in a private teaching session before. I have a gigantic wound where my mother continued to emotionally stab me as an infant every time my strength and love came out to her. I believe subconsciously that I am her and she I. I believe she has the love and warmth, and I am nothing without her.
>
> As we worked Saturday night I felt at some point a juicy, honey-like feeling or presence in my chest, where the wound is. It was sweet and warm and like nectar. I felt it again in my private session.
>
> I feel strong and more myself than before. This new depth of working still feels slightly beyond my grasp, as if some wonderful new body of knowledge just appeared and it is taking my mind a while to grasp it.

Before this session, Ruth had experienced herself as the Personal Essence, as a result of letting go of her masculine identification with her father. This brought into clear relief her identification with her mother. The combination of experiencing greater individuation and seeing her identification with her mother made her feel both unable to separate from, and longing for, the "good" mother. The experience of the gaping hole coincided with the longing for the "good" mother, and was the result of seeing her merged identification with her. We can see her process in several steps:

1. Seeing through her masculine identification with father, and understanding it as partially a way of separating from mother.
2. Experiencing the individuation and autonomy of the Personal Essence.

3. Seeing her identification with the undifferentiated representation   231
   with mother.
4. Experiencing the gaping hole and the longing for the "good"
   mother.
5. Experiencing the heart wound, and understanding it as the absence
   of love in her relationship with her mother.
6. Experiencing the Merging Essence.

Our understanding of this sequence, integrating the various facets of her experience, is as follows: Her pleasurable experiences in the symbiotic phase included the experience of the Merging Essence, and became associated with it. The gratification she felt was the Merging Essence, and the affects accompanying it. These experiences became the basis for the "all good" undifferentiated representation. In time, she lost connection with the Merging Essence, for many reasons, among them the negative experiences in the symbiotic phase. This loss is experienced as a wound related to loss or absence of love. The loss of contact with the Merging Essence resulted in a deficient emptiness, a gaping hole with the sense of the absence of the "good" mother. In time this hole was "filled" and covered up with the part of the ego structure that is connected with the symbiotic phase, the non-differentiated representation. This representation then became the deeper layer of both self and object images. The self-representation based on identification with father was built on top of it.

This process of loss of an aspect of Essence, which leads to uncovering a previously unconscious part of ego structure, occurs for all aspects of Essence. Our book *Essence—The Diamond Approach to Inner Realization* describes the process in detail; we call this understanding, as we noted above, the "theory of holes."

In the Diamond Approach, the process of inner realization is partly a retracing of the steps listed above, what is called in psychoanalysis a regression process. As this regression occurs one integrates the aspects of Essence, and the individuality of ego becomes absorbed into the Personal Essence.

Our description of the process of loss of the Merging Essence is not based only on cases like that of Ruth. There are two other sources: one is when students have flashes of memories from the symbiotic phase, they usually include memories of the Merging Essence, indicating that it is actually part of the experience of infants when they are

232   experiencing gratification. The other more important source is the direct observation of infants by the author and other people, at times of the infant's gratification during the months of symbiosis. The consistent observation is that at such times of gratification when the infant feels contented and satisfied, the Merging Essence is present in the consciousness of both infant and mother. We also observe that the Merging Essence, although it is present from the first days of life, becomes the dominant essential aspect during the symbiotic phase.

We will describe the characteristics of the Merging Essence, which should make it clear why this aspect is connected with the symbiotic stage.

- It is a presence, a state of Being, a certain form of self-existing consciousness. It is not an emotional reaction or an image.
- It feels soft, tender, gentle and very sweet. It feels like a form of love. This form of love feels like the presence of goodness.
- This love has the quality of sharing in it, of feeling it with someone else. The sharing feels like the sharing of the goodness one has.
- It has a sense of nourishment, contentment, satisfaction and happiness. When one feels Merging Essence one basically feels satisfied, contented and happy in a complete and deep way. One feels gratified.
- Its most characteristic property, which distinguishes it from all other aspects of Essence, is its feeling of melting. It feels melted and melting. It feels melted like melted butter, but clear as some kind of very light and delicate honey. It has the effect of melting one's sensations, one's tensions, one's mind. When it emerges in consciousness, one feels melted by a sweet and delicious kind of love. The heart melts and flows, and the mind becomes rested and contented.
- It has the characteristic color of clear gold. When seen with the inner senses of Essence it looks like a very delicate clear honey-like flow, which has a luminosity, as if the sun is shining through the delicate honey. This probably accounts for using the golden color in popular expressions describing intimate, romantic or gratifying situations.
- It has an intrinsic sense of pleasure. It feels like a pleasurable sensation. It has the feeling of gratification.
- The melting quality of this aspect of Essence makes one feel merged with the environment, not separate and not differentiated. So it basically melts one's sense of boundaries. The melting is felt

throughout the whole body. The whole consciousness feels melted and merged with the environment or the object.

This quality of merging is seen in object relations theory to be characteristic of the symbiotic phase. Edith Jacobson writes about the infant in this phase:

> Whenever he is fed by his mother or is physically close to her body, his wishful fantasies of complete reunion with the mother by means of (oral and visual, respiratory, skin) incorporation will be gratified. Hence, with the achievement of gratification, his images of the self and of the love object will temporarily merge. . . [Edith Jacobson, *The Self and the Object World*, p. 40]

From our point of view, the merging that Jacobson refers to is the result of the presence of the Merging Essence. It is not merely a mental image of no differentiation; it is the actual experience of the Merging Essence, which is felt as the presence of both self and mother in unity. The gratification does not lead to the merging; the gratification is the experience of the presence of the Merging Essence. So the gratification and the merging are the same experience, and it is the experience of the Merging Essence.

Jacobson speaks of incorporation; but although there might be images in the infant mind, the merging happens through the manifestation of the Merging Essence in consciousness. Mahler states:

> The essential feature of symbiosis is hallucinatory or delusional somatopsychic *omnipotent* fusion with the representation of the mother and, in particular, the delusion of a common boundary between two physically separate individuals. [Margaret S. Mahler et al., *The Psychological Birth of the Human Infant*, p. 45]

From the perspective of Being, the fusion is not hallucinatory or delusional. It is the perception of reality from the vantage point of the Merging Essence. We find it interesting that Mahler says that the perception of fusion in the symbiotic phase is hallucinatory, although she theorizes that the sense of a separate individuality is a developmental achievement which is not attained until the last stage of the separation-individuation process. If we take Mahler's theory of the development of ego seriously then we must conclude that the original state of fusion is the intrinsic condition, and the sense of there being two separate individuals is a result of constructs in the mind. In fact, the perception of

234   two separate individuals is seen from the perspective of Being as hallucinatory and delusional. The boundaries are only concepts, which
object relations theory itself in effect asserts, saying they are constructed from mental representations.

At the beginning, the organism does not have the capacity to discriminate; this develops gradually. So the fusion of the Merging
Essence is, in reality, already a discrimination from the original undifferentiated state.

Mahler correctly calls the perception of common boundaries between child and mother a delusion. However, the correct perception,
on the Being level prior to any constructs in the mind, is the absence of
all boundaries, and not individual boundaries, as she asserts. We will
see in later chapters how there can be discrimination without
boundaries. This understanding is extremely difficult for ego to grasp,
for the very existence of ego is based on the belief that physical
boundaries are real, and that the physical world is the most fundamental aspect of reality. Being sees otherwise, for Being is not restricted by
boundaries. When one realizes one's nature to be Being, these
boundaries lose their function of defining who one is. One still perceives the boundaries of physical objects, but one is aware that they
exist only on the physical level, and not in the consciousness of Being.

The most important barrier against the experience of the Merging
Essence is the belief in an individuality with boundaries. This is why it
becomes much easier to experience this aspect of Essence when one
realizes the Personal Essence; the latter is a sense of being a person
that is not dependent on ego boundaries.

As the child matures, and as ego development progresses to differentiation and separation, it becomes gradually more difficult to experience
the Merging Essence. However, if the metabolism is complete and leads
to the Personal Essence, then it becomes possible not to lose contact
with the Merging aspect.

The perception and understanding of the Merging Essence make
the conceptualizations of object relations theory even more exact. It
explains many things in a very simple way. Object relations theorists
make observations based on the assumption of the reality of separate
entities and, of course, construct their theories accordingly. But, because they do not take Being into consideration, their conceptualizations are inevitably approximate.

As we can see from our discussion so far, the perspective of Being shows the basis of some of the concepts in object relations theory, and makes them more exact. Furthermore, it produces deeper insights into the functioning and development of ego. The Diamond Approach primarily utilizes direct perceptions of the actual states of consciousness of individuals, organized in an integrated and coherent picture.

By direct perception we mean what is actually perceived when the inner capacities of Essence are functioning. These capacities are not generally experienced on the ego level, but sometimes a hint of them can be recognized from the perspective of ego. For instance, the capacity of empathy is commonly recognized, and acknowledged by some psychologists as a valid mode of perception. However, from the vantage point of Being, empathy is seen as the first vague glimmer of a capacity of Being. When this capacity is developed, one does not vaguely sense the emotional state of the other person, but one is clearly conscious of the exact inner state of the other. One knows what the other feels, where in the body the feelings are, what tension patterns accompany this state, how the other is interpreting this state, and even what is underneath the state in the unconscious.

The science of psychology at the present time is still in its infancy in terms of the capacities which can be used for observation and study. It could become a much more exact science by incorporating the capacities of perception innate to Essence. Our exploration in this book and others is a good illustration of the exactness and precision possible in psychological understanding when even some of such capacities are operative. We recognize that most readers will experience a difficulty because our discussion and exploration refers to perceptions that are uncommon, and hence rarely communicated. The problem in understanding our approach is not a logical or scientific one, for it is perfectly logical and scientific in view of the available data. We can only again note that although in currently common experience the perceptual capacities of Being are fairly unknown, they are actually not esoteric or mysterious, and a large body of traditional spiritual literature supports the existence and availability of these forms of perception. A good example of such literature is Henry Corbin's *The Man of Light in Iranian Sufism.*

We return now to our discussion of the Merging Essence and its relation to symbiosis. Just as the Strength Essence is the dominant

236   essential aspect in the differentiation subphase, and is associated with separation, the Merging Essence is the dominant aspect in the symbiotic phase, and is associated with fusion. The Merging Essence is closely related to the function of the parasympathetic branch of the autonomic nervous system, and hence it is inseparable from the discharge processes of the nervous system. [More details of this point can be found in our essay "Essence and Sexuality."] These discharge processes are intimately connected to, and in fact part of, the experiences of gratification during the symbiotic phase.

However, our observation is that during symbiosis the Merging Essence is actually present in the infant's consciousness most of the time, not only after discharge of tension. This is particularly so when the relationship with the mother is basically positive and gratifying.

The Merging Essence seems to be needed by the organism at that time for healthy maturation and growth. Its presence brings about the symbiotic connection to the mother needed for survival and psychological development.

It is a differentiated aspect of Being, in contrast to the nondifferentiated aspect of oneness characteristic of the normal autistic stage, in which there is no perception of boundaries at all. So it is a step toward differentiation, and part of the perceptual and cognitive development towards the ability to discriminate. It allows a certain limited capacity for discrimination. More accurately, it allows discrimination in perception, but it does not allow the fixation of boundaries and partitions. Boundaries and partitions are perceived but are not seen as fixed; they are fluid and changeable. It appears that one of the first boundaries experienced is that of a common boundary around mother and child, in what Mahler calls the "dual unity."

Perception becomes more discriminative when the Strength Essence dominates consciousness, in the differentiation subphase. It brings to perception the capacity to see partitions as more fixed and stable. Still, even here, partitions are seen as porous, transparent and permeable. The impermeability of boundaries is the effect of ego development, and not that of Essence.

We see that the Merging Essence is needed for the development of the perceptual and cognitive faculties, among others, and hence is instrumental in ego development. It is involved in the first inner representations, the undifferentiated ones, which are the basis for all subsequent identifications. Jacobson, assuming that merging is a wishful fantasy, writes:

> These earliest wishful fantasies of merging and being one with the mother (breast) are certainly the foundation on which all object relations as well as all future types of identifications are built. [Edith Jacobson, *The Self and the Object World*, p. 39]

Since the Merging Essence is dominant in the symbiotic phase, and is especially present at times of gratification, it becomes associated in memory with the following:

1. *Gratification.* After a while the child cannot distinguish the Merging Essence from the experience of gratification. So he cannot separate it from the perception of his needs being satisfied. In other words, he does not separate it from the mental representations of the activities or processes leading to gratification. So need for the Merging Essence becomes associated in the mind with the need for other things, such as food, comfort, protection, safety, pleasure, warmth, contact, discharge of tension and so on. This has far reaching consequences, from the compulsive need for love relations, to overeating, smoking habits, drug addiction, greed, idealization of communities and belongingness, and so on. These are illustrations of how the need for an aspect of one's Being can be directed to external objects and activities.

2. *The "all good" undifferentiated self-object representation.* The child cannot differentiate in his mind between the essential aspect and the image of the good dual unity. The child feels the gratifying pleasure of the Merging Essence, but he is not conceptually aware of it. Conceptually he is aware of the dual unity, of a common boundary around him and mother. This has a profound implication for future relationships. The individual grows up believing that he will experience the pleasure, love and melting of the Merging Essence only when he is with another person in an intimate situation. In other words, he ends up believing that he cannot experience this aspect of his Being, a part of him, except in a very narrowly defined circumstance. This puts a tremendous pressure on intimate love relationships. It probably accounts for the consuming human preoccupation with love relationships and sexual contact. The fact is that this state of pleasure and merging is an aspect of oneself, and can be experienced in any situation, whether by oneself or with a love object.

238   3. *The "good" mother image.* The ego cannot think in terms of undifferentiated representations. Since it is the result of differentiation and separation it cannot imagine what it is to be truly merged with another. It can only think of two people coming together in a very intimate way; it cannot imagine the actual experience of not being a separate person. So when one feels a need for the Merging Essence one feels it as a longing or need for the good, gratifying mother. The closest he comes to concepts of undifferentiation is in the fantasies of incorporation or of being incorporated, as in disappearing within the good love object, or returning to the golden womb.

Unconsciously, Merging Essence is equated with the good undifferentiated representation, the positive dual unity. But consciously it is associated with the good mother, or the all-good love object. A devastating outcome of this association is the development of the strong belief that the Merging Essence is not part of oneself, but that it is, or is part of, the good mother. In the usual process of ego development, the most integration an individual can have of this aspect is the belief that one can experience it only with the good mother, or with somebody who stands for her. We see this clearly reflected in Ruth's report when she says about her mother: "I believe she has the love and warmth, and I am nothing without her."

Another important factor in this aspect is its relation to the nervous system. It is a state of melting and flow, expansion and pleasure. When it is present it seems particularly to affect the nervous system, facilitating the functioning of the nerve cells and ends, as if energy and electrical impulses become smoother and more easily transmitted. It is a profound relaxation of the nervous system, and of the whole organism.

It is closely allied to the functioning of the parasympathetic branch of the autonomic nervous system. So it facilitates discharge, rest, relaxation, metabolism, gestation, which are all features of states of satisfaction and gratification. Its effect on the organism, at all levels, is that of comforting, soothing, nourishing, relieving tension and discharging energy. It is no wonder that the good mother becomes the promise of everlasting happiness for the ego. She represents a vehicle for the return to Essence.

These qualities of the affect of the Merging Essence are exactly the mothering functions, which object relations theory says are internalized and integrated by internalizing the good mother's image. Object relations theory understands ego development and autonomy to be dependent on internalizing these soothing and regulating functions, which in turn depends on the internalization of the mother's image, forming one of the two main achievements of object constancy.

> Mahler views object constancy in terms of the internal good object, the maternal image that is now psychically available to the child just as the actual mother was previously available for sustenance, comfort, and love. As Tolpin (1971) puts it, object constancy constitutes a developmental leap that involves the gradual internalization of equilibrium-maintaining maternal functions that leads to a separate, self-regulating self. [Althea Horner, *Object Relations and the Developing Ego in Therapy*, pp. 34-35]

This suggests that what needs to be integrated, at least part of what needs to be integrated, are the effects of the Merging Essence. This is exactly what the child feels he is integrating by the internalization of the good mother image. The mother naturally facilitates most of the processes of discharge, relief and gratification in early childhood, and the child becomes increasingly autonomous as he learns from her how to do these things.

However, the Merging Essence is the inner factor which actually affects the organism directly. It affects the nerves themselves, quieting the autonomic nervous system. The mother's ministrations facilitate the emergence of this aspect of Essence only at times of gratification.

When we think of the human adult who is able to regulate himself internally, is it not obvious that he only needs the presence of the Merging Essence for all processes of inner soothing, relieving and discharging to be facilitated? There is clearly no actual need for the mother's image.

Object relations theory believes that one needs the mother's image in order to acquire her regulating functions. But what happens to this belief when we know about Being, and especially about the aspect of Merging?

One might think that one can integrate the Merging Essence by internalizing the mother's image. One would then assume that the more positive the symbiotic phase is, and hence the more the Merging Essence was present in these early months, the more positive is the internalized image of mother, and the more one integrates the Merging aspect.

240   This is true, but the phenomenon cannot be completely explained by object relations theory, for the following reasons:

- The Merging Essence is an aspect of Essence, part of one's Being. There is no need to have an image of anything or anyone for it to be present or to function. Believing that a self-image is needed for it to be present is like believing that one needs a certain image for one's circulatory system to function.

- Mother's image is also a mental content. As we have seen, holding on to an image is a barrier against the presence of Being. This was illustrated in Ruth's report; when she felt her identity with the mother's image she did not experience the Merging Essence. She had to feel the loss of this inner representation, which revealed a gaping emptiness, before she became aware of the Merging Essence.

- The reason which is particular to the Merging Essence has to do with its property of melting away boundaries, which makes it antithetical to the existence of ego boundaries. The individuality of ego is based on differentiation, separation and the establishment of stable boundaries. On the other hand, the development and integrity of this individuality depends on achieving object constancy, namely, on the establishment of a unified image of mother. If we were to assume that by internalizing mother's image one integrated the Merging Essence, then we would be saying that the individuality, which is defined mainly by its boundaries, is based on the integration of the Merging Essence, which is a state that melts away boundaries. So we would be contradicting ourselves.

The fact is that ego development, as it usually occurs and as it is conceptualized by developmental psychology, is antithetical to the integration of the Merging Essence. When the Merging Essence is integrated this individuality cannot exist, for it will lose its defining boundaries. In fact, we find that one of the main resistances against the experience of the Merging Essence is the fear of loss of separateness and boundaries.

This point has profound and disturbing implications for ego development. It shows that the conceptualizations of developmental psychology, including those of object relations theory, cannot be complete, since they do not deal with the following conflict:

The individuality of ego, the main outcome of the separation-individuation process, is primarily defined by its boundaries. This individuality is dependent on the internalization of mother's image and her soothing functions. However, the soothing functions, in terms of inner experience, are those of the Merging Essence, which is characterized by the absence of individual boundaries and separateness.

Clearly, the outcome is that it is impossible to have a separate individuality and to truly integrate the regulating functions. The two are antithetical. And since the individuality of ego can never integrate these functions in any fundamental way, it can never be completely harmonious, and cannot, by its nature, experience deep contentment and happiness. Ego cannot exist without internal conflicts. This is in fact the general experience of most of humanity. It is also the assertion of most of the profound spiritual teachings, which state that ego cannot be happy or contented in any real or lasting way.

A new question emerges here: what accounts for the fact that the more mature the ego development, the more there is an integration of soothing functions? In our discussion in Chapter Eleven of the question of maturity we saw that ultimately it is the result of the ego development going through a more complete psychological metabolism, which makes ego identifications more transparent. This indicates that a more complete metabolism will make the individuality more vulnerable and open to the Merging Essence.

This happens in two basic ways: First, maturity involves a greater realization of the Personal Essence, which is a sense of being a person, a real individual, who does not need ego boundaries and thus can tolerate the melting quality of the Merging Essence. Second, more complete metabolism means also the metabolism of the identification system that is recognized as mother's image. More specifically, the metabolism of the nondifferentiated representations (the deeper layers of the mother's image) leads to the experience of the Merging Essence, just as the metabolism of the identification system recognized as the separate individuality leads to the Personal Essence.

Thus we can see that the internalization of the mother's image is an incomplete attempt to integrate the Merging Essence. When the metabolism is complete, the nondifferentiated representations are absorbed into Being, resulting in the realization of the Merging Essence.

Thus, when both the Personal Essence and the Merging Essence are realized, the Personal Essence takes the place of the separate individuality, and the Merging Essence takes the place of the mother's

242   image. We think, however, that it is more accurate to see the process not as a replacing of ego, but as a more complete development.

One question that arises at this point is why one must go through internalizing the mother's image, then metabolizing it, to integrate the Merging Essence, if this aspect of Essence already existed in the symbiotic phase. Answering this question will further illuminate the function of internalization of self- and object-images, and of ego development in general.

The Merging Essence is lost in the child's experience not only because of identification with ego structure, but also for traumatic reasons. These traumas constitute psychodynamic reasons for its repression, which arise as issues about Merging Essence in the process of essential realization.

It seems that a very gratifying overall symbiotic experience makes the Merging Essence more available to one's experience. However, it is not enough for complete integration, because of the limitations of the perceptual and cognitive functions at that stage. The infant cannot perceive the Merging Essence, or any aspect of Essence, at the early stage without associating it with the environment, especially with mother. There is still no concept of self, no concept of one's nature, and hence no possibility of knowing that one is experiencing one's own beingness. The infant's mind is basically exteriorized, in the sense that there is no conceptual perception of anything inside. The discrimination in perception begins in seeing everything as outside. However, this does not imply that the infant is aware of an inside set against the outside, for there is no concept of being an individual or self yet.

Ego psychologists have assumed that the infant perceives things somewhat similarly to adults. So when they have observed behavior that indicates projection they have concluded that the child is aware of an inside as opposed to an outside. This is probably not an accurate conclusion. From the perspective of Being, when there are no ego identifications at all, it is possible to experience perception from a certain state, which we call the experience of Absence, in which both the sense of individuality and self are absent. There is no self-consciousness whatsoever, although there is perception and functioning. The perception includes one's body as part of the environment. But the perception is not related to a frame of reference, or to a self as a center. There is the perception of all that appears to the senses, without the slightest movement of referring anything perceived to a self or entity. It is as if there is the perception of the outside without a concept of inside.

It is reasonable to assume that the infant exists in such a state, or something similar to it, before he begins to form concepts. At the beginning he behaves in ways that can be interpreted by the external observer as involving projection. But if there is as yet no concept of inside, of entity, or self, what could projection mean?

At such a very early age the infant is not able to cognize that any differentiated perception is of something relating to itself. The Merging Essence is a differentiated aspect of Being. It can be felt, sensed and even seen. The infant is bound to cognize it as belonging to the environment, and later as part of mother. In fact it is seen as part of the dual unity, but the dual unity itself is still not identified with.

Thus the projection of the Merging Essence on mother, or on the undifferentiated representation, is inevitable. Discussing the absence of differentiation between inside and outside, Kernberg writes, "Again, the child cannot yet differentiate between elements such as pleasurable bodily sensations, the perception of light, and the perception of mother's breast." [Otto F. Kernberg, *Object Relations Theory and Clinical Psychoanalysis*, p. 93]

On the other hand, the complete metabolism of the nondifferentiated representations makes it possible to realize this aspect of Essence. So the process of internalization can be seen as part of the process of essential realization, from a slightly different angle than we have seen it before.

Also, as we have discussed in the section on separation, differentiation and separation are needed for the realization of the Personal Essence. And this process, which is part of ego development, would not be possible if the Merging Essence were from the beginning seen as part of oneself.

There is another reason it is unlikely for the Merging Essence to be integrated directly, that is, in the symbiotic stage. This is the fact that the infant notices that whenever he is with his good mother this sweet feeling arises. So it is difficult for him not to assume that she is the source of it, or that it is inseparable from being in her presence.

We can say then that the Merging Essence is in a sense the "inner mother." In fact, all students in the process of inner realization relate

244   to it as if it were their good mother. One of the main issues to be worked through is that of associating it with one's mother.

It is an independent aspect of Essence, a Platonic form. It has its own perspective, or rather, one can see all of reality from its vantage point. One can see the whole process of human development as the ever-increasing merging with one's Being, as more and more boundaries are dissolved. Many associated issues and conflicts must be resolved for it to be completely realized. We are discussing it briefly only to understand its relevance to the realization of the Personal Essence.

The reason the realization of the Personal Essence requires the realization of the Merging Essence is that the realization of the Personal Essence is experienced as a profound autonomy implying a radical separation from mother, which seems to threaten the loss of the capacity for inner soothing and regulation. So the ego hardens its defenses and identifications against the experience of the Personal Essence. However, when the Merging Essence is realized, the ego experiences the presence of all the soothing and comforting it feels it needs, and this disposes it to further surrender its defenses. However, this must not be taken to imply that one realizes the Merging Essence first and then the Personal Essence. The process is not so linear. The aspects become realized gradually together. This becomes possible by dealing with the rapprochement conflicts, as we will discuss shortly.

Chapter Twenty

Negative Merging

T he symbiotic phase does not comprise only gratifying experiences; it includes many painful and frustrating experiences. When the infant's needs are not met adequately or immediately, he cannot but experience frustration, rage and other painful affects. But the infant's experience of this negativity is not experienced as his own or his mother's; it is part of a merged relationship. There are still no clear concepts of self and other, and no clear boundaries between the two. Thus the frustration and suffering can only be experienced as what we call "negative merging," in contrast to the positive merging of the experiences of gratification.

The first structures of ego develop at this time. They are defensive structures which attempt to protect positive internalizations from the negative affect of the painful ones. The pleasurable and positive merged experiences are internalized as "all good" undifferentiated self-object representations, and the painful and negative merged experiences are internalized as "all bad" undifferentiated self-object representations. These representations are then organized into overall "all good" or "all bad" undifferentiated self-object representations. Object relations theorist Kernberg investigated the development of internalized object relations, building on the work of Jacobson. He writes about this first ego organization:

> I mentioned before that the primary, undifferentiated "good" self-object representation is built up under the influence of pleasurable, gratifying experiences involving the

infant and his mother. Simultaneously with the development of this "good" self-object representation, another primary, undifferentiated self-object representation is formed, integrating experiences of a frustrating, painful nature, the "bad" self-object representation, centering on a primitive, painful affective tone. [Otto F. Kernberg, *Object Relations Theory and Clinical Psychoanalysis*, p. 61]

Thus during the symbiotic phase and a little later, ego identifications begin to appear in this merged form, in two opposite organizations, which are split off and kept separate from each other. In a sense, the infant feels he has two relationships: the positive merged one and the negative merged one. He does not see that they are parts of the same relationship with one person. This splitting gradually becomes utilized for defense, "protecting" the good relation from the bad one.

The positive merging is dominated by the presence of the Merging Essence; its representation is an attempt to internalize it. On the other hand, the negative merging is dominated by a primitive affect of frustration. The first defensive operations are those of splitting and projection. The negative merging is split off, seen as separate and unrelated to the positive merging, and projected outside; thus it is perceived as part of the environment.

It is important to consider here the genetic source of negative merging. Object relations theory would consider the source to be primarily the frustration and inadequate gratification in the interaction between infant and mother. This is clearly true, but we see another important, but rarely recognized, source: the infant is actually in a real merged relationship with its mother, not only a delusional one. In other words, the consciousness of the infant not only does not differentiate where a certain feeling is coming from, but is also in a complete state of empathy. The infant feels everything in the environment, especially in his mother. This is what it means to be in a merged state; it is a merged consciousness, not only a perception of common boundaries. Thus the mother's state has a direct effect on the infant. Mothers know this phenomenon very well. Psychotherapists know this both from their empathic capacities and from the reports of their severely disturbed patients who cannot tell their feelings from those of others.

During the symbiotic phase the infant is in complete contact with the mother's consciousness. He feels her joy, her fear, her anger, her pain, her frustration, her weakness and so on. But he is not aware that these are the mother's feelings, for he has no sense of a separate self. So what he feels and what mother experiences make up the content of his merged relationship with her.

This phenomenon has many disturbing implications. One is that the quality of the symbiosis is not dependent only on the child's interaction with his mother, but also on the general inner state of the mother. Developmental psychology has considered the effect of the mother's state on the infant only insofar as her state determines to a large extent her interactions, reactions, responses and attitude towards her child. We are seeing here that her influence is much greater than that. Her inner state, regardless of what it is, is experienced by the infant as part of the merged relationship, and internalized as part of the merged representation. This means that the totality of her emotional makeup is internalized and identified with as the merged representation.

We have seen this phenomenon on many occasions while observing a mother with her sleeping infant. The infant is asleep and peaceful. The mother becomes anxious, for some reason. The infant feels the anxiety, and wakes up fretting. The mother thinks something is happening to the infant, so she comforts him, by nursing him, for example. In this way she discharges her anxiety and calms down. Now the infant calms down and goes back to sleep. Everyone believes that the mother has regulated her infant, while the fact is that in this instance the infant helped her regulate herself.

One of the few psychologists who saw the paramount importance of this phenomenon is Harry Stack Sullivan. In fact, he considered it to be central in the development of ego; he thought that ego structure develops primarily as an attempt to deal with the negative affects picked up from the mother. Sullivan saw anxiety as the primary painful state absorbed from mother through a merging kind of empathy:

> He suggests that anxiety in those around the infant is picked up, even if the anxiety has nothing to do with the infant per se. The process through which anxiety is conveyed he terms "empathic linkage." [Jay R. Greenberg and Stephen A. Mitchell, *Object Relations in Psychoanalytic Theory*, p. 93]

Sullivan considers this affect of anxiety to be responsible for the early ego differentiations:

> Because the presence or absence of anxiety in the mother is *the* factor determining the presence or absence of anxiety in the infant, Sullivan terms this earliest discrimination in the infant's experience between nonanxious and anxious states "good mother" and "bad mother" respectively. [*Ibid.*, p. 94]

We do not single out anxiety the way Sullivan does, but we do see the importance of what he terms "empathic linkage." The symbiosis is much more profound, even literal, than it is usually taken to be. One could say that the infant functions as the mother's heart. We see here another reason the child needs to separate.

Thus during the time of symbiosis, much of the mother's personality is imbibed, so to speak. This has great significance for ego development, as Sullivan saw. When the mother is happy the infant will feel happy, even if she is not interacting with him. When the mother is suffering, the infant will suffer, even if the mother is not expressing her inner state in her interaction with him. For instance, the mother might be angry at her husband. She knows this and is not directing her anger towards the baby. She holds the baby gently. However, the baby feels her anger completely, and the resulting experience is negative merging.

This point becomes painfully clear in the deeper stages of essential development, when the student begins to deal with the merged representations. He will realize that many of his traits, conflicts and emotional proclivities are not his own at all. He will see that he is living not only his own life, but also the life of his mother (and his father to some extent), and her mother before her, and so on. One will realize, with horror or perhaps with humor, that he has literally inherited the deeper layers of his personality. One lives, to a greater extent than one cares to face, the emotional lives of people long forgotten. One is reminded of the character of Alia, in Frank Herbert's science fiction book, *Children of Dune*, where the persons in her memory of the immemorial past vie with each other to dominate her consciousness:

> She had possessed full consciousness long before birth. With that consciousness came a cataclysmic awareness of her circumstances: womb-locked into intense, inescapable contact with the personas of all her ancestors and of those identities' death—transmitted in spice-tau to the Lady Jessica. Before birth, Alia had contained every bit of the

knowledge required in a Bene Gesserit Reverend Mother—
plus much, much more from *all those others*.
 In that knowledge lay recognition of a terrible reality—
Abomination. The totality of that knowledge weakened
her. The pre-born did not escape. Still she'd fought against
the more terrifying of her ancestors, winning for a time a
Pyrrhic victory which had lasted through childhood. She'd
known a private personality, but it had no immunity
against casual intrusions from those who lived their reflected lives through her. [Frank Herbert, *Children of Dune*,
p. 64]

How can we speak of ego autonomy, when its deepest layers are
inhabited by other people, most of whom one has never known?
There is true autonomy only on the Being level, where one is who
one is, at the moment, completely free from the past.

We see that the content of the merged representations is greatly affected by the mother's emotional experience during the symbiotic
phase. The mother might love her baby dearly, and this will add to
the positive merging; but if she is unhappy, the baby is bound to experience the unhappiness as negative merging. And since most
humans, regardless of how much they love their children, are full of
emotional conflicts, uncertainties, the stresses of life and so on, the
experience of negative merging is almost always considerable.

Negative merging is one cause of most individuals being cut off
from, and unaware of, their Being. The mother's (parents') lack of
contact with, and ignorance of Being is internalized by the infant,
through negative merging. The child grows up completely ignorant of
his true nature. The greatest and most devastating ignorance of
humanity is perpetuated in the daily lives of families. Most of us do
not want such knowledge or perception; it is too painful and frustrating to confront our fears and illusions. But our love for our children
and for the human race might give us the courage to face these issues
and allow us to look inward to find the true harmony of Being.

Negative merging is a powerful force in the personality. It is the
core of suffering, the basis and the fuel of all emotional conflicts, of
all negative object relations. It is in the deepest core of the unconscious, in the merged representations, manifesting in the more superficial layers of the personality as the various conflicts and distortions
specific to the later stages of ego development.

250   Generally speaking, when an adult wants to resist separation and individuation, he resorts primarily to negative merging. Negative merging is still merging. One can always activate it at times of separation anxiety. It is painful, manifesting in frustrating affects and emotional conflicts, but when it is used for defense against separation, one feels mother is around, and therefore feels secure in some way, even though the mother might be angry or hateful. We saw this in the report of Paula at the end of the last section. Using negative merging as a defense against separation usually manifests as clinging to, or regressing to, negative patterns, manifestations, and relationships.

In developmental psychology the phenomenon we are calling negative merging is thought to be always defended against. We find that it is most of the time defended against, but frequently it is employed, in a disguised form, as a defense against separation and its anxieties. Here are a few situations in which it typically manifests:

1. *In superego attacks.* Frequently a student will make some strides towards individuation, but find himself right away under a barrage of attacks from his superego. He finds himself judging himself harshly, berating himself, belittling himself, etc., or expecting similar attacks from others. In fact he believes that others are emotionally attacking him. At these times it is difficult to see whether he is attacking himself or the attack is coming from the outside. When one observes more closely, one realizes that there is no difference, the attacks come from both without and within. What is more, not only does he feel attacked and feel badly about himself, he also believes the attacks. He cannot differentiate between inside and outside sources, or between ego and superego. So there is no differentiation and there is negativity. This is exactly the experience of negative merging. And when this issue is worked through, it becomes obvious that the whole thing is a defense, because when it is recognized anxiety manifests, and then a state of separation emerges.

An example is the case of Marilyn, a young woman working in an office setting, under a manager. She complains in a group meeting of the viciousness of her manager, who attacks her and others in the office, emotionally and verbally. The manager seems to use any excuse to yell at Marilyn for any little delay or mistake, although sometimes they are the fault of the manager herself. Marilyn needs the job and cannot do anything practical to eliminate the situation. So she is learning to defend herself emotionally, through gentle confrontations with the manager. However, in the group meeting, she starts to see that the more successful she is in defending herself and disengaging from the negative interactions, the more scared she becomes. First she sees that part of her mind supports those attacks and even believes in them. She becomes aware of her own participation in the interaction, and sees that she has needed it emotionally. As she allows the fear, she starts feeling that she will lose something if she is completely successful in handling the situation. It turns out that she has believed unconsciously that she would lose her mother. When she sees that, she begins to feel strong and expansive. This leads to the sense of separation and the capacity to deal with the situation.

2. *In love relationships.* This manifests in several ways. The most common situation occurs when an individual is in a relationship that is mostly negative in nature. He might recognize this fact but be unwilling or unable to get out. He keeps complaining about the relationship, usually blaming the other partner for his dissatisfaction, but is quite attached to it. In fact, he might become less interested and more frightened if it starts becoming more positive.

In these situations it is not generally easy to see where the negativity comes from. They are generally complex, with many intertwined emotional conflicts. But in time it becomes clear that the individual is involved in a negatively-merged relationship. He is playing out a negatively-merged representation because he does not want to be separate. Separation means letting go of the negativity, but it will also bring about intolerable anxiety.

Another way this defense manifests is when the individual has an experience of separation and individuation, which happens frequently with students in the process of essential realization. The individual becomes engaged in fights, arguments and negative conflicts with his love partner or spouse. Individuation means separation from mother, and since there is always a projection of mother's image on the love partner, he tries to increase his attachment by feeling negatively connected. It is a negative merging and not merely a negative object relation because one feels he is bad and the other is bad in the same way. The self-image has the same emotional quality as the object-image. One is angry and the other is angry, for example, and it is difficult to see who started the whole thing. One can identify these

252 negative merging situations both by seeing the absence of differentiation and by observing the quality of the negative affect permeating
them.

3. A clear example of reverting to negative merging as a defense
against separation is *when one identifies with the mother's image*. The
individual feels that he is his mother, in the sense of being just like
her, in a negative manifestation. Ruth in the case above states this
clearly, when she says: "I believe subconsciously that I am her and
she I." (This example is more of an identification than merging but
has the same effect.)

4. Another example of reverting to negative merging to avoid separation is seen *in children at the end of the practicing period*, the third
subphase of the separation-individuation process. When the child becomes aware of his separateness and his helplessness he tries to
return to symbiotic fusion with the mother. Frequently this is not possible to do in a positive way, especially because it is not phase
specific (Merging is phase specific for the symbiotic stage), and the
mother is frequently not open to it. The child reverts to negative
merging, in clinging behavior and negativistic manifestations towards
the mother. It is not always only closeness that the child looks for. It
is frequently observed that the mother is available and contactful but
the child continues to be discontented, negative and clinging, until the
mother starts getting irritated or angry. The child then has succeeded
in resisting separation by re-establishing the negative merging. This
occurs more frequently with children who have had a lot of frustration in symbiosis.

Of course, this does not mean that at such times the individual is
completely immersed in negative merging. It merely indicates that this
merged representation is brought up from the unconscious and is
more present in conscious experience than before. One is still mostly
aware of individual boundaries, except in intense experiences, where
the negative merging seems to dominate for short periods of time.

Negative merging is of course not the only defense against separation. Frequently one merely activates past object relations, usually ones
with negative affects. Sometimes, positive object relations are activated
as a defense, even positive merging. A clear example of the latter is
when an individual falls in love every time he comes close to a greater
experience of individuation. He is becoming more expanded, more

individuated, more successful in his life, and at the height of his fullness he falls in love, and becomes embroiled in a romance that takes him away from what he needs to do to actualize his newly-attained individuation.

However, more often than not, one reverts to negative merging or negative object relations. It is interesting to explore the reasons for this. The most obvious is the one implicit in the formulations of object relations theory, i.e., that positive merging and positive object relations tend to encourage separation and individuation. Mahler writes:

> The more nearly optimal the symbiosis, the mother's "holding behavior" has been; the more the symbiotic partner has helped the infant to become ready to "hatch" from the symbiotic orbit smoothly and gradually . . . the better equipped has the child become to separate out and to differentiate his self representations from the hitherto fused symbiotic self-plus-object representation. [Margaret S. Mahler, *On Human Symbiosis and the Vicissitudes of Individuation*, p. 18]

This implies that negative merging discourages separation, which is why it can be used to defend against it.

There is another, more fundamental, reason why individuals usually revert to negative object relations, and especially negative merging, in order to defend against experiences of separation and individuation. To understand this reason we need to know specifically the nature of the primitive affect that characterizes negative merging. It has in it all the negative affects: anger, rage, hatred, pain, fear, anxiety and so on. But there is a specific affect that is always present, which characterizes negative merging, and is independent from the other painful emotional states. This is the basic painful affect in the symbiotic phase, the feeling of frustration when the child's needs are not met adequately and immediately.

The child feels a need for something, such as food, comfort, soothing, discharge, warmth or holding. He either does not get it or receives an inadequate response. His need is not met, his tension is not released. The result is a state of frustration. This might be expressed in rage and/or crying.

Now, what is the specific feeling of frustration? Although people generally believe they know the feeling of frustration, the specific affect is not so easily discerned. Most people feel a general discomfort,

254 irritation and impatience. There is a sense of being pent up, edgy and discontented, that demands immediate release. One can feel dissatisfaction and discontent, but what are these? More specifically, what are the sensations in the body when one is feeling frustrated?

In anger one feels heat, energy, power and, maybe, some discomfort. In sadness one feels warmth, depth, gentleness and, maybe, some depression or hurt. But what are the specific sensations of frustration?

The sensation of frustration is very painful, usually intolerable to feel directly. What most people call frustration is really a softened and smoothed-out frustration; the frustration is usually filtered through some defense or numbing of the sensation.

It is possible to perceive the raw affect of frustration, but usually only when one goes very deep within oneself. One's consciousness must become fine, subtle and minutely discriminating. One must be able to discern one's state at the subtler levels of personality, which generally requires the aid of essential experience.

One starts feeling a kind of heat, as in anger, but it is a dry heat. It is an unpleasant feeling of heat and dryness. This makes it feel prickly, a hot prickly sensation, similar to the sensation of irritated and inflamed dry skin.

When one is willing to go deeper into the sensation one feels it as a harshness, a dry and hot harshness, prickly and almost feverish. There is a hot irritation here or there in the body, a restlessness on the skin. Even though the purest form of this affect is very subtle, the reader might recognize these "symptoms" of negative merging, which are actually very common indeed in our experience, but so ubiquitous and so filtered through defense that they are not noticed.

When it intensifies, the harshness becomes more prickly, as if one's skin is being rubbed by sandpaper from the inside. One image that many students report is that of barbed wire inside the skin. One feels as if he is being pricked by a concentration of fine barbed wire.

Many individuals believe they are getting a rash when they first experience the frustration on their skin. They might even get a rash. We believe, in fact, that many skin irritations are due to this affect. It is like an inner itching. One wants to scratch but cannot reach it.

The sensation is usually defended against by a kind of coating, or by numbness. In fact, all ego defenses are used to resist this feeling.

One knows one is frustrated only indirectly, by the sensation translating itself into restlessness, impatience, edginess and irritability.

The usual defense against it is a numbness in the nervous system, which feels like a dull, cushiony kind of coating. When this dullness is explored it turns out to be the effect of all kinds of beliefs and ideas that are false. It is the falsehood of the personality covering up the painful sensation.

If one pays a sustained and meditative kind of attention to this sensation of frustration, one finds that it is basically a contraction in the nerve ends. Frustration turns out to be a state of contraction of the organism, mainly in the nervous system. One feels his nerves are dried up and parched.

During a state of relaxation, especially in the state of the Merging Essence, the nerves feel soft, smooth, delicate, as if they are bathed in gentle fluids. They feel like gentle running brooks. But in the state of frustration they feel as if the gentle fluids have dried up, and the nerves feel dry, harsh and prickly. In this state they clearly cannot function well.

It makes sense that the state of frustration is a contraction because it is the state of the organism when there is an undischarged tension. In the original experience, the child needs something but does not get his need met. The need is like a rising tension. It is in fact sympathetic arousal, a heightening of the charge of the autonomic nervous system, similar to what happens in the fight or flight reaction. When the need is met there is a discharge of the tension and arousal reaction. The discharge, which is a parasympathetic reaction, is felt as relaxation, satisfaction and gratification. This discharge, as we have discussed, is closely allied to the manifestation of the Merging Essence. The Merging Essence, which is felt as a pleasurable contentment, affects the nervous system, discharging its tension.

When the need is not met, the heightened state of arousal and tension remains, and the Merging Essence is not released. This is clearly not healthy for the nervous system, for its function of autonomic regulation is being impeded. This state of contraction, which is the outcome of undischarged mounting tension in the nervous system, is frustration, the primitive affect characterizing negative merging.

We call this affect "negative-merging affect," expressing its relationship to the state of negative merging, but distinguishing it from the

256   undifferentiated object relations themselves, which are colored by the affect.

This frustration, this painful and primitive affect, is felt as pure suffering. It is the specific feeling of suffering. It is not just pain or anger or fear; it is emotional suffering in its purest form. It is the suffering at the core of all human pains.

We have seen that the negative-merging affect is the state of contraction of the nervous system due to undischarged mounting tension. This contraction is always the core of any contraction or tension in the organism,. any painful or stressful condition. In anger, in fear, in hurt, in jealousy, in anxiety, in any painful emotional state there is a contraction in the nervous system, and this contraction is the negative-merging affect. It is also the core, at the nervous system level, of physical contraction and tension.

Most, if not all, of human suffering can be reduced to physical pain and tension, or painful emotional states, which involve contraction in the nervous system and thus the negative-merging affect. This indicates that suffering is ultimately frustration, and that tension produces it. It is also significant that an aspect of Being, the Merging Essence, is what can eliminate this suffering; this is another reason for the infant's desperate need to internalize the good mother of symbiosis. We note also that autonomic regulation cannot be very efficient in the absence of the Merging Essence, and thus the state of the organism is kept always in a less than optimal condition.

This returns us to the observation that the separate individuality of ego cannot coexist with this aspect of Essence, and therefore the ego always experiences a great deal of suffering. This is exactly the claim of most spiritual teachings, as exemplified by Buddha's first noble truth, that the life of ego is suffering.

There is another, less obvious reason the ego is bound to live in frustration and suffering. We have seen that identification systems, by their very nature, tend to resist Being, and that they always involve some defensive function; further, any defensive quality or posture in the mind must be reflected in the organism as tension or contraction. We have described this either as a thickness in the case of defense, or a lighter dullness like a rubber cloud, in the case of pure identifications.

But this thickness, which can become hardness, and the dullness, are nothing but states of contraction in the organism, basically in the nervous system. Thus the core of the thickness or dullness of all the defense mechanisms of ego must be the negative-merging affect. This thickness is the dull coating we have discussed in relation to the feeling of frustration.

Thus all identification systems are reflected in the nervous system as the negative-merging affect. So the negative-merging affect forms not only the core of negative identifications that are based on negative merging, but also the core of what are usually considered positive identifications. The wider implication is that the experiential core of the ego is the negative-merging affect, pure suffering. Again we see the truth of Buddha's first noble truth, this time from the perspective of psychology.

Understanding the negative-merging affect allows us to see the truth in more of the Buddha's statements; we can understand, for instance, that attachment is suffering. One can see that all states of emotional attachment are those of negative-merging affect. When one feels attached to a love object, whether human or not—not in the sense of feeling love, but in the sense of possession, need and not wanting to let go—the state can be seen as a clear state of negative-merging affect (as well as negative merging itself), covered up with all kinds of ideas, emotional patterns and beliefs.

So it is not only that the loss of the object of attachment will bring suffering; the experiential state of attachment, itself, is suffering. It is this state of suffering, of negative-merging affect, that manifests when the object is lost. This explains the spiritual teaching that attachment is suffering, which is somewhat different from what most people believe this truth actually means; the usual belief is that attachment can lead to suffering. This is why most spiritual teachings advocate emotional detachment.

Another of Buddha's insights is that desire is suffering. A superficial understanding of this deep truth can inspire seekers to undertake all kinds of renunciations and deprivations in the guise of spiritual discipline. Desire is the expression of undischarged tension; this is, in fact, the usual understanding of desire. However, when we study the feeling of desire itself we find out that it is pure negative-merging affect.

When desire is a result of a real need, like hunger, then its tension can easily be discharged by the adult individual. But when it is tied up with past experience, it is the expression of a chronic undischarged

258   tension, which again is negative-merging affect. One can experience
this directly in states of expanded awareness. We see this in the following report of a student, Daniel, who usually takes the stand that he
does not need or want much:

> Working with you the other night, I felt really frustrated.
> It seems to be a clarification of the frustration that I have
> been feeling for a long time now. I am unclear about how
> to work now. I started to say want, and that has to do with
> wanting the right thing.
>
> I feel angry at you as if you did not give me what I wan-
> ted. I feel frustrated from wanting something, making
> demands about it and not getting it. This comes from the
> grandiose position that was defended by not asking for
> things that I wanted. I feel very much an "I want what I
> want" state of which I have not been conscious before. A
> flip from trying to make no demands to wanting all
> demands met. The state of frustration is very clear, and I
> see the relation of the inappropriate demands and the
> negative merging.
>
> As I finish this I am feeling the frustration coming from
> not wanting to give up the magical idea of "demand means
> satisfaction of demand."

In our understanding, Buddha's truth about desire implies that one
needs to study one's desires, instead of believing them or rejecting
them. This can lead to their source, and might bring about a discharge
of the tension.

The presence of negative-merging affect in the personality manifests
as many kinds of desires. Since it is a state of painful undischarged
tension, the desires are ultimately for discharge, though the objects of
desire will vary greatly. And since only Being is a presence without
negative-merging affect, then our ultimate desire must be for realizing
Being.

The second reason one usually reverts to negative merging as a
defense against separation is that the fear of separation brings a desire
for connection. This desire for connection is based on fear and deficiency, so it is the result of negative-merging affect, and in fact is the
same as negative-merging affect. So one activates negative-merging affect to regain or hold on to connection. But connection associated
with negative-merging affect *is* negative merging. Thus one is caught
in a double bind; one desires connection, but the very desire itself

prevents real connection. Desire is a movement towards merging with the object of desire. When one is identified with desire one cannot reach the Merging Essence, the essence of the positively merged state. One will only reach negative merging.

One cannot merge in a positive way when one starts with desire. Being has no hint of desire in it.

Reacting to the unaccustomed and perhaps frightening sense of autonomy of the Personal Essence, an individual might want the positive merged state with mother, or any other love object. One might desire even the Merging Essence itself, if one has experienced it. But although as we have seen, one cannot attain Being by desiring it, this desire can be useful if one studies it deeply and follows it to its source. Then one might learn that there is need for surrender, which is nothing but the Merging Essence.

Merging Essence is a state of pure surrender, for it is the melting of all individual boundaries. The surrender is love. It is also pleasurable contentment and satisfaction. This is what ego wants. This is what it wants when it internalizes the good mother of symbiosis. But it cannot have it because the desire, or any activity based on this desire, turns it into its opposite.

Both the ego's individuality and its desire shut it off from the contentment and happiness of the Merging Essence. Instead of an individuality based on ego boundaries there must be an individuality that does not need them. Instead of desire there must be Being. And it is the Personal Essence that is the individuality of Being. Thus the Personal Essence can live in happiness and contentment, like a precious pearl bathed in the luminous honey of the Merging Essence.

Chapter Twenty-One

Identity

B efore discussing the critical question of identity, let us review what we have seen so far regarding ego development. We have described ego development as part of the process leading to the realization of the Personal Essence, identifying the beginning of this development in the symbiotic phase as the internalization of merged representations, forming some of the first memory traces of experience. We followed the development through the differentiation subphase wherein representations begin to be differentiated. And we have discussed the organization and integration of the differentiated representations into the self and object images.

From the point of view of the Diamond understanding, we have seen that the nondifferentiated representations reflect the presence of the Merging Essence, and that the integration of representations is due to the integrating influence of the Personal Essence. We have identified the Strength Essence as the energy and drive behind differentiation and separation. However, we have not discussed what makes differentiation happen. What makes it possible for the child to distinguish self from nonself?

The Strength Essence is the driving force, the spirit behind the process of differentiation, but it is not what determines the pattern of this process. Object relations theory recognizes neutralized aggression as the energy behind differentiation, but it sees differentiation as partly due to the perceptual and cognitive maturation necessary to distinguish self from object. Mahler, writing about the two tracks of separation and individuation, says:

> One is the track of individuation, the evolution of intra-psychic autonomy, perception, memory, cognition, reality testing; the other is the intrapsychic developmental track of separation that runs along differentiation, distancing, boundary formation, and disengagement from mother. All of these structuralization processes will eventually cul-minate in internalized self-representations, as distinct from internal object representations. [Margaret S. Mahler et al., *The Psychological Birth of the Human Infant*, p. 63]

This is a general formulation of how self-representations develop. However, what makes a child at some point know that a certain part of his experience represents him and another part does not, if at the beginning, in the merged state, there is no such differentiation? This is a very important point for the understanding of development; how does a self come from no self? If there is no sense or concept of self at this early time, how then can a child build a self-representation? Why is the representation connected to self, and not to something else?

There are actually two questions involved in this inquiry. The first is, what enables a child to distinguish self from object? It is a question about differentiation. The second is, what makes the child formulate a self, an identity, instead of another category of experience? This is a question of identity and representation. This latter question is usually not approached in developmental psychology.

Mahler's formulation above is an approach to answering the first question. Jacobson, in trying to describe the content of experience that leads eventually to the establishment of self-representation, writes:

> From the ever-increasing memory traces of pleasurable and unpleasurable instinctual, emotional, ideational, and func-tional experiences and of perceptions with which they be-come associated, images of the love objects as well as those of the bodily and psychic self emerge. Vague and variable at first, they gradually expand and develop into consistent and more or less realistic endopsychic represen-tations of the object world and the self. [Edith Jacobson, *The Self and the Object World*, p. 19]

This describes the process of differentiation, but it does not say any-thing more than that certain experiences and impressions get connec-ted with one's body, and others do not. It answers our first question only, and still vaguely. She makes a more precise attempt to define the concept of self-representation in another statement. She asserts that:

> . . . the image of our self issues from two sources: first, from a direct awareness of our inner experiences, of sensations, of emotional and thought processes, of functional activity; and, second, from indirect self perception and introspection, i.e., from the perception of our bodily and mental self as an object. [*Ibid.*, p. 20]

This is a very clear way of stating how differentiation between self- (body) and object-images comes about. However, it does not yet completely explain what makes a self-representation. It explains how a self-image, or more accurately a body image, comes about, but still not completely accurately or satisfactorily. Our question about what is self, or identity, is still not answered.

Implicit in object relations theory is the idea that a self-representation is a representation, an image, or an impression, relating to a self. But there must be some feeling or concept of self for such a reference to be possible.

As adults we can speak of self and self-representation, and can make some sense of them, because we already have the concept of self. But what about the child, who has no concept of such a thing at all? The theory is that through the processes of ego development, the accumulation of self-representations ultimately leads to a sense of self. The individuality attains not only a sense of separateness, but also a sense of identity, a feeling of self. There results at some point a relatively unchanging feeling of self. One recognizes a certain flavor or sense that one feels as identifying oneself. Jacobson, for instance, differentiates between identity and the feeling of identity:

> I would prefer to understand by identity formation a process that builds up the ability to preserve the whole psychic organization—despite its growing structuralization, differentiation, and complexity—as a highly individualized but coherent entity which has direction and continuity at any stage of human development.
>
> The objective process of normal identity formation finds reflection at any stage of development in the normal subjective feeling of identity. [*Ibid.*, p. 27]

So object relations theory does not stop at the creation of a self-image or functional self. It asserts that the unified self-image not only produces an individualized entity, but also gives one a feeling of identity or self, which is of paramount importance. The two, the self or entity and the feeling of self, cannot ordinarily be separated in one's experience.

This assertion, that ego development leads to the development of the feeling of self or identity, though accepted unanimously in object relations theory, has never been truly substantiated or explained. The theory is that the child is able to construct self representations, and that through the integration of these representations he attains a sense of self or a feeling of identity.

Actually, object relations theory establishes only that images are formed, and that through the function of integration, a unified image results. The question of why representations get attached to a concept or feeling of self, or what makes the final sense of self, is never really resolved. Why is it that the development does not involve only referring the representations to the body? Why does a feeling of identity develop? And if there is no such sense of identity at the beginning, how can representations be referred to a self that cannot be separated from the identifying feeling of the same self?

The usual implication in object relations theory, in its various forms, is that the unified image gives one a feeling of self or identity. But an image is only a shape. And if we extend the concept of image called by Mahler "self boundaries" to include sensations, feelings and perceptions, as Jacobson does, we still cannot explain the feeling of identity. These impressions are mostly of pleasure and pain, in general, as Jacobson said. They are things like temperature, tension, relaxation, sadness, anger, love, fear, movement, thinking and so on. But how can such categories of experience lead to the category of identity or self? The feeling of self that individuals experience does certainly include, and is associated with, all these categories of experience, plus images, inner and outer. But still, this does not explain what is really the feeling of self, and how it comes about. The feeling of identity is quite unmistakable, and obviously the process of ego development contributes to it; but there is something here that is not understood or even usually isolated conceptually.

Mahler tried to deal with this difficult question, to some extent, by talking about the "core identity." She, however, is quite aware that it is still not understandable how this identity comes about. She writes, when discussing the differentiation subphase:

> In our observational research we could clearly see the infant-mother interaction patternings, but we could as yet only guess and extrapolate the internal patterning that contributed to the "coreness" of the primitive body image at its inception (cf. also Kafka, 1971). [Margaret S. Mahler et al., *The Psychological Birth of the Human Infant*, p. 53]

In fact she devotes a whole chapter of the above book to this issue, the chapter titled "Reflections on Core Identity and Self-boundary Formation." She begins by stating the difficulty in understanding how the overall self-representation comes about: "The steps of building the self-representation from the self-object representations of the symbiotic phase are rather elusive." [*Ibid.*, p. 220] She attributes part of the difficulty to the fact that it is not possible to tell exactly what the infant feels inside his body:

> What the infant feels subjectively, inside his own body, especially in the beginning of extrauterine life, eludes the observing eye. That is to say, behavioral referents are barely existent. [*Ibid.*, p. 220]

She then discusses some of the possible processes, reflected in the child's joyous reaction to being mirrored, like wiggling, moving his body and so on: "This obvious tactile kinesthetic stimulation of his body-self, we believe, may promote differentiation and integration of his body image." [*Ibid.*, p. 221]

It is clear, however, that this is not a sufficient explanation, and Mahler recognizes this fact. Tactile kinesthetic stimulation will give the infant familiarity with his sensations and body environment, and contributes to body image differentiation. But it says nothing about how the feeling of identity comes about. She ends the chapter by stating that not only observational methods, but also psychoanalytic reconstruction (of past experience) cannot trace the process of development of the sense of self:

> We must emphasize again that the development of the sense of self is the prototype of an eminently personal, internal experience that is difficult, if not impossible, to trace in observational studies, as well as in the reconstructive psychoanalytic situation. [*Ibid.*, p. 224]

From our standpoint, the questions, both ours and those of Mahler, lie at the cutting edge of a specific understanding of identity. They cannot be answered except through essential experience and perception.

Also, from our perspective, it is not true that "behavioral referents are barely existent." The referents do exist, but to recognize them for what they are there must be some understanding that requires essential realization. Mahler and others do see these referents in children's behavior and attitudes, but generally misinterpret them as something else, as we shall discuss shortly.

To answer the above questions one must have a certain essential experience, the experience often referred to as "self-realization." One needs to know the experience of the essential aspect of Self. Self or identity is a specific aspect of Being, a Platonic form, a pure and immutable ontological presence. When one knows the true Self, the Self of Essence, it becomes possible to see and understand the behavior and attitudes that express it.

That there is a true and timeless Self, an Essential Self, a Self that is not constructed in early life, is widely known in most religious and spiritual teachings of both East and West. All throughout the ages the quest for this real and Essential Self has been recorded in teachings, stories, poetry and art. We find it more surprising and intriguing that psychologists in most persuasions manage to overlook this fact, although much of the rest of humanity knows of it. What is most intriguing is that this fact is almost entirely overlooked by the very psychologists who make it their scientific work to study the self. Perhaps these psychologists believe that they are studying the same self in their theories, and perhaps they believe that they are studying it more scientifically. But why ignore the insights of individuals and teachings which have molded human culture and history to a greater extent than any of the modern psychological theories?

Humanistic and transpersonal psychologies try to include the concept of Essence or Being, plus the idea of inner development, in their formulations; however, as far as we can tell, the attempts are merely the addition of the spiritual perspective to the psychological one. There is no truly integrated perspective in such psychologies. Some forms of existential psychology include the concept of Being, but in a more abstract way than we have done. However, none of these systems of psychology has an integrated perspective or theory of ego development, let alone ego development seen from the perspective of Being.

As we have noted, some object relations theorists, for instance Winnicott, have discussed the idea of Being or the true self, but these

266   formulations are somewhat confusing, because Being and mental structure are not sufficiently differentiated.

Returning to our discussion of the Essential Self: our understanding, based on both direct observation of infants and reconstruction of adult experience, is that this aspect of Essence is present in the infant from the beginning of life. In fact, it can be observed even in intrauterine existence. In most infants, however, the Essential Self is present only occasionally, becoming more predominant in the differentiation subphase, and then becoming the dominant essential aspect in the practicing subphase of the separation-individuation process. The Essential Self can be seen from the earliest time, when we notice a certain look of alertness and directedness suddenly appearing in the infant. This look can appear even right after birth, but rarely, and for short periods of time. Some infants seem to have it more than others. The presence we see in the infant is, in fact, the presence of the Essential Self.

This is one of the behavioral manifestations of the Self, which Mahler actually observed. She writes:

> Observing the infants in our set-up, we come to recognize at some point during the differentiation subphase a certain new look of alertness, persistence and goal-directedness. [*Ibid.*, p. 54]

In fact, Mahler interprets this observation correctly, according to our understanding. She says: "We have taken this look to be a behavioral manifestation of 'hatching' and have loosely said that an infant with this look 'has hatched.'" [*Ibid.*, p. 54]

When the Essential Self is present then, in a sense, the child is born; he is self-realized. He is his true Self, unique and distinct from all others.

Mahler discusses the difficulty in defining such manifestation, a difficulty characteristic of defining any state of Being. She writes: "The new gestalt was unmistakable to the members of our staff, but it is difficult to define with specific criteria. It is probably best described in terms of state (cf. Wolff, 1959)." [*Ibid.* p. 54] She is accurate again; it is a state. However, what she did not see is that it is not just a state—it is a state of Being.

It is interesting that Mahler and her co-workers actually observe the manifestation of the Essential Self, understand it as hatching, which is birth, but still do not directly relate it to the sense of self. However,

this is what often happens when an individual who does not concep-
tualize the existence of Being observes the manifestation of one of its
aspects. There is recognition, but an inability to make the conceptual
leap into the dimension of Being.

The Essential Self is a central aspect of Essence, distinct from the
Personal Essence. The Personal Essence feels like an individuality, a
person, while the Essential Self feels like an identity, a feeling of self.
The Personal Essence feels like "I am," while the Essential Self feels
like "I." The Personal Essence has some sense of identity, but not as
specific and distinct as the Essential Self. The sense of beingness, of
the "am" is much more dominant than the sense of identity, the "I,"
while it is the reverse for the Essential Self.

The Essential Self is a very simple and pure sense of presence. It is
so simple that it becomes subtle and difficult to differentiate from
other feelings. It is not the usual sense of self that most people know.
The usual self is only a reflection of the true self, and we will shortly
discuss the relation between the two. What we are calling the Essential Self is not the same as the self assumed to exist in the early
months of life by some object relations theorists, such as Fairbairn.
Fairbairn's self is an entity that is functional and psychical in nature,
while the Essential Self is, rather, the presence of Being, in the aspect
of identity. It is neither psychical, the way Fairbairn meant it, nor
functional, the way he saw it. It is also not any of the four senses of
self that Daniel Stern proposes. It is closest to what he calls the sense
of a "core self" in the first few months of life. Stern writes:

> A crucial term here is "sense of," as distinct from "concept
> of" or "knowledge of" or "awareness of" a self or other.
> The emphasis is on the palpable experiential realities of
> substance, action, sensation, affect and time. Sense of self
> is not a cognitive construct. It is an experiential integration.
> [Daniel Stern, *The Interpersonal World of the Infant*, p. 71]

This comes near to the description of the Essential Self, except he
sees the "experiential realities" to be of the physical body, and the
"core self" to have "a sense of being a nonfragmented, physical whole
with boundaries and a locus of integrated action. . ." [*Ibid.*, p.71]
which makes it a different order of experience from the Essential Self.

On the other hand, the usual sense of self, the self of ego, is an
emotional content, an affect based on past experience. It has an

268 emotional coloring that differentiates each person's sense of self from
the other. It is, however, not as clear and definite as the sense of Essential Self. It is usually somewhat vague and amorphous, and most
individuals do not become truly aware of it unless they first experience its absence.

The following report from a young woman about her experience of
absence of self while working in a group session illustrates some of
the issues in such experience:

> I began to talk about the tensions I was noticing in my
> head. It seemed that the fatigue and spaciness were from
> being in my head all the time. I started to feel hot and con-
> fused about what point I was trying to make, what I was
> trying to work on here. I relaxed my eyes at some point
> and started to feel sad and angry. I noticed a hurt feeling
> in my heart. I had a feeling like something was missing in
> my body. I felt it was a sense of who I am.
>
> Then all feelings went away and I felt empty. It felt light
> and pleasant. I noticed that when I took my glasses off the
> emptiness expanded. My body was there but it was not a
> boundary. The emptiness was inside and out. It was a still,
> pleasant feeling.

The sense of absence of her usual self is clearly poignant, but she
did not recognize it at once. She first felt a hurt and the sense of
something missing, with a lot of confusion; most individuals experience this confusion when the sense of self is absent. A very specific
investigation of her feelings was needed before she recognized that it
is her sense of self that she missed. At first she felt something uniden-
tifiable was missing because she was used to experiencing it without
ever isolating it in her mind. We also see in this report what happens
when one understands the experience and does not reject it or react
to it: the deficient emptiness that is the absence of self transforms to
an essential emptiness characterized by the feeling of peace.

The usual sense of self is, nonetheless, present all the time, as a
vague but quite familiar feeling of identity. It is how the individual
recognizes himself from within. He knows it; he identifies with it constantly, but he rarely isolates and contemplates it. If he did he might
inadvertently precipitate the experience of the Essential Self.

The Essential Self, on the other hand, is a simple presence with the
specific feeling of identity. One feels simply "I am present, that is me."
The sense of identity is very distinct, very clear, very definite and very

precise. It cannot be described, but it can be recognized, just like love
can be recognized when it is felt. That is what it means to be an essential aspect. This aspect is the purest, most specific, most exact, most
differentiated feeling of the particular category of experience. It is a
completely differentiated and discriminated perception of a particular
category of experience. This complete definiteness and delineation of
experience is not possible on the ego level; it is the domain of Essence.

The Essential Self is experienced as the most definite of all aspects
of Essence. It is supremely singular, and amazingly unique. This unique singularity is recognized readily as one's true Self. One recognizes
oneself in a very direct and simple manner, with a feeling that one has
known one's Self always, even though one has always identified with
the vague sense of identity belonging to the ego.

The sense of pure identity, of pure selfhood, is completely devoid
of, and independent from, any emotion or image from the past. It is
the presence of Being, in the specific aspect of Self. The following letter is from a student reporting her experience of the Essential Self
while listening to a group discussion. She had been working on issues
related to her sense of self for some time, and this experience is the
result of an intensive period of investigation. We especially notice her
excitement and happiness to find herself, which is a common response to this experience:

> I especially wanted to thank you for your talk today. As
> I said, it seemed a perfect culmination for the aim I have
> had the last four weeks. While you spoke today I felt a fire
> inside my chest, and I felt that I am special. It was as if for
> that time I was something real—me. I felt a kindness for
> myself I have never felt and saw even more how I try to
> prop myself up or tear myself down.
> I feel so grateful for this experience and so excited about
> what I feel and have seen. I am looking forward to my work
> in this group, but what is happening now is so alive and real.

The experience is not only of pure identity, but of one's own identity. One does not recognize the self only as identity, but also as
oneself. One realizes that the vague sense of identity that one has always been aware of or identified with indirectly is only a reflection, a
distant reminder, of this singular and unique self. One recognizes
oneself immediately, as the original source and prototype of one's
usual but vague sense of identity.

270   It is interesting that in ego psychology the sense of self is the most difficult to understand, while in essential experience it is the most definite and singular. In no other area is it so clear that the absence of the concept of Being in object relations theory gives rise to ambiguity and incompleteness. As a result, the field of object relations theory contains much disagreement about, and many different definitions of the self; there is no agreement as to whether it is a representation, a process, a structure, within the ego or superordinate to it, and so on.

In essential experience, however, the Self is not only definite and singular, but also feels like a sense of freedom, lightness, joy and delight, as we saw in the report above. There is a sense of excitement, playfulness and adventure. One suddenly feels interested in oneself, excited about one's life, wanting to live and enjoy it. One feels one's own preciousness and specialness, and the preciousness and delight of living. Life feels like an adventure, of unlimited potential and exciting possibilities. The following report is from a student, James, who has been in a group for several years, and who has been dealing with very painful narcissistic issues. He has been experiencing much hurt and a sense of having no value or importance. He focused at some point on feeling not seen or recognized for who he really is. The report is of a segment of work he did in a group session:

> Before I started talking, I felt scared, burned out, and hurt—the things I had been feeling for the last month. I also felt at some point a sense of clear spaciousness, and a crystal kind of clarity. Then I started feeling something sparkling, like flashes of light. I became aware of a presence like a point of concentration in my head. It felt just like a point, no dimension to it, but seemed indestructible; there was no question of it being destroyed or altered by anything outside.
>
> When I felt this concentrated presence in my chest, it made me want to laugh and smile. I stopped myself, still holding on to the hurt. Then I felt it warm my whole chest. It felt wonderful! The hurt left, it felt like I was healing. There was an itch in the center of my chest where the hurt had been.
>
> I felt especially close to myself. Somehow I felt very different, like a child and not knowing how to relate to other people, a little embarrassed, I think. After group I felt a lot of peace and happiness. Later when my wife and

I made love I felt the pointed presence in a very wonderful way.

My mind questions this (of course!), "is it real," "could I
have such a thing?" But the experience is still there and my
questions just disappear when I sense this presence. When
I sense this presence, that feels like a point of consciousness and joy, as I move around, it seems the whole rest of
me, body and mind, is there to move it around.

We can compare this experience of the Essential Self with what Mahler
says about the practicing subphase of the separation-individuation
process:

During these precious 6 to 8 months (from the age of 10
or 12 months to 16 or 18 months), the world is the junior
toddler's oyster. Libidinal cathexis shifts substantially into
the service of the rapidly growing autonomous ego and its
functions, and the child seems intoxicated with his own
faculties and with the greatness of his own world.

The chief characteristic of this practicing period is the
child's great narcissistic investment in his own functions,
his own body, as well as in the objects and objectives of
his expanding "reality."

The child concentrates on practicing and mastering his
own skill and autonomous (independent of other or
mother) capacities. He is exhilarated by his own abilities,
continually delighted with the discoveries he makes in his
expanding world, and quasi-enamored with the world and
his own grandeur and omnipotence. [Margaret S. Mahler et
al., *The Psychological Birth of the Human Infant*, p. 71]

We could not have described the experience of the Essential Self
more eloquently. Mahler here shows her exquisite perception of the
manifestations of the true Self.

She said that there are no referents to the inner experiences of the
child. What she describes here are the exact behavior and attitudes that
are the direct expression of the Self. It is clear from her descriptions that
the Essential Self becomes dominant in the practicing period. This can
be ascertained directly by individuals with essential perception. Essential
perception makes it possible to directly perceive the inner state of the infant, and see what aspect of Essence is present in his consciousness.

Mahler further writes: "We may assume, however, that the earliest perceptions are of the order of bodily sensations. . ." [*Ibid.*, p. 220] The fact
is that sensation is the closest description of the feeling of Being. Its feeling

272   is very much like a sensation of something, but much more clear and precise than a physical sensation.

The Essential Self is not an image nor is it dependent on an image. It is the direct experience of a presence, by being the presence. An image is defined by its boundaries, which is why in object relations theory self is frequently conceptualized in terms of boundaries.

The Essential Self is a clear example of a definite presence with no boundaries; this is inconceivable under ordinary circumstances. Imagine a radiant point of light. It is definite, precise and quite clearly differentiated; it is a nondimensional point. However, because it is a radiant point of light, it does not have separating boundaries. It is the source of light, and it is the light itself. The radiant light goes on forever; it is not bounded by spacial distances. Now if we imagine the light to be consciousness or awareness, then we have a very good impression of a definite conscious presence that is boundless. One experiences oneself as a brilliant point of light, consciousness and awareness. Since one is a dimensionless point, one feels singularly definite, but one has no sense of boundaries. The Essential Self feels like a concentrated presence, a precious and pure presence of consciousness, with the characteristic sense of self. The sense of definiteness, singularity, uniqueness and preciousness are so lucid and complete that it is not really possible to appreciate without having the direct experience. Without the direct experience, one might have some beautiful image like the image of a brilliant star. But this hardly conveys the profound feeling of significance in the experience. It is an experience of pure consciousness, of lucid awareness, of alive presence, in its most singularly definite form.

Our understanding is that object relations theory erred in its conceptualization of the development of identity. It sees this development as beginning with self-representations and ending with the sense of self. The implication is that the self does not exist at the beginning but it does at the end of the development.

Our understanding, based mainly on direct perception but also on observation and analytic reconstruction, is quite the contrary—that the self exists at the beginning but not at the end of ego development. This true Self is responsible for differentiating the self-representations from the merged representations. Then the development of ego proceeds according to the formulations of object relations theory. The

various self-representations coalesce into the self-image with a sense
of identity. This final sense of identity is that of ego. One believes by
then that ego is who one is, and in this way one is cut off from the
Essential Self. Let us describe this process in some detail:

1. *During the symbiotic phase the dominant essential aspect is that of
the Merging Essence.* One result of this phase is the internalized
merged representations.

   The Essential Self manifests rarely at this time, for at this point the
infant is unable to be the Essential Self in any sustained way. This is
because the infant's perceptual capacities are still not developed
enough to be able to feel it very definitely.

2. *During the differentiation subphase the Strength aspect becomes
dominant.* This contributes to the increased capacity for perceptual
discrimination. This increased capacity affects development in two
ways. It makes it possible to differentiate one's image and manifestations from those of the object. It also makes it possible to sense and
be the Essential Self, which is a highly definite sense of presence and
uniqueness, an experience that needs the capacity for differentiated
consciousness.

   In other words, the essential aspect of Strength becomes more
dominant the more the organism matures in its capacities of perception and cognition.

3. *The Essential Self becomes the most dominant in the practicing
period,* partly due to the increased capacity of perception and cognition in terms of differentiation and discrimination, and partly due to
the development of locomotion. This is because, at the beginning of
its realization, this aspect has a dynamic quality, an excitement and
activity similar to the sense of the toddler running around full of excitement and joy. This dynamic quality is missing in other essential
aspects, but makes walking and locomotion part of the development
needed for its full manifestation.

4. *During the differentiation subphase some of the representations are
related to self,* and have some sense of self in them because of the
presence of the Essential Self during the experiences generating such
representations. Let's imagine an interaction with mother during this
time, when the Essential Self is present. The child is the Self, feels
himself as the Self, and is quite aware of the feeling of identity.
He feels definite, distinct, singular and unique. However, he is not

274   conceptually or reflexively aware of the Essential Self. He does not look at the Self and say, that is me. He is indistinguishable from the Self. He is aware of the experience of identity, but he has no image of an entity called the Self. He is completely identified with the Self, and has no distance at all from it. He does not look back at the Self, in other words, he just is it. The experience of the Self is through identity and not through reflection.

So he feels unique and singular without knowing that it is because he is experiencing the Essential Self. This is the characteristic of a full experience of Being. One is, but one is not reflecting on the isness. There is no mind in this experience. This is a complete experience of self-realization, which is so rare and difficult to come by in maturity, because of the development of the reflective faculty of the mind.

However, largely because of identity with the true Self, the child is aware of his physical sensations, emotions, expressions, body image and so on. The Essential Self is such a deep source of consciousness and awareness that when one is realized on this level, one becomes aware of all other experiences as somewhat outside. So the child is aware of the usual categories of experience, in the usual kind of perception, in the sense that there is some distance from them.

In other words, his awareness of the Essential Self is a nondualistic perception by identity, and his awareness of all other categories of experience is dualistic, through subject and object. This means that he can experience only a sense of identity, but he can have an image for the rest of his experience. So he feels a definite sense of identity, but at the same time he is aware of some kind of image connected to himself. By image here we do not mean just a picture; we are including an overall "gestalt" of physical sensations, emotions, ideas and so on.

Consequently, the child's experience includes a wordless and imageless Essential Self, and at the same time an objectifiable experience of body and mind. This objectifiable experience of body-mind is what becomes the representation in the self-representation, which is then present in his consciousness with the wordless and implicit experience of Self. Clearly, since he is not aware of the Essential Self in an objective way, he cannot but connect this sense of Self to the representation.

This explains how the infant comes to associate the representation   275
to the category of self, instead of something else. It is the Essential
Self that is present, whose definite sense of uniqueness and singularity
aids his already maturing perceptual faculties to differentiate his representations from those of the object. And because the representation is not only related to the body, but to a clearly felt sense of Self,
it becomes a self-representation.

The final result is the internalizing of a self-representation (an
image or an impression) that is associated with a feeling of self. It includes the feeling of self or identity as part of the representation, as
characterizing it, or coloring it. The feeling of self or identity is experienced by the infant as coexistent with, and in fact an important
part of, the representation or image connected to his body.

The reason for this is that when the child remembers the interaction
with the mother, he remembers an image of himself (a body-image
that includes feelings, sensations and thoughts), and the memory includes a feeling of identity. Thus the memory is of a representation
that is colored by a feeling of self or identity. So self-representations
are always connected with, or imbued with, a feeling of self.

It is important not to forget that a self-representation as part of the
ego structure is a memory. This means the Essential Self is not there
in it; what is there is only the memory of the feeling of self due to the
initial experience of identity with the Essential Self.

This explains adequately not only the differentiation of the self-
representations from the merged ones, but also how they become imbued with the feeling of self.

5. *It is these differentiated self-representations that become the building blocks of ego structure.* They go through the processes of organization and integration as formulated by object relations theory. The end
result is a unified self-image. Since each representation has a sense of
self, which is really a memory of the sense of identity of the Essential
Self, the unified self-image develops imbued with a feeling of self.

The final feeling of self is a composite of all the myriad memories
of the original feeling of Self. This feeling is obviously colored by all
the experiences in the child's history, since their impressions always
accompanied the memories of the feeling of self. It is also influenced
by all the intrapsychic processes that all the self-representations go
through in the process of structuralization of ego. So clearly this

276 feeling of self is colored by the significant emotions, sensations, images and perceptions that constitute one's experiences. It is not a pure sense of identity; it has a characteristic emotional coloring determined by the individual personal history.

This sense of self, however, is a pale reflection of the original feeling of self or identity. It is not only a memory of the original feeling; it is a contaminated memory, contaminated by all of one's history. This is in contrast to the sense of identity in the Essential Self, which is completely independent from personal history.

6. *The final outcome of ego development is a unified self-image.* This is experienced as a sense of self and a separate individuality; or one could say there is an individual with a sense of self. The Essential Self is replaced gradually by the ego sense of self, as the latter becomes increasingly established. By the time the ego development is capable of selective identification, the ego sense of self has become dominant. The process of loss of contact with the Essential Self is also exacerbated by the usual narcissistic difficulties and traumas in early childhood.

The self is no longer an ontologic presence. One is now cut off from the true Self by identification with an image. One's sense of self is now determined by a memory-image constructed from past object relations and structured by the development of internalized object relations, just as object relations theory contends. But as is clear according to our present analysis, that is not the whole story. The feeling of identity in the self-image is a vague memory of the true feeling of identity.

One important consequence of this development is its profound and disturbing implication for narcissism. Since pathological narcissism is usually understood to be a consequence of the pathology of the self—either absence of it, or a distortion of its sense and structure—then clearly the individuality based on self-image is bound to be narcissistic in a very fundamental sense. In other words, since the Essential Self is the true Self, one is either basically narcissistic or self-realized. Ego by its nature is narcissistic. We will develop this point, the relationship between narcissism and self-realization, in a future publication, to follow the present one.

We discuss now only one aspect of narcissism which is important for our discussion: grandiosity. During the practicing period the child behaves as if he is all powerful, all knowing and completely wonderful. There is much less fear of separation, a greater sense of autonomy and adventure, and a kind of blindness about his limitations, both physical and mental. Mahler described in the passage on page 271 his inflated sense of ability and fearless adventure in the attitude of relating to the world as if it is the "junior toddler's oyster." He falls and stumbles, but he picks himself up, full of enthusiasm and confidence. He makes great strides in maturation and development, but adults can see that his sense of confidence and ability is unrealistic and imaginary, for he is still quite limited physically and mentally, and is still very much in need of the mother's care and protection.

This sense of grandeur and omnipotence is understood readily when one realizes what it feels like to be the Essential Self. The experience of the Essential Self fills the consciousness with a special kind of preciousness, and with a feeling of omnipotence and omniscience. One feels completely wonderful, completely able and totally indestructible. One feels all loving, all knowing and all powerful. There is a sense of completeness and totality. When students come upon the experience of the Essential Self, these qualities are always felt, as is seen in James' report, above, when he says:

> I became aware of a presence like a point of concentration in my head. It felt just like a point, no dimension to it, but seemed *indestructible*; there was no question of it being destroyed or altered by anything outside.

The fact is that these characteristics are actually true of the Essential Self. It is an indestructible source of pure love and knowledge. It cannot be touched, cannot be hurt and cannot be marred. The late Indian teacher of self-realization, Sri Nisargadatta Maharaj, describes the Essential Self like this:

> When you realize yourself as less than a point in space and time, something too small to be cut and too short-lived to be killed, then, and then only, all fear goes. When you are smaller than the point of the needle, then the needle cannot pierce you—you pierce the needle! [Sri Nisargadatta Maharaj, *I Am That*, p. 464]

One has these characteristics on the Being level when one is self-realized. The child is self-realized, in some sense, at this early age. He

278   is completely the Essential Self. He feels these great qualities, and they feel real and definite to him. They are actually real in this realm of experience. For instance, all the knowledge of Being is available when one is self-realized; hence the feeling of omniscience.

However, as we have already discussed, he is not aware that he is being the Essential Self. He is not conscious of his self-realization. He is the Essential Self completely, but he is dualistically aware of his body-mind. So it is natural that he comes to believe that these characteristics are the properties of his mind and body.

On the Being level the Essential Self has no limitations, but the child comes to believe that his body and mind have no limitations, which is obviously a delusion. The delusion is not the feelings and attitudes of grandeur and omnipotence, for these are the actual feelings of the Self of Being. The delusion is in attributing them to the body-mind. We can see from this that the Essential Self has no physical-mental wisdom.

The grand qualities belong to the Essential Self, but they become grandiose when attributed to the body and the mind. The child's imperviousness to hurt is an expression of his solid identity with this Self of Being. It takes him a long time to become aware that these feelings of grandeur and omnipotence are false. When this happens he is thoroughly disappointed and deflated. This usually occurs in the rapprochement subphase, third subphase of the separation-individuation process. This is the big fall, the great narcissistic wound that shows him his limitations and dependency. Mahler writes about the beginning of this subphase, at the middle of the second year of life:

> However, side by side with the growth of his cognitive faculties and the increasing differentiation of his emotional life, there is also a noticeable waning of his previous imperviousness to frustration, as well as a diminution of what has been a relative obliviousness to his mother's presence. [Margaret S. Mahler et al., *The Psychological Birth of the Human Infant*, p. 76]

He also becomes aware that his wishes are not always those of his mother, which marks the beginning the loss of the omnipotence of the dual unity.

> This realization greatly challenged the feeling of grandeur and omnipotence of the practicing period, when the little

fellow had felt "on top of the world" (Mahler, 1966b). What a blow to the hitherto fully believed omnipotence; what a disturbance to the bliss of the dual unity! [*Ibid.*, p. 90]

Here both the dual unity and the sense of grandeur and omnipotence are lost, due to the maturation of the child's cognitive and perceptive faculties. Dealing with this colossal disappointment becomes the task of the rapprochement subphase, and an important fulcrum in ego development.

The truth is that the child needs to learn not that his grandeur is not real, but that it is not a property of his physical-emotional-mental self. However, he learns by becoming increasingly aware, due to both experience and maturation of autonomous functions, that he is limited in his capacities and dependent on his mother.

Since his sense of self is nonconceptual and nondualistic, he does not have the understanding that his Essential Self is truly grand and in a sense all-powerful, but his physical-emotional-mental self is not. He never learns that he is more than the psychosomatic organism. This has several far-reaching consequences:

1. *The perception of vulnerability, limitation and dependency, without the ability to separate these from the experience of the Essential Self, leads to the abandonment of identity with the latter.* The child loses his unconscious self-realization. He pushes away the sense of grandeur and omnipotence because he feels it is not true, and in the process he pushes away his Essential Self.

The significance of this step cannot be appreciated until one is deeply involved in the process of self-realization. One knows the extent of the loss in childhood only when one consciously regains the Essential Self.

2. *The child becomes more identified with the self-image, and begins to believe that he is his body, his mind and his emotions.* The identity shifts from Being to ego. The Essential Self remains only in the vague memory of its sense of identity.

3. *The most practical consequence is that the child becomes more realistic about his physical and mental capacities, which is necessary for both survival and autonomy.* He is now especially aware of his body, its feelings and sensations, its image and its abilities.

By the end of the practicing period and during the rapprochement subphase, we begin to see . . . the baby's

280   taking possession of his own body and protecting it against
           being handled as a passive object by the mother. . . [*Ibid.*,
           p. 222]

    In the next section we will address the obvious and intriguing ques-
tion: What is the relationship of the Essential Self to the formation of a
personal self defined by the ego?

Chapter Twenty-Two

Personalization

The process of childhood self-realization, along with its loss and the resulting development of the physical-mental self, can be seen as serving adaptation and development. When the child is born he is completely Being. In psychoanalytic terms, he is born completely cathected to Being. He is basically unaware of his body, its limitations and its capacities. This awareness develops slowly due to the maturation of his physical and mental faculties. During the early months of life he is completely dependent on his mother. As he differentiates and separates he becomes more himself. But even then he is still cathected to Being, by complete identity with the Essential Self.

The Essential Self is completely ignorant of the physical world and its laws. If the child continues to be the Essential Self he will not learn about his body, and how to live in the world. Under normal circumstances, he would not survive.

He must gradually cathect his physical body, and the rest of physical reality. At the beginning he is, although pure, not able to survive and grow in physical reality. The sense of grandeur and omnipotence of the Essential Self is actually quite dangerous for his survival.

The process of disappointment is a major step in cathecting the physical apparatus. The disappointment indicates his increasing awareness of his body and its limitations. He is already learning about his body in the practicing period, through the accidents of falling, knocks, and hurts, plus parental physical handling. He not only learns about his body in this period, but also learns about and

282   internalizes its image. And consequently his identification with this image increases.

> As the infant crawls and later walks on his own, the frequent falling and knocking against unyielding objects in the environment seems to augment his feeling (the cathexis) of his body-self boundaries. [Margaret S. Mahler et al., *The Psychological Birth of the Human Infant*, p. 222]

So the presence of the Essential Self, with its sense of omnipotence, helps to give the child the opportunity of having an immediate and repeated experience of both the physical world and his body, in relationship to each other. This happens as self-representations form, as we have already discussed.

The outcome is the formation of many self-representations which include experience of the body, the physical world and the relationship of the two. The disappointment and deflation at the beginning of rapprochement is a result of this experience, as is a greater and more realistic appraisal of the body and the world. It also marks the shifting of cathexis from Being to the body and its world.

Consciousness becomes increasingly anchored in physical reality, and in the mind, which is closely allied to the latter. It becomes less aware of the dimension of Being and, in most instances, loses its contact with it. The unity of Being is lost, and the world appears more and more fundamentally physical.

We see then that both childhood self-realization and shifts of identity from Being to the body-self serve the purpose of cathecting the body, and physical reality in general.

What happens in ego development is that this experience of the body (and its world) becomes integrated into the structure of ego. The final outcome is the establishment of a separate individuality, with a sense of self based on the body-image, which includes physical-emotional-mental knowledge. The individual grows up learning the ways of the body and physical reality. He develops his sense of self by learning about his mind and emotions, and about human relationships; for his individuality is the outcome of experiences gained mostly in object relations. The physical, emotional and mental wisdom gained is integrated into his individuality. It becomes second nature. He is now a person, a human individual. This is the development of the man of the world.

Our exploration in this book has shown us that ego development   283
is part of a larger process, leading to the realization of the Personal
Essence.

This indicates that the process of cathecting the body (and its
world), if it continues to its completion, will result in the development
of the Personal Essence. The Personal Essence contains all the true
learning of the individuality of ego. The Personal Essence is the essential aspect that embodies the wisdom of living in the world. When the
Personal Essence is developed, however, the identity is no longer
connected exclusively with the body. The body is recognized for what
it is: the external and physical manifestation of the Personal Essence.

Thus the process that ultimately leads to the realization of the Personal Essence begins with self-realization in childhood; i.e., with the
Essential Self, and ends with the Personal Essence, the essential person. Between these essential poles, the ego development makes up
the rest of the process. In this way, Being acquires the wisdom of the
world. It can now live in the world, although it is fundamentally not "of
" it.

Thus the realization of the Personal Essence can be understood to
be the way that Being learns to be in the world. The Personal Essence
is the aspect of Being that embodies the wisdom of the world.

We have discussed the Personal Essence as the aspect of Being
connected with functioning. We have seen it as an integration of the
functions of primary autonomy, on the Being level. So the development of the Personal Essence is the way Being becomes functional in
the world.

We can see now in what way ego development is part of a larger
process, a process by which Being becomes a human being. This
process, which includes cathecting physical reality, is that of the realization of the Personal Essence. So it is a process of personalization
of Being.

Winnicott understood the process of ego development to be centered around the cathecting of the body. He saw that this process of
learning happens through the formation of the person, as a process of
Being learning to inhabit the body. In the words of two of his students:

> Personalization was the word used by Winnicott to de-
> scribe psychosomatic collusion, or the "psyche indwell-
> ing in the soma." . . . Psychosomatic collusion is largely

taken for granted by most people, but Winnicott saw it as an achievement. It is a development from "the initial stages in which the immature psyche (although based on body functioning) is not closely bound to the body and the life of the body." . . . Personalization means not only that the psyche is placed in the body, but also that eventually, as cortical control extends, the whole of the body becomes the dwelling place of the self. . . . Like the achievement of "I am," that of indwelling in the body relies upon good-enough environmental provision. [Madeleine Davis and David Wallbridge, *Boundary and Space*, pp. 40-42]

We use the term personalization similarly to Winnicott, with some differences. We do not see it exactly as indwelling. It is more a matter of cathecting the body and focusing on it, for the body is only part of the unity of Being. In other words, Being and body are not two distinct things (this can be seen from the perspective of undifferentiated Being, but not from that of ego). This is a very subtle point to discuss; we will leave it to a future chapter dealing with the undifferentiated aspect of Being. The other difference is that it is not just the psyche that becomes allied to the body, but Being itself; but the terminology will stand if with psyche we include Being.

Winnicott seems to have had some essential experience, and some understanding of Being. His concept of the true self indicates that he had some understanding of the Essential Self. He seems also to have had some understanding or experience of the Personal Essence, indicated when he talks of the person or the "I am." It seems, however, that his concepts mix the Essential Self, the Personal Essence, and ego, as can be seen in his definition of the true self. He also did not make it clear that the individuality of ego is quite different and distinct from that of Being. He took the attitude that when ego development is healthy it should lead to the person of Being. This is definitely true, but the word "healthy" means one thing when considered by ego, and a completely different thing from the perspective of Being.

The final outcome of the process of personalization is the development of the Personal Essence, with the Essential Self as its center and source. So, in some sense, it is true that the world is the child's oyster. Being, by manifesting in the world and interacting with it, develops the Personal Essence, the Pearl Beyond Price.

We have seen that the Essential Self is instrumental in forming self-representations. Self-representations contain the worldly experience and wisdom of the organism. These self-representations ultimately lead to the realization of the Personal Essence. This happens through the complete metabolism of experience. The Personal Essence absorbs all the true wisdom relevant to living in the world, while still being Essence. It has some sense of identity, reminiscent of the Essential Self, but with it there is growth and development.

The development of the Personal Essence can be considered an outgrowth, a development, from the Essential Self. It is as if the Essential Self becomes filled out through the metabolism of personal experience. The understanding of the relationship between the Personal Essence and the Essential Self is a certain realization in the process of inner realization, which occurs in its deeper stages. The relationship is seen as that of love and value, as the true and essential object relation. The Personal Essence is the true person, and the Essential Self is his true source. One experiences oneself as an alive and sensuous fullness, as the expression of the love, joy, pleasure, appreciation and light of the Self. One is Being, but fully grounded in the world.

Chapter Twenty-Three

Rapprochement

The rapprochement subphase of ego development in childhood begins when the child becomes conceptually aware of his separateness from his mother. This coincides with the deflation of his grandeur and omnipotence. He becomes actually aware of his vulnerability and dependence. One possible recourse for him is to defend against the perception of vulnerability and dependency by continuing to believe in his omnipotence. In this case he develops a self that is based on this defensive sense of grandiosity, an inflated sense of self that covers up emptiness and deficiency. The result is what is called the narcissistic personality. Or he can defend himself by withdrawing inside, and isolating himself from the difficulties of object relations. He becomes detached, and does not feel needy, vulnerable or dependent. By cutting himself off from the world of love objects, he cuts himself off from his own inner resources. This results in the formation of a schizoid character.

The more normal development is that the child acknowledges, to some degree, his vulnerability and dependency, and attempts to revert back to more infantile behavior of needing and wanting mother, and seeking closeness to her. This does not happen so easily though. The mother often finds this development unexpected, and even disappointing, which can lead to her failing to respond appropriately to the needs of the child. She might resent the child's new behavior of clinging and demanding.

One can readily see how it might be regarded as regressive behavior and an imposition on the mother's freedom just when she is beginning to enjoy the child's independence from her. [Gertrude and Rubin Blanck, *Ego Psychology: Theory and Practice*, pp. 58–59]

Both mother's reaction to his new behavior, and the child's fear of losing the separateness and autonomy that he has gained so far, lead to a conflictive relationship to her. This manifests in approach-avoidance behavior. He wants to go to her, be with her, even merge with her, but he is afraid of losing his boundaries and autonomy. So he reacts by avoiding her or pushing her away. This behavior dominates this important subphase, which can last up to 18 months.

This rapprochement conflict is usually reenacted in our work, after the Personal Essence is experienced in a sustained manner. The student goes back and forth, from feeling individuated and autonomous, to feelings of longing and yearning for closeness and merging, indicating the wish for mother. It is possible to recognize the conflicts, the feelings and behavior of clinging and demanding, on one hand, and those of separation and avoidance, on the other, in love relations, and in the transference with the teacher, and even with the group

We find that every individual, regardless of how integrated he is on the ego level, has an unconscious rapprochement conflict. The conflict is usually resolved in childhood by the child ultimately finding some kind of a compromise between the wish for individuation and the wish for closeness with mother. Mahler observed that this happens usually at around 21 months of age, when the emotional struggle appears to calm down.

> The clamoring for omnipotent control, the extreme periods of separation anxiety, the alternation of demands for closeness and for autonomy—all these subsided, at least for a while, as each child once again seemed to find the optimal distance from mother, the distance at which he could function best. [Margaret S. Mahler et al., *The Psychological Birth of the Human Infant*, p. 101]

This can be seen in the following report by a student about one of his work sessions in a group meeting. He was preparing for his vacation when he discovered he was scared. He writes:

> I asked you about trying to pack my suitcase to go on a vacation. It was the first time I knew I was feeling hysterical when I was feeling hysterical—blind panic. We focused

288

on my suitcase. I felt a great deal of dread and then sadness. I remembered how I felt, when I was sent away to
school in the seventh grade.

As you suggested that I imagine approaching the
suitcase, I felt panic the closer I drew. I also felt panic if I
became too distant from the suitcase. When you asked me
how close to the suitcase I could get and still feel okay, it
was two feet. I was scared to learn this. One and a half to
five feet is all I can take. At greater distance my mother
disappeared. I had a great deal of fear acknowledging her
loss. She is gone, that brings fear.

The session gave a meaning to a symbol, but I did not
resolve the problem as I had hoped it would.

He was supposed to go on a vacation with his wife, an occasion of
being closer with each other. The suitcase represented this closeness
with his wife, the symbol of mother. It is interesting how Mahler's
concept of optimal distance can be made so concrete.

It is interesting that in this case, even though some understanding
has occurred, the issue is not resolved. He found his optimal distance,
but the rapprochement conflict is not over. The solution is a compromise which is bound to be challenged by life circumstances.

It is clear that for ego the solution must be a compromise; for ego,
autonomy and fusion are contradictory states. When one is dealing
with the issue on the Being level it attains another dimension of significance. It becomes a conflict in the student's mind between the Personal
Essence and the Merging Essence. Autonomy becomes the Personal
Essence, and closeness with mother becomes the Merging Essence.

The rapprochement conflict becomes reflected on the Being level in
the deep belief that it is not possible to experience the Personal
Essence and the Merging Essence at the same time. The longing for
closeness with mother is really a longing for the Merging Essence. The
individual feels he wants his mother, but really he wants the feeling of
merging, which is the Merging Essence, as we saw in Chapter
Nineteen. Mahler puts it this way:

> The fact is, however, that no matter how insistently the tod-
> dler tries to coerce the mother, she and he can no longer
> function effectively as a dual unit—that is to say, the child
> can no longer maintain his delusion of parental omni-
> potence, which he still at times expects will restore the
> symbiotic status quo. [*Ibid.*, pp. 78-79]

The realization of the Personal Essence is not seen only as the loss
of the mother, but also, and more profoundly, as the loss of a part of
oneself, the Merging Essence. This is for two reasons. The first is that
the sense of complete autonomy, attendant to the experience of the
Personal Essence, is experienced as a much larger distance than one's
own optimal distance from the mother which was established in the
rapprochement subphase. Thus the compromise attained then is
bound to be challenged by the experience of the Personal Essence,
which is experienced as total autonomy.

The second reason is that mother's image stands, in the unconscious,
for the state of the Merging Essence, as we have already discussed.
One usually cannot tolerate its loss. The loss of mother is experienced
as terrible. But a complete loss of part of oneself, an aspect of one's
Being, feels completely unacceptable. One reacts from the depth of the
unconscious. Even though he may not know of the existence of the
Merging Essence, his unconscious knows, and will revolt against the
possibility of losing it.

Sometimes, a student will consciously miss the Merging Essence,
and become terrified of completely losing it. This can happen especially after one has had some experience of it. The fact is that unconsciously the individual cannot differentiate between mother and the
Merging Essence. So the realization of the Personal Essence is always,
at the beginning, experienced as a threat of the loss of both mother
and the Merging Essence. This can manifest as fear of loss of mother,
of her love, of closeness to her, of merging with her, of the Merging
Essence, etc.

The loss of the symbiotic mother, which is associated with Merging
Essence, implies a lot more than one can see at the beginning, because of the properties of symbiosis and of the Merging Essence. The
loss is experienced as equivalent to the loss of, or the loss of the possibility of, security, pleasure and company. The fear of loss of security
becomes reflected in fears of loss of support, money, nourishment
and so on. This accounts for many phobias, like fear of being in
airplanes, of earthquakes and so on. The fear of loss of pleasure is
generalized to all kinds of pleasure; eating, comfort and so on; but
more particularly it manifests as fear of loss of sexual pleasure. This is
enhanced by the fear of loss of company, which manifests mostly as
fear of aloneness. In other words, the gratification of what can be

290 seen as the three primary instincts—sexual, social and survival—becomes endangered.

On the other side of the rapprochement conflict is the fear of loss
of autonomy. This manifests as threat of loss of independence,
separateness, individuality, boundaries, being, self and so on.

The student experiences the Personal Essence for some time,
minutes or months, feeling happy and expanded. Then a longing
manifests. By understanding the longing he reaches the state of the
Merging Essence. He then experiences contentment, love, pleasure,
security and boundlessness. This happens until the longing for autonomy surfaces again. This process does not stop; there is no such thing
as compromise here. Autonomy is total and merging is total. One is
either one or the other. When there is compromise then there is no
essential experience, for compromise is possible only for ego. The
student's immovable conviction is that it is not possible to experience
the Merging and the Personal Essence together. This is a reflection of
remaining identifications with ego.

This conflict manifests in an individual's life in many forms. It can
be a conflict between love relationships and freedom or work. It can
manifest as conflict between security and autonomy. It can manifest as
a conflict between marriage and free sexual life. The well known mid-
life crisis is an expression of this conflict, as are many of the conflicts
of adolescence.

It takes long and deep work, mostly working through one's relationship to one's mother, before the experience of a final resolution becomes possible. Each student works through differently, depending on
his particular relation to his mother. But the resolution is always the
same, and it is only on the Being level. In the following report we find
Mark dealing with this particularly difficult issue to its final resolution.
He is a professional man in his early forties, who has been in a group
for over five years. He has gone through many changes, and been
through many essential realizations. We find him here dealing with this
issue in his transference to the author in a group session:

> What prompted my work was the intensity of feelings I
> had about not being appreciated. I knew I was sad and hurt
> because something in me had been ignored and taken for
> granted; which was much more than my feelings, but which
> was real. I was afraid to bring it up because I have been
> wanting to experience my Personal Essence for a long time,

but mostly in the past few weeks. At times I thought I had. I was afraid you would not see me this way or would not acknowledge me this way, or would see it mainly as something else. I think I wanted something acknowledged and seen, that felt just like me as a very little boy.

You called my attention to the melting state which brought up anxiety in different parts of my body, a lot in my legs and pelvis. It was a fear of letting go, that I would shit in my pants, because that part of me was relaxing. I was afraid that I would dissolve and melt.

It felt soft, nice, and I felt like a sweet loveable boy. I was afraid of this. He is not supposed to be this way or want this, or want mommy.

You then asked if I noticed my chest. I just had and knew what I felt there. It was what I wanted but I was afraid to acknowledge it. But it was me, the fullness of who I am. I wanted to laugh but was afraid to be too happy and proud. I realized I was feeling both the Personal Essence and the Merging Essence. I could feel my usual conflict. It was a real dilemma, about which I want most. It is starting to soak in today more what the conflict is about, and that there is really no conflict. I can experience both.

I really appreciated you telling me that it was me that recognized me. I had not noticed that and I had thought you were the one who recognized the presence in me. This feels really important to me and I could easily have overlooked it. It also felt that all those issues I have been having so intensely in the last 6 months or so have lost their significance, which has been happening in the last month or so. I am learning to appreciate who I am, and I want to more.

Mark was clearly projecting his mother's image onto me. He experienced his mother as not acknowledging, approving or understanding his desire for autonomy. He longed for the autonomy of the Personal Essence, but was afraid I would respond the way his mother had. He wanted me to acknowledge and value him. He felt, obviously unconsciously, that if he got this acknowledgement then he would have both his mother and his autonomy. He first experienced the Merging Essence, because he was first in touch with the longing for his mother. This happened when he allowed himself to be the loving and sweet boy he was, which was possible because he had worked through a lot of his masculinity issues. The Personal Essence manifested, but he did not want to acknowledge it right away because of

292   the rapprochement conflict. He was afraid that if he acknowledged the merging he would lose it. He believed he had to choose only one part of himself. Seeing that clearly allowed him to experience both at the same time.

This kind of resolution is not possible on the ego level, where only an uneasy compromise is possible. There is no compromise here at all. Both the Merging Essence, which implies a state of union, and the Personal Essence, which implies a state of complete autonomy, are present, at the same time. One feels individuated, autonomous, completely real, present as who one is. At the same time there are no individual boundaries, no sense of individual separateness. There is a sense of melting, sweetness and love. There is a sense of being present as one's own person, in the midst of a sense of union, love and contentment.

Recalling that the Personal Essence is a sense of being a real person, which does not depend on ego boundaries, we can see that there is really no conflict between it and the presence of the merged state. The conflict is in the mind, due to childhood rapprochement. This is what Mark finally understood.

There is never a real conflict between one essential aspect and another. Conflicts arise, but they are due to lack of understanding. The real and objective understanding is not available because of ego issues. When these issues are resolved objectively the understanding spontaneously manifests.

The resolution of the rapprochement conflict usually leads to resolving its expression in one's personal life. It is not only an inner resolution. We see this in the report of another man, James, whom we discussed before. For a long time he had an overriding conflict in which he felt that if he were himself he could not be with his girlfriend, and if he were with her then he could not be who he genuinely is. He writes of the end of a work session:

> I experienced feelings of being scared and alive. I felt a sense of strength and identity of my own and a closeness and love towards my girlfriend. As a result I feel a fullness and warmth that is expansive, through my belly and chest. My feeling of losing her does not seem to overwhelm me as before. A sense of taking responsibility for my own feelings and growth is paramount. I feel that I want to work on myself and find out what I want with my

girlfriend. My earlier feelings of desperation and grabbing are not there.

It is important to see how the resolution of his situation with his girlfriend manifests. He is no longer projecting his mother's image on her. There is an objectivity about the situation and a sense of responsibility, all within a feeling of both merging love and autonomy. We also notice in his state the presence of the Personal Essence, the Merging Essence, the Strength Essence and the Essential Self.

The resolution of the rapprochement conflict implies much more than a pleasant inner state accompanied by a harmony of object relations. This is because the conflict of rapprochement, which manifests as a contradiction between the Personal Essence and the Merging Essence, means a conflict in adaptation. The Personal Essence, and before it the individuality of ego, is the functional part of oneself. It is the capacity to function as a person. On the other hand, the Merging Essence, and before it mother's image, is needed for the inner regulation of the organism. We have seen that the soothing, discharging and comforting functions, i.e., the functions of inner regulation, become integrated into the ego through the internalizing of the mother's image. On the essential level, such inner regulation is reflected primarily in the relation of the Merging Essence to the autonomic nervous system, and is attained by realizing this aspect of Essence.

The presence of the rapprochement conflict means one cannot both have inner regulation and be functional. The reality is that these two aspects of functioning of the organism are interdependent and inseparable, and constitute the capacity for adaptation. One cannot adapt with either inner regulation or external functioning.

Thus the resolution of rapprochement on the Being level indicates the simultaneous capacity for both inner regulation and external functioning, which is, obviously, a balanced, efficient and mature capacity for adaptation, and hence, growth.

Chapter Twenty-Four

Autonomic Regulation

Inner regulation is dependent not only on the Merging Essence, but also on the Strength Essence. The inner regulation of the organism is coordinated primarily by the autonomic nervous system (ANS). The sympathetic branch is responsible for the charging up and mounting of tension accompanying any manifestation of organismic need. The parasympathetic branch is responsible for the discharge of tension and relaxation of the organism. The process of charge and discharge, tension and relaxation, is the process of inner regulation. The heart of this process is the functioning of the ANS, and is called autonomic regulation [see *The Wisdom of the Body* by W. B. Cannon, and *Autonomic Regulation* by Ernst Gellhorn].

In childhood, the mother is needed to facilitate this regulation, which is critical for the maintenance and growth of the human organism. Her ministrations, such as feeding, cleaning, comforting and so on, are needed to begin the process of discharge. That is why she is referred to sometimes in object relations theory as an auxiliary ego. The infant is almost completely dependent on his mother for his inner regulation.

Throughout ego development, this role of the mother is integrated by internalizing her unified image. This is a great step towards autonomy, for the child learns to do more of his own inner regulation. This autonomous capacity for inner regulation is partially dependent on the capacity for external functioning. For instance, the child learns to feed himself, and in this way he not only gets the nourishment he

needs, but he also autonomously discharges the rising tension of hunger in the nervous system.

We saw in our discussion of the Strength Essence that it is closely
allied to the functioning of the sympathetic branch of the ANS. So the
process of autonomic regulation is reflected, on the Being level, as the
alternation of the Strength and Merging aspects of Essence. This
means that the process of autonomic regulation can be interfered with
when there are difficulties with either of these aspects. On the ego
level, this is reflected in the issues of separation and merging. Difficulties in separation indicate difficulties in the functioning of the
sympathetic branch of the ANS. Difficulties with merging indicate difficulties in experiencing the Merging Essence, which implies difficulties
in the functioning of the parasympathetic branch of the ANS. All of
this is reflected in the individual's capacity for autonomic regulation.

The rapprochement conflict is thus reflected in the ANS as a
difficulty in autonomic regulation. The ego resolution of rapprochement in the compromise of the optimal distance clearly influences,
and is influenced by, the patterning of autonomic regulation. When
the resolution tips more towards closeness with mother, the autonomic regulation will tend more towards discharge. The individual
will have more ease with the discharge than with charge. This is
reflected in a relatively lower active energy, since sympathetic charge
is allied to the Strength Essence, which is characterized by an excitatory kind of energy. It is also often reflected in a flaccid kind of
body armor.

When the ego resolution of rapprochement tips more towards
separation from mother, autonomic regulation will weigh more
towards the charging up and mounting of tension. This is reflected in
an individuality with a higher active energy, and more difficulty in rest
and relaxation. It is also reflected in a more rigid kind of body armor.

Of course, there are many other factors determining the final outcome of ego individuality, but we are discussing the factor of the
resolution of the rapprochement conflict. It is interesting to see that
the organism functions as a whole system, integrating all levels of
functioning. The state of the organism reflects early childhood development, the status of the nervous system, and existence on the Being
level. All these dimensions, and many others, cannot be separated in
any real way.

296   The ego's capacity for autonomic regulation, which is the core of its capacity for inner regulation, is reflected in the capacity for having a stable sexual relationship. Sexual activity and discharge is the most efficient way the ego develops for autonomic regulation. It was Reich who made the greatest contribution to the understanding of sexuality in terms of inner regulation [See *The Function of the Orgasm* by Wilhelm Reich].

In our essay "Essence and Sexuality" [*Energy and Character*, Vol. 14], we discuss sexual intercourse in autonomic regulation, from the perspective of Being. We develop the understanding that the energetic function of genitality is that of autonomic regulation. We discuss the development of this genital function in its relation to the development of object relations. The capacity to have a stable sexual relationship, and hence the capacity for autonomic regulation, on the autonomous level of ego, requires the attainment of the following conditions: object constancy, genital primacy and orgastic potency.

Object relations theory already describes the importance of the resolution of the rapprochement conflict for the attainment of object constancy. In our essay, we develop the understanding of how this is important for the attainment of both genital primacy and orgastic potency. The instinctual drives are explored in relation to object relations. We find that this understanding is possible when we include the concept of Being. In our view, sexual energy, as it is usually known, does not exist in early childhood, but the interaction of the stages of ego development with the stages of psychosexual development, as set down by Freud, leads to its development. We develop the idea that sexual energy is basically an integration of two essential aspects: the Merging Essence and the Strength Essence. The Merging Essence contributes to sexual energy its object-seeking drive, the qualities of closeness and intimacy, and the capacity for sexual discharge. The Strength Essence contributes to it its excitatory quality and its capacity for building a charge.

We see that the constitution and the development of sexual energy are closely allied with the functioning of the ANS, as reflected in its capacity for autonomic regulation. This shows the importance of the rapprochement conflict, and its resolution, not only for sexuality but also for the constitution of sexual energy itself. Rapprochement resolution affects the development of sexual energy insofar as the individual's attainment of it is tipped more towards the excitatory or the merging pole. Some individuals are more excited and active in terms of their sexuality, while others are more interested in closeness, merging and sweet contact. This exploration shows how ego development influences the sexual temperament of the individual. It also shows how realizing the Strength and Merging aspects of Essence leads to a greater capacity for both sexual excitement and orgastic release.

This happens through the resolution of the rapprochement crisis in a slightly different form than the one we have already discussed. We find that the rapprochement conflict manifests in primarily three forms, generally related to different periods in the rapprochement subphase. The one we have already discussed, the conflict between the Personal Essence and the Merging Essence, seems to be connected primarily to the later part of the rapprochement subphase.

In the middle period of the subphase the conflict usually manifests as between the Merging Essence and the Strength Essence. So it is a conflict between merging and separation, instead of between merging and individuation. This is expressed in childhood in the approach-avoidance behavior, which Mahler calls the "shadowing and darting away" pattern.

In the work of inner realization, the student comes to a point where he finds it impossible to embody the Merging and Strength aspects simultaneously. He cannot conceive of how he can be merged and separate at the same time. When this conflict arises he usually reports difficulties in sexual functioning, for sexual energy is an integration of these two essential aspects.

The fact is that the conflict is in his mind only; it is not objective. There is never, in reality, any conflict between two aspects of Essence, but he cannot see the objective situation because of his rapprochement conflict, among other things. To believe that two aspects of Essence can be conflictive is like believing that two organs of the body, like the heart and liver, are antithetical in their functioning. The separation of the Strength Essence has nothing to do with rigid boundaries; it is more the capacity to discriminate by perceiving differentiated qualities.

The resolution of the rapprochement conflict between the desire for separation and the desire for merging is the psychodynamic and structural outcome needed on the emotional level for the simultaneous

298   realization of the two essential aspects. The rest of the work is of an existential, phenomenological and epistemological nature. The following case shows how resolution of the emotional conflicts lead to this realization.

Jill is a professional woman in her early forties, successful in a field that is competitive and demanding, particularly with respect to her external image. She has been working with the author for several years, and many things have changed for her, both in her inner experience and external life. One thing, however, which did not change much, was the question of her weight. Although she did not like how much she weighed, she could not do much about it, regardless of what she tried. She tried many diets, worked with various specialists, and tried to understand it in her work with me. Finally she felt she could accept the weight, but felt she had to do something about it, both for her health and for her relationships with men, which have been suffering for some time. She then started a certain diet and discipline. She also focused on the emotional issues that would result from losing weight.

One time she came to her private teaching session feeling good and her body looking healthier and more vital. In the course of discussing some situations in her life, she started seeing the kind of relationships she engages in with others. An overriding pattern is that she invariably takes a role that has mothering connotations; she is helpful, comforting, nourishing and lovingly supporting. She saw that there is nothing wrong with this role, except that she is attached to it. She realized that it is her way of having her mother, especially the good mother that she always wanted. And she believed she would lose this mother, which represented the Merging Essence, if she lost her weight, which is part of the mothering image. This meant that if she accepted her separateness from her mother, which implied feeling strong and sexy, then she could not have the nourishing sweetness of the good mother. In other words she believed she could not experience both the Merging and the Strength aspects of Essence at the same time.

As soon as she saw that, she started giggling and feeling quite wriggly. She started to laugh and blush and felt very naughty, although it was not exactly sexual. This made her feel even more separate. She was able to see that this state of feeling sexy and naughty, playful and light, is that of the Merging and Strength aspects of her Being.

The presence of both the Merging and Strength aspects of Essence is a specific state of consciousness, the essence of sexual energy. One feels sweet and soft, but also strong and hot. One feels the simultaneous presence of both closeness and distance, alternating in dominance. One feels playful, but in a very specific way. The playfulness has a flavor of teasing and flirting. It can become sexual, but it need not. One feels innocently naughty, the kind of clean and joyful naughtiness or mischievousness frequently observed in young children. It is a state of play, pleasure and delight.

Frequently this brings about the emergence of the Personal Essence. Then there is added to the experience a sense of fullness, sensuousness and presence. The state attains a pure kind of voluptuousness, where body and Being are indistinguishable. When it becomes sexual it does not become full of desire or longing. It is more the happy interplay of sweetness and excitement, now experienced with the fullness of the Personal Essence. The physical contact becomes enhanced and filled with the sensuous contactfulness of Being. It is play, involvement and pleasure, in which bodies are merged as part of the interplay of the colorful qualities of Essence.

The Will Essence

The third form that the conflict is observed to assume in essential development is that between the Merging Essence and the Will aspect of Essence. In childhood this manifests usually at the beginning of the rapprochement phase, in the behavior of the child when he realizes that his omnipotence is not real. He tries to coerce his mother back into the dual unity, by all kinds of attempts at control. He tries to control his distance from her. He wants to have the control of the situation in his own hands, and it is very important for him to have his own way.

Attempts at control and wanting to have his own way can be seen as a reflection of the child's need to assert his own will. The rapprochement conflict is between having his own way or submitting to mother's wishes. This is obviously dependent on perceiving mother's wishes as not identical to his own.

His wish to assert his own will can manifest as a negativistic behavior and a need to control because such behaviors imply separation and autonomy for him. However, when his wishes are different from

300   those of mother, he feels he has to submit to her wishes if he wants her love and wants to be close to her. But this means abandoning his own will, and hence his autonomy. So he sees the situation as a conflict between having his will or having the merging with the mother.

This is actually a reflection of two desires, both important, but often experienced by the child as antithetical: the desire for merging and the desire for autonomy. Autonomy is seen here as the capacity to assert his will, by having his own way. On the essential level, this manifests as a conflict between the Merging and the Will aspects of Essence.

The Will Essence is very important for separation and individuation, as important as the Strength Essence. Strength gives the individual energy and the initiative capacity. Will, on the other hand, is a kind of strength, but it is the strength of persistence, of being able to stay with a task till the end. It is the capacity for endurance, persistence and carrying through. It feels like a sense of solidity, of inner support, of determination and confidence. If the Personal Essence feels like "I am" and the Strength Essence feels like "I can," then the Will Essence feels like "I will." It is confidence in one's abilities.

Its loss leads primarily to a state of castration and ego inadequacy. The individual then feels no confidence in himself or his capacities. He feels no inner support or fortitude, no backbone, nothing to fall back on.

This aspect is needed for individuation because it is the confidence that one can be on one's own. It is really the will to be, the support to be oneself. That is why it becomes most dominant at the end of the practicing period, and at the beginning of the rapprochement subphase. It is most needed then for the child to continue in his already partially acquired autonomy.

It is apparent how important mother's attitude is at this time for the child's growing autonomy. If it is important for her to have her own way, which is a reflection of her own issues about Will, then the child learns that he cannot have his own Will without sacrificing his mother's love and closeness. Most often, in these situations, the child will choose the merging, and accept the state of castration. On the other hand, if the mother is a castrated person, and lets the child run all over her, he will also lose his Will; for he is, at some place in his structure, identified with her. What he needs at this juncture in his development is a mother with an intact Will, who will support his Will with the presence of her own Will. The role of the father will become important here, as a support for the child's growing autonomy.

It is interesting that depth psychology, including object relations theory, sees the manifestation of Will or its absence as the expression of the anal phase of psychosexual development. Attempts at control are seen as an expression of anal aggression, and yielding is taken to be a sign of anal submission. The concept of Will is almost absent in modern depth psychology. This is amazing in view of the prevalence of this concept in the everyday life of most people. The concept of Will is used in some systems of psychology, such as Robert Assagioli's psychosynthesis, or the existential system of logotherapy. However, we are not aware that the concept of Will is explored in terms of its relation to the development and structure of ego in any modern psychological school.

In the Diamond Approach we find the concept of Will indispensable for understanding ego and its development. Its importance for essential realization is even greater. Many systems of inner work, including Gurdjieff's, are based on this aspect of Essence. Schools that use the martial arts are using the aspect of Essential Will. In terms of ego development, structure and conflicts, the understanding of Will can bring a greater clarity and specificity. The absence of Will is reflected in the following situations, which we discuss only briefly:

- The moment one identifies with a defensive structure one cuts himself off from the Will of Essence. Understanding this can bring a precise understanding of the difference between the beingness of Being and the activity of ego.
- Castration anxiety is a direct consequence of being cut off from the Will Essence. The Oedipal situation augments the situation, but does not create it. For more detailed discussion of this point refer to our book *The Void*. It is enough for us here to mention that the state of castration itself is nothing but the state of deficiency resulting from the loss of contact with the Will Essence.
- The exaggeration of masculine identifications and qualities in some men and women is a reflection of absence of Will. Will is considered in most cultures to be a masculine quality. Thus having a masculine image becomes a way of covering up the hole of the Will by an ego structure with masculine characteristics; this is an emulation of Will.

302
- Rigidity and inflexibility in ego structure is a way of covering up the Will deficiency by creating something that emulates its sense of solidity.
- Predominance of anal traits in the personality can be seen as the expression of conflicts regarding Will.
- The need for external mirroring in the practicing period, reflected in narcissistic needs, is the need for the parents' support of one's own Will.
- Kohut's concept of the self-object that is needed in the development of the sense of self is a reflection of the need of the child to be supported by the Will of the parents.
- The experience of falling or of falling anxiety is a reflection of the absence of the support of the Will. This can result in many kinds of phobias.
- Ego inadequacy is a direct result of losing touch with the support of Essential Will. This point will be explored more exhaustively in a subsequent chapter.
- Confusion in gender identity. Gender identity is based on actual sexual differences when the Will Essence is realized.

We could make a very long list, but it is enough to mention that the Will Essence is an essential aspect, a Platonic form of Being, with its own perspective and its own issues which must be resolved for its realization. Most students have their first encounter with the Will Essence by resolving the castration complex. Some of them have the most difficulty with this aspect when it is involved in their rapprochement conflict. Daniel, whom we have mentioned before, had his greatest difficulty with this aspect because of the rapprochement conflict. He always seemed to have difficulty with the experience of Will. It did not become clear why till he started seeing it in terms of rapprochement.

At some point he started experiencing much emptiness and lack of fullness. He felt himself to be an empty shell. This brought out hurt and anger that his mother had not given him much until just before her death. This led to feelings of rebellion and anger, because she did not allow him to do things his way. He saw that he experienced her as not being there as a support for him, to feel his true feelings and do what he wanted. Many things became evident about his early relation with his mother, especially how he had to deny his Being so as not to lose his mother because she herself was not very real. This led to his seeing how he felt that he would have no sense of existence apart from his mother. In other words, he depended on maintaining the merged relation with his mother in his mind to support his identity. Seeing this led to a state of disintegration, which resulted in the experience of the Strength Essence, indicating the separation from mother.

In the next session he came with strong feelings of absence of Will, although in the previous sessions he had been dealing with merging and separation from mother. He saw the feeling of absence of Will as an emptiness in the solar plexus. This led to feelings of falling and lack of support. By accepting the emptiness he experienced feelings of peace and spaciousness, and then the feeling of the solidity of Will in his pelvis and back.

He came to the following session feeling sad and wanting a relationship with a woman. After some work this led to recognizing his belief that if he had his own Will, which is the support for his sense of Being, he would end up alone, which conjured up for him fears of death. Here, the rapprochement conflict is explicitly a conflict between the experience of Will and that of Merging.

Since autonomic regulation becomes primarily the energetic (orgonomic) function of genitality, then the absence of Will will have an important adverse effect on its efficiency, and even its functioning at all. It is difficult to use sexuality in a harmonious and efficient way for the pleasurable discharge of accumulated tension when the individual suffers from feelings of castration and castration fears at a very deep place in himself.

Will is also related to autonomic regulation at a more fundamental level. When inner regulation fails to happen, or does not happen adequately in early childhood due to deficient symbiotic experience, the organism slowly loses its innate confidence in being regulated. This is because its innate confidence is not adequately supported by the symbiotic relationship, but is instead challenged. This loss of innate and unquestioned confidence is the beginning of the loss of the Essential Will. The child loses his sense of support in terms of inner regulation.

This experience of loss of Will leads to the child trying to get the regulation through the exertion of effort. This he does by trying to control either himself or his environment. This activity of trying, effort

304   and control is the false will that the child starts building. This is, obviously, linked to the building of ego structures, particularly the defensive ones.

When there is objective understanding of the Will Essence, we find that trying, effort, control and so on, are antithetical to the presence of the real Will. Real Will is an implicit confidence that the organism will function correctly. This allows the attitude of surrender, which brings about the manifestation of the Merging Essence. So we see that the loss of Will, resulting in effort and willfulness, impedes the smooth functioning of autonomic regulation.

This in turn disturbs the capacity for functioning in the world. There is no sense of inner support, or confidence in one's capacities. The final result is a deep sense of inadequacy, of not being able to function in the world as an integrated and mature individual. It is illuminating to see the organic, multileveled interconnections in the functioning of the various essential aspects. Essence is not only the ultimate ground of human existence, it also governs our functioning.

Generally speaking, women have more difficulty with this aspect than men, because its characteristics are culturally associated with masculinity. The generally held belief is that to have Will is to be masculine. And since the characteristics of the Merging Essence are associated culturally with femininity (mostly through the mothering function), they tend, more than men, to resolve the rapprochement conflict by abandoning the Will for the Merging. It is interesting to see women pushing away their Will, even when they experience it, because its realization means often to them the end of the possibility for marriage, child bearing and the like. The tendency is to project the Will aspect onto the man. This contributes to their oedipal situation with the father, which develops into the fantasy of marrying Prince Charming. They are often contented to have the support of a man. They acquire Will, in other words, by marrying Prince Charming, who personifies Will. This way, as the fantasy goes, they attain both Will and Merging, both support and love, both father and mother.

We see here that the tendency for women to be dependent is based, partly, on the cultural myth that Will is a masculine quality. Of course, trying to have Will by adopting masculine qualities does not work; Will is much more subtle and profound than any character quality. Our clinical observation is that realizing the Will actually leads to the integration of one's genitals in a healthy and realistic body image and sensation, and hence contributes to gender identity. It makes the man masculine and the woman feminine.

We will discuss now in some detail the process of dealing with the rapprochement conflict in a way that leads to the realization of real gender identity, in the case of a young woman, Lucy, who started her work with the author when she was in her late twenties. She is good-looking, healthy, and usually dresses well. She is successful in attracting men for sexual and love relations, but not in keeping the relations for any appreciable length of time. She did have a relationship with a man for several years, but was mostly dissatisfied in it.

Her main neurotic difficulty is the occasional occurrence of anxiety attacks. She was suffering from several phobias, which were situational, so she experienced them as anxiety attacks. Exploring the phobias revealed several kinds of emptiness, which were associated with fears of disintegration, disappearing, weakness, inadequacy, disorientation and falling.

At some point she broke up with her boyfriend, after she realized she did not respect him. This started several short-lived relationships that revealed the stance she takes with men. It turned out she is frequently hard, aggressive and sometimes castrating towards them. This revealed her masculine identification with her father, which she believed she needed to be able to take care of herself in the world. Seeing through such identifications brought about more anxiety attacks, and more persistent feelings of emptiness.

This showed how she projected her Power, Strength and Will on her father. Thus she could feel safe either by being with a man whom she could respect, which meant he reminded her of her father, or by identifying with his masculine qualities. The loss of either always led to anxiety attacks and a sense of emptiness. In time, seeing that she merely projected such qualities on her father, that he was actually a cold and dry person, and was not really loving or soft towards her, led to her feeling like an empty shell, powerless and with no self.

This started some negative feelings in relations with some of her girlfriends, which led to her exploring her relationship to her mother, whom she always felt that she hated. This led to her having to explore her sexuality, feeling longing, emptiness, hatred and hurt in her

306 genitals. She realized she was terrified of experiencing pleasure in her pelvis, because it revealed all these painful feelings about her sexuality. She finally realized she had all these feelings because she felt she was not accepted as a female, so she unconsciously rejected her gender, as part of rejecting her mother, and adopted masculine identifications.

Rejecting her femaleness meant also cutting herself off from her essential qualities of Power, Strength and Will, although she believed she had them by identifying with her cold and rigid father. Being cut off from her own essential resources turned her into an empty shell of identifications, the loss of which always produced intense anxiety and emptiness.

These revelations led to her feeling the deep longing for the sweet merging with mother. In her private teaching sessions fantasies of merging with women and sucking on women's breasts, and feelings of missing her mother, started emerging. At this time she started dating a man whom she felt loved her. This brought up much sadness and hurt.

In one private session, she reported feelings of wanting to be pregnant. She even reported lactating. During the session we explored some tension in her belly, which led her to experiencing the fullness of the Personal Essence in the belly, which felt to her like being pregnant. This led to feeling sweetness and contact at the same time. This produced sucking motions in the mouth, which resulted in the experience of the essential aspect of Nourishment, which is described in the following chapter.

The next session she reported experiencing the Strength and Personal aspects of Essence, which made her feel both guilt and deficiency about feeling separate. Exploring the deficiency led to the experience of absence of the sense of support and confidence in being herself. This revealed a big emptiness in pelvis and belly. She felt she was weak and empty because she was a girl. She believed she could not have Will if she was female like her mother, but she felt guilty about being separate from her. This exploration progressed to the experience of the arising of the essential Will in the solar plexus.

The following is her report of a group session, right after the private session in which she experienced Will:

Saturday night when I meditated I felt as if my body was shooting upwards at a very fast speed. I have felt this feeling before but I had always stopped it because of fear. This time I let it happen. I felt an explosion in my head and then a rush of a tingling sensation ran down my body to my feet and my hands. Then there was a feeling of stillness and calmness that I have never experienced before. For the first time meditation seemed like it lasted only a few minutes. My body felt totally relaxed and comfortable.

Then a burning sensation started inside the hole in my genitals that I had experienced earlier that day in our private session. The burning spread through to my belly and my back. My belly felt round, soft, and full. I felt two burning points on either side of my belly which turned to two balls of fire as I talked to you. I knew them to be my ovaries. I felt pulsing sensations all through my genitals and belly. I felt as if I could almost feel my vagina.

Then I felt fear and you asked me what the fear was about. My first thought was that every one now knew that I am a girl and they would reject me. Then the fear turned to joy. I felt very proud and excited that I am a girl. I had a feeling of being loveable, sweet and very soft. I felt a sense of incredible freedom.

Today I keep feeling like I want to yell out to the world that I am a girl. I feel real proud of it. Also, today I felt so much love and warmth towards you and I felt like you knew that I felt that way.

It is clear in Lucy's case that both the Personal Essence and the Will Essence are needed for establishing gender identity, the integration of one's genitals into one's personal identity. We also see here the importance of the rapprochement conflict for gender identity. Lucy partially resolved the issue of gender identity in childhood by believing she was a female, but she actually rejected her feminine parts and idealized the masculine organ, culminating in the unconscious fantasy of having a penis. Although she idealized men because of her projection of Will on her father, she tried to castrate them. She could not experience her femininity in a pleasurable and proud way until she was able to undo this projection. She had to work through the rapprochement conflict between Merging and Will before it became possible for her to own her genitals. And this did not happen until they were integrated into her sense of herself as the Personal Essence, the fullness she experienced in her belly.

308   We find that in both men and women Will and Personal Essence are needed for gender identity. The Will leads to accepting one's genitals, and having confidence in them. The Personal Essence makes them an inseparable part of who one is. The significance of such deep integration for personal functioning, especially sexual functioning, is obvious. One's personal life becomes richer and more fulfilled, and one's relationships attain a new depth of pleasure.

PART III

PERSONAL ESSENCE
AND
ESSENTIAL ASPECTS

F or an essential aspect to be realized means for it to become permanently integrated; that is, it is always present when its mode of consciousness is what is objectively required by the situation. So it is not necessarily present all the time, but is present whenever it is objectively needed.

The realization of the Personal Essence is the same as the permanent attainment of the state of the essential person. One is present as the fullness of the Personal Essence whenever one is existing or functioning as a person. This is different from the attainment of ego individuality, where it becomes the conscious experience all the time. On the essential level one is present as the aspect, or aspects, required by the objective situation. One does not decide or determine his state of presence, for the mind is not able to function in such a complete and organic fashion as to be able to make such a determination.

The incapacity to be present in the objectively-required essential state is due only to the presence of conflicts around the state. The

309

310   conflicts around any essential aspect make it difficult for the individual to allow its presence. When it does become present in spite of issues, then these issues become apparent to one's consciousness.

The conflicts can be due to the lack of understanding of some dimensions of Being, but this understanding is usually unavailable due to the presence of emotional issues. Some teachings make it sound as if one lets go of ego, and then Being starts unfolding. The implication is that the development that occurs on the Being level requires only existential understanding. This is definitely not accurate; every development or unfoldment of a new dimension of Being involves the understanding of certain emotional issues. So the unfoldment of Being cannot be separated from the progressive understanding of, and detachment from, some ego identification systems. The deepest and most subtle functionings of ego are usually not conscious in the beginning student, and include aspects of his existence that he firmly believes are objective and immutable.

In the Diamond Approach, self-realization involves the complete realization of all aspects of Being. Each aspect manifests, its issues are understood, and it finally becomes a permanent attainment, as segments of the ego are abandoned. It is a lengthy, deep process, rich with surprises, full of difficulties of all kinds, and replete with color and significance.

The essential aspects are not sought after, but are allowed to emerge on their own. One merely lives fully, in close contact with one's personal experience, but is continually and deeply curious about, and open to, reality. One's life is governed by the love of truth, and understanding is experienced as inseparable and indistinguishable from the unfoldment of one's potential. The emergence of Essence in its aspects can be seen as due to interest in understanding oneself and one's reality. But Essence can equally be seen as emerging on its own, in response to life situations, and thus influencing one's consciousness, as it approaches from the depths. As each aspect of Essence pushes towards consciousness it naturally confronts the identification systems that were developed to bury it and to emulate it. It exposes this segment of the personality, making it feel ego alien (contrary to one's sense of who one is), and bringing about an objective understanding of that part of the personality. This understanding is the truth that is absorbed, which leads to the conscious emergence of the particular aspect.

The Personal Essence is central partly because its realization requires the realization of all aspects. It also requires that its relation to each aspect is worked out and objectively understood. We have explored its relationship to some of the aspects in the previous part. Its realization can be considered from the perspective of ego development, as in our discussion of its significance in the separation-individuation process. Its relation to the other essential aspects can be looked at from this perspective, which clearly delineates the significance of each aspect in its realization.

Alternately, one can look at the process as the realization of the Personal Essence and its relation to all other aspects. In this context, object relations theory, especially its description of the separation-individuation process, can be useful. For instance, the realization of the Essential Self can be aided by the understanding provided by the Self Psychology of Heinz Kohut. Some of the aspects cannot be understood from the perspective of any system of modern psychology, as, for instance, the aspects of Consciousness and Impeccability.

We have discussed so far the relation of the Personal Essence to a few essential aspects, by considering the issues of separation and individuation. We have followed the logic of the understanding more than the actual sequence in the process of realization. We will now consider its relation to some of the other aspects. We will do this only briefly for each aspect, except for a few, because although all the aspects are significant, with their own perspectives and issues, to discuss everything in detail is beyond the scope of this book. For additional discussion of these aspects, see our book: *Diamond Heart: Book One—Elements of the Real in Man*.

1. *Compassion:* This is the aspect of loving kindness that is needed to experience and accept one's hurts and wounds, without defense and without resentment. One cannot have an objective understanding about anyone if there is no Compassion. When there is Compassion it becomes possible to experience one's deep wounds, an experience which readily leads to the aspects related to these wounds. Each time an aspect is buried there results a deep wound in the psyche, and the experience and acceptance of this wound is indispensable for the emergence of the buried aspect.

Compassion is usually recognized in its manifestations such as consideration, regard, concern, sympathy, empathy, warmth and the like.

312   However, it is a mode of consciousness, a presence of Being, in a certain differentiated form.

Its real significance is not exactly to remove suffering, but to lead to the truth by providing the capacity to tolerate suffering. This increased tolerance for emotional suffering gives the individual the ability to refrain from ego defenses. This allows one to look objectively at one's experience, which facilitates its metabolism. It eliminates suffering in a more ultimate and fundamental sense, by allowing the ability to see the deeper causes of suffering.

Also, the increased tolerance and acceptance of experience allows one to just be, instead of trying to manipulate. This allows both objective understanding and personal presence. To be who one is is a compassionate act. It is compassionate towards oneself and towards all others.

2. *Will:* One cannot be the Personal Essence, and function from its perspective, if there is an unconscious state of castration. On the other hand, the realization of Will means the cessation of ego activity. So Will is basically the support to be. When there is no Will there is bound to be fear, which can be experienced as a sensation of falling endlessly. Or there might be tension in the body against this sense of "falling." When Will is present, and there is no identification with the ego individuality, then one is naturally the Personal Essence.

3. *Strength:* The right hand of Essence, related by the Sufis to the "rouh," spirit. It is the energy, the drive, the force, the élan vital, necessary for the realization and development of the Personal Essence. It is the passionate involvement in the process of understanding, the discriminating force behind the process of evolution. It is what gives the heart the courage to embark and continue on the journey of discovery.

4. *Joy:* The force and consciousness behind curiosity. This is a very subtle aspect to understand, and a very difficult state to realize.

It is, just as Freud thought, the happiness that results from wish fulfillment. Whenever there is an unfulfilled wish Joy closes and disappears. This means that it becomes permanently realized only when there are no unconscious wishes. So, more objectively speaking, Joy manifests when there is fulfillment. But there is no lasting fulfillment as long as there is any aspect of Being not realized.

One cannot seek happiness, for it is the result of realizing the Truth. The personality, which has security and pleasure as its aims, cannot be happy. Pursuing pleasure or safety will entail covering up any unpleasant or frightening truths. This automatically closes Joy. For Joy is the radiance of the heart when Truth is appreciated.

One of the main emotional issues that blocks Joy is the rapprochement conflict. One can be happy for a short time exercising one's autonomous functions in the experience of the Personal Essence. But then sadness returns, for one misses the Merging love. One has one or the other but not both. And when one is in the merged state, one can be happy only for a short time, for one will shortly be sad for not being present as who one is. When the rapprochement conflict is resolved, and both the Personal Essence and the Merging Essence are present, then the radiant sun of Joy will fill the heart with its lightness and merriment.

The state of Joy is that of lightness, delight, enjoyment, happiness and sweetness. One becomes a radiance, a playfulness, a carefree presence. One delights in reality. One sees life as a light and playful adventure. Every moment is a source of singular Joy, for it is the very presence of the Truth. One realizes that Joy is the radiance of Love, which is the breath of Truth.

5. *Peace:* It is not an emotional state or merely the absence of conflict; it is rather the presence of stillness, which is an aspect of Essence. It is the presence of Being as absolute stillness and calmness. This stillness is not experienced as dull or vague, but as an exquisitely alive kind of consciousness.

Peace involves the cessation of the torturous ego activity, with its hopes, desires, efforts and resistances. That is why it is often equated with ego death. Peace is actually both death and life in the same consciousness. One learns that death is nonexistent on the Being level. More accurately, one learns that death, in terms of consciousness, is really nothing but an aspect of Being. The associations that most of us have with death are actually related to an aspect of Being which we call Death Space. By following these associations one can experience a certain state that feels like death, but which is actually a certain black spaciousness [see our book *The Void*]. Also, from the perspective of boundless and nondifferentiated Being physical death is seen as a transformation of form, and not as ultimate in the way most people think of it. What most people think of as death is actually the presence of the essential aspect of Death Space. Also, the aspect of

314 Peace has experiential qualities similar to that of Death Space, such as stillness and silence.

The issues of this aspect are deep and difficult. Its realization requires that one deal with one's own hatred. It also means dealing with the primitive defense of ego splitting. It involves dealing with issues of power, both constructive and destructive.

When this happens, Peace descends on the consciousness. The life of the Personal Essence is the life of Peace. We have discussed the example of Jesus of Nazareth as an embodiment of the Personal Essence, and now we can make the connection that his message, as it is known, is that of Peace.

The relation of Peace to the Personal Essence becomes most clear when the issues of splitting, hatred and power are resolved. Then one realizes that this aspect, Peace, is also Personal Power, the power of Being. These issues are very deep, and most people are not willing to confront them. Students usually do not resolve such issues until they are quite deep in the process of inner realization.

This aspect also manifests as the capacity of intuition, of paramount importance for understanding. It is connected to the inner capacities that are related to extra-sensory perception.

The above five aspects make up the Sufi system of the "lataif," or subtleties. This system is also found in esoteric Christianity and some forms of alchemy. They are connected to specific locations in the human body, regarded as centers for their operation or concentration. The Sufis see them as elements of subtle consciousness, or organs of perception. Their activation is taken to be an important part of the Sufi work of inner realization.

> The human being is stated, in Sufi presentation, to contain five elements of the "relative" and five of the "absolute." Five, that is, which belong to secondary things, referred to as The World, and five which are beyond limitation of dimensions, and which refer to the different manifestations of the various levels of consciousness beyond ordinarily recognizable physics.
>
> There are said to be five centres of spiritual perception, corresponding to these ranges of experience. They are conceived of as having physical locations in the human body.
>
> These Five Subtleties (*Lataif-i-Khamsa*) do not exist literally. They are located in the body because the postures of extending attention to these areas are held to orientate

the mind towards higher understanding and illumination.
[Idries Shah, *A Perfumed Scorpion*, p. 89]

6. *Consciousness:* This is another aspect that is sometimes regarded as a part of the lataif system. It is the presence of Being as pure and undifferentiated consciousness. It is consciousness of consciousness; as a delicate, fine, restful kind of presence. It is the capacity for inner absorption; for contemplating one's consciousness, by being absorbed in it. It is connected with the state sometimes called samadhi, because there is no mental activity or agitation in it.

The experience is of a delicious kind of restfulness, at all levels of the organism. Anyone who has taken morphine for pain knows the delicious and pleasurable kind of restfulness, almost like a numbness, as the drug begins to take effect. This is close in feeling to the state of pure Consciousness.

The particular issues related to Consciousness are those of ego agitation and the affect of negative merging. This ego state manifests in the mind as worry, in the heart as guilt, and in the body as attachment. All these reflect the ego state of desiring, which is the specific barrier against this aspect. When one goes deeply into these ego states, one realizes that they are different manifestations of the state of contraction itself, of negative-merging affect, and also that they are differentiated emotional expressions of the undifferentiated state of negative merging.

This aspect's relationship to the Personal Essence is reflected in its effect on ego boundaries. The pure aspect of Consciousness is ultimately what dissolves the partitions between the various manifestations of consciousness. So it contributes to the dissolution of the boundaries of the separate individuality of ego. When this happens one realizes that one can be a person without the need for ego boundaries. This precipitates the experience of the Personal Essence.

This can happen in the reverse direction. The ego will not easily let go of its boundaries, and hence will resist this aspect, because it believes it will be the end of being a person. However, the presence of the Personal Essence makes it easier for the ego to let go, for it now knows that one can be a person without the presence of its permanent boundaries. This letting go is the relaxation of contraction, the melting away of the affects of negative merging, which is the manifestation of the aspect of Consciousness.

316 The experience then is of oneself as an infinite and boundless consciousness, like a clear and vast blue sky. We will explore this issue more completely in a later chapter.

7. *Space:* This is the aspect that is the open dimension of the mind, which is its most inner nature. It is the experience of Being as a vast, clear and empty space. It is not an emptiness in the sense of lack, of something missing. It is the presence of Space; clear, light and immaculate. We have devoted a book, *The Void*, to this aspect. In that book, we develop the understanding that ego development is not only a matter of building mental structure, but that, because Space is the ontologic nature of the mind, these structures are built in the emptiness of Space. So ego structures are seen as structuralization of Space, building content in it instead of letting it be in its purity. This leads to the loss of this aspect.

The particular issue for this aspect is the presence of the self-image itself. When one can let go of one's self-image Space arises. Space becomes the agent that is needed for eliminating any self-image, which is necessary for the realization of the Personal Essence. In other words, Space dissolves the self-image. The individuality of the ego, being based on the self-image, loses its defining boundaries, which leads to the emergence of the Personal Essence. The sense of self of the ego, which is dependent on the self-image, loses the mental content that defines it, which leads to the manifestation of the Essential Self.

These three aspects, Space, Personal Essence and Essential Self, are the most central aspects of Essence. In the process of inner realization they, in some sense, replace the self-image, the separate individuality of ego and the sense of self of ego, respectively. Most traditional spiritual teachings can be grouped according to which of these three aspects they emphasize. Buddhism emphasizes Space, the prophetic tradition emphasizes the Personal Essence, and most of the Hindu systems emphasize the Essential Self, which they term the "atman."

The aspect of Space is related to the Personal Essence in yet another, more specific way. It is one of the aspects needed for an important part of the process of psychic metabolism, i.e., that of elimination.

We have seen that for metabolism to proceed to its completion, which is absorption, the false in any experience must first be eliminated. The greatest falsity, in any identification system, is the

central belief that the image defines who one is. The content of iden- 317
tification systems is either part of an image, or used to build and fixate
an image. So the elimination of image amounts to dissolving all of
what is false in the mind. The truth contained in the mind becomes
absorbed into Being, and does not remain as an image, which is a
mental content. And since Space is what dissolves, or what accompanies the dissolution of, any image, then it can be regarded as the
aspect needed for elimination.

When an image is eliminated the mind becomes empty (of its content), clear, spacious and light. This is the experience of Space, mind
with no content, the nature of the mind. The dullness of mental content dissipates as the lightness and clarity of Space penetrates it.

This is obviously a significant step if there is going to be any fundamental change or transformation. There is no transformation, but
only modification, if the image remains. This distinction is what differentiates therapy and conversion from essential realization. The latter is more of the nature of a metamorphosis; existence based on
image dies and the life of Being is born. This cannot happen without
the aspect of Space.

8. *Acceptance:* This aspect is extremely subtle to experience. Its
nature is the exact opposite of that of ego. Ego, of its very nature, has
a rejecting attitude. Its defenses are based on the rejection of parts of
experience. Its structure is never devoid of defense, which is rejection.
The very presence of identification systems implies a subtle rejection
of Being.

This means that no part of ego is capable of accepting. The individuality of ego is incapable of Acceptance, because its very existence
depends on a subtle attitude of rejection. Ego can only cease rejecting, but it cannot accept. The complete cessation of rejection is the
absence of all defense and resistance. This precipitates the aspect of
Acceptance.

Thus Acceptance involves the cessation of ego, or of a segment of
its structure. We see here the intimate relationship between the aspect
of Acceptance and the process of absorption. Acceptance is really
necessary for absorption to occur, for absorption cannot proceed if
there is still resistance, which is rejection.

The word acceptance is somewhat misleading, for the aspect is not
an active attitude; there is no activity of acceptance. It is a presence of

318   Being when there is no attitude of either "no" or "yes." A "yes" could mean a prejudice, a certain point of view. But this aspect does not have any attitude. It is a pure, delicate and gentle presence, of utmost humility and exquisite refinement. It is like a gentle rain, that brings freshness and life. Most individuals, when they experience it, refer to it as blessings.

9. *Forgiveness:* This is the complete letting go of the past, and the full embracing of·the new. It is a freshness, an openness, a new beginning.

When there is no Forgiveness, there is an attachment to what has happened in the past. The memory of the past determines what one experiences in the present, and disposes the future towards certain patterns. This eliminates the possibility of essential experience, for Essence is Being, and Being is the Now.

We are briefly mentioning some of the subtle aspects like Acceptance and Forgiveness partly to show that they are not emotional states. They are not ego states, for ego is, in its very nature, a rejection of the present and a holding on to the past. All these aspects are necessary for the realization of the Personal Essence.

Chapter Twenty-Five

The Mother Aspects of Essence

There are certain essential aspects which are consistently connected in the minds of students with the mother or her image. Our observation is that in the unconscious these aspects cannot be separated from one's experience of the good mother. This is because they were experienced mostly in conjunction with good merging or good object relations with one's mother in infancy. So they are associated with the good mother or with closeness to her. It becomes almost impossible for most individuals to imagine experiencing these parts of one's Being except in intimate physical contact or similar contexts.

We have already discussed one of these aspects, the Merging Essence. In the unconscious, this aspect is not only related to the good mother, but is experienced as the good mother herself. The basis of this identification, which is actually a projection, is the good mother of symbiosis, who is equated with the good merged experience. The Merging Essence-mother is related to as the source of the other aspects of this group. Thus one of the main issues about each one of these aspects is the belief that they cannot exist without the Merging Essence, i.e., without a merged kind of relationship or contact.

Some of these aspects are the Platonic forms of Love, Value, Nourishment, Pleasure, Fulfillment, Satisfaction, Contentment, and Gratitude. These are heart qualities, or forms of love, that are differentiated aspects of Being, not emotional or ego states. These aspects, plus the Merging Essence, constitute the essential heart,

320   which the unconscious cannot differentiate from the gratifying experience with mother.

Separation and individuation often seems to threaten the ego individuality with the loss of these delicious states of Being, because of their connection to the good mother of symbiosis, while in fact they are aspects of Being, part of the human potential. They cannot be completely integrated until they are dissociated from past experience with one's mother. We will discuss three of these sweet and gratifying qualities.

The first quality is *Value*. Its reflection on the emotional level is usually experienced as self-esteem. Self-esteem is always seen as a result, either of some performance, accomplishment, success or excellence. Value, on the other hand, is a state of Being. Like other states of Being, it is not a result of anything, but is an existence. One experiences oneself not as having Value but as being Value itself. One's presence is Value: full, pleasurable, sweet and quite satisfying. The main issues around this quality are those of narcissism. Value arises when one appreciates oneself, when one values one's own personal presence.

It is intimately connected to the Personal Essence, as if it were the specific affect that describes it. Many times the Personal Essence is born from within the state of Value, so it is the expression of the Value of Being. Its presence allows one to cease seeking external appreciation and recognition, and thus to let go of some related identifications. The objective understanding of Value is that ultimately Being itself is the self-existing Value, and all human values are reflections of it.

The second quality is *Love*. Object relations theory contends that object love, which is love for a separate and differentiated human person, does not develop until object constancy is attained. In fact, it is part of the definition of object constancy that when it is achieved the individual has the capacity to love another as an individual in his or her own right.

According to our perception, Love as a state of the essential Being exists from the beginning of life. Babies exist in this state of Being a great deal of the time. It is this state that we are perceiving when we see a baby as cute and adorable. This aspect is experienced as a gentle and soft presence, that feels fluffy, pure and sweet. One feels the affect of "liking," of finding pleasure in something or somebody.

The development that is called "object love" in object relations theory is simply the channeling of this state by restricting it to one human object. In other words, one directs this aspect of one's Being to a differentiated other. At the beginning this state exists as the child's beingness. He feels Love regardless of who or what is there. It is not directed to anything or anybody; it is a state of Being.

As the individuality develops this state becomes restricted, or rather conditioned, so that it becomes available only according to the conditions of the particular ego structure. The final result is that the child can feel love only for certain individuals, and under certain safe circumstances.

This can be called the development of the capacity for object love, but it is actually more of a loss than a gain. One gains the capacity to direct Love to real human objects, but loses the freedom to experience it independently of one's personal history.

We can understand what object love is on the essential level when we remember that ego development is a prelude to the realization of the Personal Essence. So essential (real) object love can be realized when we understand the relation between the Personal Essence and this aspect of Love. What happens is that when the Personal Essence is present with the Love one feels not only Love, but personal Love. This is the real object love, except that with the Personal Essence this capacity is not restricted or conditioned by one's particular ego structure. Since the Personal Essence is independent of past object relations, it actualizes the capacity for personal love that is free from the past.

The person who has developed the Personal Essence experiences personal love not according to his experience of the past, but according to the objective requirements of the particular situation. So he can experience it towards any living being, in any situation, if that is what is objectively needed. The state of Love, which was not personal in early childhood, now has the added dimension of the personal element. So it is certainly a development, a gain. The following report, by Pamela, whom we mentioned before in relation to the Merging aspect, shows some of the connections between Love, the Personal Essence and the belief that the Merging Essence is its source:

> My experience of last night's work was to discover more what being separate means to me. My experience of separation seems to mean being on my own, having no requirement of me, being able to say "no" to anyone. Separate is

me with me, no commitment or particular behavior required. And my separateness is precious to me. Me being
separate feels precious to me and I do not want to lose
myself again like I did when I was small. My experiences
recently have felt like separation means fulfillment. I do not
need anyone or want anyone for this fulfillment, just me. I
feel like me with myself is the sweetest, most warm and
loving feeling I have felt in my life. I feel a warmth in my
heart that makes my chest burn. My head feels like liquid
tears, and as if these tears descend to my heart. I feel a
warmth and a glow like "pink rain" and "golden nectar." I
feel sweet and warm and full inside—fulfilled.

When I think or feel desire for someone else, I feel
threatened and scared. I want to recede, get small and disappear, so that no one will see me or try to influence me,
try to get me to do what they want instead of what I want.
My desire to merge with someone else makes me feel
scared, angry, and resistant. I feel afraid they will try to
take me away from myself. I feel I want to say "no" to
them and "yes" to myself. I want to keep myself and my
preciousness at all costs.

In the past, in order to love my parents I had to surrender to them; become someone different from me, in order
to have their love. Now I love again and feel resistant to
give up myself. I see I need to trust the part of me which
seeks itself: Essence, Love and Merging with separateness.
This I feel will take some time.

We see here that although Pamela had developed object love, and
was able to love her parents, she had to do so by renouncing her Personal Essence, which is the preciousness that now she wants to keep
at all costs. The Personal Essence allows her to feel personal love with
no restrictions.

We also see in Pamela's report how she came to feel this personal
love, now towards herself, in conjunction with the Merging Essence.
First she had to experience the Merging Essence as part of her, and
thus separate it from the good mother image. Her usual associations
with her mother are negative, and that is why she is so afraid of
losing her precious separateness if she desires merging. She had always believed that she could not feel fulfilled unless she were loved
by somebody who wanted her, that is, unless there were merging
and Love. In this new experience of herself she actually realizes the
aspect of Fulfillment, the "nectar," when she experiences the Merging

Essence and the Love Essence, in conjunction with the Personal Essence.

She still has much more work to do to integrate the capacity for personal love, for she still associates Love with the merging feeling. Usually the Love aspect appears with the Personal Essence, when one finally loves oneself for who one is, and not for anything else. It is when one experiences something like:

> I am who I am. What I have is good and valuable, although not perfect. I do not need to prove myself, I do not need to get recognition or Love from outside of me. My Being itself is loveable.

The third aspect is *Nourishment*. This aspect of Being is equivalent to mother's milk on the physical level. Its issues are those of the oral stage; of nursing and weaning, of oral gratification and frustration. Its relationship to the Personal Essence is equivalent to the relationship of mother's milk to the infant—it is the essential nourishment needed for the realization and development of the Personal Essence. It is the material needed for building the substance of the Personal Essence. That is why the longing for this aspect usually starts right after experiencing the Personal Essence.

It is no wonder, then, that it is associated with the mother's image and with the symbiotic connection with her. The specific identification system that must be metabolized to realize this aspect is mother's breast, which is probably the first image of the object. Jacobson writes about this primitive part object image:

> It is the combined oral-visual experience of the breast—or primal cavity, respectively (Spitz, 1955)—that not only equates the mother with the breast but turns the latter into the first image of the gratifying mother. [Edith Jacobson, *The Self and the Object World*, p. 35]

Thus to permanently realize this aspect one must deal with the deepest structures of the internalized mother's image. This is a very deep and subtle process, which ultimately exposes the deepest object relations, such as the sense of being a hungry mouth relating to the world as a breast. The deficiency relating to the loss of this aspect always feels like a big hunger, or an empty stomach. A student writes of this experience: "I went into the emptiness, which felt like a huge hungry stomach."

324   The hunger can manifest as the need to be fed by the world, or for
success, recognition, money, food, love and so on. This hunger under-
lies many cases of drug addiction and compulsive smoking. One such
case is of a married woman, Jacqueline, satisfied in her marriage and
holding a professional position. She has had an alcohol problem that is
by this time very much under control. She asks in one group meeting
about her need for success, and its relation to her previous alcoholism.
Discussion. finally leads to a longing for a sweet nurturing love, a
nourishing fullness, a longing that was accompanied by a sense of
emptiness in her mouth and throat. By staying with the emptiness and
hunger she starts feeling a flow of sweetness down her throat that
makes her feel gratified. She describes part of her experience this way:

> I see that I can have what I really want. I never knew con-
> sciously that I wanted sweetness regularly. I thought I wan-
> ted success, etc. I need to listen more to that part of me
> that knows what I really wanted. As you talked I realized
> that what I also deeply want is some place to rest my
> head—I felt real sad—something sweet regularly, a place
> to rest my head—they seem so simple, yet what a treasure
> to me. I think I used to drink large quantities of wine to
> get back that feeling. When you talked to somebody else
> in the group I felt the sweetness in my chest like an in-
> finite pool, which can heal what is sour in me.

This Nourishment, or Milk Essence, is a state of Being, and is always available to the human being. But because it becomes associated with the mother's physical milk it becomes almost impossible
to experience. Every individual has a deep longing for this nurturing
presence, but it is not allowed into consciousness, because one is
now an adult. One student writes when he feels the deep longing:
"When I experienced the emptiness of not having my mother's nurturing, I seemed to be faced with staying a child or being an adult,"
meaning that as an adult he cannot take the need for Milk seriously,
because one can have it only as a baby.

So the longing for this aspect is usually deeply repressed because
the adult individual feels it is too late to have mother's milk. But this
aspect is part of oneself; it can be realized, and it is needed for complete autonomy, which is the Personal Essence.

Fairbairn so thoroughly understood the centrality of the oral object
relation between the mouth and the breast that he took it to be the

core of ego structure. He saw difficulties at this stage of ego development as the main genetic cause of schizoid manifestations, which he
considered to be the deepest structural difficulties for the ego. He
wrote in 1940:

> The ego of the infant may be described as above all a
> "mouth ego" . . . The first social relationship established by
> the individual is that between himself and his mother; and
> the focus of this relationship is the suckling situation, in
> which his mother's breast provides the focal point of his
> libidinal object, and his mouth the focal point of his own
> libidinal attitude. [W. Ronald D. Fairbairn, *Psychoanalytic
> Studies of the Personality*, pp.10-11]

In another part of the same paper he wrote:

> The child's oral relationship with his mother in the situa-
> tion of suckling represents his first experience of a love re-
> lationship, and is, therefore, the foundation upon which all
> his future relationships with love objects are based. It also
> represents his first experience of a social relationship; and
> it therefore forms the basis of his subsequent attitude to
> society. [*Ibid.*, pp. 24-25]

All this substantiates our understanding of the importance of the
Nourishment aspect for the development of the Personal Essence, the
true individuation. If it were not for the fact that Nourishment exists
on the Being level, and hence its presence is independent of age, the
development of the Personal Essence would be impossible for people
who were inadequately nourished in childhood.

Being is a magnificent reality. It has all that a human being needs to
grow and develop. It does not matter what one missed in childhood.
If one looks within, and is genuinely interested in the truth, one finds
treasures beyond imagination. Only purely physical needs cannot be
fulfilled with Essence. Any need that is emotional, mental, spiritual or
moral, can be completely fulfilled by the richness of Being.

The aspect of Nourishment is a kind of love; a gentle, delicate and
lightly sweet presence. It has a warm sense of nurturance, and a
unique quality of stilling inner hunger. It is closely allied to the process
of metabolism, important for the realization and development of the
Personal Essence. It is the food absorbed from personal experience.

When this aspect is present it becomes easy to see what is of real
value in any experience or activity of life. One can discern what will

326   lead to growth and development, and what must be discarded. It also means that one can absorb the nutrient in any personal experience; in other words, the realization of this aspect implies that the individual can now absorb true Nourishment. When there are conflicts about this aspect then it becomes difficult to absorb the truth in experience; for one has difficulty in taking in true Nourishment.

The absorption of experience is equivalent to the feeding of the Personal Essence. The more one gains from true experience, the more the presence of the Personal Essence grows, and attains more capacities, and a greater maturity.

It might seem to the reader by now that the emotional issues in essential realization are all related to one's relationship to one's mother in early life. This impression will be remedied shortly. But it is important to note that the early relationship with the mother is the most important factor in the development of the ego structure, which is the relevant material in regaining one's identity with Being. The relationship with father becomes more important later in ego development, when there is enough separation from mother.

Chapter Twenty-Six

The Father Aspects of Essence

T he father is important to the child as a person separate and different from mother. His presence aids the child's differentiation and separation from mother. Most children experience the availability of the father as a support for them to differentiate and separate from the mother in early childhood. Mahler writes about this point:

> The child's desire for expanded autonomy not only found expression in negativism toward mother and others, but also led to an active extension of the mother-child world: *primarily, to include father.* [Margaret S. Mahler et al., *The Psychological Birth of the Human Infant*, p. 91]

So the father becomes important for support of individuation, for guidance in the world outside that of mother, for protection, and for identification. This makes him the focus of the projection of a group of essential aspects. These aspects, we have observed, are always associated with father or with the relationship to him. Students consistently report these aspects to be associated with masculinity or maleness. They are very different, in terms of experience, from those of the mother group. One might gain an intuitive sense of this difference by learning that the mother group is represented by the color gold, the father group by the color white or silver.

The Father aspects include Universal Will, Diamond Guidance, Intelligence, and most of the boundless aspects of Being. These aspects usually do not manifest until later in the process of essential realization.

327

328   Some aspects are associated with both father and mother, depending on one's specific personal history. Some individuals, for instance, associate Love with father. This usually reflects a more loving relation with father than with mother. When we speak of a father or a mother group of essential aspects we do not imply an absolute differentiation; we are speaking only statistically.

One of these aspects is *Universal Will*. This is different from the aspect of Will already discussed. That aspect is a personal Will, one's own inner support, for one's own presence and functioning. Universal Will is the capacity to support others. We use the term "universal" to differentiate it from personal. So a universal aspect is for everyone, and not just for the individual. This differentiation is clearly seen in the essential realm.

Universal Will creates a sense of immense strength and solidity, a confidence in one's capacities in relation to others. Hence, it is quite important for personal relationships. When Universal Will is present the feeling is that one's personal Will is supported by a bigger, more immense and more universal presence. It is quite impossible to appreciate what we mean when we say it is an immense presence, without having the direct experience. It is like feeling one is solid, immense and immovable, like a mountain. There is nothing like it in ego states.

Universal Will is usually projected on the father, and becomes associated with his image. The issues around it are basically those of father's support for one's own Will. The specific identification system related to it is the identification with father's masculine strength and solidity. The issue is generally different for women, for whom the identification is with a self-image that is receptive to the father's support and solidity.

A second aspect related to the father is *Intelligence*. This label does not do justice to this aspect; it is more like the essence of intelligence, or what enables the mind to be brilliant. It is the aspect of pure intelligence, of luminosity, of brilliance. It gives one the sense of completeness, of protection, of being contained and looked after. Its immediate presence feels so fine that it is the smoothest sensation or consciousness that one can experience; it has an effect of imbuing the mind with a uniquely penetrating quality. At the same time there is a sense of largeness, expansion, immensity and majesty.

The consistent experience of our students is that when they feel a desire for the father, they ultimately find this aspect. So its relation to father is like the relation of the Merging Essence to mother. Thus the father's image is the identification system that covers it up, and replaces it. So realizing it means working through one's relation with one's own father. It is also experienced in relation to father in the religious sense. It is the first aspect encountered that is related to God the Father.

We present the experience of Donna, whom we mentioned before, as she now realizes both the Universal Will and Intelligence. We find her at this juncture dealing with many conflicting feelings towards me: anger, hurt, jealousy, disappointment and deficiency. Dealing with the sense of deficiency results in her experience of personal Will. This then brings about feelings of anger and disappointment in me. Exploring these reveals that they are due to her belief that I know something about her that I am not telling her. This becomes then the feeling that I have something that she does not have, but should have, which she associates with a penis. This makes her feel flattened in her sense of her body. She reports that she had been feeling her body stiff and hard, with a stubbornness; which now she understands as her attempt to make her body into a penis.

This then brings about fear of loss of her relationship with her boyfriend if she owns her Will. She also starts experiencing her recurrent feelings of rivalry and jealousy in relation to some of the women in the group, her feelings that I like them more than her. This centers then on the issue of support from me and from her father. Exploring this issue brings about the emergence of the Intelligence Essence, which she feels as smoothness, but does not yet recognize. It is also interesting that part of her hurt came from her belief that I did not recognize her intelligence, which led to a feeling of deficiency in which she saw herself as being not very smart. Dealing with her father transference on me, her oedipal feelings of wanting father's penis or mine, which is related to having support, finally leads to the emergence of the Universal Will, which she experiences as a dense and solid presence filling all of her body.

In subsequent sessions she started experiencing the Intelligence Essence more and more as she understood her father transference. She liked its presence, especially when she felt it as a very delicate

330   presence. The Personal Essence emerged, and she felt herself, as the Personal Essence, wanting to melt into the brilliance of the father aspect. This brought about the emergence of the Merging Essence in her heart indicating the feeling of union with the brilliance.

Subsequently she recognized the Intelligence aspect and its relation to her father. She was filled with awe when she saw its majestic brilliance, and she asked me if it was God.

This brought about a great happiness, the arising of the aspect of Joy. This did not last long, and she started feeling sad. She found out that she believed she did not measure up to her father, especially after she felt her deep love for the brilliant Essence. This led to more understanding of her relationship to her father, her anger towards him, and so on. This made her feel the presence of the spaciousness of Space, indicating the change in self-image. She then, at some point, in a private teaching session, started feeling the exquisite brilliance showering her with its delicacy and luminosity.

It is interesting that Freud thought that the idea of God the Father is mostly due to the idealization of one's own father. This is clearly partly true, but more fundamental is the archetypal or prototypical relationship between child and father. When this aspect, which we call Brilliancy, is realized, and experienced in relation to the Personal Essence, the experience is of feeling safe, secure and protected. When one finally works through the relationship with the father and Love is experienced, then it becomes possible to experience this aspect with the Personal Essence. Then the relationship between the two aspects becomes the presence of all the heart qualities. Individuals with a religious bent become filled with a deep love for God, and an awe for His majesty.

The realization of this aspect involves the integration of pure Intelligence. One attains the qualities of brilliance in one's work and manifestations. This intelligence is related to the central nervous system. It has the functions of balance and organization and, hence, is important for the inner regulation of the organism.

The third quality associated with the father is *Diamond Guidance*. We have already discussed this aspect, as Diamond Consciousness, in some detail in a previous chapter. It is the aspect of objective consciousness. Its function is objective perception and understanding, functioning primarily through the integration of analysis and synthesis.

It is the guidance for the realization and development of the Personal Essence. So one of its main issues is father's guidance in one's process of separation and individuation. This issue can manifest as conflict in one's relationship to one's father, that led to doubting his guidance, and thus a lack of trust in him. To regain the trust, one must become objective about one's father. This ultimately leads to the perception of splitting of father's image, of seeing him as either all good or all bad. When this splitting is understood and resolved and one becomes objective about the father and his guidance, the true objective guidance is realized. The more one frees one's capacity to trust guidance and to perceive it, the more one trusts the guidance of the Diamond Consciousness.

This aspect, naturally, becomes projected on the teacher, as the guide for the process of inner realization. But this then brings about the father transference, and facilitates its understanding in terms of understanding one's relationship to father, if the teacher is able to undertake the guidance. This leads to the process of separation from the image of father, which becomes experienced as separation from the teacher, culminating in the integration of the Diamond Consciousness.

An example is the case of David, whom we discussed earlier in relation to the experience of the Personal Essence, here dealing with his relationship to me. He feels very ambivalent about me. He feels gratitude and affection, but then starts feeling defensive because he starts remembering his relationship with his father, in which he was not able to be openly affectionate and loving. This then turns into feelings of competition with me and a desire for separation.

Gradually he begins to see the extent of his identification with me, in terms of capacities and expressions. This brings about conflicting feelings; for he feels that his identification is partly an expression of his love, but partly also an expression of lack of independence and identity. He starts feeling rejecting towards the way I work with him, that it does not work for him, and is perhaps not so accurate. As he speaks out his mind about me and the approach I use, he starts seeing the beauty of the approach, but still denies its effectiveness. By being truthful about what he feels, he starts feeling a certain presence in his chest which turns out to be the aspect of Truth. He was not truthful with his father, and their relationship was mostly superficial, so he felt that he got no guidance from him about what is real in him.

332 Being real and truthful with me, although he was expressing doubt and anger, led to him experiencing his own presence as Truth.

This shows him the correctness of my approach in working with him, what I have called the Diamond Approach. He starts feeling a desire to be friends with me. At the same moment he becomes aware of the gentle and subtle presence of the Diamond Guidance in the middle of his forehead. It is interesting to mention here that this aspect is also connected to the need for a real friend who sees and appreciates. who one truly is. In fact, the guide for inner realization, whether inner or external, is referred to by some traditions as the "spiritual friend."

David's identification with me as the father he never had, who guides him in learning to be himself, actually involved an identification with the aspect of Guidance, which I use in my work with him. This then became increasingly his own integration of Guidance, which was decreasingly dependent on the identification. This is a clear example of a change in character structure through what is called in psychoanalysis transmuting internalizations. The difference between internalization and integration of one's own potential disappears when it comes to essential experience, as we see in David's case.

> Don't forget the nut, being so proud of the shell,
> The body has its inward ways,
>
> the five senses. They crack open,
> and the Friend is revealed.
>
> Crack open the Friend, you become
> the All-One.
> [John Moyne and Coleman Barks, *Unseen Rain—Quatrains of Rumi*, p. 19]

The integration of this aspect begins the process of the *development* of the Personal Essence, which starts after its realization. This is the subject of the next part of this book.

There are many aspects that we have not discussed. They are all important on their own, and in their relation to the Personal Essence. Some of these are the aspects of Truth, Reality, Sincerity, Passionate Love, Clarity, Awareness, Death, Extinction and Existence.

The completion of the process of realization of the Personal Essence involves integrating the main aspects related to ego development. This is the simultaneous presence of the Personal Essence, the

Diamond Guidance, the Intelligence Essence and Merging Essence.   333
This reflects, on the psychological level, one's own person, one's own
objective understanding, father-image and mother-image. This is a
very profound state of integration, indicating an expanded state of
autonomy and maturity.

The
DEVELOPMENT
of the
PEARL
BEYOND PRICE

BOOK THREE

The
DEVELOPMENT
of the
PEARL
BEYOND PRICE

BOOK THREE

Table of Contents

PART I

IDENTITY: EGO VERSUS BEING

The realization of the Personal Essence is not the end of its story; in fact, its story does not have an end. It is a continual process of growth and increasing maturity. We divide this process into two major parts: realization and development. Realization means it becomes a permanent personal attainment; the Personal Essence is present whenever its mode of functioning is objectively indicated. One's life becomes rich with the profundity, beauty and joy of essential life.

However, this does not necessarily indicate the complete transformation of ego or the complete disidentification from its structures. At this stage the usual condition is that there is always essential presence, but there is still some identification with ego structures. The individual consciousness is alternately dominated by essential presence and ego individuality. Identity with Essence alternates with identity with ego. One feels there are two parts, in a kind of dialogue—the old, familiar personality with its ego states, and

340   the ever fresh Personal Essence with its essential experience and perception.

The next step in essential realization is the shift of identity from ego to Being. This is a long and arduous process and, in some sense, much more difficult than anything before it. It deals with the deeper, more subtle and more fundamental identification systems, mostly ones that have been ego syntonic until this point. In this process the Personal Essence goes through a change and transformation, a development. So the development of the Personal Essence is not a matter of its being experienced more of the time or more fully; it is rather that the Personal Essence itself goes through a transformation. It grows and develops, attains more qualities, more capacities and wider ranges of experience. It is like the body, which matures and actualizes its potential as it grows. The Personal Essence develops and matures as more experiences are metabolized. The metabolism can be seen, from the inner point of view, as the experiences of essential realization themselves. All aspects go through a process in which they become more closely integrated in the individual consciousness into the Personal Essence.

Chapter Twenty-Seven

The Personalization of Essence

T he realization of the Personal Essence can be seen as the attainment of individuation on the essential level. The consciousness of the individual has by now integrated itself not only as a living presence but also as a *personal* living presence. It can experience itself as a person of Being, instead of only as a person defined by ego identifications. This consciousness can now integrate itself further by integrating the other aspects of Essence into the presence of the Personal Essence.

We discussed in the previous chapter how the relationship of each essential aspect to the Personal Essence is worked out and understood, resulting in the harmonious presence of all aspects with the Personal Essence. This is the first step towards a more complete integration of the aspects. The aspects will become synthesized into the presence of the Personal Essence, and not only be present with it. Each aspect ends up being not only present with, but an indistinguishable part of, the Personal Essence. Then there is no longer a relationship between, but rather an identity of, the Personal Essence and an essential aspect; it becomes an identity, a fusion of the two that results in the metamorphosis of the Personal Essence.

Each aspect becomes so deeply integrated that it is no longer experienced as part of oneself, but *as* oneself. In other words, each aspect becomes absorbed into the Personal Essence. This process is the gradual development of the Personal Essence. It attains the qualities and capacities of each aspect, as the latter is absorbed into it.

342   We refer to this process as the personalization of Essence, because each essential aspect becomes personal as it is integrated and absorbed into the consciousness as a further development of the Personal Essence. Joy becomes a personal Joy, Peace becomes a personal Peace, Truth becomes a personal Truth, and so on. This can be seen in two ways.

One way is that the personalization of an aspect indicates that it is a personal attainment and actualization of that part of one's potential. It becomes recognized as an undifferentiable part of oneself, and not as a state that one experiences once in a while. For instance, the Diamond Consciousness is the capacity for objective understanding and direct insight. At the beginning one has insights once in a while, especially under certain conditions. After this aspect is personalized one permanently attains the capacity for insight and objective understanding. One now uses this capacity whenever it is needed, just as one can use one's legs to walk whenever walking is needed. It is completely part of who one is. It is no longer a state, but an organ of one's organism and consciousness.

The second way we can see this process is from the perspective of the Personal Essence, as its process of development and maturation. In psychological terms, it can be seen as a change in character that coincides with maturation. The issues to be dealt with here are those of identity. The aspect is no longer felt as a state one can experience, but as part of the very substance and nature of who one is. So, because of ego identifications, the individual might find it difficult to tolerate his identity shifting and attaining new qualities.

The sense of self of ego has deeply fixed characteristic emotional qualities and predispositions. One individual might have a pervasive sense of sadness as part of the feeling of self, another might experience a quality of being active and aggressive as inseparable from who he is. The first individual will have difficulty in the personalization of the aspect of Joy, because it is felt as alien to his sense of identity. The process of personalization will bring out the subtle parts of his ego that are structured in a way that excludes Joy, and the history of the object relations that structured these parts. The second individual will have difficulty in personalizing both the Peace aspect and the Consciousness aspects, because both are quiet, still and restful.

As we have said, this process is really a matter of altering one's
character, which otherwise retains the stability and inflexibility it acquired very early on. Kernberg writes about the relationship between
the character structure and the ego self:

> The character structure represents the automatized, pre-
> dominantly behavioral aspects of ego identity. A reciprocal
> relationship exists between the self-concept and the char-
> acter structure: the more integrated the former, the more
> consistent and harmonious the latter, and, conversely, the
> more integrated the character structure, the closer the cor-
> respondence between the self-concept and the actual be-
> havior and personality as they are experienced by others.
> [Otto F. Kernberg, *Object Relations Theory and Clinical
> Psychoanalysis*, p. 74]

So the development of the Personal Essence, through the personalization of essential aspects, is actually a change in the qualitative
character of the personality, and hence is bound to be resisted by the
established self of ego, which is closely related to it. This personality
character is largely the outcome of the process of ego integration and
organization, reflected in one's self-image and inseparable from the
various defensive operations of the ego.

Thus the process of personalization confronts the individual with very
deep anxieties, vulnerabilities and conflicts that he would usually rather
forget for good. We give the following report, by Mark—whom we have
already mentioned in Chapter Twenty-Three—of one private session,
where he is involved in the process of personalizing the Love aspect:

> I have been experiencing vulnerability and fear about
> being the Personal Essence in front of you. Seeing how
> much of it was really connected with oedipal issues was
> useful, and I always resisted that a lot. I just did not want
> you to see the Love-Personal-Essence, and see it directed
> towards you or any other man. It made me feel vulnerable
> and afraid of being a sissy or queer. It is okay to experi-
> ence myself this way in front of women, unless men are
> present, and then I subdue it. I see that the amount and
> range of contact I had with my mother was broader than
> with my father. I tend to have my personal presence larger
> and denser, and not recognize it when it is more delicate.
> Now I feel quite vulnerable and exposed.

Mark's character is habitually that of being reserved, dignified, and
markedly masculine, especially in contact with men. This reflects both

344   his relationship to his father, who had an image of dignity, respect and reserve, and his ethnic background. It also reflects his identification with his father, which helped him deal with the oedipal situation in childhood, and hence is defensive. Here, however, Mark was confronting the fact that when Love is personalized the experience of oneself is of being soft, fluffy, sweet, delicate, innocent and loving in an openly personal way. He was never able to be that way with his father, although he very much wanted to, and felt so in secret. To experience himself this way meant a change in his personality, which reflected a change in his self-concept. It made him feel exposed and vulnerable, partly because he did feel personal Love towards his father which he hid from him, and partly because it left him without a part of his structure. He tends to idealize and admire the kind of strong character his father has, but he secretly longs for the softer and more open parts of him. The fact is that they are all parts of him, but because of the self-concept he developed, he got to be more comfortable with only a limited part of himself, which restricted the range of his personal contact.

The relationship between the character structure and the new personal qualities is not always so direct as in the above example. In the following report we find Jackson, whom we mentioned in Chapter Five, married and divorced, and still having problems with women, describing part of the process of personalizing the Essential Self. His character includes being original, authentic, inquisitive, intelligent—all reflections of what might seem to be the Self aspect. However, once in a while he reports isolated experiences of feeling mentally deficient, unable to focus mentally or to sustain concentration. He writes after a few sessions and encounters with this subprocess:

> An issue, actually two, have been stirring for about two months and during the Monday evening session were focused even more. (1) I am afraid to be curious or ask questions and (2) somehow I am supposed to know even before I am told what the information is. My feeling is that I will be rejected if I do ask questions or if I do not know "all"—as you say, to be omniscient. This fear is very old and has been with me for as long as I can remember, and as of a couple of months ago it has become much more intense—it is crippling and hindering my understanding, causing frustration and slight anger. Now as I begin to talk about it I feel very sad, especially when you begin to ask

me questions, pointing out that there are two issues and
not just one. I became aware that these feelings were
much a part of the way I related to my mother; I became
sad, as she had, when you questioned me. You ask me
about relating empathically, becoming aware of the other
person, "losing" oneself and becoming that person. If my
mother had never separated from me, she would feel that I
should know her feelings without her having to tell me,
and asking questions, especially emotional ones, would
make her sad. Asking the question would seem to her that
I was more separate, which is what she did not want. My
mother never has separated from me or let me go, and for
years I have felt this, at some level. This has kept me from
admitting how much I wanted her; if I did I would feel like
I was being resubmerged. In the process of my life I have
not only taken my mother into me—through sad reactions—I have also projected her onto the world, bringing
the fear of being rejected for not knowing something.
When you ask what I feel I become immediately aware of
the large, shiny, and personal presence, that had manifested during the private session. I feel this is my real individuality, my real separateness, which had been pushing
from within, and guiding my attention toward this self-
limiting relationship with my mother. It feels so natural and
so wonderful at the same time.

He had to adopt a character of being all-knowing to deal with his
relationship to his mother. This is clearly a grandiose defense against
separation, an imitation of the Essential Self. This grandiose defense of
omniscience is unconscious, and is covered up with normally inquisitive character traits. These character traits themselves are a reflection,
an imitation, of the true inquisitive, interested and lively qualities of
the Essential Self. These two layers of defense hide behind them the
actual absence of the Essential Self.

This aspect, the singular point of brilliance and awareness, gives to
understanding the capacity of focus and concentration. It makes one's
consciousness one-pointed. So its absence is reflected in Jackson's
experience of mental deficiency, when he cannot focus and con-
centrate. It is interesting to mention that this issue began to surface for
Jackson after a long process of dealing with his narcissistic tendencies,
which ultimately led to his discovery of his true and Essential Self.

For Jackson this process of personalization started after some integration of the Essential Self. He started becoming aware of the

346   absence of its qualities in his personality, initially when his habitual
       character was challenged with the increasing awareness of his sense
       of mental deficiency. After this process Jackson manifested an in-
       creased excitement in his life. He started becoming more curious
       about aspects of his life that he had never questioned before, and
       raised again the whole question of intimate relations with women.

       The personalization of the Essential Self brings about a significant
       transformation of the Personal Essence. The sense of identity and the
       sense of being a person become inseparable. The Personal Essence
       begins to attain a sense of delicacy, exquisiteness, refinement and
       lively excitement about the essential life. One becomes more inter-
       ested in others, and more disposed towards serving humanity.

       Sometimes the character is such that it purports to manifest a cer-
       tain aspect, which is actually not experienced as part of oneself. In
       such a case the character is largely defensive, hiding a certain defi-
       ciency of character. In this situation, personalizing the missing aspect
       is difficult and painful, but its completion brings a singular joy, a great
       revelation, and results in a major change in one's life. One such ex-
       ample is of a businessman, Martin, who finds jobs easily but has
       difficulty keeping them. His inner feeling regarding his career is
       usually that of failure. He habitually loses interest in his jobs, and
       leaves them for one reason or another.

       At this juncture he has a job in a business institution, which is
       bringing out the same conflict within him. In a private session he
       complains of feelings of nausea in the morning. Exploring these
       feelings we find out he is feeling rejecting of the praise for the good
       job he is doing at work. He cannot accept the praise because, he
       feels, it is not okay to want excellence. It turns out that if he accepts
       the praise then he has to accept his success and excellence, which
       means to his unconscious the loss of the image of his mother, who
       lacked the quality of excellence. So the quality of excellence in his
       character means loss of his connection with his mother, in this case
       his identification with her. In other words, if he is successful and does
       a competent and excellent job then he will feel alone. This brings to
       consciousness feelings of emptiness and aloneness, which lead to
       deep crying. He starts feeling a black emptiness in the belly.

       In this emptiness the Personal Essence arises in the aspect of per-
       sonal Will. Martin experiences a sense of dense presence, power and

groundedness. It turns out that this new form of the Personal Essence has in it the sense of excellence. He feels the excellence as a state of Being, which goes along with a confidence that he can do an excellent job. He remembers how he wanted his father to be this way, and how he himself wanted to be this way for his siblings, which brings out much sadness.

This example indicates that although Martin typically appeared to embody Will, he in fact had deep conflicts about actually owning this part of his Being. This is a reflection of his rapprochement conflict with his mother, which is obviously centered around both the Personal Essence and Will. The process of personalization did not give him the chance to experience both, but rather to integrate them into one unified presence, the experience of himself as an embodiment of personal excellence.

The process of personalizing the essential aspects does not render them unavailable to experience on their own, or in their original form. It simply makes them available in another form, the personal form. So it is a matter of gaining new capacities and ranges of experience, without losing the original ones.

This is characteristic of essential development in general. Nothing real is ever lost. There is only gain, and ever-expanding richness. Some aspects or dimensions might lose their importance, but not their existence. They merely become a part of a larger, expanding whole, manifesting when they are needed.

Chapter Twenty-Eight

The Actualization of Being

T he more the Personal Essence is realized and developed, the more one experiences one's life as integrated with who one is. One's life becomes the natural expression and extension of one's personal realization. One literally fills one's life with one's integrated qualities and capacities. Defensive, superficial and unnecessary activities, interests and engagements drop away. One's interests and activities become a direct reflection of one's essential attainment. Life becomes rich, profound, significant and fulfilling.

This does not happen through planning or premeditation. The mind does not and cannot know what needs to happen. The Personal Essence exerts the influence of all its qualities and dimensions on the consciousness of the individual. One becomes naturally and spontaneously interested and involved in the activities, interests and situations that are in harmony with one's realization. This realization determines one's life, and one's life leads to a greater development of the realization. One begins to feel that everything that happens in one's life is meaningful and necessary. It's as if nothing wrong can happen, or that whatever is perceived to be wrong turns out to be ultimately in the service of one's development.

The inner realization and development becomes expressed in life, becomes the source of one's life, the substance of this life. Everything in one's life becomes a reflection of this realization, an expression and an intimate extension of it. In this way, realization becomes an actualization. It is not only an inner experience, but an

actualized life. Life becomes a continuity of Being, instead of a   349
string of events.

It is as if the fullness of the Personal Essence pervades every corner of one's life, filling it, expanding it, transforming it and authentically actualizing it. One's Being and one's life are one thing, inseparable and unified. One is a personal living presence. Living one's life, doing one's job and relating to others, are the same as being oneself in the world.

Actualization involves the fusion of Being and living. One is simply being oneself, and this naturally translates into the life of Essence. One feels in direct and immediate contact with one's life and activities. There are accomplishments, achievements, tasks, jobs and so forth, but they are not of the same quality as those activities conducted by the ego individuality. They are completely inseparable from being oneself. One does not achieve for any reason; it is the natural expression and extension of one's Personal Essence. Achievements are not looked at as ways to gain recognition, love, self esteem, success, fame, power and so on. They might bring such things, but they are not for such ends. They are merely the natural expression of being oneself, living and functioning authentically. One does not care about gain from success in the world; success in the world can happen, but only as a side consequence of gaining one's authentic Being.

In other words, one does not gain value from one's accomplishments; these accomplishments are, rather, the expression of one's self-existing value. When one depends on any external manifestations, such as performance, achievement, excellence, or anything, to feel a sense of value or love, then one has not yet personalized the essential aspect of value. To depend upon external manifestations for self-esteem means one has to use one's mind; one has to remember these accomplishments. But the value of Being is self-existing, is a presence independent of the mind, and of the past.

This is not possible on the ego level, where self-esteem is always inferred from one's manifestations and accomplishments, and always somewhat removed from one's Beingness. This distance between one's value and one's Beingness becomes especially obvious in the case of the narcissistic personality. The narcissistic personality has no sense of value except from external approval, admiration, recognition, acceptance and appreciation. This need for such external mirroring is incessant and bottomless. One must keep performing and achieving

350   in order to keep the narcissistic supplies flowing. So achievements are
not expressions of who one is, but are pursued to give oneself significance and identity. One's life, with all its activities and accomplishments, constitutes a shell that is empty and devoid of any sense of self
or Being. In such a character, a momentary failure of or disidentification with one's external achievements makes one feel that one's life is
empty and insignificant.

The essential person may or may not have many external achievements, but his achievements are more meaningful to him, giving him
a sense of pleasure and value because they are the expression of essential qualities.

It is not uncommon that an individual is successful, accomplished,
and even creative, but feels no pleasure or value related to these
manifestations of his life. He still feels empty, insignificant and shal-
low, with low self-esteem. What has happened in this character is that
some of his ego functions have been developed and integrated so that
he can function well. However, this was not accompanied by sufficient emotional integration and development. So he is an adult on the
functional level but an immature child on the emotional level. His
functioning capacities have exceeded his emotional development. The
final result is that he does not feel connected to his functioning, and
hence, to his accomplishments. His functional self is disconnected
from his sense of self or being, and his actions are mechanical, even
though efficient. He does not derive pleasure or value from them because he is not connected to them. He feels as if somebody else has
done all these things.

Object relations theory views this type of character development as
a result of precocious ego development, when the ego capacities mature, for one reason or another, faster than emotional development.
One grows up on the surface, but one's inner growth lags behind.
Functioning, in other words, develops outside of object relations. As a
result, a gap is created between who one feels oneself deeply to be
and what one can do in the external world. Blanck and Blanck explain it this way, referring to it as

> . . . premature ego development—an unevenness in devel-
> opment characterized by pseudo-self-sufficiency in which
> part of the ego replaces the symbiotic partner, and by con-
> comitant absence of object cathexis. [Gertrude and Rubin
> Blanck, *Ego Psychology: Theory and Practice*, p. 340]

The implication is that deficiency in the symbiotic stage sometimes impels the child to separate and mature faster in terms of ego functions, to get away from the frustrating symbiosis. "This comes about if the maternal partner fails in her function of constituting an auxiliary ego. The infant has to take over her functions." [*Ibid*., p. 56]

This is experienced by some individuals in the feeling that they had to grow up too early, that they did not have the chance to be children, etc. Another reason for precocious development is that the child's ego capacities develop too early, before he can manage this development emotionally. One example of this is the early development of the perceptive capacity through which the child becomes aware of his separateness from his mother before he can emotionally handle separation. The precocious development of some ego capacities creates character types which are considered by object relations theory to involve borderline or narcissistic pathologies.

However, looked at from the dimension of Being, regardless of how mature and integrated ego is, it is always a precocious development. We have seen that the ego becomes the system that structures, and includes in its structures the ego functions. It becomes, in other words, the functional part of oneself. We have also seen that ego development is an incomplete process, short of the realization of the Personal Essence. Ego structures are always alienated from the true Being, so the functional part of oneself is separate from who one is.

Thus from the perspective of Being, ego development is a development of functioning that is separate from who one is. When there is appropriate emotional development, the individual is better off than the narcissistic character we have just described. However, it is intrinsically the same kind of situation, for in both cases—normal and pathological ego development—there is dissociation from one's Being.

In normal ego development, the mother's image is internalized, and this provides some basis for a certain kind of satisfaction and connectedness, but only on a superficial level. For true integrated development the Merging Essence must be realized, creating the possibility of the development of the Personal Essence and the sense of being intimately connected to one's life and achievements. In fact, the Personal Essence is the factor responsible for actualization.

When the integration progresses to the essential level one's accomplishments and attainments become one's contribution to

352   humanity. It is not only for oneself, and it is not only for humanity. On this level of experience the two are inseparable. One then knows and actualizes one's true contributions, by the mere fact of living one's personal life. One's personal history is now seen as the way one has been able to actualize one's personal realization and contribution. Personal history finally becomes metabolized in the realization and the development of the Personal Essence. Its fruit is one's life and the attainments of this life, as one and the same thing.

Cultural Values

Actualization involves not only attainments, accomplishments and contributions, but also the realization and manifestation of the various qualities, capacities and ranges of experience possible for a human being. The individual consciousness gradually realizes and manifests the following qualities, among others, of the Personal Essence: freedom, autonomy, maturity, efficiency, competence, confidence, reliability, regality, respect, integrity, dignity, excellence, fullness, sensuousness, firmness, resilience, integration and wholeness.

These are some of the characteristics of the essential person, which become realized as the essential aspects are personalized. It is interesting to note that different cultures or countries value and idealize some of these characteristics but not others. The idealized characteristics distinguish the cultural values of each nation. The individual is judged by his own culture, or ethnic background, according to his realization of these characteristics. Their realization and manifestation is taken to be the sign of maturity, which can lead to success, admiration or recognition. It is interesting to observe, however, that the absence of the other characteristics is not taken to mean lack of maturity. These other characteristics are not even missed, but are in fact misunderstood, and when observed in other cultures they are taken to be extreme or ridiculous. The fact is that each culture goes to great lengths attempting to realize its idealized characteristics. But its own extremism is not perceived, and is taken to be normal.

In the United States, for instance, the characteristics that are idealized and admired are those of autonomy, individuality and, to a lesser extent, efficiency. The characteristics of sensuousness or dignity, for instance, are not necessarily rejected, but in general are not valued as much. It is the opposite in Japan, where dignity, integrity and respect are the idealized cultural values. Individuality, autonomy and personal freedom are not usually sought or respected.

In most countries of the Middle East the qualities of respect and dignity are idealized, but personal autonomy or efficiency are certainly not. The British idealize competence and integrity, while in India sensuousness and personal contact are valued. The Swiss admire and embody excellence, while the Germans go more for efficiency and reliability. The South Seas culture emphasizes fullness and sensuousness, and is low on efficiency and excellence.

It is not possible to understand all these qualities if one remains on the ego level. Ego is restricted by its character structure, which limits it to the experience and appreciation of only a few of the qualities. The Personal Essence, on the other hand, is the embodiment of all the essential qualities. These qualities are the external manifestations of the developed and mature Personal Essence.

PART II

THE OBJECTIVE DIMENSIONS OF ESSENCE

We have seen that the personalization of Essence involves a process in which each aspect is absorbed and integrated into the Personal Essence. Absorption, however, requires that what is absorbed be true and undistorted. Thus an aspect is not absorbed if one's understanding of it is not objective. One can experience an essential aspect, such as Love or Joy, but lack objectivity about it if there are emotional issues that make one connect the quality with associations on an ego level. In the case history of Mark in Chapter Twenty-Seven, for example, there was difficulty in being present personally as Love because he associated femininity, and hence castration, with the state. He had to look at his issues about these matters and isolate them from what Love is, before he could experience it objectively. The process of personalization is to a great extent a matter of understanding an aspect as it actually is, and not as one has come to believe it is.

356   Understanding an aspect of Being objectively means knowing it from its own perspective, and not from one's own point of view, which is necessarily prejudiced by personal history. Objective understanding has the effect of altering the experience of the aspect, taking it to a new dimension of Essence. This dimension is that of objective understanding, which we have discussed as the Diamond Guidance. There are additional dimensions of Essence, in which each aspect becomes realized on a different dimension of objectivity. This is difficult to understand, but is easily grasped when there is direct experience.

To put it differently, in the process of essential realization, it is found that not only are there many differentiated aspects of Being, but also several dimensions in which these aspects can be experienced. The first dimension is what we call the human realm, because the aspects are most easily recognized here, and are closest to the usual emotional affects. Then each one of these aspects can be experienced in several other ways, where the aspect retains its original sense, but is experienced from a different perspective, which gives it an added meaning and significance, or rather, a clearer and more objective meaning.

For instance, the aspect of Sincerity is first experienced as a kind of sweet presence, with an austere quality. When it is experienced on the first objective dimension it is still experienced as a sweet presence with an austere quality, but now it has an objective (unemotional) feeling to it, that gives it a clarity and sharpness. This first dimension is Understanding, so that Sincerity is now perceived as a kind of understanding.

The second objective dimension is that of Pleasure, where all aspects are experienced as different forms of pleasure. Here Sincerity is still experienced as a sweet presence with an austere quality, but the experience is dominated by the sense of pleasure that it involves. This is still an objective dimension, because the qualities of clarity, precision and sharpness remain as part of the experience.

There are at least seven objective dimensions of Essence, each of which brings about an added dimension to the experience and understanding of the aspects. The aspects are experienced in the seven dimensions, respectively, as or related to: 1. *Objective understanding*; 2. *Pleasure*, or delight; 3. *Conscience*, related to action; 4. *Knowledge*, by identity; 5. *Love*; 6. *Will*, or support of Being; 7. *Nothing*, the level of understanding concepts.

The realization within each dimension is like going through the
whole process of essential realization all over again, but from a different and more profound level. Each brings new ego issues, or rather
the same issues now understood in deeper and subtler ways. It would
take us too far afield to discuss these dimensions of experience in any
depth, so we only note here that the process of personalization of
Essence involves the realization of these dimensions. Seeing that
realization proceeds through each of these dimensions points to the
magnitude of the task, but also to the magical richness of Essence.

Realizing the objective dimensions amounts to the shifting of identity from ego to Being. It also means a much more comprehensive
and objective understanding of ego, on all of its levels, and in all of its
structures. Ego, both in terms of self and individuality, becomes
known and understood, inside out. Its relation to consciousness,
Essence and Being is also understood, which leads to its gradual absorption. The amount of knowledge, understanding and experience
that results is beyond imagination. It makes one realize in what a
small realm of experience ego exists.

The process of personalization of Essence is also the process of development of the Personal Essence. Two particular issues, among
myriad others, stand out in this process. The first is one we have
already discussed, the rapprochement conflict. The second is related:
the issue of ego deficiency or inadequacy.

Chapter Twenty-Nine

Being
and
Ego Deficiency

T he realization of the Personal Essence, the personalization of aspects, and essential development in general, are processes of radical expansion. One experiences a steady expansion, in continual tiny increments, in one's experience, consciousness, capacities and life. One's mind is almost constantly being stretched, its limits pushed farther out. The changes are profound and deep, and affect the organism even at the cellular level. In fact one finds oneself always changing one's mind about who one is and what life is all about.

The experience of expansion involves delight, beauty and a sense of adventure. But sooner or later one does come upon one's personal limitations. When an individual is experiencing expansion in a certain realm, a part of him that feels he cannot do it, that the expansion is too much, comes to the surface. He starts feeling a sense of deficiency, smallness, weakness and inadequacy. This inadequacy is rarely felt as directly related to the process of realization itself, but manifests in some situation in the student's life.

The root of this inadequacy is the sense of smallness and incapacity that keeps one at a certain level of development. We find that each individual functions at a certain level of capacity or expansion, and in general does not go beyond an unspecified limit, in terms of range of experience, depth of understanding, capacity for perception and ability for functioning. On the level of work or in social relations, one must deal with limitations, which can manifest as a feeling of inadequacy or the fear of it.

Essential realization puts a much greater pressure on one's capacities, and sooner or later a sense of inadequacy emerges. It usually does not indicate emotional disorder or immaturity, for under normal circumstances this inadequacy would probably never surface to consciousness. Every student, however normal and integrated he is on the ego level, at some point becomes aware of this sense of inadequacy; it is a universal phenomenon. One must deal with ego inadequacy in order to break through personal limits and attain a greater expansion; the sense of inadequacy is the main thing holding him back.

The state of inadequacy manifests in many forms, according to its various sources. We will discuss its main manifestations, and the defenses against them.

1. *The most typical is a state of feeling deficient, inadequate, unable, and, at the same time, scared of these feelings.* The inadequacy here is an emotional state, a painful affect of not being up to what one has to do in life. In the following report, Jordan, whom we introduced in Chapter Seven, describes this state:

> I have been bouncing back and forth between feeling inadequate, afraid, deficient, etc., and feeling grandiose, manic, like I could do anything I wanted. Both of these poles are painful. I have been aware of all the energy it takes to maintain the illusion that I am the best, most advanced, most together, etc. Both feelings of inadequacy and feelings of grandiosity lead me to compare and judge.

Jordan's defense of grandiosity points to one genetic cause of his sense of inadequacy. Grandiosity is one of the main defenses employed at the beginning of the rapprochement subphase, to ward off the perception of one's helplessness and dependency, which results from perceiving one's separateness: When the child becomes aware that he is separate from his mother and at the same time discovers that his omnipotence is not all real, he becomes aware that he is too small, helpless and dependent to be able to function on his own, to be autonomous and independent. If there is not enough support forthcoming from the mother or father, this sense of smallness and dependency is experienced as helplessness, deficiency and inadequacy. The child feels too inadequate to be autonomous, or to continue in his independent expansive achievements.

360   In this situation a typical defense is a regression to the sense of omnipotence that the child experienced at the height of the practicing period, at around age one and a half. The child continues to believe that he can do anything he wants. This grandiose sense of ability usually becomes unconscious, but dominates the consciousness when the inadequacy starts emerging.

Thus a possible source of Jordan's inadequacy is a conflict at the beginning of the rapprochement phase, when he discovered his smallness and helplessness but did not receive enough attuned response from the environment to deal with it realistically. So he felt abandoned and alone in his helplessness, and had to repress the feelings of inadequacy. This corresponds with Jordan's recollections about his relation with his mother in early childhood, and also corresponds with his character, which is always busy with many activities, usually more than he can handle.

2. *The inadequacy can manifest as a state of extreme helplessness*, in which an individual feels so helpless that he cannot even lift his arm. He feels weak, unable, incapable. The feeling is that one cannot function. One both feels helpless and believes that the feeling of helplessness reflects a true state of incapacity to function. This helplessness is sometimes accompanied by an affect of extreme anxiety, even panic, especially when one feels called upon to function. A report by Andrew, last mentioned in Chapter Eighteen, describes these affects:

> Friday night I talked to you about my fears around the war when I was 6. We explored the feelings which were being covered up by the fear. I felt an emptiness in my solar plexus region, and a great deal of anxiety. We talked about another fear, the fear of total helplessness and aloneness, and about what it feels like to be unable to do anything about something. This feeling had been triggered by my having to work with a man who is crazy and does not respond in any rational way. I have been working on enduring the feelings of helplessness.

Sometimes he feels so helpless that he cannot do anything, and he believes that he cannot. This happens in episodes, and usually does not last very long. However, sometimes these episodes can reveal a deep-seated depression caused by physiological or structural-dynamic factors.

3. *The state of inadequacy is frequently experienced as a state of inner emptiness*, as reported by Andrew above. This emptiness is felt as a

sense of deficiency and lack. The lack can be of Strength, Will, firmness of psychological structure, Value, purpose, Love, etc. The affects can then be of feeling castrated, impotent, weak, spineless, inept, awkward and so on. One might react to the state with feelings of shame, degradation and humiliation.

4. *The state of emptiness and the related affects of the various deficiencies are sometimes graphically experienced.* One feels not only a big emptiness, but a sense of many holes in one's psyche. One feels perforated and deficient at the same time. Many students refer to this experience as the state of Swiss cheese. One feels parts of oneself missing everywhere.

5. *The state of inadequacy and helplessness is frequently experienced as a sense of weakness, of having no structure and no sense of inner support.* Sometimes one will feel as if there is no inner structure to one's body, as if one has no bones, nothing to hold one up, support one in taking action. One feels as if one's body is made of jelly, with no firmness, solidity or structure. Some students report feeling like a jellyfish that can move but has no structure at all. This is how a student, Penny, described it: "Now the feeling of inadequacy spread. It felt like a blob, like a squishy, fleshy mass, a gooey mass with no definition."

6. *The state frequently manifests as a feeling of smallness.* One feels too small to do grown-up things. One experiences oneself as not up to big tasks, not ready for expansive states. The feeling of smallness is not only a matter of feeling emotionally young in years. One feels actually and literally small, sometimes as small as a pea. Lily, a young woman who has been in a group for about two years, describes this state, which arises as a result of contemplating going to a group work retreat:

> The problem I spoke up about was that I was afraid to go to the retreat, or rather that I was afraid my life would be so dramatically changed by the retreat that I would not be able to cope with it. I felt very small, helpless, and out of control, and these feelings made me feel very frightened, and smaller yet.

In her case, the smallness went along with a feeling of not being able to cope with expansion, which is here seen as change.

7. *One of the most difficult manifestations of inadequacy is a state of feeling alone and not supported.* One feels as if one is hanging in

362   mid-air, with nothing to support one underneath, and nothing any-
where to hold onto. One finds it difficult to be present or be aware of
one's body or Being. One feels as if one has no handle or connection
to anything, no Strength and no Will. One feels out of touch and completely unsupported from all directions. There is no fear of falling, but
there is a panicky feeling of needing to hold onto something. Some
students report this condition as a lack of traction, as if one cannot get
a hold on anything for support or balance. Frequently this state is accompanied by feeling castrated and impotent.

8. *The state of inadequacy appears in dreams in unmistakable symbols.* One image is of trying to reach something with a stick, to finally
realize that the stick is too short. Another image is of fighting a duel
with a sword, to finally find the sword bending like a rag. Another
image is to be shooting with a gun, but to be disappointed when you
see the bullets falling just short of the target. It also appears in dreams
of taking an exam, in which one feels unprepared.

There are two specific primary defenses, and one general one,
which are typically employed to repress inadequacy. The state itself is
emotionally very distressing and threatening, and the emotional
reactions to it are very painful. The difficulty regarding this state
depends on the extent to which it is believed to be a fact and not just
an emotional state. When an individual is experiencing this state there
is usually a deep degree of identification with it. It does not seem like
a feeling, which will pass away or be resolved, like other emotional
states. Very often the individual completely believes that it is an actual, accurate description of who he is. He does not think that he is
feeling inadequate, he is convinced that he *is* inadequate, and that
now the truth is out. This point is very important for our later discussion of this issue. But it also explains why there are such strong defenses against awareness of this state.

When one believes that the inadequacy is the actual fact about
oneself, there is a deep, almost complete, hopelessness that it can
ever be different. Believing it is hopeless, one has no reason to
bring it to consciousness and deal with it. One finds no other alternative but to repress it, if possible, and hopefully completely forget
all about it. Frequently, in fact, the repression is so deep and effective that only very deep, expanded states of Being push it into
consciousness.

It is our understanding that this deep hopelessness is the primary reason most individuals do not grow and expand in any significant way in their lives. They deeply believe that they are too small and inadequate to do much growing. This leads us to the general method of defense against awareness of the state of inadequacy.

Since one deeply believes (usually unconsciously) that the inadequacy is not a state but a fact, and this causes a deep hopelessness about the possibility of expansion, one defends against this awareness by settling for a mediocre life. If there is any expansion it is small and usually only external.

The greater the state of inadequacy, and the deeper the hopelessness, the more restricted and confined one tries to keep one's life. One becomes conventional, pedantic, even petty, actively resisting movements towards expansion, and deliberately, but usually unconsciously, thwarting one's possibilities of growth. One becomes satisfied with a very small portion of one's potential, without even missing the greater unactualized part. One lives the small life of a small person.

This defense manifests in many ways: in intolerance of new truths or ways of living; in prejudices against different dimensions of experience and perception; in blindness about the true human potential, sometimes fortified with very logical, scientific, or even religious, arguments. It can manifest as the lack of interest in understanding, growth and development. It even manifests as the outright rejection of the dimension of Being, and hence of one's true nature.

One interesting manifestation of this defense, which partially expresses the defended-against state of inadequacy, is the belief, which many individuals have, that inner transformation is so special and unique that it is almost impossible for it to happen to them. It is definitely true that essential transformation is difficult, but it is equally true that it is our human potential. It is difficult but possible, and, with the right understanding, even probable.

From these observations we can see why inadequacy, and the defenses against it, inhibit many individuals from embarking on the process of transformation, and why many of those who do embark, do it in such a half-hearted way that nothing of significance happens. To actually expand, or to truly believe in the possibility of expansion, challenges one's entrenched belief in one's hopelessness and inadequacy.

364   Identifying with the inadequacy makes one feel and believe one cannot deal with it, because one will be then feeling inadequate! This is the paradox at the bottom of this issue which constitutes one important reason a teacher is generally needed for the process of realization. He is not needed only for guidance, but also for support, without which most students will feel helpless and inadequate to engage in the process. The fact that the teacher has successfully gone through the process makes it possible and believable that the student might do so, and thus shakes his deep conviction in his hopelessness.

Nevertheless, some individuals manage to believe in their inadequacy and helplessness in spite of the presence of individuals who embody essential expansion, in spite of the available knowledge and guidance. These individuals end up believing that the realized individuals are special in some way, or that their expansion is not real, and hence can be dismissed. Many students report this defense in some of their friends, who fail to see the students' expansion and growth, and thus are not awakened from their comfortable slumber about their own condition.

This general defense is sincerely and innocently manifested by Lily in the above case report. It is rare that someone will admit this fear of expansion; most individuals will regard it as shameful and humiliating.

One of the main ego defenses against the state of inadequacy is that of grandiosity, as we discussed at the beginning of this chapter. One comes to believe, and to behave as if, one has no such inadequacy. The defense is not only that one is not inadequate, but that one is the best, strongest, most able. One feels one can do anything. This defense is a complete denial of the state of inadequacy through a reaction formation, which is usually called the grandiose self, or a grandiose belief about one's omnipotence. In most individuals, this defense is unconscious, and one must look with a discerning eye to see it in operation in one's life. But it always comes to the foreground when the state of inadequacy is pushing towards consciousness.

We again give the case report of Jordan from the beginning of this chapter, for it shows clearly how the grandiosity defense relates to the state of inadequacy. He has been in a group for over five years, and has gone through some of his main character defenses and inhibitions. He now has the success that he always wanted. the job he desired and a satisfied married life. But for months now, he has been feeling agitated. He cannot stop doing one thing after another, managing so many jobs and commitments and interests that he now has no time to relax. None of his activities is particularly difficult, but to be involved in all of them is very demanding and takes all his time and energy. He does not truly need to do all of them, but he somehow cannot see that. He keeps complaining about how busy and hurried he is, but he will not stop. Exploring this manifestation finally reveals its dynamic cause, which he described in the report above.

His excessive activities and involvements are the expression of his grandiosity, of his belief in his unlimited capacities. The grandiosity has always been present in his life, but did not become so clear until he was truly successful, and was able to see that there is no real need for all that he is doing. This then exposed the inadequacy that had been warded off with his belief in his omnipotence. So for a period of time he was feeling either the state of inadequacy or the grandiose defense against it. It was a trying period for him, for which he had to marshal all his true capacities and sincerity. In time he managed to resolve the issue.

The second defense normally employed against the state of deficiency is negative merging. The individual avoids the feeling of helplessness and impotence by becoming embroiled in all kinds of negative states and interactions; thus he also avoids feeling separate and alone. The negative merging is a way to feel contact and union with another—unconsciously the mother—and hence supported. This defense has many important functions, although it is emotionally painful. It protects the individual from feeling helpless and alone. It protects him from feeling suspended in midair without anything to hold on to. It gives him a sense of traction, and hence relieves him from the terror of feeling he is going to slip into oblivion.

The following report by Penny, quoted earlier in the chapter, clearly shows how this defense is employed. She writes about a certain group session:

> In talking to you on this Saturday night meeting I spoke of my response to my private session with you on Friday. I said I had a great deal of preference for the sandpaper state I was experiencing. I was experiencing it as a sense of negative merging with my mother. It is a reliving of my negative connection to her.

   I was feeling a desire to get through this, and see what is on the other side of it. You wanted to know why I wanted the change. I told you I felt scared but wanted to know what else was there. You asked what I was afraid of, and I said "loss of attachment, losing mother, being all alone, floating in space, etc." Then you wanted to know why I was afraid of being alone, unattached, and so on. After feeling totally spaced out came the answer. I felt inadequate. The reason I did not want to let go of the sandpaper state (or negative merging) was that I feel inadequate without mother. It is not that I so much loved the negative merging, but it is preferable to feeling totally inadequate as a person. Next I began to feel sad and scared, scared to look forward, and sad about feeling I needed to have the negative merging around me. Then I felt even more terrified in my chest. This led to deep sadness, compassionate sadness because I really had no choice when I was a baby. There was nothing I could do because I was inadequate in the world, and my mother was the only one to take care of me.
   Now the feeling of inadequacy spread. I felt like a blob, like a squishy, fleshy mass, a gooey mass with no definition. I felt hopeless, empty, worthless, useless, like nothing at all. I did not want anything because I did not know enough to know what I wanted; totally dependent and yet unaware of who or how or where the source of my dependency might be, totally deficient and inadequate.

Penny's description is very lucid regarding both the defense of negative merging and the state of inadequacy in its various manifestations. It is clear in her report how difficult, painful and terrifying this state can be. We must also note that it took her several years of deep exploration to be able to confront and tolerate this state, which was deeply hidden in her, and quite unapparent in her usual manifestations as a successful, warm and well-functioning human being. We will finish her report, in which a real resolution becomes possible, in a later chapter.

Another defense against inadequacy, less common than the above two, but related to them, is the schizoid defense of isolation and withdrawal. The inadequacy is sometimes experienced as an incapacity to interact with others, to engage in human object relations. One feels too inadequate and deficient to make contact. Then one defends oneself against this deficiency in relating by abandoning interpersonal relations altogether. One isolates oneself from others, builds a detached wall around oneself, and withdraws deep within. Guntrip recognized this relationship between the schizoid mechanism and inadequacy. He saw that the schizoid defense of isolation and detachment is a defense against, and is primarily due to, a fundamental inadequacy, which he termed ego-weakness. He writes:

> *Ego-weakness consists not in lack of energy or innate ability, but in this unremitting state of basic fear and distress and lack of self-confidence of which the individual feels ashamed, and of which he develops considerable secondary fears.* . . .
> The most obvious ways in which the person with a basically weak and immature ego seeks to protect himself in face of outer world pressures and inner world fears, is to hide the part of himself that is a child facing a life that feels too big for him, behind central ego detachment. . . . All the psychoneurotic defences come into play. [Harry Guntrip, *Schizoid Phenomena, Object-Relations and the Self*, pp.183-184]

The issue of inadequacy is a central question in Guntrip's book. He develops the understanding that it is the core problem of ego structure, that all structural problems and conflicts are ultimately due to this basic ego-weakness:

> The unremitting and strenuous efforts to overcome or hide this weakness, which they do not know how, genuinely, to grow out of, constitutes, together with the weakness itself, the mass of psychopathological experience and behaviour, as seen not only in patients but also in the general low level of mental health in the community. *The struggle to force a weak ego to face life, or, even more fundamentally, the struggle to preserve an ego at all, is the root cause of psychotic, psychosomatic and psychoneurotic tensions and illness.* [*Ibid.*, p. 177]

He sees this issue also as the main problem to be resolved in therapy. He sees the various neuroses not as due only to repression of drives, but mainly as ways to deal with this basic weakness of ego. He regards the neurosis, in a sense, as specific defensive constellations to ward off this ego deficiency:

> The psychoneurotic defensive states represent rather the struggle to force a pseudo-adult pattern which masks the frightened child inside. [*Ibid.*, p. 184]

368   Guntrip's analysis is fascinating, and certainly in accord with our findings in the process of inner realization for normal and neurotic individuals. His understanding that ego weakness is the basic problem of psychopathology is in our estimation a brilliant breakthrough in understanding ego structure. His emphasis on this issue, we believe, reflects a deep understanding of ego, which regretfully has not been absorbed by mainstream object relations theory. It is understandable that he has this emphasis, because, as we have noted before, he understands the role of Being in ego development. We will show, in some detail, the importance and centrality of ego inadequacy in the structure of ego. We will develop an understanding of this state, that will bring about a very deep and profound understanding of ego and its structures.

Ego inadequacy is one of the issues that we call "diamond issues" in the Diamond Approach. It is a universal issue, which is not due to specific personal history but is a consequence of the nature of ego. A diamond issue is an ego issue that results from identification with ego. Its presence is inseparable from ego identifications, regardless of how pathological or healthy the ego structure is. Only the severity of the issue is determined by the particular personal history. Guntrip has a deep and detailed understanding of the issue of ego inadequacy, but he does not go all the way to seeing it as an issue for all egos.

Since it is a process of moving from ego to Being, the process of inner realization deals largely with diamond issues. All the major emotional issues and conflicts we have discussed in this book are diamond issues. They are characteristic of ego structure, and do not necessarily reflect mental pathology. Of course, there are individual variations in the way an issue manifests, which reflect personal history, but the basic pattern and resolution are universal. So our discussion in this book of the various issues applies to everyone. Every individual has them as part of his ego structure, unless he is not identified with ego.

Chapter Thirty

Origins
of
Ego Deficiency

Depth psychology, and object relations theory in particular, understand ego inadequacy or weakness as a structural problem resulting from lack of sufficient ego integration. Thus it is seen either as a result of incomplete ego development, or as a distorted or unbalanced development, which has resulted in a self-image which is not quite stable or unified, an individuality which is not whole and integrated, and a sense of self which is diffuse and lacks coherence. This type of development is usually attributed to what are called "subphase inadequacies," resulting from the absence of the needed support or environmental factors in each subphase of ego development, which absence is usually due to difficulties in the early mother-child relationship.

For example, in the symbiotic phase this inadequacy is due to the lack of sufficient gratifying symbiosis; in the differentiation phase it is the absence of support and understanding of the child's need for separation; in the practicing period it is the absence of sufficient mirroring and support for the child's growing autonomy, and so on. So ego weakness is a general result of all difficulties in the process of ego development. This weakness, however, is generally seen to be a pathology of ego, and not a basic characteristic of it. It is thought that normal ego development will result in ego strength and adequacy.

Kernberg, in fact, regards ego weakness as a characteristic of borderline pathology, in which there is inadequacy of ego integration reflecting insufficient integration and synthesis of internalized object

370   relations. Describing what he calls the lower level of organization of character pathology, the most pathological structures, he writes:

> Their lack of integration of self-representations is reflected in the absence of an integrated self concept. . . .
> The absence of both an integrated world of total, internalized object representations and of a stable self concept produces the syndrome of identity diffusion (Erikson, 1956). [Otto F. Kernberg, *Object Relations in Psychoanalytic Theory*, p. 147.]

He lists additional factors which contribute to this lower level of pathology, but emphasizes the characteristic borderline defense, which is the splitting of good and bad internalized images. He ascribes ego weakness primarily to the lack of integration of the good and bad images, object relations, affects and drives. He sums up this description in the following way:

> All these factors, in addition to the disintegrating effects of the predominant mechanisms of splitting and related defenses and the lack of crucial ego organizers such as an integrated self concept and an integrated superego, contribute to severe ego weakness. [*Ibid.*, p. 147]

While these aspects of object relations theory are undoubtedly correct, the theory refers mainly to what Kernberg called "severe ego weakness." Only such severe manifestations of ego inadequacy as are manifested in borderline pathology are explored. There is no exploration of ego inadequacy in the normal individual, except by Guntrip, whose perspective we discuss below; the overall implication in the literature is that a normal and integrated ego will have no such weakness.

We have stated that ego weakness is a universal issue characteristic of any ego existence, and that psychopathology indicates a severity of this issue. From our previous discussion of ego development and the development of the Personal Essence, it is simple to see from the perspective of the Diamond Approach why this is so. Since, as object relations theory states, ego weakness is due to incomplete or inadequate ego integration and individuation, and since, as we have discussed in great detail, ego development as conceived of in object relations theory is an incomplete process, every ego structure will naturally have some inadequacy. The individuality of ego is not the real, true and final integration of the person.

This means that ego weakness will disappear only in the realization of the Personal Essence, the real person of Being. As long as one takes himself to be an individual and a self based on self-image, there is bound to be a basic sense of inadequacy at the core of the identification. Ego inevitably contains a deep, basic sense of, and fear of, inadequacy. This is of course why the development of the Personal Essence ultimately exposes the inadequacy; it is the antithesis of the arising fullness, integrity, confidence and strength of Being. In the following case report by Dwayne, we see how the sense of ego inadequacy disappears when Essence arises, indicating that the state of deficiency is due to lack of contact with being:

> I worked with you Tuesday night on understanding my concept of working to earn a living. I am either afraid to do anything because of my feelings of inadequacy, or I work on grandiose plans to get rich. It is very hard to just work every day to earn a living.
>
> I felt a lot of fear while working on this issue, and it was around my inadequacy. When you worked on getting me to feel this I kept going back to my grandiose ideas. This happened a few times, and finally I stayed with the feeling of inadequacy. I felt an emptiness and fear that I did not exist. As I explored the feeling of emptiness it felt like a hole and then a big cave. There was substance there and as I felt the substance I began to feel strength in it. It felt like the strength I try to get by being grandiose, except that it felt real and it felt like my strength. It is hard for me to feel this real strength because I am so identified with the feelings of inadequacy and grandiosity. They are both in my head and neither are able to give me the strength I need to function, as Essence does.

In fact, the realization of the Personal Essence makes it more tolerable for the individual to confront and deal with ego weakness. It gives him both the inner support and the hope that it is possible to deal with such a profound sense of inadequacy.

The study of the severe ego weakness seen in psychopathology is useful for our exploration because its extremity exposes something that is usually not seen; it exposes a characteristic of ego by exaggerating it. It is true that the more integrated one's ego the less one feels, or is affected by, this sense of deficiency; but if one goes deeply into himself, exposing the deeper layers of the ego structure, he is

372   bound, sooner or later, to come face to face with this dreaded basic characteristic of his individuality.

Guntrip, in fact, shares this understanding of ego weakness. He rightly understands it to be due to an ego development that is separate from one's beingness. He sees ego weakness as a result of the ego developing through reactivity instead of through the personalization of Being:

> *It is the individual's capacity for experiencing a sense of "being" that is primarily dissociated, left unrealized at the start of development. He cannot get at his capacity to feel real*, because at the start of life no one evoked it, his mother gave him so little genuine relationship that he actually came to feel unreal. This emerges with startling clarity in those patients who feel so undermined that they feel they will never be strong enough to cope with living. [Harry Guntrip, *Schizoid Phenomena, Object Relations and the Self,* p. 255]

His understanding is that normal and healthy development arises out of, and is a continuation of, Being, and not antithetical to or separate from it. He writes:

> An absence, non-realization or dissociation of the experience of "being" and of the possibility of it, and, along with that, incapacity for healthy natural spontaneous "doing" is the most radical clinical phenomenon in analysis. Patients realize that they have been working hard all their lives busily "doing," not in a natural but a forced way, to create an illusory sense of reality as a person, a substitute for the experience of "inbeingness" in a solid and self-assured way that is the only basis of the self-confidence nearly all patients complain of lacking. . . . *The experience of "being" is the beginning and basis for the realization of the potentialities in our raw human nature for developing as a "person" in personal relationships.* [*Ibid.*, p. 254]

This corresponds with our understanding in this book, except that Guntrip believes that it is possible for ego to develop and not become separate from Being. This can be true only if one's development results in the realization of the Personal Essence, which both Guntrip and Winnicott seem to point to, but confuse with the individuality of ego. This confusion actually seems to be unavoidable; all students of essential realization, at least in the Diamond Approach, become subtly confused in this way, until the deepest

stages of development of the Personal Essence. We will discuss this 373
point further in the next chapter.

Not only is the understanding of ego inadequacy as a basic characteristic of ego individuality a necessary, logical outcome of the
perspective we are developing in this book, it is also a result of actually exploring the condition of ego inadequacy in the cases of
hundreds of normal individuals, some of whom have come to the
point of its actual resolution.

Here we will describe some of that exploration, which substantiates
our understanding of ego inadequacy. We can begin by investigating
the specific defenses against the state of inadequacy. Each of these
defenses can be understood to reflect an absence of a certain essential
aspect, and involves a regression of ego in an attempt to reach the
needed support equivalent to the missing essential aspect. To summarize the main defenses as they relate to this regression:

1. *Grandiosity.* This is a regression which is an attempt to return to the
feelings of grandeur and omnipotence that characterize the practicing
period of the separation-individuation process. We have pointed out
that in this period, though the grandiose feelings are delusional with
respect to the psychophysical apparatus, they are actually characteristic
of the Essential Self, the aspect which is dominant in that period.

2. *Negative merging.* This regression is an attempt to regain the om-
nipotent comfort and support of the good merged state, characteristic
of the dual unity of the symbiotic phase; in other words, it is an attempt to regain the loving support of the Merging Essence. We saw
when we discussed the issues of merging in Chapter Nineteen that
trying to regain this aspect inevitably results in negative merging.

3. *Isolation and detachment.* This regression is an attempt to regain
the sense of differentiation and strength characteristic of the differentiation subphase. This defense gives the individual a sense of isolation
which is actually an extreme sense of separateness. This happens
when one feels too inadequate to be present and still feel separate,
reflecting the absence of the Strength Essence.

An extreme development of the defense of grandiosity in childhood
leads, of course, to the development of the narcissistic personality organization. Kohut and Kernberg agree that grandiosity is the main
characteristic of the narcissistic personality, although they differ as to
its origin.

374   The extreme of the defense of negative merging in childhood leads to certain forms of psychosis. Reverting to negative merging is termed a refusion of self and object representations. Describing Jacobson's contribution to ego psychology concerning psychosis, Blanck and Blanck write:

> In psychosis, self and object representations that had dif-
> ferentiated in infancy as a normal developmental process,
> merge again regressively to form an undifferentiated self-
> object bringing distortions which adhere to it. [Gertrude
> and Rubin Blanck, *Ego Psychology: Theory and Practice*,
> p. 67]

The extreme of the defense of detachment leads to the development of the schizoid character, as Guntrip has amply shown.

We have observed that these defenses, which are generally associated with psychopathology—regressive refusion with psychosis,
grandiosity with pathological narcissism, defensive detachment with
schizoidism, and splitting with borderline conditions—do not really
completely disappear in normal ego development. Our exploration of
the deeper layers of the normal personality reveals that these defenses
are still present and are in fact employed extensively. They become
more active, or rather more consciously active, in the deeper stages of
inner realization, revealing, in the presence of every ego individuality,
structures that are, or are similar to, psychotic, borderline, narcissistic
and schizoid structures. The individual does not usually become
pathological when these structures emerge in consciousness, indicating that they are not the dominant structures in the personality, but
they do cause considerable distress and anxiety.

Thus we see that, although in the normal individual the well-adapted
or "conflict-free" segment of ego predominates, the structure actually
contains all the forms of the major pathologies, both structural and
neurotic.

We have seen that the various defenses against ego inadequacy
involve regressions to various subphases of ego development, in the
attempt to contact the support of the dominant essential aspect of
each phase. Furthermore, the state of deficiency itself is a reflection
of difficulties in the rapprochement phase, indicating the absence
of the aspect of the Personal Essence. This is in accordance with
Kernberg's view that the state is a characteristic of the borderline

condition, which is taken to be primarily a reflection of difficulties in   375
the rapprochement phase.

From the perspective of Being, then the major mental pathologies can be understood thus:

- Psychosis is a reflection of the absence of, or conflicts about, the Merging Essence in the symbiotic stage.
- The schizoid condition is a reflection of the absence of, or conflicts about, the Strength Essence, mainly in the differentiation subphase.
- Pathological narcissism is a reflection of the absence of, or conflicts about, the Essential Self, primarily in the practicing subphase.
- The borderline condition is a reflection of the absence of, or conflicts about, the Personal Essence, primarily in the rapprochement subphase.
- Neurosis is a reflection of the absence of, or conflicts about, the essential aspects involved in the Oedipus complex. We will not discuss the oedipal phase here, but will only mention that it is possible to see that there are three essential aspects involved in it: the aspect of Passionate Love related to oedipal love; the aspect of Power related to oedipal hatred; and the aspect of the Personal Essence in one of its developments which involves the sensuous and sensual qualities. This last aspect has to do with personalizing the physical body, i.e., integrating it into the experience of the Personal Essence.

This is only a suggestive picture of different ego characters seen from the perspective of Being, and is not meant to be rigorous or complete.

The defenses against inadequacy—negative merging, grandiosity, and defensive detachment—are typically resorted to by the child at the beginning of the rapprochement phase, as we discussed in our exploration of the issues of that phase. We saw that the child resorts to these defenses especially when the environment does not respond in a phase-appropriate manner, in order to ward off the sense of helplessness, deflation and dependency that results from two developmental realizations at that time. The first is the disappointment resulting from the collapse of the sense of his grandeur and omnipotence. The second is the realization of his separateness from the mother, due to perceptual and cognitive maturation.

Thus it seems certain that ego inadequacy originates in this phase, at the end of the practicing period and the beginning of the rapprochement phase, around age one and a half. At that time the sense

376   of omnipotence and grandeur is lost, as we discussed in Chapter Twenty-One, due to the increasing cathexis of the body. At that time the child has substantially shifted his cathexis from Being to the psychophysical apparatus, as part of the process of ego development. He gains physical and mental wisdom in this way, but at the same time loses his connection to Being.

Thus his identity has largely shifted from Being to ego, through the developing cathexis of the body, and also due to the decathexis of the Essential Self. This process is of course taking place through the formation of self-representations.

In object relations theory, the sense of helplessness and inadequacy at this critical time of development is seen to be due to the realistic abandonment of omnipotence and the equally realistic perception of separateness. From the perspective of Being, however, this is not completely accurate; these realizations are a result of cathecting the body and identifying progressively with it, and then looking at reality from the perspective of the body and the physical senses. Since at the same time there is a decathexis of Being and a loss of identity with it, the child is no longer perceiving the world from the perspective of Essence with its different capacities.

It should now be clear that the ego inadequacy which appears at the beginning of rapprochement, which occurs simultaneously with the shift of identity from Being to the psychophysical apparatus, is due to the loss of contact with Being, just as Guntrip and Winnicott have indicated. We have also seen evidence that the defenses against this state are actually attempts to connect with certain essential aspects.

However, object relations theory in general, as we have discussed, views the psychophysical organism as our deepest self, and physical reality as the most real of all existence. This is because it is a theory constructed after the fact of cathecting physical reality, by theorists identified primarily with ego. Knowledge of Being allows one to see that this perspective is just part of the truth.

The various modes of the sense of inadequacy are connected with the absence of certain essential aspects. The sense of castration is the absence of the Will aspect, while that of impotence is absence of the Strength aspect. The sense of worthlessness is the absence of the Value aspect, and the sense of insignificance (or being nothing, as

Penny described it) is the absence of the Essential Self. These connections have been made by many students who experienced the state of inadequacy as a deficient emptiness (which is always a result of losing Essence), and then explored the deficiency [see our book *The Void* for more discussion of this point].

Chapter Thirty-One

Resolution
of
Ego Deficiency

G iven that ego is so cut off from the real resources of Being, one might wonder where it gets its strength and energy! Part of the answer is that individuals vary in terms of the rigidity of their identifications with ego structures, and as we saw in our discussion of maturity and metabolism, the less rigid or the more flexible the ego individuality is, the more permeable it is to Essence and its resources. Under such conditions, one has available some real strength and energy, at least some of the time. However, the sense of who one is is never devoid of the state of inadequacy. The self of ego is what is inadequate, even though one might not really be inadequate to the demands upon one. This is seen in students who are experiencing essential states but still believe they are inadequate. This is a result of identifying with the ego individuality. Individuals believe consciously or unconsciously that they are truly inadequate, because they believe they are the ego individuality, and this individuality is actually basically inadequate. It is hopeless for the ego individuality to become free of its inadequacy; this is why most individuals identify so much with inadequacy and hopelessness. When one identifies with ego then one is, in a manner of speaking, truly inadequate and hopeless.

This fact confronts all students of essential realization at some point. As they experience essential states and perceptions, they become hopeful that they can become adequate. But they are ultimately frustrated and disappointed when they realize, over and over, that

378

this is completely impossible. They cannot be completely adequate while they continue being who they have been in the past. They must ultimately let go of the identity with ego. This is the metamorphosis known in spiritual traditions as "self-realization," and constitutes a profound shift of identity.

Ego, however, has a kind of energy available for its functioning that becomes more available due to the state of inadequacy. When one looks deeply into the personality, before ego inadequacy is revealed consciously, one finds the state blocked in a specific way. Our experience is that many people complain of kidney tension and pain when they are dealing with this issue. Its blockage is always connected with physical contractions at the adrenal glands, especially the one over the left kidney. If one looks closely, one will perceive a very small hole in that area, with strong defenses against it. This is the state of inadequacy as it is seen in the unconscious and reflected in the body.

This contraction at the adrenal glands, which is usually subtle and not available to normal consciousness, seems to affect them in a way that makes them generate more adrenalin, which creates an excess of a particular energy that feels active, speedy, unsettled, agitated and excited. This is the primary energy that ego uses, which is clear in states of fear, agitation, anger and worry. One then cannot sit down, cannot be calm, cannot settle, physically or mentally. This is what Jordan meant in the report in Chapter Seven when he said he felt manic when he was feeling grandiose. This is in contrast to the energy of the Strength Essence, which is calm, and also excited in the sense of vibrant aliveness and which makes one feel more present and clear.

When the blockage against the inadequacy dissolves, and one feels the state itself, the hole at the left kidney expands and is felt to be centered at the solar plexus. The solar plexus is the location for the emergence and operation of the Will aspect, and so with a hole there the feeling is of the absence of support, confidence and solidity of the Will. This shows the importance of the Will for the resolution of the inadequacy. We have already discussed how any ego activity leads to blocking the Will. We will now turn to the discussion of how ego inadequacy is resolved.

It is clear from our discussion so far that complete resolution is possible only with a thorough shift of identity to Being; later chapters will

380   elucidate what this means. Here we will discuss the major steps in this process of resolution, focusing in detail only on the points relevant both to resolving ego inadequacy and to developing of the Personal Essence. Although the process of self-realization is much larger and more involved than what we can cover here, we can understand its main steps and issues by understanding the resolution of inadequacy.

A major step towards resolution of the state of inadequacy is the integration of the third objective dimension of Essence. The entry to this dimension occurs by confronting and understanding the defensive nature of ego. One need not exert any effort to focus one's attention on this aspect of ego. The defensive function is usually at its peak when one is dealing with ego inadequacy. The strongest and most tenacious defenses and resistances come up to ward off the awareness of inadequacy. One's whole consciousness contracts. One might feel heavy, thick and defended. One feels defensive and resistant to going within. The consciousness becomes dull and insensitive. The tensions in the body become intense; they can become so severe that one gets headaches. The impression at such times is that the individual is defending himself as if he is fighting for dear life. In fact, it turns out that this is one of the fears generated by ego inadequacy. Some individuals become afraid that if they feel so vulnerable and helpless they might die. Others become afraid that they will get so small that they will disappear.

The defensive function of ego is at its height, against both the inadequacy and its feared consequences. These fears are reasonable in two ways. The first is that ego inadequacy is a reliving of an earlier experience in very early childhood, when one was actually vulnerable, helpless and dependent. Although we discussed the state of inadequacy in terms of the beginning of the phase of rapprochement, its emergence or development is a gradual process that starts much earlier, in the first months of life, because the process of cathecting physical reality starts so early. Many students actually remember themselves as infants, alone, helpless and scared.

This kind of memory might be a composite of many experiences at different early times, but it does reflect some experiences in the earliest months of life. Since the individual normally identifies deeply with the state of deficiency it becomes understandable why, when this state becomes conscious, it generates so much terror and fear of death. This reflects the actual helplessness of the psychophysical organism at such early times.

The other reason for the terror is that at such early times, at the beginning of ego development, ego structures are still unstable, shaky and not unified. Since one identifies with such structures, in these experiences there is a natural fear of disappearing, for one is aware of one's sense of self as shaky, unstable, weak and vulnerable. In fact the experience can lead to a kind of death, which is the disappearance of these unstable and early-formed structures. This is obvious in the cases we discussed above, where at some point the individual disappears completely, and only emptiness is left. We see this in the following report from Jackson, as a result of his working on the pain he feels with the people he works with. He writes:

> You ask me about the pain—to understand it and where it comes from. The pain makes me feel very small, very young. I feel as though I am supposed to be strong even before I could sustain my own life. I am very young and I am crying, no one comes—I cry harder and still no one comes—I feel more alone and isolated and smaller—I hurt and am sad to be so alone and feel smaller. You said, let these feelings happen and when you say this I feel a shudder of terror go through me, a deeper terror that if I get smaller there will be nothing left—nothing even to feel the pain. At first I do not want to get smaller—then I see and feel me getting smaller and more alone, until puff— there is nothing there. No me—no crying—no sound. Just quiet, a deep quiet—still, dark—black dark—calm, no sound. A strange kind of awareness that nothing is being observed and I am not present to observe. There is nothing except Blackness—empty, yet not lacking—black and not devoid of light—a rich emptiness—nothing desired and nothing wanted.
>
> Something on the periphery is moving fast and jumping up and down, as if to catch my attention, as if it did not understand (or maybe it did all too well). And even this fades and again only Black. It is difficult to explain this richness and fullness. I even taste a sweetness in the back of my mouth. I have no desire to move away or move—I seem to move without moving. My body seems to be of no value. Peace—quiet—fulfillment. I hear your voice as though it is in the Blackness. I have no fear, as if I already know somehow.

The result of experiencing such emptiness is usually peace and clarity, but the ego does not know that will happen. This peace is anticipated as death by various structures of ego.

When one finally allows the state of vulnerability, it can manifest as a state of defenselessness. This indicates the dropping of the defensiveness of ego. Such letting go means the abandonment, usually transitory, of certain deep identification systems. These constitute the core of the defensive structures of ego. The result is again the manifestation of emptiness, this time vast and of immeasurable depth. It is a deeper dimension of space.

This development then leads to the emergence of a new essential aspect, the central aspect on the third objective dimension, the entry into the third dimension of Essence. This aspect is actually a certain combination of essential aspects, specifically of Universal Will and Truth, now functioning as one aspect or presence. When this presence is embodied, it feels awesome in its power and solidity. One feels that he can handle anything, that nothing can sway him if he does not want it to. This presence is that of Will in a deeper, more expanded form: more powerful, more solid, more immovable, and its support is awesome.

An example of this development is the case of Jill, whom we discussed in the section on rapprochement. We find her here in the middle of a big expansion in her work, both in terms of working with more people and using different modalities. She has been working hard and feeling successful and fulfilled personally in terms of her work. She has been complaining of being tired, in her private teaching sessions. We work on a dream of hers, of being small and young. This leads to the perception of some distortion in her body image. She then starts experiencing the fullness of the Personal Essence, which is not a new state for her. But she realizes the presence of a hard plate of tension, as if she needs such a plate to support her presence. The hard plate of tension turns out to be an ego defense she uses as support in order to do what she needs to do in her life. This exposes a contraction at the spleen and left kidney area. This then exposes some deficient emptiness that expands into Space. She then starts experiencing a sense of a solid presence in her lower body but there is still resistance to it. This leads to a discussion of her life, how she lives it, and the need for inner discipline.

The more she understands the meaning of inner discipline and the need for it in her life, to support her true accomplishment and work, the more she feels the solid presence of will expanding with its sense of power and immensity. She then experiences herself as an immense and powerful presence, solid and immovable, which gives her the feeling of being an adult.

The experience of this new dimension of Will is of being supported in a specific way. One feels one does not need ego defenses, because one now has the real "defense." This aspect of Essence is sometimes specifically experienced as the defense of Essence. This is one reason why we call this aspect the Citadel. The sense is of being supported, protected, defended by a presence that is as formidable and invulnerable as a citadel. It is the presence of Essence as the defender of the Truth.

One realizes that the defensive functions of ego are actually a reflection of this aspect, an imitation of it, and hence unreal and distorted. Here one begins to understand what is needed to protect one's essential realization, so that it is not lost, but rather continues to develop securely. It is the need for the defensive functions of ego that cuts one off from Being. And this need is due, to a large extent, to the unconscious identification with the inadequacy of ego.

While the aspect of the Citadel gives one a sense of solid support and formidable protection, one feels it is okay to be. The presence of this aspect gives one the feeling of being grown up, able to take care of oneself and live one's life the way one chooses, in a real, undefensive manner. As far as we can tell, this aspect seems not to be available in early childhood, which might partly account for the fact that, in the process of cathecting the body, Being is decathected. This point needs more exploration, but this aspect does feel like such an immense and solid sense of presence that it is difficult to imagine the toddler's organism being able to embody it.

When the Citadel aspect is present, it gives the individual the possibility of looking at ego inadequacy in an objective and unemotional way. One feels so supported that the state of inadequacy loses its threatening property. The Citadel gives one a sense of solidity and support, with no grandiose ideas. One is clearly aware that it is an essential presence, and not a physical or mental power, that it is a support for Being and not for ego.

384   The sense of support and protection related to this aspect is much deeper than the state of awesome immensity. One begins to learn that the realization of this aspect requires from one something specific. It is not a matter only of inner understanding. It is a state in which Will and Truth are harmonized, are functioning as one state. This means that its influence is to manifest Will in the service of Truth. It is actually solid Will in the service and support of objective Truth. To embody (realize) this aspect, one's actions, and all of one's life, must function according to objective Truth.

At this point one learns, usually through the difficulties of trial and error, that one cannot continue to experience Being if one lives his life according to the belief that he is the ego individuality. One's action, behavior, style of life (all manifestations of Will) must be in harmony with the Truth of Being. One cannot indulge in false identifications, regard essential experience as some sort of reward, and expect to live the life of Essence.

The aspect of the Citadel provides guidance for how to live one's life according to the Truth of Being. It is referred to as "objective conscience," for it is like the conscience of Essence. It gives one support and protection, i.e., is present and available, only when one is living according to the Truth of Essence. In other words, its presence (realization) is equivalent to living according to the laws of Being.

Realizing this aspect means many practical things. One must change one's practical life in a way that supports essential life, rather than impeding it. One's activities, interests, associations, relationships and so on, now have to be according to the Truth, in the service of, and in harmony with, Essence.

Living the life of Truth is the true meaning of inner discipline. One actually must discipline oneself in a certain way. However, it is not the usual understanding of discipline. It is not according to rules one has in the mind—which is the control of the superego—and it is not according to someone else's idea of discipline. It is very personal, and depends on the particular person and his situation in life. He has to find his own way, his own application of objective Truth in his life. And he can do this by realizing the Citadel, by using it as his true conscience.

This true life is seen to be the real support and protection of Essence and its development. The inner state itself is not enough. The state itself, in fact, will not be present if one lives according to lies and delusions. One has to become real or this aspect is not permanently attained. If it is not attained then one cannot resolve ego inadequacy. This aspect becomes primary for such resolution.

This is understandable when we remember that the inadequacy is primarily due to abandoning Being and identifying with the body (the psychophysical organism), and looking at life and living it only from this limited perspective. The way of life of the individuality of ego is based on partial truth, and hence, on falsehood. To live according to the ego perspective is to live a life that supports inadequacy, in fact, that is based on it. To live without taking into consideration the Truth of Being is to perpetuate inadequacy by living according to it. This is exactly what the child learns to do in the process of ego development, creating the defensiveness of ego.

The hope of resolving inadequacy is in the realization of the Citadel aspect. This implies that one is willing to live one's life from the perspective of objective Truth, which takes into consideration the fact of Being, without denying physical reality. Although all students deal with ego inadequacy, only a minority move steadily towards resolving it. This is because not many are willing to adjust their lives according to objective Truth. This deep surrender is rare and requires a great deal of maturity.

When the Citadel is realized it creates the possibility of experiencing the first major resolution of ego inadequacy. It is the presence of the Citadel that allows the hole, or deficient emptiness, of inadequacy to be replaced by the various aspects of Essence. This happens specifically first by the emergence of the Merging Essence in the solar plexus—the location is important but not absolutely necessary—exactly where the inadequacy is usually experienced.

We return to the case of Jill, whom we have discussed in terms of realizing the Citadel. In her next session two weeks later, she tells me how efficiently she has been functioning in her life, especially in terms of doing the right things to support her work with her clients. After a while in the session she starts feeling the usual tiredness. She starts having images of decay and death, as she experiences some separation from her mother, in her mind. This leads to feeling something like a golden elixir in the area of the spleen. This emergence of the Merging Essence coincides with feelings of happiness

386   about her life and for knowing me. This leads to several sessions of her dealing with issues of support, in terms of others supporting her, or she supporting them, which leads to more reliance on her own resources and inner support, and more responsibility for herself and her life.

We must remember that the state of inadequacy experienced in childhood is due primarily to two causes: the feeling of impotence and castration when the sense of omnipotence is lost, and the feeling of helplessness and dependency when separateness is perceived and believed. The presence of the Citadel remedies the impotence and castration. It is also a state of Will, which gives one innate confidence. This allows one to stop the ego activity and desire that block Will and create negative merging. This in turn leads to the Merging Essence, which remedies the helplessness due to separateness.

The important point here is that the Merging Essence manifests— the good mother is gained—without sacrificing the Truth. Because of the presence of the Merging aspect, one does not feel alone and isolated although one is living the life of Truth. The individuality of ego sacrifices the Truth of Being to avoid isolation and the loss of mother's good image. But with the support of the Citadel one lives connected to Being, in real conscience, and is able to experience the sweetness and love that the mother's good image is supposed to provide.

The realization of the Citadel actualizes the Merging Essence right at the site of the inadequacy. This then brings about the presence of the Personal Essence, along with the heart qualities and the Diamond Guidance. It is the same as the state we discussed as indicating the realization of the Personal Essence, plus the supporting and protecting presence of the Citadel, which is also reflected in a certain style of life.

This resolution is not final, because it is not complete. We will come back to this issue and its deeper resolution in the final chapters. However, it is crucial for the process of development and realization. It does not completely eliminate the state of inadequacy. This state is present whenever there is identity with self-image. Nevertheless, the state becomes much less intense, less significant, more understood and easily tolerable. Basically, with this resolution, one attains a much greater measure of disidentification from the state of inadequacy. When the inadequacy manifests it is regarded as an emotional state, just like any other, that is transient and conditional on certain identifications. One stops believing it is a true description of who one is. It will manifest whenever there is a major expansion, but it does not stop one's expansion.

Disidentification from inadequacy allows the expansion necessary for the development of the Personal Essence without fear or distortion. This opens the way to the ever-expanding process of personalizing Essence.

Chapter Thirty-Two

The
Complete Person

Realizing the Essential Citadel and absorbing its perspective is a big shift in the process of essential realization. It is a movement towards greater actualization, which precipitates numerous changes in practical life, as well as many further essential experiences and perceptions. In one's environment, one's work and one's personal relationships, Essence becomes the primary driving force, the central inner reality.

This naturally puts pressure on the ego sense of self, the identity of ego, which has been based on a life of images and inadequacy. The ego self becomes increasingly ego alien; it is felt to be the central source of psychological contraction and suffering. This ego self becomes the focus of the work of understanding the personality.

Living according to objective Truth automatically exposes the part that is unwilling to live in this way. This part is the ego self, whose development involved the increasing cathexis of physical reality and the abandonment of Being. So this self becomes the main identification system challenged by this level of development.

Exploring this identification precipitates the entry into the fourth objective dimension, which is the experience of Essence as objective knowledge. It is knowing by being, rather than through mental activity. This dimension is also that of the teachings of Essence; it makes possible the understanding of how the perspective of each aspect can be a whole teaching, a path for essential realization. All existing teachings regarding Being become comprehensible in this dimension.

The perspective of each aspect is seen as a way of freedom from the self of ego. Each aspect becomes understood in its relation to the self, and to the experience of dissolution of this self. This is a wide and deep level of essential experience, which ultimately leads to the experience of ego death, or the annihilation of the self. This happens through the detailed, specific, and objective understanding of the identity of ego. The work is deep and profound, involving realizations that are shattering to one's identity with ego. The gist of the understanding has to do with what is called ego activity. This is the inner activity, psychic activity, which is the life of the ego self, which cannot exist without this activity. This realization crystallizes in a direct, experiential understanding of hope and desire, which are the main activities of ego. The ego activity is fueled by hope and desire for the good, the pleasurable and the safe, along with movement away from the bad, the painful and the frightening.

To hope is to hope for something in the future that is not present in the now. This implies that the now is not completely accepted. It is judged as not good enough, if not actually bad. It indicates the absence of complete acceptance of one's experience. Since Essence is Being, it is always in the now. So the movement of hope is automatically a rejection of the now, and a rejection of Being.

Desire exists, on the other hand, because there is hope. If there is no hope at all then what is the point of desire? One can argue about original and natural desire that is independent of hope. It is debatable whether there is such a thing, but here we are discussing the desire that is normally experienced by ego. This desire indicates the presence of hope (for gratification). We see then that ego activity is primarily a cycle of rejection, hope and desire.

This is not difficult to understand conceptually, but to actually see this cycle in operation, to actually feel the ego activity, and understand it directly, is an extremely subtle, and hence difficult task. For instance, the moment one says, "Okay, I will look and try to understand this," one is now desiring this understanding. One is thus identifying with the cycle of ego activity, which makes it difficult to look at it in an objective way. The experience of disidentification from ego activity simply occurs on its own in some situations, when one is being, and is not caught up in this cycle.

This initiates a cataclysmic transformation that finally results in the repeated experience of the cessation of ego activity. When this happens

390   it is experienced as an annihilation of the identity that one has been familiar with since one was conscious of existing. The experience itself is the absence of all inner activity, psychic or mental. Annihilation is then experienced as nothing but the presence of an aspect of Essence. The self is extinct, and Essence is present as Annihilation. It is a state of complete and total peace, of no stirring of ego. This is a difficult experience to imagine without having the taste of it, because it does not make sense to the mind to experience a presence that feels like annihilation. This is due to the limited range of experience of ego and its concepts. When one recognizes Essence the range of what one can experience expands in amazing and unexpected directions.

One experiences one's source now as peace, instead of the feverishness of ego activity. There is no sense of self, and no feeling of need for self. This state is not necessarily permanent, nor always present, but does become available to experience. In other words, one learns that one can live without a sense of identity.

If disidentification from ego-inadequacy opens the way to expansion and supports the development of the Personal Essence, then the annihilation of identity does even more. The ego sense of identity has a restrictive influence on expansion, because it is a specific, and, to a great degree, fixed sense of self. We have already discussed how this limits the process of personalizing essential aspects, when an aspect is contrary to this sense of self. Now this unchanging sense of self becomes restrictive because it cannot allow the presence of qualities that seem to it contradictory, not only to its sense of self, but to each other. This latter limitation prevents one from experiencing one's personal presence as having many qualities at the same time.

The ego self cannot allow the experience of being alive, joyful, compassionate, strong, peaceful, and so on, all at the same time. This is because in the process of its development the ego identity is solidified through the process of selective identification, which occurs after some integration of this identity; thus there is a selection of identifications that do not contradict its already established feeling of self, but rather go along with and support this identity. Jacobson describes this selectivity in terms of identifying with parents:

> Moreover, the selectivity of identifications increasingly expresses the child's rebellious struggle for the development and maintenance of his own independent identity, since it

means: "In this respect I like you and want to be like you, but in other respects I don't like you and don't want to be like you; I want to be different, in fact myself." [Edith Jacobson, *The Self and the Object World*, p. 66]

So the capacity to be without this ego sense of self eliminates selectivity in one's personal experience of essential qualities, opening the consciousness to an unlimited range of qualities.

The absence of inner selectivity due to cessation of the feeling of self, coupled with the openness to expansion due to disidentification from ego inadequacy, allows a new possibility of realization. It makes it possible to complete the process of personalization of Essence, which is the absorption of all essential aspects into the Personal Essence, or the synthesis of all aspects into a personal presence. The essential aspects now constitute the very substance of the Personal Essence.

One not only feels one is a full personal presence, but that this very same presence includes the presence of Love, Joy, Strength, Compassion, Merging, Peace, Intelligence, Will, Consciousness, etc. Aspects are simultaneously personalized, with their capacities and functions integrated. This is a condition of completeness, of an amazing degree of integration. One is full and firm, strong and soft, sweet and warm, and so on. One is a complete person. This does not mean that one's personal presence from now on is always this complete state. It indicates that one is able to be present in this expanded state of Being.

The Personal Essence is an organic and fluid presence; there is no rigidity in it at all. All its states, through the whole process of its realization and development, are available to it now, manifesting according to the situation. Practically, this realization allows the capacity to be personal in any of the essential aspects, or any combination of them, depending on the demands of the situation.

The complete state of the Personal Essence brings a perception of one's presence as preciousness, beauty and regality. It is no wonder that the Personal Essence is called in some stories, the Princess Precious Pearl.

Chapter Thirty-Three
Personal Essence and Ego Boundaries

E ven at profound levels of realization of the Personal Essence, one can retain a certain sense of separateness and bounded- ness. This chapter will explore the reasons for the tenacity of this sense, the functions of the sense of separateness, and the means of moving through them to the cosmic or formless realms of Being.

The sense of being a separate individual is challenged only very far into the process of inner realization. This is partly because, although there is a clear but subtle experiential difference between the individuality of ego and the presence of Essence, the absence of the sense of separateness in the experience of the personal Essence is rarely noticed in the early stages of realization. The subtlety of this difference is not the only reason for the failure to perceive it. The main reason is that to see this difference one must be able to disidentify, to some extent, from the sense of being an individual. This is certainly not easy nor even desirable at the beginning.

One's ego boundaries are so much a part of ordinary perception that one never questions them; the sense of oneself as a separate entity is taken to be an objective and absolutely necessary characteristic of being a living human being. However, the ever-expanding development of the Personal Essence gradually puts pressure, by the mere fact of its presence, on the sense of being an ego individual, exposing the ego individuality as unreal.

Ignorance of this fundamental difference between Essence and ego in terms of the sense of being a person creates a subtle contraction in the psychophysical apparatus that becomes increasingly obvious as one becomes more familiar with the Personal Essence. This contraction becomes a pressure, a resistance or a sense of constriction against the full presence of the Personal Essence. The lack of clarity causes a confusion in one's mind between the Personal Essence and the ego individuality; one sometimes takes one for the other. One typically attributes to the Personal Essence characteristics that do not belong to it, but to the ego individuality.

Eventually one realizes that he has been attributing to the Personal Essence a sense of boundaries, which separate him from others and from the whole environment. It gradually dawns on him that the Personal Essence has no sense of boundaries at all, no sense of separateness whatsoever; and that the separateness one attributed to it belongs to the ego individuality. One starts to see that there has always been a subtle identification with the sense of separateness with respect to being a person.

As we have discussed, the sense of being a separate individual develops through the construction of ego boundaries. The ego individuality always has two characteristics: the sense of being a separate entity, and the sense of self, that is, the feeling of identity that differentiates the entity subjectively from other entities.

The sense of separateness is different from the sense of identity. The separateness involves the belief in individual boundaries, while the sense of self, which is like an emotional coloring of the entity, differentiates it from other entities.

People differ in their senses of self, but they all agree that they are independent entities, separate individuals. The sense of being an individual is more basic than the feeling of identity. A person can sometimes not know who he is, but he always knows clearly that he is a separate entity. It is inconceivable to ego how one can be a person, and not be separate. One may rightly ask how he would know where he ends and where others start, if he has no individual boundaries. How would he know what is his and what is another's? How would he know what is his personal experience and what is not? How could he live and act, without a sense of boundaries? These are deep questions, and ego cannot answer them.

Although it is true, as object relations theory states, that the sense of being a separate entity is a result of construction of bounded ego

394   structures, the fact remains that the human being does exist in an objective sense before he has any sense of individual boundaries. Thus, ego boundaries are not necessary for bare existence. The adult ego, however, cannot even conceive of how one could exist without being an individual. The closest he can come to such conception is the possibility that one might not be consciously aware that he is a separate individual, but is still existing as a separate individual. For instance in times of complete absorption in some activity, or in sleep, one is not aware that he is an entity, but one naturally thinks that certainly he is.

Most people, including psychologists, believe that an infant is a separate entity, but that he does not know it yet, only gradually coming to this realization. However this is not exact. The infant does not come to the realization that he is a separate individual. It is not a realization; it is a development, the creation of something that was not there to begin with. From the perspective of Being, as we have discussed, it is very clear that these ego boundaries are actually concepts, which involve emotional attachment to a certain image of the self. They are seen as ideas, empty of any fundamental or objective validity. In other words, the perception of Being is that there is no such thing as a separate individuality.

Confronting this truth is positively terrifying to ego. We have seen how difficult it is to surrender the sense of self, but that is nothing compared to the letting go of one's separating boundaries. It is not only difficult and terrifying as it approaches; it is completely inconceivable by the individual. This impossibility of conceiving of personal existence without the separating individual boundaries causes many misunderstandings:

- It is why individuals confuse the ego individuality with the Personal Essence. One cannot conceive of being without boundaries, so one automatically assumes that the experience of the Personal Essence includes the sense of boundaries. This causes a contraction against the presence of the Personal Essence in the latter stages of its development, in the form of holding on to these boundaries.
- It is the main reason why the man of spirit usually thinks of Being as impersonal or nonpersonal. Many teachings believe the personal element indicates the presence of ego boundaries.
- It is clearly the main reason for the division between the man of spirit and the man of the world. The first wants Being and the latter

wants to be a person. Since they both believe that Being does not have boundaries, and being a person is inseparable from having them, they cannot come to terms with each other. Each one believes that the other is missing something, and they are both right. In our understanding, they are both overlooking the Personal Essence; thus each has only half of the truth.

Only the objective understanding of the Personal Essence can show how it is possible to be a person and not have ego boundaries. The continued presence of the Personal Essence, along with its further development, slowly shows that the sense of separateness belongs to ego and not to itself. The student becomes aware of certain tensions and constrictions, and by exploring them finally realizes that they are nothing but ego boundaries. He realizes that these boundaries have been almost impossible to perceive, because he has been so identified with separateness. He gradually learns that the boundaries are what give him the sense of separateness, the sense of being a separate individual. He then longs for their dissolution, but he is at the same time terrified of this possibility.

This is a paradoxical situation, in which one wants to be free from separateness, but the one who wants that is the sense of separateness itself. The separate individuality wants to be free from the constricting boundaries, but this means it wants its own cessation. This produces extreme frustration, conflict and anxiety. We let Penny, whom we introduced in Chapter Twenty-Nine, describe this situation, as she starts becoming aware of this issue:

> I noticed today I have a sensation around my body that feels like a film around me, like some kind of a protective coating. It is very difficult to experience, feel, or verbalize how I am behind this coating or film.
>
> I felt it took a lot of courage to talk to you today. I have a very hard time seeing myself behind or without the coating. I feel protected and safe within the boundaries of my "shell" as it were. I see the shell or coating reflected in my eyesight, everything is slightly out of focus. The film seems to put some area, some thickness, some filter between myself and others, and between myself and myself. I feel tough on the outside with my coating, sort of like a scab that protects a wound.
>
> Right now I feel my scab is getting "muscular-like," soft and less and less hard and protective. I am feeling alarmed

as if signals are going off in my head to warn me of danger. I have always needed to keep a shell between me and the world, a separation. I feel some push from within to break the barrier, however terrifying it seems. I feel terrified to think of living without the boundaries, the separateness, distance, the film. I feel extremely fragile underneath the coating, as if the coating really is a scab protecting a raw, open sore underneath. Anger is part of this barrier; I'd rather be pissed off than almost anything. And, anger is part of the fragility. Fear is also both inside and out. I am afraid on the outside for the barrier to be broken and I am terrified on the inside of everything, like my guts, spilling out.

I feel isolated behind the screen, the wall, the boundary. My life somehow touches no one here, and no one can reach me, no matter how hard they try. I think I trust you more than anyone in the world, and somehow I cannot let you through nor really reach out to you. I yearn for contact, for closeness with one other human being and see that I don't have it. However, right now I feel I cannot survive without this sense of separateness.

This report contains several important points regarding the direct experiential perception of one's sense of separateness (and we should note that this report is typical of the experience of many students at this stage):

1. *The sense of boundaries can be experienced in a very definite way.* Penny felt it as a kind of film around her body, as a thickness like a scab, a hardness, a barrier. This might sound strange, but only because to experience individual boundaries so clearly is a rare experience; it is not something one often hears discussed. The immediacy of the physical perception is not unusual among students who have learned to distinguish very subtle states. Also, it is not easy or simple to come to this perception. We notice that Penny started by stating how difficult it is for her to experience this state, or verbalize it.

The direct perception of ego boundaries requires lengthy and deep work, letting go of ego identifications, and a great refinement and depth of awareness that is usually not available without the presence of Essence. It took Penny more than six years of intensive inner exploration to become able to experience the boundaries that give her the sense of separateness.

We have discussed how any ego identification system is, at some level, a contraction in the organism. The ego structure that composes ego boundaries is experienced as a contraction around the body. The boundaries are, at the core, the boundaries of the body. This is common experience, and reflects Mahler's description of the beginning formations of the self:

> The body ego contains two kinds of self-representations: an inner core of the body image, with a boundary that is turned toward the inside of the body and divides it from the ego, and an outer layer of sensoriperceptive engrams that contributes to the boundaries of the "body self" (cf. Bergmann, 1963 discussing Federn's concepts). [Margaret S. Mahler et al., *The Psychological Birth of the Human Infant*, p. 46]

Then she goes on to say about the boundaries of the body self:

> The sensoriperceptive organ—the "peripheral rind of the ego," as Freud called it—contributes mainly to the self's demarcation from the object world. [*Ibid.*, p. 47]

So, according to Mahler, it is the perception of, and sensations at, the boundaries of the body that lead to the formation of the ego boundaries which separate the individual from the object world.

It would be a mistake to assume that the mere perception of having physical contours creates the sense of separateness. The sense of separateness is created by the formation and maintenance of ego structures, which are cathected; i.e., held onto with emotional (libidinal) energy. This can be clearly seen in the many cases in which there is a distortion in the body image, indicating that the image is a mental structure and not an objective perception. [For more on this subject see our book *The Void*.]

Without these structures there is no sense of separateness. Some aspects of Being involve perception of body contours without those contours bounding the sense of presence. Ego boundaries are experienced as a film or thickness around the body, because their reflection in the body is a surface tension. This subtle contraction, which is characteristic of all identification systems due to the presence of the defensive element, is experienced in different states of hardness, or thickness, depending on the degree of tension, like any other physical tension. It becomes particularly hard or thick or rigid when there is anxiety regarding it. This happens particularly when one becomes aware of the possibility of its dissolution. The extreme anxiety about loss of boundaries causes the surface tension to increase, which makes it easier to perceive.

398   To believe that one's boundaries coincide with the external contours of the body indicates that one has not only cathected the body, but also has decathected Being. Belief in ego boundaries involves the conception that one is primarily the body.

2. *Ego boundaries create not only a sense of separateness, but, in a fundamental way, a sense of isolation and lack of contact.* This was painfully felt by Penny above. This is also a subtle perception, requiring a great deal of disidentification. As we discussed in the section on contact, the individuality of ego feels like a kind of personal contact, but only the Personal Essence can make real, direct contact.

Our present discussion of boundaries makes it clear why this is so. It is not only because ego individuality is a mental structure and not a beingness, but also because its very existence is based on its boundaries. These boundaries separate it from the rest of the world much more profoundly than is usually assumed. When one experiences the quality of contact of the Personal Essence, it becomes clear how thoroughly ego is shut off within its boundaries, as if behind walls. It is painfully isolated from true human contact.

It is common understanding that deep contact requires that one relax, let go of one's boundaries, and become vulnerable. The essential contact of the Personal Essence is made possible by a complete relaxation of defensive boundaries, a total vulnerability. This immediate, real contact is possible only for a personal presence that does not have the isolating boundaries of ego. This quality of the Personal Essence is mysterious, even miraculous.

One might think that the sense of isolation and painful separateness in this process, as reported by Penny, is not normal, but rather the result of a kind of schizoid defense. In fact it is a manifestation of schizoid-type defenses, but this deep level of schizoid defense is present in all egos, regardless of how integrated and developed they are.

The truth is that the sense of separateness of ego is a schizoid phenomenon, but it is usually experienced in a mild form. The ego boundaries are a manifestation of the schizoid sector of the personality, of which no ego is devoid. The schizoid experience becomes intense and more manifest, and therefore more visible, when this separateness is challenged.

The separateness of ego individuality is the outward, usually acceptable, manifestation of ego's schizoid characteristics. The markedly schizoid character is basically a personality crystallized around this sector of ego.

In the process of essential realization, the issue of ego boundaries is resolved by dealing with the schizoid sector in one's personality, among other things. It is one of the most painful to deal with, but not necessarily the most subtle.

3. *Ego boundaries always have a defensive nature.* This is what Penny meant when she felt the boundaries as protection, or as a scab that is hiding a rawness. This is part of the reason for the fear of losing the boundaries.

4. *The fundamental fear, however, is the terror that without ego boundaries there is no separate individual existence.* Penny expressed the feeling that she could not conceive of herself existing without boundaries. This terror is virtually impossible to allay. The individual cannot, on his own, let go of the boundaries. He *is* the boundaries, and hence, he cannot do anything to be free from them. That is why it is said in spiritual teachings that the freedom from boundaries cannot be accomplished with method or technique. At this stage one must drop all methods and techniques. This segment of the process of inner transformation is termed the "no-method" path. Zen Buddhism emphasizes the no-method approach, as we see in the words of Huang Po, one of the most respected Zen masters in history:

> Whoever has an instant understanding of this truth suddenly transcends the whole hierarchy of saints and adepts belonging to any of the Three Vehicles. You have always been one with the Buddha, so do not pretend you can AT-TAIN to this oneness by various practices. . . . The approach to it is called the Gateway of the Stillness beyond all Activity. . . . Not till your thoughts cease all their branching here and there, not till you abandon all thought of seeking for something, not till your mind is motionless as wood or stone, will you be on the right road to the Gate. [Translated by John Blofeld, *The Zen Teaching of Huang Po*, pp. 79-80]

One cannot free oneself from boundaries for several reasons:

- One is the boundaries. The sense of being an individual is the presence of boundaries. So if one does anything to try to free himself, he will be automatically asserting his presence, which is the presence of boundaries. If he even desires, wishes or wants the absence of boundaries he will be merely expressing the desires, wishes and wants of his individuality; and hence he will be asserting the presence of boundaries. Being has no desires. Being, even the Personal Essence, is completely desireless. The presence of any desire is the presence of the ego individuality, and hence of ego boundaries. Most spiritual teachings say that one cannot attain enlightenment if one desires it; only when one lets go of all desire, even desire for enlightenment, can it happen.

- Doing anything at all indicates the presence of ego activity, and the action of hope and desire. It involves rejection of the present, which requires the presence of a rejecting individual, which again implies the presence of ego boundaries.

- Using any technique or method, doing anything intentional, means also asserting the will of the ego, which is inseparable from the ego individuality. Exercising this separate will, and asserting one's own choice, at this point of inner transformation, is contraindicated because it means not only asserting one's individuality, but also blocking the essential Will. The presence of the Will Essence is indispensable for resolving the issue of boundaries, and it is present only when one does not desire, or exert any effort towards, anything. We illustrate this point with the report of a student of his experience in a group session. Ben writes:

> I said that I was feeling hot, my lips were burning. And that there was a lot of energy present. I said that I was aware that I was angry at the whole world, at you, at the group, at my clients, for telling me what to do.
> I said that I felt like I would rather be a mechanic or a carpenter; however if I became a mechanic, then nothing would get done unless I exclusively did the work. You pointed out that I wanted to be alone, but that I was resisting being all alone. I felt and said that I must look at why I do not want to be alone.
> Then I felt that I was experiencing myself as if I were hanging in mid-air with my arms and legs flailing. You then pointed out to me how you saw that it was interesting how one's will gets blocked by trying to act. Seeing this, right away I felt solid, calm, and clear.

Ben was resisting aloneness by engaging in the negative manifestation that indicates movement towards negative merging. Seeing that he resisted aloneness, he allowed himself to drop the negative merging. This exposed the state of ego inadequacy (hanging in mid-air) that he was resisting the aloneness for, for aloneness meant facing this inadequacy. Letting go of his ego activity precipitated the presence of the Will aspect, which made him feel solid, clear and supported, rather than suspended.

Understanding ego activity brings about (among other things) the personalization of the Intelligence aspect. The Personal Essence becomes present in a precious, brilliant, exquisitely smooth and luminous form. The experience is to be, completely, with no concern or attempt to be anything. This seems to move emotional and instinctual libido towards Being. It is interesting that this state of the Personal Essence is connected to the sense of responsibility; one understands that one's ultimate responsibility is to be.

This also resolves the deep guilt that one experiences when one lets go of ego activity. One feels guilty just being, instead of doing things to help others. One feels just to be is selfish, and involves abandoning others, not caring for them. One then realizes that the best that one can do emotionally for another is to be, to be there, to be present for him. This is real responsibility.

Before we proceed to describing how this issue of boundaries is resolved, we will first discuss the various manifestations of ego boundaries.

These manifestations become clear at the stage of development in which the Personal Essence is in a state of completeness, and the capacity to be without the ego sense of self exposes the main remaining issue of ego, that of individual boundaries. Boundaries begin to be seen as antithetical to the full experience of Personal Essence, being a remnant of ego identification. In other words, one finds that he can be the Personal Essence, and sometimes be without the sense of self, but that there is a remaining contraction. Understanding the relationship of boundaries to the Personal Essence brings about the emergence of the fifth objective dimension of Essence, the dimension in which each aspect is experienced as Love. Compassion is felt as Love, as are Peace, Joy, Will, Truth and so on. This is a vast and magnificent dimension.

402   The dimension of Love might manifest as a result of understanding ego boundaries, or it might manifest first and uncover the issue of ego boundaries. It is what is needed to resolve this basic issue of ego.

The process of becoming aware of ego boundaries involves perceiving the tensions and images regarding the contours of the body, which are experienced as having some property—thickness, tension, peculiar sensation—that distinguishes them from the inside of the body. The perceived boundaries do not always fit the actual contours of the body. Sometimes they extend slightly around it, as some kind of a ball, or as a distortion of the objective shape of the body. Sometimes they are experienced all around the body, when their function is to give the sense of individuality. Sometimes they are clearly experienced in some places in the body, but not in others. There are different kinds of ego boundaries, which feel different and have different functions. However, they all give the sense of being a separate individual. Each set of boundaries forms a sub-issue, which can be resolved separately. The resolution of ego boundaries in general means the letting go of all boundaries. This is a very dramatic and cataclysmic experience.

The issue of ego boundaries is much more difficult to understand and resolve than that of the ego self or identity. Paradoxically, although working with this issue requires a great deal of work, it is only the complete abandonment of all effort that brings the resolution. This part of essential realization is the main step towards freedom from ego, and is considered by some spiritual teachings to be the experience of enlightenment. The issue of separating boundaries is expected to be the most difficult barrier on any spiritual path.

A lot of the work on this issue can be accomplished by exploring the various functions of boundaries. Here are the main types of ego boundaries, in terms of their functions:

1. *Individuality*. This is the sense of being a separate individual. In this most general layer of ego boundaries, one feels one's boundaries as a soft and smooth surface, with a kind of dullness of sensation. This dull sensation feels like a thickness around oneself, but feels warm, comforting and familiar. One recognizes it as the familiar sense of himself. This familiar sense usually reminds one of his early life, for it reflects the basic emotional tone of his childhood home.

The individuality is composed of ego identifications which have the function of giving it not only its separateness, but its sense of identity as well. There is a recognition of one's person in it. It reflects one's personal history, and feels very familiar. It is actually the sense of being the individual that one has been aware of for most of one's life. It is, in a sense, an imitation of the Personal Essence; for this reason we sometimes refer to this state as the false pearl.

This false pearl is actually what one is ultimately afraid of losing; it is what dissolves when one makes the transition to the formless dimensions of Being. It is a universal phenomenon; in a sense it is inherited or transmitted throughout the ages, from one generation to another in human history. It is the most universal and the deepest human conditioning. It is the condition of the overwhelming majority of humankind, ignorantly taken to be the real human element, when it is only an imitation or at best an incomplete development.

The remaining types of ego boundaries are, in a sense, the building blocks of this overall sense of bounded individuality; they can be seen as the functional differentiations of this layer of the personality.

2. *Restraint.* This is a sense of boundaries that feels harder and thicker than the first. The sensation is thick and leathery. The function is to restrain oneself, one's feelings, impulses and energy. Restraint is more conscious than defense or resistance. Some individuals seem to manifest it much more than others, reflecting demands in their early life, when they felt they had to restrain themselves.

3. *Resistance.* This is even a thicker and a denser sensation than the above. One feels one's skin thick and dull but not hard, as if it is made out of rubber. This is a sense of boundaries, an identification system, whose function is resisting experience, especially any experience that threatens one's sense of separateness and individuality. This is the state of the ego individuality in the mode of resistance. In this state one cannot help but resist. Whatever one does, whatever one says, whatever one thinks, is resistance. One *is* resistance; sometimes students in this state say that they feel like a thick rubber ball, resisting any intrusion.

4. *Defense.* This is the presence of the boundaries in the function of defense. The defense is usually unconscious. Here one feels one's boundaries to be very hard and rigid. One feels defended, like a gladiator with iron armor all around his body.

404   One feels not only armored, but feels that he is nothing but armor. He feels very strong and impenetrable, strong willed and rigidly determined. He also feels completely isolated from others, totally shut off from human contact. There is a sense of emptiness, of alienation, of the absence of human gentleness and softness.

Here the boundaries are functioning as the schizoid defense of isolation and defensive detachment. One defends himself against the vulnerability of being human by becoming only boundaries, hard, rigid, harsh and alienating. One feels untouchable, unaffected by others, without any human emotion. One feels almost nonhuman, as if he were from an alien planet, except that he still feels he is a separate individuality.

This state of individuality lacks all other elements of being human, except for the sense of existing as an individual. It shows the ultimate outcome of identifying with separating boundaries. This is the most alienating of ego boundaries, and the most painful to work through. Its dissolution feels like a painful, terrifying and completely helpless state of fragmentation. But every student has to go through it, in order to dissolve this basic defensiveness. Its resolution involves working through the schizoid sectors of one's ego, and leads to personalizing the human aspect of Essence, which feels like a clear and fresh running mountain brook. One then feels defenseless and vulnerable, but the vulnerability, rather than being threatening, is accepted as a quality of being human.

This can be seen in the case of Jackson, whom we discussed previously in relation to personalizing the Essential Self. As we mentioned, one of his defenses was that of isolation and defensive detachment. At some point he started feeling a great deal of love and compassion for the suffering of people around him. States of gentleness, kindness and boundless love dominated his consciousness for weeks. This was followed by feelings of fear and a powerful sense of vulnerability. He became aware, especially in his private teaching sessions with me, of his head feeling very hard. Working on this manifestation he became aware of a sense of arrogance and defensiveness. The hardness, which had the quality of a sheet of iron around areas of his body, but especially around the head, would make him feel alienated to the point of experiencing everything as unreal. He started understanding the sense of indifference he feels sometimes in relation to women, alternating with feelings of vulnerability, helplessness, emptiness and aloneness. When he accepted these difficult feelings he began to feel the vulnerability becoming a state of gentleness, humanness and delicacy, in conjunction with the loving kindness he had been feeling previously.

5. *Hope.* The state of the personality based on hope is composed of identifications that give one the hope for various gratifications. One is then a hopeful individual. This is a very subtle boundary, for hope is rarely questioned. Almost all people believe they cannot exist without hope; this is definitely true for the ego individuality.

When this sense of boundary is experienced it feels somewhat clear, although thick. It feels like a kind of thin film, the way Penny reported it. However, although it does not necessarily feel uncomfortable, it does make one feel that he is superficial and fake. It makes one feel he is a fake person, living a fake, plastic life.

This is difficult to perceive directly, and even more difficult to let go of. The moment one feels he wants to let go of hope or work on it, or tries to do anything to get rid of it, he only reinforces and hardens it. For any movement toward doing anything about it implies the hope that something can be changed.

6. *Contraction.* This is the state of ego boundaries in its purity, devoid of any other function besides that of separateness. This is the specific state of separateness. Here one clearly, definitely and distinctly feels separate. It is as if the separate individuality has been bared to its bones. It is the inner and most elementary structure of ego boundaries. It is the bare minimum of individuality, the sense of separateness itself. It is the basis of all other layers of boundary, and of the ego individuality.

Experiencing this ego state gives the final understanding of what ego boundaries truly are. Here one knows that a boundary is not an objective and ontologically real phenomenon, but a reaction, a contraction. In this experience, typically the skin is a little hot, a little prickly, a little dry. One feels somewhat frustrated, but also empty. One feels like an empty shell, and the shell is nothing but a very thin layer of a frustrating kind of prickliness. This state of boundaries is nothing but the sense of surface tension itself, a slight contraction all over the skin. It is ego boundaries in the state of pure contraction, the presence of negative merging affect all around one's body.

406   The dissolution of this boundary can bring about a state of emptiness, a deep level of Space. One feels as if he is going to fall on his face, and fall forever. One feels so open, so spacious, that there is nothing between one and the world. As these boundaries dissolve one frequently feels as if he is going to lose his breath, because there is no control on the breathing function. One feels directly in touch with everything, as if one's chest contains the whole universe. One feels as if he extends forever, for then, one *is* the spacious, boundless void.

It is interesting that this level of ego boundaries is related to the state of negative merging. Although one feels distinctly separate, one still feels somehow connected to his mother, the primary object of ego. This indicates that the development of ego boundaries is closely related to the negative experience in the symbiotic stage. Another reason for this sense of connection to mother is the fact that the ego boundaries developed through the integration of internalized object relations, and thus always feel somehow related to the object. However, this state of negative-merging boundaries does have a direct connection to the state of dual unity. It is related to the desire for, or attachment to, the dual unity.

Now, if the individual can do nothing to be free from boundaries, then how can this issue be resolved? How do these boundaries dissolve? They dissolve through the action of Essence itself. This can be called blessing, or grace, or divine intervention, and in some sense it is, but it is really a natural phenomenon, with its own immutable laws. One cannot do anything to dissolve ego boundaries, but if one truly loves truth then one is bound to explore and eventually understand this whole issue of boundaries, separation and individuality. The issue arises and will finally become clear, and distinctly uncomfortable, because of the continued experience of the Personal Essence. One's curiosity based on love of truth for its own sake will turn one's attention naturally and spontaneously to understanding this issue. One does not have to have any attitude towards boundaries. He is only interested in the truth, not for any end, but because he loves Truth deeply. Truth will expose this issue as an issue because in reality there is no such thing as a boundary; Truth is ultimately a boundless presence, as we will see in the next chapter, and this will emerge first as the dimensions of Essence that will expose and dissolve the falseness of boundaries.

As we have noted, understanding boundaries will precipitate the dimension of Love. Part of understanding this dimension of Essence is seeing that the action of Essence is love. One realizes that it is Love that ultimately dissolves ego boundaries. Love is not bound by separateness; it is what penetrates it. Love is also what gives the individual the security and the trust that makes it possible for him to cease identifying with ego activity. When there is Love then there is no need for desire and no need for hope. One can relax, let go and even forget the whole issue.

Love is what the personality needs in order to feel secure and safe. It is the absence of Love that brings the need for defense, resistance, restraint, hope, desire and so on. But when Love is present one can afford to just be, and not engage in the feverishness of ego activity.

The following factors are important in allowing the dissolution of boundaries:

1. *Understanding.* This is the specific understanding of ego boundaries, which we discussed briefly. It is also the understanding of the nature of ego activity. This is the basic factor. Even the spontaneous experience of letting go of boundaries can be seen to be due to understanding. The understanding might not be integrated; it might be merely a simple flash or recognition of truth.

The direct, complete perception of oneself as a separate individual can allow the disappearance of separateness. The understanding by itself does not lead to the dissolution of boundaries, but it does lead to seeing that one's activities are the primary difficulty. It is also instrumental in developing the other factors.

2. *Love.* Love, as we have just said, allows the individuality to relax. It also eliminates fear, which is the original cause of contraction. Also love bridges boundaries by its very nature.

When Love is present with boundaries then the individuality does not feel threatened. When one wants to get rid of his boundaries, there is self-rejection; the presence of Love, however, allows one to disengage from this rejection of and opposition to boundaries. The rejection of boundaries is nothing but the individuality rejecting itself, which gets it into a frustrating mess. So Love disengages it from this civil war. As it relaxes it lets go of the defensive attitude. The absence of defensiveness and the presence of objective understanding of this

408   segment of the personality are the conditions needed for its complete metabolism. This leads to the absorption of this identification system into the essential aspect of Love, followed by the emergence of the Personal Essence.

This emergence means that the presence of Love is what is needed for the absorption of ego boundaries. This is why Love, the fifth objective dimension of Essence, is what is needed to understand and resolve the issue of boundaries.

The understanding of any set of boundaries brings about the emergence of some aspects of Essence on this dimension, i.e., as Love. The effect of these aspects on the boundaries is to finally absorb them, and allow them to be transformed into the Personal Essence. As each of these particular aspects is integrated on the dimension of Love it gives the opportunity for the absorption of a set of ego boundaries.

The process of absorption of identification systems becomes very clear and definite in this dimension of Essence. This dimension is really quite miraculous. The aspects of Essence do not appear here merely as Love, but are also experienced as having a personal element to them.

This dimension generally manifests after the process of personalization of Essence is complete; when all aspects are experienced as personal, it becomes possible for this dimension to appear. This is because on this dimension each aspect is not only objectively experienced as Love, but is felt also as a personal Love.

We are not saying that each aspect manifests in this dimension as the Personal Essence characterized with the respective aspect, but that each aspect manifests as an objective kind of Love, with a *personal* sense to it. This is a very subtle point that indicates the close relationship between Love and the personal element. Even universal Love has some sense of being personal.

On this dimension of Love the process of personalization of Essence becomes objectively understood. One can see here that an aspect becomes personalized, i.e., becomes personal, when it is finally understood that it is Love. When this happens, whatever identification system one happens to be identifying with becomes absorbed into the particular aspect. The result is the personalization of that aspect.

The absorption of boundaries into Being through the action of Love is the easiest, and the most available way to dissolve boundaries.

Boundaries can dissolve through disintegration, fragmentation, disappearing and so on, leading to other essential aspects, usually different levels of Space. But this is a difficult and painful process, and is much harder for most individuals, who will of course tend to resist the dissolution. However, they will resist less when there is Love. And when Love is personal, it lends the greatest support possible for the process of melting of boundaries. This leads to the third factor:

3. *The Personal Essence.* This is the experience of personal presence, the sense of being a person which does not have, and does not depend on, a sense of separateness. The individual's greatest resistance to letting go of his boundaries is due to the fear that he will cease being a person. Loss of boundaries means to him the loss not only of his separateness, but the loss of his personal life, and more importantly, the loss of his functional capacity. Thus the presence of the Personal Essence makes it much easier and more attractive for him to let go of his boundaries. The Personal Essence is his true personal element, and it is also the functional aspect of his Being.

The realization and development of the Personal Essence becomes the greatest support for the process of boundary dissolution. We give the example of a student, Jane, who is at the time a student in college. She is complaining, in a group session, that she feels frustrated in school because it is not easy for her to be alone, focusing on her studies. She is feeling frustrated while talking with me. I ask her to describe her state. She says she feels empty and airy, but she is aware of her skin feeling somewhat prickly. She realizes that this sensation is the source of frustration. She feels herself only as a boundary around the body, a negative merging boundary, prickly and uncomfortable.

By exploring the feeling of aloneness and frustration she finally starts feeling the fullness of the Personal Essence in her belly. Then she feels the fullness filling all of her. As she becomes the fullness she feels the prickly boundaries just disappearing, melting away, easily and effortlessly. She changes from being a frustrated, empty individual, to the fullness of the personal presence. She no longer feels a sense of boundaries. Although she feels a full, personal presence, she also feels a spaciousness all around her.

The presence of the Personal Essence allows the ego boundaries to melt and dissolve. Then one feels oneself as a full presence and a spaciousness. One is both the fullness and the openness. So instead of

410   the contracting boundaries around one's personal presence, one feels the openness, spaciousness, lightness and clarity of Space. The experience of the Personal Essence without boundaries is nothing but the experience of one's personal presence in clear and empty space. One suddenly feels so much room, so much space, so much clarity, all around one. This is not even exact; one feels one is both the presence and the Space. There is no sense of boundaries, no sense of separateness. One is a boundless spaciousness, continuous with a fullness of presence.

What a delight, what a joy and a lightness, is this personal presence without heaviness. One feels in direct open contact with everything, without barriers between one's presence and the rest of the universe.

Chapter Thirty-Four

Aloneness

T he dissolution of boundaries both intensifies and clarifies a certain state, the state of aloneness, which is encountered all the way through the process of realization and development of the Personal Essence. It appears from the beginning of experiencing the autonomy of the Personal Essence, and becomes more frequent until it becomes connected with the issue of ego boundaries. It is usually not understood objectively until one is deeply involved in the process of inner realization.

Most people believe that they understand aloneness, but this initial understanding is superficial and faulty. At the beginning the student is not able to differentiate between the state of aloneness and the affect of loneliness. He feels usually both alone and lonely, which state is usually considered undesirable, and so is resisted along with states such as the Personal Essence that bring it about. It becomes one of the main barriers to the experience of the Personal Essence. Many students resist their autonomy, and cling for a long time to the negative merged state, to avoid this state of aloneness. There are many reasons why aloneness is resisted; some of the most important are the following:

1. *Aloneness is frequently considered synonymous with not being with the mother, or with loss of the mother.* This produces all the reactions that have to do with separation. Aloneness in this case is seen as an extreme state of separation. This indicates that there is still an identity with ego, and the sense of autonomy of the Personal Essence makes

412   one feel one is alone, or going to be very alone. This brings about fear, deep sadness and longing.

Aloneness is equated here with loss of love, pleasure, intimacy, security, support, etc.; all the libidinal supplies that can come from the love object. Sometimes students associate with aloneness the feelings of abandonment, rejection, hurt; so they react with feelings of loneliness.

Babs, a wife and mother who is having difficulty with both her family and her job, has been experiencing much aloneness, mostly by choice. She writes:

> I am afraid of the aloneness I feel around my sadness. I just feel very alone at this time in my life. My earliest memories of this aloneness were when my mother left me in my crib crying for hours, not getting any love or food. Every time I feel alone I feel desperate, abandoned, and those terrifying feelings of that time in my life.

Clearly the state of aloneness brings with it unconscious associations, which are early and painful experiences of abandonment. The interesting thing is that in these cases aloneness is considered from the perspective of the body. One feels the aloneness in the experience of Being, which is really the absence of past object relations, but reacts to it as if one were physically alone, or were going to be alone. This indicates the identity with ego, which is based on the body.

2. *Aloneness is frequently resisted because of identification with ego inadequacy.* So to be alone means to have no support when one is still small and helpless. This brings fear, sadness and longing. Pia, a young woman in one of the helping professions says, in reporting a group session:

> I talked some about my eyes. I was sad to realize that I do not believe people will listen to me. I want to be able to see so I can at least see if you are looking at me or away, if you are looking interested or bored. When I am not wearing contact lenses, and my vision is blurred I fear other people will know I am inadequate. That somehow, with my vision blurred, they will be able to look at me and see how empty I am. They will know I am inadequate.
>
> It seems also that vision is connected to boundaries, and blurred vision to loss of boundaries. It seems easier to feel things while I was talking with you. I remember feeling shaky and cold, as if in a blizzard, very alone with "nothing

to grab onto." I like that phrase, "nothing to grab onto."
Sounds very nice actually. No grabbing. . .

It is clear again that when aloneness is related to inadequacy
there is still identity with some ego structure, for it is only ego that
has inadequacy.

3. *Aloneness is also resisted because it is basically equated with loss of
the Merging Essence.* This is because this aspect is associated, in the
unconscious, with the dual unity, that is, the stage in which the infant
experiences a common boundary around him and the mother.

It is understandable that one will resist the loss of the Merging
aspect, for it means the loss of the capacity for inner regulation. So
here aloneness is resisted because of the rapprochement conflict. One
believes it is not possible to be alone and still have the Merging
aspect. This belief is so deep and crystallized that it persists right up
until the deepest inner realizations. Every new essential development
brings aloneness, in a more profound sense, and the belief that there
will be no merging, with its sweetness, melting softness and soothing
qualities.

Aloneness is, in fact, accepted only when one is able to experience
the Merging Essence in the state of aloneness itself. Obviously, this
depends on resolving the rapprochement conflict.

4. *One deep resistance against aloneness is due to guilt.* One feels that
if he is alone, and especially if he is happy in his aloneness, then it
means he is selfish and uncaring about others and their suffering. We
let Mark illustrate this with a session report:

> I asked about a certain hurt in my chest which was
> about my isolation from my brother. I had been angry at
> him for getting a lot of attention and me getting less. I saw
> that when I really looked honestly, I did get all I needed,
> enough or more than enough in the group. I had fear in
> my lower chest that I was not clear about. I began to see
> that I had to take all I could get from my mother or she
> would get hurt and angry and that I'll take and take from
> many people, even though I don't really need. This results
> in endless wanting that produces frustration. I began to
> feel more aloneness. I asked about my feelings that many
> in the group reject me when I am alone and I feel I isolate
> myself. I could see that I transfer my mother onto the
> group. The part I have difficulty with is that my isolation
> really is true sometimes, at least so I believe.

When I thought about that afterwards there was no
answer and the question made no difference. From the
work that evening I experienced a fullness in my head,
and a clear state in my chest.

This report illustrates that sometimes one takes aloneness to be
one's own rejection of merging or contact with the other. This is the
other pole of the rapprochement conflict. It again implies to the mind
that aloneness means lack of the Merging Essence.

These usual associations with aloneness imply the continued identification with ego, and the lack of understanding of Being. Understanding aloneness requires the willingness to just be. Then aloneness
is experienced as an expansive state of freedom. To finish the report
of Pia, after she began to like the feeling of absence of grabbing: "The
feelings changed so that alone became more pleasant, warm and full."

Here aloneness became, for Pia, the state of the Personal Essence.
This is not only because the Personal Essence is a state of separation
and autonomy, but also because to truly be the Personal Essence is to
be alone, in a fundamental way, not known by the self or individuality of ego.

The Personal Essence is a state of Being, and hence it is a now-
ness—an existence in the now that is completely independent from
any past object relations. To be is to exist totally independent from
any relationship, to anybody or to anything. So it is not independent
only from past object relations; it is also independent from present
ones. One can be totally alone when one is relating.

The sense of aloneness arises because one loses the sense of being
related to others in a conceptual way. This sense of being related to
others is inseparable from all aspects of ego, because the self-image,
which is by nature conceptual, is always seen from the perspective of
a relationship to an object-image.

When one is experiencing Being, as in the state of the Personal
Essence, then one is not the self-image. This means one is not engaged at that time in any inner object relation. This feels like a state of
aloneness. One is actually alone; one is not engaged in the inter-
minable object relations that are the basis and origin of the self-image.

This means that Being is not only the absence of relating to the object or his image, but it is complete independence from all inner past
object relations. If one is identified with any part of the ego structure

then there is no true aloneness yet. There might be a sense of separateness, but not aloneness. There might be a fear of aloneness, or a
movement towards aloneness; and this causes the customary feelings
of fear, sadness, longing and loneliness.

But when one is finally alone then there is no loneliness, for there
is no ego structure to feel alone. Aloneness means that Being is alone.
It means one is present without any psychic structure; for psychic
structure indicates the presence of internalized past object relations. It
is freedom, from ego. It is pure beingness.

Hence, aloneness is not a matter of one being separate or physically alone. It means one is existing without ego, without self-image.
For if there was self-image then one would be engaged in internalized
object relations, and one would not feel alone then. Krishnamurti said
one time that ego cannot exist in aloneness. And we see here how
true this is, for ego involves internalized object relations.

That is why the experience of the Personal Essence feels like
aloneness, and brings about strong reactions from ego; ego reacts because it starts seeing the end of its story. Aloneness means the death
of ego, the false personality based on past mental object relations.

The loss or dissolution of boundaries frequently feels like aloneness; for it is the dissolution of the last identification systems of ego.
Although boundaries make one feel separate, even isolated, one still
does not feel alone. These ego boundaries are based on self-images
that are part of internalized object relations. As they dissolve one
starts feeling alone, but this means that one is entering the state of
freedom, Being without ego.

Aloneness is actually inner aloneness; one is alone in one's mind.
There are no umbilical cords (internalized object relations) connecting
one to the past. One is here, now. This is a state of purity. One is,
and there is no self-image.

This indicates that all states of Being, all aspects of Essence, bring
the state of aloneness, when experienced with no self-image. The absence of self-image means the mind is empty and immaculately clear.
It means the presence of the aspect of Space, which is what dissolves
the self-image.

The aloneness of the Personal Essence is slightly different and more
paradoxical than that of the other aspects of Being. The Personal
Essence is a personal presence that is capable of making direct personal

416   contact. So with it one can be relating to another human being and still be alone. One can be in intimate human contact, but feel completely alone within. This means one is being the Personal Essence in the presence of Space. One is an aloneness relating to another aloneness. One is an aloneness contacting another aloneness. This sounds paradoxical, but this is exactly the state of two human beings who are relating with the Personal Essence, from Being to Being.

One can be in a social setting, such as at a party, and be totally alone. One is then the Personal Essence without boundaries, and without their basis of internalized object relations. Only in such a state of pure and total aloneness is complete contact possible. For then there are no boundaries, but there is the contactful presence.

One feels no sense of boundaries, no separateness and no contraction. One feels an openness, a clear space all around. And one feels a full presence, pure, clean. One is this presence, instead of being the body. And instead of body boundaries, there is boundless Space.

One, in fact, is both the Space and the presence. The presence gives the functional capacity in space and time. When this aloneness is complete there is no longer even any feeling of aloneness. The sense of aloneness is only in contrast to the feeling of ego individuality. So one has this sense of aloneness as this individuality is dissolving. But after a while it is forgotten, and there is only freedom.

Even the freedom is experienced in relation to the constrictions of ego. After a while the sense of freedom disappears too. One merely is. There is presence, and there is boundless Space.

The objective understanding of aloneness includes the following points:

- I am the fullness of the Personal Essence. I am the person of Being. I am independent from time and space, but I am functional in time-space.
- My autonomy is the freedom from object relations. My beingness is completely independent from any object relations, past, present, or future. In fact, object relations are irrelevant to who I am; they do not define me. I can engage in them but they do not determine me.
- Aloneness is being me. Aloneness is freedom, which is who I am. I am pure presence, and spaciousness is my limit.
- Wanting anything from object relations is the expression of identifying with ego or the body. Aloneness is not only a matter of letting

go of the mother's image; for ultimately the whole world, for ego,   417
is mother. I do not want anything from the world. I am in the
world, for the world, but not of the world.

- Realization is a completely private affair. It happens in total aloneness, and it is not related to anybody else. It is a private affair
between me and my origin, my nature.

PART III

THE
FORMLESS DIMENSIONS
OF BEING

I n the process of essential realization, as in human development in general, when a certain stage is experienced completely and fully, a deeper and more expanded one begins to manifest. The complete realization of any aspect or dimension of Being or Essence is a complete metabolism, which leads to further growth. Therefore, the full realization and development of the Personal Essence naturally and spontaneously leads one's consciousness to realms beyond the personal.

The realization of the Personal Essence, which involves the personalization of essential aspects and dimensions, leads to the complete development and objective understanding of the essential person, as we saw in the last chapter. This realization makes it possible, even easy, to move to the nonpersonal or formless realms.

These realms have been called "nonpersonal," "cosmic" or "boundless" and we will sometimes use these terms, but generally we use the term "formless dimensions," for these reasons:

• In these realms there are no personal or individual boundaries, so there is no sense of entity or separate existence. This is why the dissolution of ego boundaries is the primary requirement for experiencing them.

• The experience is beyond the body, and hence the dichotomy of inside-outside is transcended, and there is freedom from the restriction of consciousness to a center in the body. Thus these dimensions are beyond form; it is the body image that gives us our personal form.

• The experience is also beyond the person, beyond personal life and transcending personal history.

The man of spirit is mostly concerned with these realms; they are the object of many religious and spiritual traditions. However, as we discussed in Chapter Two, these realms are unimaginable by the man of the world, and his impressions from the communications of those who do know them definitely do not necessarily make him want to know more. They are outside the confines of ego states, and are usually viewed by ego as threatening to its survival. Nevertheless, most traditions and teaching systems orient their methodology toward the attainment of these formless realms, which attainment is considered spiritual realization or liberation.

The Diamond Approach looks at these formless realms as part of the human potential, in fact as the acme of human consciousness. But we see the idealization of these realms to the exclusion of the personal realm and of the other aspects and dimensions of Essence as a limited, even prejudiced, view. Our approach does not value or judge one realm above another; we simply observe that these formless realms become spontaneously available in the process of actualizing the human potential, thus expanding what is normally thought to be the nature of this potential. In time, these dimensions dominate the consciousness, influencing one's experience and determining one's view of reality.

There is no need to make them an object of seeking. When the student merely lives his or her life fully, metabolizing his or her experience totally, motivated and guided by the pure love for truth, the formless dimensions manifest. The point of transition to these dimensions arrives when the Personal Essence is finally integrated and understood. No particular guidance or practice need be added.

The beingness of the Personal Essence is in its very nature a bridge   421
to these dimensions.

In this chapter we will explore the formless dimensions primarily
from the standpoint of their relationship to the Personal Essence.
Much more could be said about these realms, but here we will discuss
them only briefly, focusing on the following lines of inquiry:

1. How the experience and understanding of the Personal Essence
   leads to these dimensions.
2. The relationship between the formless dimensions and the Personal
   Essence.
3. The personalization of these dimensions. The attainment of these
   dimensions can be seen as part of the development of the Personal
   Essence. This point, which is developed in some detail in the
   Diamond Approach, is rarely discussed by traditional teachings.
4. How the understanding of ego and its development, gained mainly
   from object relations theory, can assist the movement toward these
   realms of experience. This involves an understanding that is almost
   completely ignored by the various traditional teaching systems,
   which is how understanding psychodynamic and structural issues
   can lead to the nonpersonal and formless dimensions of experience.

It is not possible to understand completely what a human being is
without understanding the relationship between the Personal Essence
and the formless dimensions. The human being cannot be completely
comprehended without appreciating his place in the scheme of things.
And this appreciation can come about only through seeing his relationship to realms beyond form and personhood.

Chapter Thirty-Five

The Impersonal
versus
the Personal

It is important to note that when we refer to an essential aspect as personal, we are not implying that all other aspects are impersonal. Other aspects sometimes feel personal and sometimes not. The same is true of all the differentiated aspects; other aspects may include their qualities. For instance, the fact that there is an aspect of Peace does not mean that other aspects are not peaceful. All aspects of Essence have a peaceful and serene quality to them, but except for the aspect of Peace itself, peace is not their central, characteristic quality.

However, the Personal Essence is different from other aspects, such as Peace and Love; it feels like a person. But the personal element in it is not restricted to it alone. Thus the Personal Essence is not the only quality that can feel personal. It is simply the aspect which is the personal element in a Platonic form, a quality of consciousness.

There is as well an aspect that is specifically impersonal. When one experiences it there is no personal quality present at all. This is one of the formless dimensions of being, which is in a sense the entry into the formless realm. Its manifestation is a direct consequence of realizing the Personal Essence and understanding the personal element. The full realization of the Personal Essence brings about the longing for the impersonal. This happens when one realizes that subtle ego identifications still exist (because some dimensions of Being are not yet integrated), and one begins actually to perceive these ego structures. One realizes slowly but steadily that although there has been tremendous transformation, there is something that has not changed.

422

It is not easy to see what it is that has not changed, although it is becoming more and more ego alien. It creates contractions in the psychophysical organism, discomfort and loss of complete identity with Being.

It finally dawns on the student that the totality of his personal experience still has the same old flavor, and because of this ego boundaries and self keep being reinstated. This unchanged quality begins to feel undesirable; one feels clearly, without any sense of condemnation, "I am the barrier."

The further exploration of this overall issue takes the student through the process of realization of the Essential Self, a subject we will discuss in detail in a future book. Part of this realization is the capacity to disengage from ego activity, which is now experienced as the activity of the person as a whole. One learns finally, then, that the realization of the Personal Essence is not final until one goes completely beyond the personal life. This is because ego boundaries and sense of self do not stand on their own but are supported by the personal life and personal history.

This insight usually appears as a perception that one is lost in one's personal life. One has the strong impression of being imprisoned by everything in one's life, desirable and undesirable factors alike. The student is not usually aware that the impersonal aspect is approaching; he is simply experiencing more and more that the fact of being a person is a barrier to freedom and harmony. He perceives that the totality of his person, including his personal life and history, has not changed. This makes him aware that he is lost, enmeshed in his personal life, that he is so involved in his relationships, work interests, house, family, friends, projects, activities, plans, ideas, thoughts, preferences, prejudices, everything that is the content of his life, that he is trapped by it, and hopelessly limited within it.

One becomes aware of the subtle but deep tendency to take the totality of the content of the personal life to define who one is. This is particularly obvious in the case of one's thoughts. One can think only of certain things, along certain lines, unique to one's person. One starts to feel one's roles, one's personal uniqueness, as limiting and stifling.

This brings about a deep yearning to be free from all of one's personal life; one wants to be beyond it all, and senses that he actually is beyond it. One feels it is not right to identify with one's personal life

424 and manifestations, that no content can contain or define who he is, that it is wrong for personal details to limit his nature.

At the beginning one cannot tell what it is about him that is beyond the personal life and its content. The longing not to be caught by the content of one's personal life is felt as a desire motivated by love. There is no rejection of the personal life, just a feeling coming from an unknown place.

There is still no direct awareness of the impersonal, although it is putting pressure on the personal. It is beautifully clear in this instance how an aspect of Being, as it approaches consciousness, brings about the delineation of the specific barrier against its realization, making it feel undesirable, producing the understanding of its nature, and leading to the deep, true longing for its reality.

The Impersonal aspect usually begins to appear in flashes of perception of a new reality. One becomes aware of a strange kind of awareness or perception, which is in some way constant, always there, but is not involved in whatever is happening. One becomes conscious of an awareness which is in complete contrast to one's ordinary personal awareness, which is always involved in the particulars of one's experience.

At this point an awareness arises of the totality of the life process, sometimes in unexpected flashes, and one sees the complete involvement of the personal consciousness in this life process. The awareness is perceived as separate from the personal consciousness, as if there is a background of constant, unchanging awareness that is always aware of what is happening, even though the personal consciousness is sometimes so involved in events that it is lost in them.

For the first time ever, then, there is an awareness that is aware of the personal consciousness itself. This is a peculiar experience; one feels sometimes as if there is someone looking from behind him, encompassing him. This is the beginning of experiencing the Impersonal aspect, but still from the perspective of being a person. One sees for the first time the fact of one's personal consciousness and the extent of its involvement in the particulars of one's personal life.

We find Mark, whom we discussed last in Chapter Twenty-Seven, in a private teaching session, becoming aware of what does not change about him, the personal and specific character of his personal identity and personal life. He has been dealing with this perception within his accustomed pattern, wanting to change by using his will. Discussing this leads to a greater awareness of the totality of his personality. He then starts becoming aware of how his personality is inseparable from his personal life and personal history. When I ask him how he is aware of the totality of his personal experience he becomes conscious of something that is aware of the totality without involvement in it. He also perceives how any movement on his part enmeshes him more in this personal experiential totality.

He then becomes aware of experiencing himself in a silent background of awareness. Working further on his mental holding and tensions releases some fear. He experiences himself then dissolving in the silent vastness. The transition for him is complete dissolving of his manifestation. He then experiences himself as infinite, as an aware vastness that contains the world.

The process of moving from the personal to the Impersonal is subtle and profound. One must see oneself and the totality of one's life, all at once. This can happen only when the real personal—the Personal Essence—is completely realized.

The psychological issue here is that the ego individuality is not separate from the totality of one's life, and also it is dependent on, and in continuity with, one's personal history. So far, we have explored how to go beyond the ego individuality in the process of the realization and development of the Personal Essence. Now we see that this cannot happen in a final way unless one is detached from his personal life, and free from his personal history.

This of course accords with the object relations view that the individuality cannot exist separately from its past, since that individuality is a product of the integration of past object relations. It is a continuation of the past, part and parcel of the personal history, and cannot be separated from its world and its personal life.

Thus there cannot be freedom from this ego structure as long as one is attached and completely lost in his personal life, and as long as one continues to view himself as an extension of his unique personal history. For complete freedom from this ego individuality, which is the same as completely establishing the Personal Essence, one must be free from the supports of this ego structure, the personal life and personal history. Only when these supports are exposed and then transcended does the true support for the Personal Essence arise,

426   through the action of the Impersonal aspect. In other words, just as the Personal Essence exposes the individuality of ego, the Impersonal aspect exposes the support of such individuality.

One could say that the full realization and understanding of the Personal Essence shifts the sense of being a person from ego to Being. This then exposes the deep supports for the individual ego structure, which is seen as inseparable from the personal life and history. This latter perception is possible only from the Impersonal aspect. It is interesting to notice that this transition happens only through the combined influence of the full realization of the true Personal Essence and the transcendent awareness of the Impersonal aspect.

One resistance to the Impersonal aspect that each student must surmount is the belief that there will be no personal life if there is no involvement in it. It seems that there is a universal belief that one must be attached to the personal life, or it will be lost.

Finally one is able to go beyond the inertia supporting everything personal. This happens through the process of personalizing the aspect of Existence. The fear is that there will be no existence for anything personal if one lets go of the supports of ego personality. This fear is transcended when the Personal Essence is experienced in the state of Existence. This is another Platonic form, a pure differentiated aspect of Being, where the sense is just existence. Personalizing this aspect one feels a sense of personal existence that is real, and not based on mental structure or the supports of this structure in past or present. The usual experience of the Personal Essence is of fullness and personalness. But when Existence is personalized it attains a density and an immensity that gives the experience the specific feeling of existence. In other words, existence becomes a more dominant feeling than fullness. Existence is present implicitly in Beingness, but now it is specifically delineated.

Experiencing the Personal Essence in this state is the stepping stone towards the complete, clear arising of the Impersonal aspect. As the Impersonal, one experiences oneself as a vast, dark, silent emptiness. It is a sheer emptiness, boundless, infinite and absolutely silent. One experiences oneself as an emptiness that has no characteristic except that of being a totally silent Impersonal Witness. There is a stupendous vastness, an absolute silence, a complete impersonality, and a singularly clear but absolutely uninvolved awareness of everything.

One is merely a witness, a silent and unchanging witness. The witness is a pure emptiness, which is at the same time awareness. So the Impersonal aspect turns out to be an Impersonal Witness. In India this aspect is called the "silent Brahman." The silence is so complete that it is eerie. One feels one is absolutely this ultimate, but singularly aware, void. Here the perception unfolds of how one is beyond the personal. One individual speaking from this state relates:

> I am not the body, not the personality, not the mind, not the Essence, not even God. I am nothing that is a content of experience or awareness.
>
> But all experience happens within me. Everything, at all levels, from the physical to the spiritual, all happens within me. I see the personal life as a drama that I am not involved in. It is like a movie that has a beginning and an end.
>
> But I am untouched and untouchable by any of it. I am beyond anything and everything—the person, and his whole universe. I am the Beyond, absolutely transcendent. I am a silent witness, that contains all there is. I am unchanging.
>
> I am the deathless, the unborn, the uncaused. I was never born, will never die. I have no beginning and no end, but all beginnings and all ends are within me. The concepts of life and death do not apply to me.
>
> I do not need to be freed or enlightened. I am always free, always have been, and will always be free. I see life and death as nothing but a process of constant transformation happening within me. All existence, from the lowest to the highest, is always in a state of flux, but I am the unchanging witness, where all transformation and change happen. I am the background against which this flux is seen.
>
> I am static, unchanging, unreacting, unresponsive, but singularly and purely aware.
>
> I am beyond time and space. I am beyond timelessness and spacelessness. All time is a movement within me. I see it as the movement of the timeless within the immensity that is me. This movement creates time, which is the axis of personal history. But all of personal history, all of time, and all of space is a time-space continuum that is a small and insignificant thing within me.
>
> I see mind, the totality of it, as a small process, like a little storm, within me. It is always busy with itself, trying to grasp me. But how can it grasp what transcends it absolutely!

Time and mind are not contrary to me, are not a disturbance in my silence. They are little happenings within my
vastness. I am beyond, but contain, all time, space, and
mind.

This is not a particular, person-centered experience, it is merely becoming, or realizing that one is, the ultimate, silent background for all
of existence. This state is not necessarily the highest; it is not seen in
terms of high or low. It is beyond high and low, for it is the background for all levels of experience. So it exists at all levels, as the
background. Experiencing it is not a matter of development, of reaching a certain level. It is more a matter of exiting from the experiential
universe, physical, mental and spiritual. This is what is needed to go
beyond the personal. One realizes here that the personal is nothing
but a manifestation in the Impersonal. This experience jolts the mind,
by absolutely transcending it.

It is not the experience of no-mind reported by many spiritual
traditions; it transcends mind, but allows it to exist within it as a small
thing of no consequence to it. It is beyond mind and no-mind.

It is also not the timelessness reported by the traditional teaching; it
transcends time, but allows it as a small movement within it. It is
beyond both time and timelessness. In fact, in this experience one can
see the relation between time and timelessness.

The Impersonal Witness is an aware vastness that contains, and is
beyond, the time-space continuum which is the manifest universe. It
is generally not possible to imagine what Einstein meant by saying
that the universe is a four-dimensional time-space continuum. Mathe-
maticians and physicists have this concept and deal with mathematical
equations regarding it, but in the experience of the silent Impersonal
Witness, Einstein's four-dimensional universe is actually, directly perceived. It is as if one is looking from a continuum of more than four
dimensions.

This realization brings a new clarity and understanding to one's
personal life. It makes it possible to see the role one is identifying
with in one's life, and to know one's function, work and unique contribution in one's personal life. One can see how some characteristics
or skills are developed in one's life, for some unique role or purpose.
Here one understands the role of conditioning, as a tool towards the
development of personal characteristics and skills needed to actualize
a certain role, to facilitate a particular contribution.

One here understands one's personal maturation as a unique development exemplified in the Personal Essence. This development is a unique manifestation in the Impersonal background. One knows one's unique, real function or work, as a specific contribution to the totality of life. One's personal realization, including one's real personal life and work, become seen as a unique manifestation of the Real, which is the same as one's unique contribution to the universe. This is a direct insight, not the result of a thought process.

Here, everything in one's life, including all of the past history, becomes meaningful. One realizes one's place from the perspective of the ever-existing background. This is something that the man of the world always longs for. He always wants to make his unique contribution. He always wants to know what is his real function, his real work, his real place in the universe. But we see here that this is not easy to realize, but comes about only through realizing and understanding the relationship between the Personal Essence and the Impersonal and Cosmic background. We see then that this dream of the man of the world is not simply a dream—it is a possibility—it is, in fact, part of the realizable human potential.

Chapter Thirty-Six

Cosmic Consciousness and Individuation

U nderstanding the Personal Essence from the perspective of the Impersonal Witness gives a meaning to the person in relation to the nonpersonal, formless realm. However, we have not yet clearly seen the connection between the two realms. How does the personal emerge from the Impersonal? What is the continuum, if any, between the personal and the Impersonal? What is the final relationship between the personal and the Impersonal? Considering these questions leads to the manifestation of the other formless aspects or dimensions of Being.

The next aspect that becomes dominant is what is often referred to as Cosmic Consciousness, as distinguished from personal consciousness. We can look at this from two points of view. We can see Cosmic Consciousness from the perspective of the Impersonal background, or from that of the Personal Essence. From the Impersonal it can be seen as part of the continuum that connects it to the Personal Essence; or, in other words, it is one level of reality that emerges from the Impersonal background in the process of creativity (creation) that culminates in the essential person. Sri Aurobindo describes how the silence of the Impersonal becomes filled with Cosmic Consciousness:

> Overpowered and subjugated, stilled, liberated from itself, the mind accepts the Silence itself as the Supreme. But afterwards the seeker discovers that all is there for him contained or new-made. . . then the void begins to fill, there emerges out of it or then rushes into it all the manifold Truth of the Divine, all aspects and manifestations and

many levels of a dynamic infinite. [Sri Aurobindo, *The Synthesis of Yoga, "Arya"*, p. 133]

However, it is more instructive to study this dimension of Being from the other side, that of the Personal Essence. In this way we can see what ego structures need to be metabolized in the process of realizing this formless dimension.

This dimension usually begins to manifest before the emergence of the Impersonal Witness; but it is not easily understood in its relation to the Personal Essence until the latter is experienced. Students usually encounter it when going beyond the ego structures of self or boundaries. The diamond issue that leads to its emergence is the belief that one is the body. As one goes beyond the ego sense of identity or the ego boundaries, one learns that these ego structures are based on the belief that one is the body. We recall Mahler's description of the "body ego:"

> The body ego contains two kinds of self-representations: an inner core of the body image, with a boundary that is turned toward the inside of the body and divides it from ego, and an outer layer of sensoriperceptive engrams that contributes to the boundaries of the "body self" (cf. Bergmann, 1963 discussing Federn's concepts). [Margaret S. Mahler et al., *The Psychological Birth of the Human Infant*, p. 46]

The first kind of self-representation becomes the ego sense of self, and the second kind develops into ego boundaries. So to go beyond such structures one must see that one identifies with the body, and surrender the identification. This belief that one is the body, although it is easily seen and commonly acknowledged, is such a deep, hidden and crystallized identification that under normal circumstances it is not possible to become aware of its deeper levels. Most individuals are aware of it rather vaguely and indirectly, actually being aware of the consequences of their identification (for instance a self-image), rather than the identification itself, which is so difficult to directly perceive exactly because one believes that the perceiver *is* the body. When one becomes directly and specifically aware of this identification with the body, disidentification happens spontaneously. This occurs usually only after deep and intense work on recognizing and surrendering self-representations. Of course, it can happen accidentally under unusual circumstances, or as a result of some spiritual practices. Rajneesh describes his experiences of going beyond body identification which resulted from his

432   meditations. He would sit on a tree branch and meditate. One night he became so absorbed in his meditation that his body fell to the ground without him knowing it. He says: "How it happened that I was sitting on the tree and my body was lying on the ground I could not understand at all. It was a very queer experience." [Joshi, *The Awakened One*, p. 55]

This is a dramatic and singularly clear way of seeing that one is not the body. But obviously this is not the usual way it happens. In the Diamond Approach it occurs by first directly perceiving the specific identification with the body. This objective understanding spontaneously leads to disidentification, not only from self-representations but, most importantly, from the psychophysical organism. We see this in the following case presentation from a private session.

We find Donna, whom we mentioned in a previous chapter in relation to the characteristics of the Personal Essence, dealing with the fourth objective dimension of Essence that has to do with objective knowledge. She has been working, especially in her private teaching sessions, with her sense of identity. This has manifested in many ways: as her tendency to cover up some deficiency in her identity; as hurt for her love not being seen; as desire for annihilation, for her sense of self to dissolve. She came to a session feeling scared; she had been waking up in the middle of the night afraid of leaving her body. Exploring this she feels a longing to go deep into the starry night. It turned out that she was seeing a deep inner black space as the physical night sky. When I asked her about why she thinks of it as a starry space, instead of just black space, she realizes she is thinking of reaching more people, and the stars represent people for her. Exploring how she can reach more people lovingly we came upon her sense of identity, which she equates with her body. In other words it does not make sense to her how she can be connected to everybody because she is separate, because she is a separate body. Seeing how her separate identity is based on the discreteness of her body she starts to feel happy and giggly. She starts feeling pretty, open, light and happy. But these are not the usual characteristics of her identity. She realizes she is experiencing herself as a Loving Light, delicate and conscious. When she realizes that she is actually being the Loving Consciousness, instead of merely experiencing it she feels quite expanded. She feels herself as not the body, but as the Loving Light. She now feels connected not just to everybody but to everything.

This experience has far-reaching consequences. When one realizes   433
in a very distinct way that one is not the body, one has taken a very
significant step in the movement from ego identifications to Being.
Rajneesh describes the importance of his experience for his spiritual
awakening:

> "And from that day death also ceased to exist, because
> that day I experienced that the body and spirit are two dif-
> ferent things, quite separate from each other. That was the
> most important moment: my realization of the spirit that is
> within every human body." [*Ibid.*, p. 56]

When there is transcendence of the body through disidentification
from the self-representations based on it, the Cosmic Consciousness manifests. One realizes that one is not only not the body, but that one is a
boundless consciousness. One becomes aware of being a presence that
transcends the body in a very specific manner. One feels one is a
presence that is conscious, but that is not centered in the body. In fact,
one becomes conscious of the body in a total way, as if from outside.
One experiences oneself not as in the body, but as containing the body
within oneself. One is a boundless and infinite consciousness that contains the body. One feels "I am not the body, the body is in me." This is
a very new and unusual experience for ego; in fact, ego cannot actually
experience such a state, which transcends ego and its boundaries.

Cosmic Consciousness has the following characteristics:

1. *It is a presence.* It is a very soft presence; gentle, delicate, smooth
and flowing. One is like a wisp, like a delicate and soft cloud.

2. *It is conscious.* This presence is experienced as the very stuff of
consciousness.

3. *It feels like light itself, but more like the substance of light, not as
rays of light, but as a flow of light, as an ocean of light.* It is "light
upon light."

4. *It is Love.* This conscious substance of light is soft, gentle, tender
and sweet. It is loving. It is as if one becomes an ocean of Love that is
conscious. So one can call it conscious Love, or loving light. In traditional literature this is sometimes referred to as Universal Love or
Christ Love. It is both Consciousness and Love in the same presence.

5. *It is boundless.* There is no sense of individual or personal
boundaries in this aspect of Being. The conscious and loving
presence is felt to pervade everything, to extend infinitely, as a

434   homogeneous soft medium. It is not felt to be personal, in the sense that it does not belong to oneself. That is why it is sometimes referred to as universal consciousness. It is the consciousness of all beings. There are no boundaries here between individuals. That is why when a student experiences it he cannot help but feel one with everyone. And the oneness is felt in Love. One becomes full of Love and gratitude towards any being. One realizes he is not separate from the other. That he and the other are the same, are both of the same nature of conscious Love.

This is beyond merging. It is the recognition of nonseparateness, of the universality of Essence. And it is a delight that separateness is eliminated by Love. This aspect of Being is the most effective for transcending ego boundaries. One lets go of his personal boundaries through Love. There is no fear or loss, for one merely becomes a loving presence that transcends and contains all boundaries. One's identity is now not with the body, so it has no physical boundaries. One is this conscious Love, that pervades and transcends everything. From this place, one can be conscious of one's body walking or moving, but not be involved in it. One is merely a witnessing consciousness. But it is not like the Impersonal Witness. It does not have an impersonal sense to it. It is also a pervading sense of presence of Love, and not a background emptiness.

It is important to notice here that the detached witness state can exist on several dimensions. Most spiritual teachings speak of the detached witness as if there is one such state. The fact is that one can be a witness from different dimensions, for instance as the Impersonal Awareness, or the Cosmic Consciousness.

When Cosmic Consciousness arises, it feels familiar. It reminds one of normal personal consciousness, except that it is boundless. This points to the fact that the normal consciousness is really this Cosmic Consciousness, but that it is restricted by identification with the body and its boundaries. One learns that one's personal consciousness has the same quality as this aspect; it is like daylight. But it is focused, narrowed and made heavy by attaching it to the body.

It is possible to see that the process of cathecting the body in the initial stages of ego development is really a matter of focusing Cosmic Consciousness on the body to the extent of feeling and behaving as if one's consciousness comes from the body. But consciousness is consciousness, and personal consciousness owes its conscious capacity to this aspect of Being.

The end result of cathecting the psychophysical organism is, as we have seen, the development of ego identity based on the body. One forgets that he is a boundless conscious presence, and comes to believe that he is a body that has personal consciousness. This insight, that one is basically a conscious presence, but mistakenly takes oneself to be an individual based on the body, is part of some of the old teaching traditions. Nisargadatta Maharaj, the late Indian Vedanta teacher, puts it this way:

> The body is only an instrument, an apparatus which would be totally useless but for the energy within, the animus, the sense "I am," the knowledge of being alive, the consciousness which provides *the sense of being present.* Indeed, this conscious presence (not ABC or XYZ being present, but the sense of conscious presence as such) is what one *is*, and not the phenomenal appearance that the body is. It is when this consciousness, feeling the need of some support, mistakenly identifies itself with the body and gives up its unlimited potential for the limitation of a single particular body, that the individual is "born." [Nisargadatta Maharaj, *Pointers from Nisargadatta Maharaj*, p. 118]

It is important to note here that a developmental psychologist cannot objectively see how the ego sense of being an individual develops, without taking into consideration first that the initial beingness of the human being is this Cosmic Consciousness and not the psychophysical apparatus. Object relations theory does note the gradual cathexis of the body, but is not aware of what it is that becomes focused on the body. Hence it is not aware of what is lost in the development of ego. The cathexis of the body is usually seen as the realistic comprehension that one is the body.

Object relations theory can be seen as a very specific and detailed way of explaining the above statement by Nisargadatta Maharaj that consciousness mistakenly identifies itself with the body, leading to the birth of the individual. Maharaj focuses his attention on what is lost through this process of psychological birth, while Mahler, for instance, emphasizes how this birth happens through the process of ego development. The Diamond Approach sees the whole process as one, in which understanding is very useful in the process of moving backward from the ego individuality to the boundless conscious presence.

436   6. *The Cosmic Consciousness is responsible for the appearance of form.*
This can be seen in a deeper experience and appreciation of this
aspect of Being.

One realizes that this conscious presence is not only one's own
nature and substance, but that it is the nature and substance of all existence, including the physical universe. One realizes at a deeper
level, that not only does this consciousness transcend and contain the
body, but that ultimately the body itself is made out of this subtle substance. At the beginning one experiences Cosmic Consciousness as
pervading everything. After a while one learns that it is the inner
nature of everything; that everything is a manifestation of this consciousness, as individual multifarious forms. This conscious presence
is not only one's presence that is within, or transcending the body,
but is the very stuff of the body, and all of physical reality.

This is a very deep and profound perception, which is at the very
heart of many of the great teaching traditions. That is why this consciousness is sometimes referred to as God, and why sometimes God
is referred to as Love. The Christian saint, St. John, is reputed to have
said, "God is love," and, "He that dwelleth in love dwelleth in God
and God in him." And more clearly in the words of the Christian
English author of *The Cloud of Unknowing*, speaking of God: "And
thus, also, he is one in all things and all things are one in him. For I
repeat: all things exist in him; he is the being of all." [Edited by
William Johnston, *The Cloud of Unknowing and the Book of Privy
Counseling*, p. 150]

And we find Nisargadatta Maharaj asserting:

> This beingness, this conscious presence that he is, is the
> beingness of every sentient being on the earth, the very soul
> of the entire universe,—and indeed, therefore, *this-here-
> now, this conscious presence, cannot be anything other than
> God.* [Nisargadatta Maharaj, *Pointers from Nisargadatta
> Maharaj*, p. 116]

One realizes that all of existence is a manifestation of consciousness; that ultimately everything is made out of consciousness. This can
happen only when one transcends identity with the body.

There are many ways that this realization appears. One is the perception that there is an infinite and boundless ocean of presence-
consciousness-love, and that all physical forms appear to arise out of

this substratum. One's body and the rest of the universe appear as 437 forms arising out of this primordial substance. One feels direct affinity and divine Love for everybody and everything.

Another way of seeing this fact is the direct perception that everything is made out of Love. The body, the walls, the air, the space, the atoms, all seem to be made out of the same continuum, which is this Cosmic Consciousness. There is unity and oneness, although there is variety and difference.

A third way is in relation to the Impersonal Emptiness and the Personal Essence. One is aware of total emptiness, and out of this emptiness there manifests, as if from nowhere, this divinely beautiful consciousness that then condenses in one drop, which is the incomparable Personal Essence. All beings and physical forms are seen as condensations from this Love that is sometimes experienced as grace.

This third way of perceiving the nature of everything as consciousness has many implications:

1. *The manifestation of Cosmic Consciousness as a human being appears in the form of the Personal Essence.* The Personal Essence is seen directly here to be the real individualization of Cosmic Consciousness. This is in contrast to the ego individuality which is cut off from everything else by its separating boundaries. It is obvious from this perception that the Personal Essence is the real human person, the true development, which is nothing but the individuation of the divine. This is what we feel Jesus Christ meant when he said that he is the son of God.

It is the potential of every human being to realize himself as the son of God, which is the Personal Essence. The relationship of the Personal Essence to the Cosmic Consciousness will become even more clear when one goes completely beyond identity, as we will discuss shortly.

2. *In this perception it becomes clear that the physical body is an external extension of the Personal Essence.* This is in contrast to the ego individuality, which is an extension of the body. One experiences oneself as a continuity starting from the boundless conscious presence, individuating as the Personal Essence, and manifesting physically as the body.

3. *The relationship between the Impersonal background and the Personal Essence is Love.* The Impersonal becomes personal through

438   Love, as an expression of Love. Universal Love is the continuum between the Impersonal and the personal, and hence, it partakes of
both.

Also, not only the personal, but all of existence is the expression of
the Love of the Impersonal. All the forms in existence are but
differentiations and discriminations from the basic substratum: the
conscious presence. Nisargadatta Maharaj puts it this way: "It is consciousness indeed that manifests itself in individual forms and gives
them apparent existence." [*Ibid.*, p. 4]

Universal Love and Ego Identity

In the process of realization and development of the Personal
Essence the representations that are metabolized are primarily the self-
representations. This ultimately leads to the surrender of both the ego
boundaries and the sense of self. This means that what is surrendered
(absorbed) is the integrated self-representation or the self-concept. However, since this self-concept is a structure built through the integration
of past object relations, it does not exist on its own, in isolation. It
exists always in relation to the object image, or more accurately, in
relation to the various internalized object images. The totality of all
object images are integrated into what is called the representational
world (a concept introduced by Sandler). The self-concept plus the
representational world constitute an overall psychic structure, what
Erikson and Kernberg refer to as ego identity. Kernberg writes: "Ego
identity refers to the overall organization of identifications and introjections under the guiding principle of the synthetic function of the
ego." [Otto F. Kernberg, *Object Relations Theory and Clinical Psychoanalysis*, p. 32]

Thus the self concept cannot be separated from its milieu, which is
the representational world. One is always conscious of being a person
in relation to the overall world. The world the individual is relating to
is not the real objective world, but the "representational world." We
repeat a passage from Kernberg about the representational world:

> It has to be stressed, however, that this internal world of
> object representations ... never reproduces the *actual*
> world of real people ... it is at most an approximation,
> always strongly influenced by the very early object-images
> of introjections and identifications. [*Ibid.*, p. 33]

This means that one cannot let go completely of the self-concept 439 unless one lets go of the totality of ego identity, including the representational world. One cannot be the Personal Essence relating to the representational world. The self-concept will eventually reassert itself through the presence of its milieu, the representational world. But if the Personal Essence is truly integrated then the representational world will start being perceived as not the real world, and will become an issue to be understood.

When the ego individuality associated with the self-concept is finally perceived objectively, it is experienced as a kind of an empty shell. One feels the presence of boundaries that give one the sense of being an individual, but one feels fake, unreal and empty of any true substance or nature. Usually this leads to the absorption of ego boundaries into the Personal Essence. However, one can still perceive the world in the usual way, as real and full of significance. This means one still is not seeing through the representational world. One is still projecting this ego structure onto the real world, and is filtering one's perceptions of the world through it.

The realization of both the Personal Essence and the Cosmic Consciousness now make it possible to see through the projection of the representational world. The continued experience of the Personal Essence and the Cosmic Consciousness begins to expose a contraction in the psychophysical organism that has been very deeply hidden. One slowly starts realizing that this disharmonious contraction has to do with focus on, or cathexis of, physical reality in general, and not just on one's own body. Understanding this exposes the self-concept again as an empty shell. However, now the empty shell feels like an individual who is emotionally and mentally trapped by the physical world. Sometimes one feels as if he is fat, or full of fat that covers a deep emptiness. One becomes aware that this sense of being a fat empty shell is coexistent with a state of greed and lust for food and physical comfort and pleasure. One realizes the consequences of the exclusive cathexis of physical reality, which is basically how ego sees the world. One relates to the world as if it can fill one's emptiness, can satisfy one's greed for all kinds of physical rewards. One is deeply, though unconsciously, aware of one's deficient emptiness, and is seeing the world as the source of gratifications.

440   Staying with this realization of the deep underlying relationship to the world will spontaneously lead to a new perception, hitherto totally unsuspected. One begins to become conscious that one's empty shell feels continuous with, and not separate from, the rest of the world. One feels as if one's individuality and the rest of the universe make the same entity, at the same level, with the same significance. This is the beginning of the objective awareness of the totality of the ego identity. One starts becoming aware of the totality of the ego structure projected on all of reality.

Then one starts becoming aware that this reality, which includes both self and world in a continuous manner, does not seem to have any real significance. Both self and world turn out to be one big shell, empty and insubstantial. Now it is not only one's personality that is perceived to be fake and empty, but the whole world is experienced in this way. It is strange to see physical objects, including people, having no substance, no density and no reality. They feel empty and flat like cardboard, colorless and devoid of vitality. Everything still looks the same, but one realizes that one has been projecting a significance, fullness and reality that is not really there.

Here one is objectively perceiving the totality of ego identity, and realizing for the first time that it is empty, unreal and, in fact, feels like images or thoughts, which it is. So not only one's individuality, but the totality of the world that one has been familiar with, turns out not to have the reality that one believed in so unquestioningly. One realizes, for the first time, that the world does not have the richness and gratification that one always believed it had. The world of ego is as empty as ego.

This is a stunning discovery for the ego, and shattering to some of its most basic beliefs. One can never forget such a realization. The usual experience of the personality is that one feels oneself as real, full and existing, and the world also as real, full and existing. The usual sense of significance and substantiality of the personality is experienced as continuous with that of the significance and absolute reality of the world that one perceives.

But now one experiences the ego personality as an empty shell, full of greed, lust and desire for physical pleasure, comfort, security and power. And this state is continuous with that of the world, including the physical universe, as empty, flat and lacking any real

significance and value. The material which has filled this shell in the   441
past, all the past object relations, is no longer there. And the
representational world is revealed in its true nature, as empty, as a
shell covering a huge, infinite deficient emptiness. Just as the experience of Being finally exposes the self as a shell covering a hole, it
now exposes the representational world as a big "cosmic shell,"
covering a huge "cosmic hole." This means that without the connection to Being the world we usually see is really empty, a cosmic
deficient emptiness, covered by a shell, which is the content of the
representational world. It is this experience that many mystics refer
to when they say the world is an illusion. A Christian contemplative
relates such an experience, which was a terrible realization for her,
as follows:

> Suddenly I was aware that all life around me had come to
> a complete standstill. Everywhere I looked, instead of life, I
> saw a hideous nothingness invading and strangling the life
> out of every object and vista in sight. It was a world being
> choked to death by an insidious void, whereby every
> remaining movement was but the final throe of death.
> [Bernadette Roberts, *The Experience of No-Self*, p. 42]

Bernadette Roberts seems to understand that the loss of self leads automatically to the cosmic emptiness: ". . . I understood this thing called
self: it is man's defense against seeing absolute nothingness, against
seeing a world devoid of life, a life devoid of God." [*Ibid.*, p. 43]

In terms of the individual, when a deficient emptiness is accepted it
usually becomes displaced by the essential aspect lost, as we have
discussed. This applies to the cosmic emptiness as well. If and when
one remains with this universal deficient emptiness it slowly starts
filling up with the beautiful loving softness of Cosmic Consciousness.
The whole universe becomes filled with this aspect of Being. The
universe regains its soul. Both oneself and the rest of the world are
one unified existence now, and its beingness is the Conscious
Presence. One realizes here that the cosmic hole is due to the loss of
the boundless conscious presence.

One starts experiencing oneself as this loving conscious presence,
as if one is this consciousness and the universe is one's body.

At this point students typically encounter a particular object relation:
the experience of oneself as a child relating to a parent who is not
loving. Usually this parent is the father. The more one becomes the

442 Loving Light the more the self-concept or the personal shell is perceived as a child who is scared and small. Frequently a dialogue
ensues between the child and the Loving Consciousness. The child
feels angry at the loving presence, feeling abandoned by it, during
difficult times. One can realize that one is projecting the father's image
on this cosmic presence, which is sometimes equated with God. But
seeing this presence as Love brings out the loving object relation to
father. One starts remembering the love between father and child.

It is interesting that this particular object relation between child and
father becomes activated during the time of dealing with ego identity.
Sometimes the relation is with mother, but usually, especially at the
beginning, the relation is with the father. We consistently find that the
father image is projected on, or associated with, the aspect of Being
that appears as divine or cosmic, God the Father. We just mention this
here, without any more discussion, except for a case presentation.

This happened to Donna around the time that her father was dying
(a few months after her experience of Loving Light). It started as a
hurt, and a sense of boundaries around her body. In subsequent sessions she started feeling weak, small, deficient and hurt. She wanted
me to see her as beautiful, elegant and graceful. She recognized she
was wanting things from me that she wanted from her father, needs
that were becoming pressing due to his impending death. Now, in a
subsequent session she experiences much hatred towards friends and
colleagues, sibling rivalry related to her sister. This becomes clearly
understood as the expression of a rejection object relation with her
father. This understanding finally exposes her identification with her
body again. This brings up the experience of feeling her body cold,
dead like clay. This leads to a loss of her personal boundaries through
disidentification with her body-image. The experience that arises is
that of boundless Love. She first feels it personally towards me. She
now feels touched and grateful, instead of not seen or appreciated.
The boundless and universal qualities of Cosmic Consciousness become more dominant in her life, as she feels her loving relationship
with her father and me more consciously.

The activation of the loving object relation with father, after working through the unloving one, leads to an identification that is more
with the loving presence. One then feels oneself as the conscious
cosmic presence in a loving and compassionate relationship to the

child or the personality. There can arise a perception, as if from the outside, of one's anxiety, frustration and suffering. There is a compassionate and loving understanding of the individual. He is accepted and welcomed. This resolution is the understanding and the working out of the relationship between the Personal Essence and the aspect of Cosmic Consciousness.

As the individual is accepted, loved and welcomed by the universal Love one starts feeling oneself again as a person. One starts becoming conscious of a subtle sense of being an individual. It is similar to the ego sense of individuality, except that there is no contraction. It is a fullness that encompasses all the body, and more. One realizes that one's whole body is suffused by the tender softness of the conscious presence.

Here one realizes one's personal relation to the Cosmic Consciousness. There is the definite experience of being an individual rooted in the loving presence. There is no sense of boundaries. One is a presence, a personal presence, but with the quality of the Loving Light. Not only does one feel and see the personal loving presence as directly connected to the boundless Cosmic Consciousness, but one also feels oneself to be a personal expression of the divine presence, and still part of it.

When there is focus of attention on the personal presence one feels oneself to be an individual continuous with the cosmic presence. When the attention is focused on the cosmic presence one feels oneself to be the divine infinite presence. One is both the infinite and the individual. This is a very beautiful and fulfilled state. One feels oneself as a fullness grounded in the boundless presence. The mind is crystal clear, and one is a rounded fullness, bathed in the delicate tenderness of the conscious Cosmic Presence, and connected to it from one's depth and center. One feels connected to the Cosmic Presence, supported by it and enveloped by its lovingness.

This clarifies in a very singular way, more distinctly than ever before, some of the differences between the ego individuality and the Personal Essence, which is here experienced on the level of Loving Light:

• The Personal Essence is connected from its depth, as if through an umbilical cord, to the Cosmic Loving Consciousness. It is, as a result, completely and directly connected to the universe. The ego

444   individuality, on the other hand, is disconnected, because of mistaken identity, from the cosmic presence, and from the rest of the world, except in the fantasy of past object relations.

- The Personal Essence has no sense of separateness or boundaries, while the ego individuality is separate, and is the very presence of ego boundaries.
- The Personal Essence is an ontological presence, while the ego individuality is an identification with past object relations, through memory.
- The Personal Essence is surrendered to the will of the cosmic presence and is in harmony with all of existence, while the ego individuality has its own separate will, which covers up a deficiency.
- The Personal Essence knows no fear, while the ego individuality is scared, because it is separate and isolated from the universe.

We have been discussing the process of personalization of the Cosmic Consciousness, which shows the direct relation of the Personal Essence to the formless realms of Being. It indicates, in an actual personal experience, that individuation is really the Cosmic Conscious Presence individualizing and manifesting as the Personal Essence.

This process is also the deeper resolution of ego inadequacy. It is easy to see here that ego inadequacy is not only a consequence of the loss of contact with Essence, but also due to the separateness of ego boundaries that isolates the ego individuality from the Cosmic Presence. The Personal Essence has no inadequacy because it is directly connected to, and hence completely supported by, the Cosmic Loving Presence. Ego boundaries leave the ego individuality without the inner support of the various aspects of Essence, and without the comprehensive support of the Cosmic Essence (Consciousness). So just as we saw before that ego inadequacy is due to a mistaken sense of self, now we see that it is also due to the presence of ego boundaries. Both intrapsychic self-structures, the sense of identity and the sense of separateness, although indispensable to ego existence, are the reasons for its deep and basic inadequacy. Inadequacy is the deep nature of ego, due to the mere presence of its structure.

Chapter Thirty-Seven

Oneness
and
the Person

The dimensions of both the Impersonal Witness and the Cosmic Consciousness, although nonpersonal and formless, are still differentiated aspects of Being. All the essential aspects we have discussed so far are differentiated, discernible Platonic forms. Love is definitely love, completely delineated, as are Will, Compassion and so on. The Impersonal Witness is singularly impersonal. The Cosmic Presence is very clearly a consciousness that is boundless love, a loving conscious light.

The realization of the various differentiated aspects of Being leaves the door open to the manifestation of pure Being, nondifferentiated presence. Manifestation and realization of this basic and supreme aspect is a long and difficult one, but it is a natural process that spontaneously occurs at some point of personal development. We will discuss this supreme aspect of Being only enough to explore its relationship to the Personal Essence.

Nondifferentiated Being is simply the nature of everything, including all aspects of Being, and all of physical existence. One realizes that everything, on any level of perception, is nothing but a differentiation of this nondifferentiated sense of Being. This is different from the Cosmic Consciousness, which is the soul of all existence. Pure Being is not only the soul and Essence of the universe, it is the universe itself, and beyond. So it is a deeper and much more basic reality. It is seen to be the nature of Cosmic Consciousness, its beingness, the beingness of all aspects of Essence, and the nature and

446   beingness of everything perceivable. It is difficult to conceptually see
        the difference between Pure Being and Cosmic Consciousness, but
        experientially the difference is significant and clear.

        This level of Being is discussed in most spiritual teachings and
        traditions as the ultimate nature of reality. In Sufi metaphysics it is
        regarded as the first manifestation, or as the first plane of Being, seen
        as the dimension of unity. A fourteenth-century Sufi explains:

> Attributed to God, the Unity designates the purity of the
> Essence isolated from all the Names, from all the Qualities,
> from all cause and effect. It is the supreme revelation be-
> cause all other revelation will be necessarily particularized
> by something, with the exception of the "Quality of
> Divinity" (*al-ulûhiyah*) which is distinguished only by its
> non-exclusivity. Unity is then the first manifestation
> (*zuhûr*) of the Essence. [Abd al-Karîm al-Jîlî, *Universal
> Man*, p. 22]

        The manifestation of Pure Being is the experience of awakening.
        One merely wakes up and realizes one's pure nature. It is as if one is
        usually dreaming, but is taking the dream to be reality. Then he
        wakes up and spontaneously realizes the true state of affairs. Al-Jîlî
        puts it this way:

> Now, there does not exist for the Unity, in all the cosmos,
> a single place of manifestation (*mazhar*) more perfect than
> thyself, when thou dost plunge thyself in thine own
> essence, forgetting all relation, and thou dost seize thyself
> by thyself, stripped of all thy appearances, so that thou art
> thyself in thyself and that all the Divine Qualities or the
> created attributes—which belong to thee in any case—
> none any longer relate to thee. [*Ibid.*, p. 21]

        There is no sense of discontinuity of experience in awakening. It is
        not that something that was not there is now manifest. It is more like
        becoming cognizant of the presence of something that has always
        been there, and known to be there, but ignored. It is the only aspect
        of Being that is never lost, and when one experiences it, one realizes
        it was never lost, and cannot be lost. One merely wakes up to the fact
        that "Oh, that's it." There is no beginning of experience and no end of
        experiencing here. It is waking up to the fact that this is one's nature,
        it always has been, and one has always known that, but did not pay it
        notice. As Pure Being, one realizes:

Nothing can exist without me, not just because I am the very nature of everything; for I am everything. There is no separation here between appearance and Essence of nature. I am both and beyond.

I am the nature of thought. The moment the mind turns towards me it disappears. It becomes me, and there is then only me, Pure Being, as I have always been. Mind disappears as mind and appears as Being.

There is no Essence and personality, no Being and ego, for me; for I am both. I am the nature and being of both. Only in me, Pure Being, does the differentiation between personality and Essence dissolve.

I am unknowable, in the sense that there is no differentiated quality to be discerned. I am merely being, without reflecting on Being.

The Personal Essence is an easy access to this aspect because it is a personal Being. One merely has to be and, by and by, one is the supreme reality.

The relation between this pure aspect and the Personal Essence becomes evident by working through some object relations, similar to the ones of the Cosmic Consciousness. We illustrate by giving the report of Mark, a student whom we have discussed before, on his work in one group session:

I have been wondering about my Personal Essence, feeling that it is not existing these days, especially that I have been experiencing the death state. I had experienced Pure Being that afternoon, when I had been wondering about what is it that is alone. I began to see tonight that I did not feel connected to this supreme reality, that it just seemed like another state that did not really mean anything to me. I saw that I felt that the supreme did not include me personally. Also I felt that I felt this way with my father, that we were not connected, even though he really did love me and I really did love him. This was rarely expressed between us, except in very indirect ways. I felt sad and incomplete and unresolved with my father, and that there was nothing I could do because he was dead. I had been feeling this way since the summer retreat. I felt the love I had towards my father which was my personal love. While talking to you I saw my father's love, but at first felt disconnected from it until I saw clearly that he did love me and that he could not express it directly or tolerate my expressing it towards him. I also felt hurt and sadness around not being able to connect. I remember always wanting to let him know that I really loved him, and that we may have expressed it once shortly before he died. When I saw this, my personal love and the universal love, which first felt like my father's, blended. I felt the Personal Essence within it. And then I saw the Supreme as my father and I felt myself within it, complete and completely resolved with my father. Since then, I have been very happy about this, like I have always wanted this.

Several points in this report can illuminate our exploration:

1. *Mark dealt not only with his personal relation to the Pure Being, but also to Cosmic Consciousness, in the same process.* He had not understood and resolved his object relation to his father before this time, although he had experienced the Cosmic Consciousness before. Here the work on both formless dimensions of Being is telescoped into one process.

In the case of the student who has resolved this object relation at the level of the Cosmic Consciousness, the issue in relation to Pure Being manifests in a slightly different form. It typically appears as attachment to the formless dimension of Pure Being, with some subtle rejection, or absence of valuing, of the person. There results frustration, because rejection of anything indicates the presence of some ego identification. At some point there is the direct realization that the totality of the individual—the personality, the Essence, the mind, the heart, the body—has a place and a value of its own. Then one experiences Pure Being as the source of the deep, juicy kinds of love—all the essential heart qualities plus the Loving Light, flowing towards the individual. The individual, in all its aspects, is loved and accepted, and is experienced itself as Love and Value. This leads to the emergence of the Personal Essence in union with the Pure Being. One is both the Supreme and the person, in a kind of dual unity.

2. *In Mark's experience the person is felt as within Being, as the direct expression of Being, as is the case with Cosmic Consciousness.*

3. *However, in this case, the person is the expression of the Love of Pure Being.* Pure Being is seen as the source of the Cosmic Consciousness, which then differentiates further into all the essential aspects. The differentiation finally becomes integrated into the Personal Essence. So the Personal Essence is the individuation of Being through a process of differentiation and integration that is the expression of Love. This is

similar to the Sufi doctrine that God created the universe out of himself
as an expression of Love:

> It is to this apparition of God in all the least particles of exis-
> tence that the initiates allude in speaking of the penetrating
> Being (*al-wujûd as-sârî*), penetrating all existences. The
> secret of this penetration consists in that He created the
> world of Himself; but, as He is absolutely not divisible, every
> thing of the world is as it were entirely Himself. [*Ibid.*, p. 28]

And with regard to love in its relation to creation, Izutsu writes, in
discussing the work of Ibn 'Arabi, the greatest saint of the Sufis:

> The Divine Love is, after all, the same thing as Mercy, but
> looked at from a somewhat different angle. It is, theologi-
> cally speaking, the fundamental motive of the creation of
> the world by God, and in terms of the ontology peculiar to
> Ibn 'Arabi, it is the driving force of the self-manifestation of
> the Absolute. [Toshihiko Izutsu, *Sufism and Taoism*, p. 136]

4. *We notice that Being is associated with father, as is Cosmic Consciousness.*

5. *It is important to notice that part of the process of realization of
Pure Being is the metabolism of some object relations.* This means
psychodynamic and structural work can lead to this dimension of experience. This is usually completely ignored by spiritual teachings,
which makes the realization of this dimension difficult and extremely
rare. We see here that a large part of the barrier against this dimension
of Being is the existence of nonmetabolized past object relations. Most
spiritual teachings focus on the existential and epistemological barriers, which are only some of the relevant issues. In the Diamond
Approach, we see that consideration of the psychodynamic and structural issues is very helpful in realizing these deep aspects of Being,
and integrating them in a deep personal way. In fact, we see such
issues to be the primary ones, and the phenomenological-existential
and epistemological ones as much easier to deal with.

6. *Contrary to the assertion of many traditional spiritual systems, there
is a real person, and this real person has his place and value, even
from the perspective of Pure Being.* Once in a while, we find a spiritual
teacher acknowledging this fact. Nisargadatta Maharaj, although he
does not emphasize the aspect of the person, says:

> The person, the "I am this body, this mind, this chain of
> memories, this bundle of desires and fears" disappears, but

450   something you may call identity, remains. It enables me to
        become a person when required. Love creates its own
        necessities, even of becoming a person. [Nisargadatta
        Maharaj, *I am That*, p. 488]

Here Nisargadatta is not seeing the real person as the ego individuality. He understands the person to be the expression of Love, as we saw
above, although he usually identifies with a formless dimension.

7. *The relationship between the Essential Person and Pure Being is between the unique personal individuation and the ultimate ground.*
Jesus Christ put it in the form of the relation between the son and his
father. When one is the Personal Essence then one is a person supported by, and is an expression and extension of, Pure Being. When
one is Pure Being then only nondifferentiated pure Being is. In the
world of differentiation Being exists as the essential person. There is
no human life, nor any life at all, when there is no differentiation. As
Being, one is beyond life and death, form and formlessness.

This resolution and understanding of the relationship between the
Personal Essence and Being opens the door to the process of the latter's
personalization. This is a very subtle, and usually difficult, process. It
deals with extremely subtle perceptual and cognitive considerations.
However, the main barriers are mainly issues relating to ego structure.
The deepest and most subtle defenses of ego are resolved here. These
are the borderline defense of splitting, and the schizoid defenses of
isolation and withdrawal.

The story of the defense of splitting in relation to Being is a long
and complex one. Here we will note only that resolving the primary
split in the ego, the split between the bad and good representations,
involves integrating the essential aspect of Power. The defense of
splitting entails splitting away one's Power, because it is associated
with the all-bad self-representation, and projecting it outside. The
result is identification with a self-representation that is all-good but
powerless. This all-good, innocent, and powerless sense of self is experienced as confronting a world that is all-bad, hateful, and powerful. In this situation of powerlessness one experiences an excruciating
vulnerability in one's contact with the world, vulnerability to powerful
and destructive objects. So the individual resorts to the schizoid
defense of isolation (no engagement in object relations) and withdrawal (regression to primitive ego identifications). The defense of

schizoid isolation is seen then to be related to the defense of splitting. Working through this defense of isolation, or defensive detachment, is involved in the process of personalization of the Human aspect of Essence, which is related to vulnerability.

Working through this sector of the personality, which involves dealing with very primitive ego identification systems, ultimately reveals the most elementary form of the personality. It is the regressed, at the same time undeveloped, part of the ego that forms the basic and most rudimentary sense of self and personality. One sees here that splitting, isolation and withdrawal are in a sense the same thing; they meet in one manifestation. One experiences one's identity in a form of consciousness that is very subtle and delicate, but is characterized by being separate from Being, the nondifferentiated reality. One sees that the final, or conversely the most primitive, resistance is against Being, remaining separate from nondifferentiated Pure Being. The personality has an autonomous and differentiated existence, and hence the ultimate defense is a resistance that keeps the personality separate from Being. This defense is a withdrawal from contact with Being, which creates an isolation from it, with the final result being a primary splitting of Being and personality.

We have already discussed this issue briefly in discussing absorption; we will now focus on other elements of it.

One can possibly become conscious of a complete identification with this primitive state of personality. The state feels ordinary, simple, soft, somewhat warm and cozy. One is being the membrane of the personality, which we discussed previously. It is a simple warm feeling of being oneself. One becomes the feeling itself, that is not experienced to be directly connected to body, or mind, or boundaries. It is like a pure and undefended state of personality, like a simple but primitive individual consciousness. It is feeling the state of being the person that one is familiar with, with no defenses whatsoever, except for the separateness from Being.

But then one realizes it is a state of deep withdrawal, because one feels disinterested in feeling anything, especially an intense affect. There is a subtle belief or feeling that any intense sensation, like pleasure or love, will be too much. One feels comfortable in one's cozy defenselessness, not wanting any intrusion, even of aliveness or pleasure. There is no fear of judgment, exactly. It is more like an

452 organismic response. Any feeling is experienced as too much, as when a sensation feels too much and the body shudders against it. It is like tasting something too sweet or hearing something too loud. Any feeling is experienced as too intense, disruptive and disintegrating. So this ego or personality state, although soft and comfortable, has the innate tendency to reject any intensity. This manifests as a simple lack of interest in any feeling or activity. If any intense sensation intrudes, a thickness or hardness manifests in the state of personality, to avoid feeling the sensation.

One way of understanding this state of withdrawal is that it is the condition of the individual consciousness when this primitive form of ego structure was in its inception. So it is vulnerable and, in fact, inadequate when it comes to experiencing anything intense. It is the state of ego inadequacy in its original form, as incapacity to tolerate any intensity in feeling or activity.

We can say it is the initial cause of ego defense. The original defense must be against feelings, and not only against anxiety or hatred, for feelings are experienced as disruptive to structure at the primitive stages of its organization, at the inception of ego development. The ego structures are so primitive and vulnerable at the beginning that any pressure will be disintegrating. So there is a need to resort to defense. The first defenses are the schizoid withdrawal and isolation, followed by the borderline splitting and primitive projection.

Finally, as we have already discussed, this relatively defenseless state of the personality turns out to have a very subtle defense in it, which keeps it separate and differentiated from Being. We see here that not only the most primitive defenses are of the schizoid type, but that they are defenses against merging with Being. It is no wonder that in the schizoid character there are deep fears of being devoured. This was seen by Guntrip: "So the schizoid not only fears devouring and losing the love-object, but also that the other person will devour him." [Harry Guntrip, *Schizoid Phenomena, Object Relations and the Self,* p. 35]

We see, however, that not only for the schizoid character, but for every ego, there is a deep fear of being completely devoured and absorbed. This is not due only to difficult early object relations, as in the etiology of the schizoid character, but due to the vulnerability of primitive ego structures in the face of Being. This must be the case at the time in ego development when internalizations are just beginning to be set up. The identification with Being is still strong at this time, and these early and primitive ego structures are probably easily absorbed at times of complete letting go and relaxation. It is reasonable to assume that at such times the primitive infantile ego must experience repeated absorptions. This in turn assumes that the nondifferentiated aspect of Pure Being is part of the undifferentiated matrix of the neonate; but this seems like a most reasonable assumption in view of the universal experience of those who experience this realm of Being, that it was "always already there."

It is understandable that at such times the ego will first resort to schizoid defenses, especially those of withdrawal and isolation, not from object relations, but from the omnipresent sense of Being. This makes the schizoid sector of the personality the deepest core of ego structure. Fairbairn and Guntrip arrived at similar conclusions, through different considerations. They attribute the schizoid core to maternal inadequacy. However, we see it as a basic property of ego structure, based on the fact that it actually is weak and defenseless at its inception, and hence vulnerable to the presence of Being.

This explains completely why ego identification systems must include a defensive property, in order to exist at all. It is also in harmony with our findings that in the advanced stages of the process of essential realization, students seem to deal increasingly with schizoid defenses and issues. Thus the schizoid phenomenon has deeper origins than are recognized by object relations theory. Of course, one can say that such defenses are not schizoid but autistic in nature, corresponding to the autistic stage of ego development, the state of nondifferentiation of ego, as conceptualized by Mahler, for instance. She describes this stage, which is the earliest forerunner of the separation-individuation process:

> This is the period when the stimulus barrier (Freud, 1895, 1920), the infant's inborn unresponsiveness to outside stimuli, is clearest. . . . The infant is protected against extremes of stimulation, in a situation approximating the prenatal state, in order to facilitate physiological growth. [Margaret S. Mahler et al., *The Psychological Birth of the Human Infant*, pp. 41-42]

It is possible that this primitive form of ego structure originates in this autistic phase at the first few weeks of life. But asserting this means claiming that ego structures have their inception earlier than what

454 object relations theory has believed. It also means that ego defenses begin earlier than is usually believed, as early as the first few weeks of life. This might be the case but, for our purposes, it is enough to assume that at the inception of ego development the structures are still weak and vulnerable, and the first defenses are schizoid in nature, and are related, at least sometimes, to the presence of Being.

So at this advanced stage in the process of inner realization, vulnerability must be completely understood and accepted. It is experienced as the human adaptive capacity for being permeable, penetrable and impressionable. It is intrinsically adaptive, being open to a great range of experience and learning.

At this stage, the student learns that for the individual consciousness to be completely without defenses means to be completely vulnerable, not only to human love objects but, more basically, to Being itself. This means no resistance, no defense, no separateness and no isolation. So for the personality to be completely vulnerable to the reality of Pure Being means ultimately that it will become so transparent and permeable to it that there is no longer a difference between the two. It is complete absorption of ego structure by Being; the complete integration of personality into Being. The result is the state of unity and oneness of Being.

It is also the process of personalization of Pure Being. We see that the following are equivalent:

• Complete cessation of ego defenses and resistances
• Complete vulnerability
• Complete absorption of personality into Being
• Personalization of the supreme aspect of nondifferentiated Pure Being
• Total oneness of Being.

This process leads to two important essential realizations: that of supreme oneness, and that of supreme Personal Essence. The latter involves the Personal Essence attaining a new state, that of nondifferentiated Being. This is not the same as the oneness of Being. One here feels oneself still personal, but in a very pure way. One is a pure person, without any roles, free from all roles. There is freshness, newness and a sense of eternity. One perceives the passage of time, but one is not touched by it. One stays the same, changeless, eternal and feels no personal passage of time. There is fullness, openness, clarity

and eternity. It is a sense of freedom, where freedom is a complete 455
openness and lightness, where action is spontaneous and unimpeded.
It is freedom from object relations and the world of object relations,
while retaining the full capacity for human contact and relating. It is
the Personal Essence on the level of Pure Being, where the person is
completely synthesized with Pure Being. It is difficult to imagine such
a state, for it defies logical categories.

An interesting question arises at this point: In the process of personalization of the supreme aspect of Pure Being, is it that when the
personality is completely devoid of defense one realizes it is nothing but
the Personal Essence with the Pure Being quality, or that the personality
becomes integrated into Being resulting in the emergence of the Personal Essence in the new quality of Pure Being beyond differentiation?

It is possible to see that both perspectives are accurate; in other
words, there are experiences to substantiate both. There are experiences and perceptions where one realizes as the last primitive defenses
dissolve that the supreme Personal Essence is nothing but the completely purified and clarified personality. One learns that the sense of
separateness is completely due to the presence of subtle defenses.

On the other hand, there are definite experiences where one actually feels oneself, as the personality, being absorbed into Being. As
the last primitive and subtle defenses dissolve, due to objective understanding of vulnerability, one feels oneself being steadily absorbed or
reabsorbed. One feels taken in, eaten, swallowed, completely integrated. There is no fear and no resistance. The deepest fear of the ego
is now actualized; there is a loss of one's individuality, of one's separate identity. But it is experienced as a matter of fact perception,
without reaction of any sort, and without a sense of loss.

At some point one perceives—usually suddenly—that one is the
formless oneness of Being. The supreme, pure aspect of Being is now
experienced in its aloneness, without the presence of ego structures
and identifications. For this reason, the issue of aloneness sometimes
resurfaces just before this experience of pure oneness.

This state of oneness is in contrast to that of the Personal Essence,
but without any contradiction. One feels that one is everything; there
are no personal boundaries, and no partitions between objects. One is
the supreme aspect of Being, is pure nondifferentiated presence, that
is the nature of everything, that is also everything.

456   Pure Being is experienced as both everything and beyond everything. As beyond everything it is experienced in its suchness as a pure sense of Beingness. This is referred to usually as the state of unity. As everything, it is experienced as the nature of everything, and this is usually referred to as the state of oneness. In Sufism, unity is seen as the first manifestation of Being, and oneness as the second. In Taoism, oneness is seen as the second stage of manifestation of the Tao, or the Way:

> At this second stage, the man becomes conscious of the Way which contains all things in a state of pure potentiality. The Way will diversify itself at the following stage into "ten thousand things." But here there are no "boundaries" yet between them. The "things" are still an undivided Whole composed of a limitless number of potentially heterogeneous elements. They are still an even plane, a Chaos, where things have not yet received "essential" distinctions. [Toshihiko Izutsu, *Sufism and Taoism*, p. 355]

Oneness is not experienced as a something, an object of perception. It is known by being it, directly, without subject and object duality. One is aware of one's body as part of all appearance, of all the perceived universe. All appearance that one can perceive through the senses is perceived as one and whole; there are differences but no partitions. One, in fact, feels as if the whole universe is one's body. Everything is one, Pure Being, which is the ground and nature of everything.

There is no localization of consciousness in the body. The body is completely in unity with the rest of physical reality. All of physical reality is experienced as a unified whole, which is inseparable from Pure Being, that is the ground, essence and substance of all existence.

The condition of oneness is seen as a fact; it is seen to be the objective truth. One is certain that this is not a transient condition, but the actual condition of reality. It is really nothing but the total perception of reality. The perception is at all levels, the physical and the spiritual. This is in contrast to ego perception, where it is only physical, based on the physical, and exclusive of any other reality that is not an extension of the physical.

There is certainty that the experience of oneness of Being is an objective perception because one is aware that the perception does not exclude anything (including the normal perception), but adds another dimension, that of nondifferentiated Pure Being.

Transcendence and Embodiment

The realization of both the condition of oneness and that of the supreme personal Essence now shows the deeper and objectively true relationship between Being and the person. As Being one experiences oneself as all of existence, boundless and eternal. One is a oneness, which is the universe, but also beyond it. There are differences and varieties in the universal oneness, but no separation.

As the Personal Essence one is a pure person, a personal presence of eternity. But one is continuous with the oneness, as a form co-emergent from Pure Being. One perceives oneself as a cell in an infinite body.

One's identity goes back and forth, according to the needs of the situation. Sometimes one is the cosmic body, the state of oneness itself. At other times one is a cell in this body, as a personal presence. The two realities, the oneness and the person, are both Being; they are complementary. One is both. This is important to understand, because many believe that once ego boundaries dissolve there will be no longer a sense of the person, that only oneness will be left, forever. Many people are afraid of this prospect, and some are simply not attracted to it. In our understanding, the human potential allows the possibility of both conditions, without contradiction. We believe that those who teach that the two conditions are contradictory and exclusive of each other simply do not know of the Personal Essence.

The main difference between the two conditions of Being is that oneness is a transcendence of the body, and the person is an embodiment of Being. Understanding the relation between these two conditions can add a great deal to our understanding of the human being.

The state of transcendence can be experienced on many dimensions, not only on the plane of Pure Being. We have seen it in all the formless dimensions of Being. But it always involves a transcendence of the body. It is not only a matter of not identifying with the body, but also of not locating one's presence or consciousness in it. The consciousness, presence or beingness is experienced as larger than the body, usually infinite, containing the body, but never excluding it. One then knows oneself as beyond the body, transcendent to it, and of a nature that is not physical. Oneness always includes the body, but unity does not; for there is no differentiation in unity. Unity can

458   be considered a condition of transcendence, but it is not in relation to anything, while oneness is a transcendence of the body.

As a person one is not exactly the body, but one's presence and consciousness are located within it, or more accurately, coexistent with it, and inseparable from it. However, one's nature is still that of Being, just as in transcendence. So the person is nothing but the embodiment of Being. It is being Being but acting through the body. One is Being, in all of its dimensions and aspects, but one is living in time and space. The person is the presence of Being in the world, as a human being.

We have seen that ego development is a part of the process of realization of the Personal Essence. We have also seen that it is a process of cathecting physical reality, especially the body. Winnicott has called this process of psychosomatic collusion "personalization," or "indwelling" in the body. This is described in a book about his work:

> The basis for this indwelling is a linkage of motor and sensory and functional experience with the infant's new state of being a person. . . .
>
> Personalization means not only that the psyche is placed in the body, but also that eventually, as cortical control extends, the whole of the body becomes the dwelling place of the self. [Madeleine Davis and David Wallbridge, *Boundary and Space*, pp. 40-41]

We agree with Winnicott in taking the cathexis of the body to be a process of personalization. But we also understand that this process of personalization must continue through the realization of the Personal Essence, when Being is embodied. Now it is possible to talk about human beings and human life.

The understanding that is arising here is that ego development is part of the process of embodiment of Being. It is part of the process of Being finally learning to manifest and live in embodied existence. At birth the infant lives as Being, in a state of undifferentiation that is not linked to the body. A process then starts, of consciousness gradually cathecting the body and physical reality. This process of embodiment of Being is a process of personalization, of Being finally emerging as a person, a Human Being.

This process of embodiment includes the process we have described, the personalization of Essence, in which the various essential aspects become integrated in the presence of the Personal Essence. Now we see that this process also involves embodiment of these essential aspects; for the Personal Essence is the embodiment of Being.

In embodiment one is both Being and a person, a human being. One is the fullness and richness of Being, manifest as a unique person, living a human life in the world. One is both Being and the expression of the love of Being.

Being is transcendent, and ultimately nondifferentiated. It is possible to see that the person is a result of Being differentiating into the various aspects, which then become integrated again in a process of embodiment, forming a new synthesis, the Personal Essence. When this process is complete then the human being has attained maturity. This maturity includes the capacity for transcendence; for the Personal Essence is in actuality a cell in the oneness of Being. In other words, transcendence and oneness, the concerns of the man of spirit, are part of the maturity of the Personal Essence, which is the truth behind the hopes of the man of the world. This maturity is related to the realization that the Sufis call the station of the Perfect Man, sometimes symbolized by the Koran. Corbin, giving Ibn 'Arabi's understanding of this condition, writes:

> To be a "Koran" is to have achieved the state of the Perfect Man, to whom the totality of the divine Names and Attributes are epiphanized and who is conscious of the essential unity of divinity-humanity or Creator-creature. But at the same time the Perfect Man discriminates between the two modes of existentiation encompassed in the essential unity; by virtue of which he is the vassal without whom his Lord would not be, but also by virtue of which he himself would be nothing without his Lord. [Henry Corbin, *Creative Imagination in the Sufism of Ibn 'Arabi*, p. 211]

The human being comes from Being, ultimately goes to Being, and is the embodiment of Being, as an inseparable cell in the eternal oneness of Being.

Chapter Thirty-Eight

Nonconceptual Reality and Functioning

We can still ask, however, why personalization is needed. Why is there a need for the development of the Personal Essence? Why is the person needed for Being to be in the world?

The various ancient traditions give different answers. Some even deny the need for the person altogether. Some, like the Sufis and the Kabbalists explain that (divine) Being has manifested the human person so that it (Being) can see itself in its entirety, when the person is complete. A Kabbalist writes:

> Man, that is a full human being, is there not only to develop his Soul for himself, under difficult but highly stimulating conditions, but also as the sight, hearing, touch, smell and taste of the Lord at this level. As a Self-conscious Soul he remembers and is Remembered, Knows and is Known. Because of this, the Lord perceives directly through human experience the World he has Called forth, Created, Formed and Made. [Z'ev ben Shimon Halevi, *The Way of the Kabbalah*, p. 171]

In our exploration, we will discuss the need for the person in more down-to-earth terms, by understanding the characteristics of the Personal Essence. We can understand this need, at least partially, when we remember that the Personal Essence is related to functioning. It is the aspect of Being responsible for actual functioning in the world of space-time. Pure Being, in its state of eternal unity and nondifferentiation, cannot function in the physical world; it does not even make

sense to speak about functioning in relation to this aspect. It is completely separate from, and transcendent to, functioning. Functioning
presupposes differentiation and discrimination. The Personal Essence
is the integration that is the outcome of the synthesis of the differentiated aspects of Being; it is the functional aspect of Being.

To thoroughly understand in what sense the Personal Essence is the
functional aspect of Being, we must explore the relationship of the
Personal Essence to the ultimate reality. This ultimate reality is not exactly that of nondifferentiated Pure Being or oneness. It is beyond all
conceptualizations. Oneness still retains a concept of oneness. Nondifferentiated Pure Being still retains the concept of Being or existence.
Pure Being is none other than the ultimate reality, but is still not seen
completely objectively. It is devoid of all differentiation, but it is not
devoid of concepts. It is beyond all concepts except one; one is still
adhering to the subtle conceptualization of existence. There is still a
sense of presence, of beingness, which is very clear experientially.
And we find that ego ultimately will use this sense of presence to
support its existence and identity. So the next development in the
process of inner realization is for Pure Being to lose the last concept,
that of Presence.

Absence

The loss of the concept of Presence happens through the realization of
the ultimate void (Sunyata), which is the absence of conceptualization.
This is another radical departure from one's previous experience. One
goes from a sense of absolute presence to a sense of absolute Absence.
One here realizes that for the first time a complete cessation of the sense
of self is attained. There is no experience of self or person, *without consciousness* that there is no self or person. When the sense of presence is
lost, the last foothold for the sense of self (identity or person) is gone.

In the state of Absence there is no self-consciousness at all, and one
realizes that it is the self-reflective movement of the mind that is the
core of the sense of self. Roberts describes her discovery of this truth
this way:

> Before this event took place, I had never noticed how
> automatically and unconsciously the mind was aware of it-
> self, or how continually conscious I had been of my own

462   awareness in all mental processes, or in all my thoughts,
         words, and deeds. But when this reflexive movement came
         to an end, I suddenly realized the profound roots of self-
         consciousness, roots that unknowingly had infiltrated every
         aspect of my existence. [Bernadette Roberts, *The Experi-
         ence of No-Self*, p. 148]

It is not until this realization of Absence that one realizes that usually there is a continuous and incessant sense or feeling of self or I. Every experience is related to this I. Now there is experience and perception of experience, but it is not related to an I, not even to the I of oneness. There is pure awareness of phenomena, with complete absence of self or center. The Absence is so complete that there is not even consciousness of the Absence. The complete absorption in this condition is the cessation of all sensation and consciousness of oneself. There is Absence and there is absence of the consciousness of Absence. It is like deep sleep but one is not asleep. Absence is what the Buddha termed the cessation of perception and sensation, which he took to be the ultimate state needed for the end of karma. Here he states, in a passage translated from the Samyutta-Nikaya:

      And moreover, O priest, I have taught the gradual cessa-
      tion of karma. Of one who has entered the first trance the
      voice has ceased; of one who has entered the second
      trance reasoning and reflection have ceased; . . . of one
      who has entered the realm of the infinity of consciousness
      the perception of the realm of infinity of space has ceased;
      of one who has entered the realm of nothingness the per-
      ception of the realm of the infinity of consciousness has
      ceased; of one who has entered the realm of neither per-
      ception nor yet non-perception, the perception of the
      realm of nothingness has ceased; of one who has entered
      the cessation of perception and sensation, perception and
      sensation have ceased. Of the priest who has lost all
      depravity, passion has ceased, hatred has ceased, infatua-
      tion has ceased. [*The Harvard Classics: Sacred Writings*,
      Buddhist Volume II, p. 245]

The cessation of perception and sensation is considered the trance of cessation, the final step of the path of cessation, leading to eradication of ego life. Complete Absence is a radical experience, and students usually approach it slowly and tentatively.

One student, Katy, in a private teaching session, encountered this condition in a way that throws light on its peculiar quality. She was having difficulty being present, her consciousness moving away from the situation. She thought she was avoiding something. But it did not seem that way to me. When I asked her to describe her condition objectively, without judgment, she started seeing that her consciousness kept wanting to go away because it did not have anything to return to. Instead of feeling herself in her usual way, there was complete absence of sensations and consciousness, and hence she could not feel anything there. She could not be present because there was Absence. Realizing this allowed an acceptance of a condition she did not know or anticipate. She began to perceive that there was awareness of everything except her own presence of consciousness or self. Awareness became clear although she was not there to be aware; this experience was so outside the realm of her normal experience, it was astonishing and incredible to her, although at the same time it was very simple and clear. Complete Absence means just what the Buddha said, cessation of perception and sensation. Like being in deep sleep but without being asleep, there is a state of no consciousness.

In Absence one experiences oneself to be a pure subject, that is not an object. One is the source of awareness. One is not the witness, not the witnessing, not the witnessed. One recognizes oneself as an Absence, unknown and unknowable. When one looks inward there is no perception; there is absolute Absence without consciousness of Absence, because Absence is not an object of perception. It is in fact the absence of an object of perception.

When one looks at phenomena one observes functioning. There is absolutely no self-consciousness, so there is complete spontaneity. There is awareness of phenomena and functioning, but there is no involvement at all. It does not feel that there is someone or something observing or aware of phenomena. Everything is the same as usual, except that there is no self. There is no person or presence who feels or thinks he is doing or perceiving. The perceiving is present, the doing is present, without being related to a perceiver and doer. This is completely incomprehensible to ego. Ego cannot conceive of perceiving or functioning if it is not present at the center of it. For ego, functioning is always the functioning of the person or self.

This experience is dumbfounding to the mind. One realizes that one has always assumed, and has taken it to be the absolute truth, that there cannot be functioning without a functioner. But here, in the

464 experience of Absence, one realizes that one has been wrong all along. Functioning happens smoothly and spontaneously, and does not need the presence of any self or personality.

There is perception of the body moving, doing what it normally does; eating, talking and so on. However, all this is seen as functioning, completely spontaneous, not belonging to a person or a self. It is also not seen as separate from any other functioning in the universe. There is Absence and the awareness of the oneness of existence, which is experienced as in a state of functioning. Or as Roberts puts it:

> Here on the first step of the transition, the "logical subject" has evidently given way to a state of consciousness in which there is no known subject, and the one real object of consciousness remaining is the Oneness of all that exists. [Bernadette Roberts, *The Experience of No-Self*, p. 149]

This is a surprising and, of course, rare condition. There is no doer whatsoever. Everything is happening as functioning; each part, body or mind, is doing its functioning smoothly, and spontaneously, without a center.

The experience of ego is that functioning, including perceiving, is the doing of the ego individuality, at the center of which is the sense of self, the I. Ego never experiences functioning differently; as far as it can remember, functioning has been the manifestation of parts of its structure.

Now, in this condition of Absence, one realizes that this is not the case, that the feeling "I am doing, I am perceiving," and so on, is not an objective perception of the situation. It is only a subjective feeling based on a belief in the existence of a sense of self. When this belief is gone, and the sense of self or I is seen only to be a concept, functioning is seen to happen on its own, independent of any center.

We are quite aware of the fact that this state cannot be imagined or conceived by ego or mind. The conviction that one is at the center of functioning is so deep, total and crystallized that it is taken by the mind to be an absolute natural law. However, it is important for us to describe this functioning which is free from a functioner in order to explore its relation to the Personal Essence.

In the state of Absence there is no presence, consciousness or functioning. As functioning is needed there is then the awareness of consciousness arising. This consciousness is experienced as a loving

presence, spontaneously arising in the voidness of the Absence. It is   465
perceived to gradually transform itself into the presence of the Personal Essence. The functioning is then experienced as inseparable
from the presence of the Personal Essence. Functioning and Personal
Essence are seen to be equivalent. One is still Absence here, with
complete lack of self consciousness. But there is the perception that
the Personal Essence is an expression of oneself, as a specific formulation of Loving Consciousness, and is directly involved in functioning. One does not experience oneself as the Personal Essence, but
experiences the Personal Essence as an arising conscious presence
that is the source, and part and parcel of functioning. In other words,
as Absence, one needs the Personal Essence for functioning. There is
here no ego structure whatsoever. Functioning is completely spontaneous, in some sense, automatic. But it is a direct response to the
situation, totally devoid of premeditation. This capacity is the result of
the profound and completely organic integration of all organs of perception and action into the Personal Essence. It shows the unique
place of the Personal Essence both to Being and to the world, to the
Reality and to the appearance of things.

The Nameless

Although there are no concepts in the state of Absence, when there
is functioning there is duality. Absence is experienced as separate
from, transcendent to, and totally uninvolved in functioning. One experiences oneself as not involved in functioning, and hence, there is
the duality of Absence and functioning consciousness. Absence can
be seen as the ultimate transcendence, but it is still not the ultimate
reality. We can say it is the first glimpse into ultimate reality, and is
still not complete. It is the absence of presence, and of all other concepts. However, there is a subtle conceptualization here, because
Absence can be experienced as a definite state. Its definiteness is its
absence of concepts. In other words, the concept of the absence of
concepts becomes the subtle concept in the state of Absence. One is
quite aware of the absence of presence, in particular.

These considerations of the perception of duality and subtle conceptualization, amongst others, precipitate spontaneously the ultimate
reality, the truly nonconceptual truth. Here, words will not say

466   anything positive. Nonconceptual Reality is how things are. It is direct perception of reality without the involvement of the mind. It is both presence and absence, but also neither. It is neither self nor no-self, nor the absence of both self and no-self. It is both being and non-being and neither. It is everything and it is nothing. Whenever there is negation or affirmation there is conceptualization, and the true reality is gone. And hence we call reality as it is the Nameless; it cannot be named.

In Zen this Nameless Reality is expressed in paradoxes and enigmatic actions, called koans. One such koan is: "Show me your face before you were born." Technically speaking this ultimate reality, the Nameless, is experienced when Presence and Absence are integrated, when Pure Being acquires the property of Absence.

The Fourteenth Dalai Lama, the head of Tibetan Buddhism, speaks of this reality as the ultimate fruit of meditation. He says, in one of his lectures, referring to Absence as emptiness, and taking Presence to be that of the aspect of Clear Light:

> As the mind grows even more subtle, reaching the subtlest level, it is eventually transformed into the most basic mind, the fundamental innate mind of clear light, which at once realizes and is of one taste with emptiness in meditative equipoise without any dualistic appearance at all, mixed with emptiness. Within all having this one taste, anything and everything can appear; this is known as "All in one taste, one taste in all." [Dalai Lama, *Kindness, Clarity, and Insight*, p. 71]

Or as the Zen master Huang Po puts it: ". . . the One Mind, which is the substance of all things, is co-extensive with the Void and fills the entire world. . ." [Translated by John Blofeld, *The Zen Teaching of Huang Po*, p.79]

The relation of the Personal Essence to this nonconceptual reality is again seen in functioning. Functioning in this realm is like that in the state of Absence, in the sense that it is not related to a doer or a center. However, there is no duality, no differentiation between the presence of Nameless Reality and functioning. The experience is of the ultimate reality, which is everything and beyond everything, and is seen to be the source of functioning, without functioning being any different from the presence of the Nameless Reality. One is the Nameless all, without the mind saying so. One is the functioning, without

the mind saying that one is functioning. The Reality is functioning, 467
and functioning is the Reality.

In other words, the Nonconceptual Reality is what functions, without functioning being perceived as separate in any way from the presence of Reality. There is no conceptualization whatsoever, so there is no differentiation between functioning and what functions. It is as if when the hand moves it is not your hand, but the hand of the true Reality, which is nothing but the true Reality. The Nameless Reality is .you, is the hand, and is the movement of the hand. This condition is expressed in a famous Zen Koan: A Zen master, Joshu, was approached by a disciple. The disciple asked the master to teach him the essence of Zen. The master asked: "Have you had your breakfast?" The disciple answered affirmatively. The master said: "Then go wash your bowl."

The understanding is that the disciple, the bowl and washing the bowls, are all the essence of Zen, the Nameless. This is a direct perception, and not just merely a belief in such condition, or an insight about it. Roberts calls such functioning, which she sees to be characteristic of what she considers the ultimate Reality, "doing":

> The reason for using this term is because the doer, as well as that which the doer acts upon, falls into the realm of the unknown; only the act of doing falls into the realm of the known. We do not know "that" which smiled or at "what" it smiled; all we know is the smile itself—even though all three are identical. This means that what Is can only be known because it is identical with its acts (or doing).
> [Bernadette Roberts, *The Experience of No-Self*, p.69]

What we observe is that in functioning what is unified with Absence is not only Being, but also the Personal Essence. Alternately, we can say that, in functioning, the Personal Essence is present with the Nameless, but not at all separate from it. It is one truth then, that is both Nameless and functioning. This truth is both personal and impersonal, but also neither. It is the personalization of the Nonconceptual. However, there is no mind, so who is to say?

This perception is extremely subtle, but it is nothing unusual. It is merely the normal state of affairs, all the time, without the mind saying anything. It is the simplest reality, but the mind cannot comprehend it. Mind can comprehend only complexity, which is nothing but the interplay of concepts that it is constantly creating.

The Absolute

Inner realization is a process of shedding, of losing what one takes oneself to be, to ultimately become what one is, without need for any external support, not even one's mind. This description is not metaphorical; one actually experiences the disappearance of great realms of one's identity. As one goes deeper and deeper, one realizes that one is shedding concepts that one had taken to be absolute truths. The shedding of all concepts is the realization of the Nonconceptual Nameless Reality, what is. Nothing can be said to describe it because one can only use concepts to describe.

Yet the shedding is still not absolute. It is true that all concepts are gone, but there remains one more thing—consciousness itself. The nature of the Nameless is pure consciousness, consciousness that is conscious of consciousness, without labeling or knowing anything. There is consciousness, but there is no knowing of what is known, or what knows; there are no conceptual categories. Huang Po says: ". . . you would find it formless, occupying no point in space and falling neither into the category of existence nor into that of non-existence." [Translated by John Blofeld, *The Zen Teachings of Huang Po*, p. 87]

Even consciousness, which is not exactly a concept, can be shed. At some point, usually without anticipating it, one realizes that one is perceiving the Nameless Reality as external to oneself. One becomes aware that one is beyond the Nameless, and the world that it supports, as an unknowable mystery. The Nonconceptual Reality, which is the ground of the world of concepts, is experienced here as not absolutely real. In fact, it is experienced as a radiance, ephemeral and insubstantial, in relation to and emanating from an unfathomable Absolute. One realizes that one's most absolute nature, which turns out to be the underlying nature of all of existence, transcends not only the mind, but consciousness itself. One is the beyond, beyond whatever can be experienced or perceived. Absence is seen as an incomplete glimpse into the Absolute. One is the ultimate subject, which cannot be an object of perception, and hence is unknown and unknowable. The Absolute is not aware of itself, but awareness of everything else proceeds from it, while what characterizes consciousness is that it is conscious of itself. Nisargadatta Maharaj says of himself as the Absolute, the noumenon:

> All I am, all I have always been, and will be, is what I was before I was "born." Not being a body, how could I have been born? Being Awareness itself, how could I be aware of awareness? I am no "thing" and know no "other," to be aware of.
>
> Noumenally (absolutely) unknowable, phenomenally (relatively) I become an object of knowledge. Noumenon-I-is what remains after all phenomena are totally negated. *I am this-here-now, total phenomenal absence. How then can I, noumenon, be known, experienced, cognized?* [Ramesh S. Balsekar, *Pointers from Nisargadatta Maharaj*, p. 96]

The Absolute dimension is considered by the various spiritual traditions to be the deepest possible realization; when one does have a taste of such truth there is certainty of its absoluteness. There cannot be anything beyond the Absolute, because if there is any perception or experience then by definition it is within consciousness, and the Absolute is precisely the transcendence of consciousness. It is the Father of Christianity, the Divine Essence of the Sufis, the Parabrahaman of Hinduism, and the Nirvana of Buddhism. Sri Aurobindo, wrote of his experience of the Absolute, which he termed nirvana:

> *It threw me suddenly into a condition above and without thought, unstained by any mental or vital movement; there was no ego, no real world—only when one looked through the immobile senses, something perceived or born upon its sheer silence a world of empty forms, materialized shadows without true substance. There was no One or many even, only just absolutely That featureless, relationless, sheer, indescribable, unthinkable, absolute, yet supremely real and solely real. . . . What it (this experience) brought was an indescribable Peace, a stupendous silence, an infinity of release and freedom.* [Satprem, *Sri Aurodindo or The Adventure of Consciousness*, pp. 151-152]

The Absolute is sometimes referred to as emptiness or void, and this is so. However this does not truly describe this mystery, for although it has the nature of voidness it is also nonconceptual, and hence beyond the concept of void. It is in fact more real than physical reality, more solid and substantial than anything else. Nisargadatta Maharaj, from the tradition of Vedanta, and perhaps the most explicit representative embodiment of this dimension in modern times, describes it this way:

470

> By itself the light can only be compared to a solid, dense, rock like, homogeneous and changeless mass of pure awareness, free from the mental patterns of name and shape. [Nisargadatta Maharaj, *I Am That*, p. 34]

And again:

> This state is entirely one and indivisible, a single solid block of reality. The only way of knowing it is to *be* it. The mind cannot reach it.
>
> It is not perceivable, because it is what makes perception possible. It is beyond being and not being. It is neither the mirror nor the image in the mirror. It is what *is*—the timeless reality, unbelievably hard and solid. [*Ibid.*, p. 36]

It is the underlying reality behind all of existence, the source of all dimensions. In one private session, Pamela, whom we have met before, was working with me on a very difficult, old issue of hers. For some time she had been working on states that caused her much disintegration and loss of identity. In her life it turned out she was engaged in an object relation in which she was to blame for the negativity of the object. She then found out that was her way of protecting the all-good image of her mother and thus not losing her. Seeing how she was splitting her image of her mother, she started seeing her mother more objectively. First this brought about fear, then deep sadness for the loss. This sadness became deep warmth and compassion for herself, her mother and the suffering of all humanity in their ignorance. This universal compassion expanded, and led to deep aloneness, which turned out to be a deep and vast black spaciousness, starting at the heart. Sinking into this aloneness and space she felt it becoming more real and solid, as if the emptiness attained a density. After a while she was perceiving all of existence as a thin film over this immense reality. She realized that all of existence is of the nature of thought in relation to this reality, which was both a voidness and a solidity, but really a majestic mystery, that supported all. We see here how the vulnerability and the loss of self due to seeing through the splitting of the mother's image led Pamela finally to the experience of the most fundamental self, the Absolute, which was also the fundamental reality underlying all other realities.

This case illustrates the relationship between the world and the dimension of the Absolute, but it also shows how the realization of even this absolute dimension requires working through some object

relations and psychodynamic issues. We find that even after the dis-   471
covery of this dimension, its complete realization is mostly a matter of
freeing one's consciousness from very deep object relations and self
representations.

The Absolute is the realm of complete mystery, or of bedazzlement,
as the Sufis say. And only here will the heart feel it has arrived home,
at long last. There is wonder, there is beauty, there is majesty, but it is
all mystery upon mystery. The peace is stupendous, the certainty is
absolute and the beauty is dazzling. It is the ultimate Beloved of the
heart, the Spirit of spirits, and the mystery of all existence. It is the absolute presence of absolute annihilation, which is then seen to be the
primal cause of all. Obviously such words make no sense to the mind,
but when consciousness finally reaches this its final abode, the heart
will hear these words as music.

Understanding functioning from this dimension leads to further integration and actualization of the Absolute. Functioning is seen here
to happen in several ways, depending on from what dimension it is
seen. One way is similar to functioning from the perspective of Absence, another similar to that of the Nameless Reality. In the next
chapter, in which we discuss the dimension of the Logos, we will explore such functioning. The functioning most relevant for us has to do
with the dimension of the Personal Essence, where the personalization of the dimension of the Absolute becomes the issue.

It is here that the understanding of personalization reaches its peak.
It is again a long and difficult process, in which one must pass
through the dark night of the spirit, and attain the station of complete
mystical poverty. This means divesting ego, and personal consciousness itself, of all existence. Then one realizes at some point that to be
the Personal Essence here is to be a personal expression of the Absolute, a particular but pure manifestation of the ultimate mystery. As
the Personal Essence at this dimension one is part of the very fabric of
the ultimate mystery. In other words, to be a particular unique expression of the Absolute in ordinary life one must have realized the
Personal Essence. But one realizes that only the Absolute has true existence. So, is one here the Absolute or the expression of the Absolute? This mystery, the relationship—which is not an object relation—
between the lover (the individual expression) and the Beloved (He,
the Absolute) is expressed by a Sufi poet:

472   Look close: all is He—
              but He is manifest through *me*.
          All ME, no doubt—
              but through Him.
          [Fakhruddin 'Iraqi, *Divine Flashes*, p. 79]

Functioning here is absolutely spontaneous, without any trace of self-consciousness. It is the Absolute functioning through the integrated human being, but not separate from it. It is a mystery, where one is both an individual personal expression of the Absolute and the immensity of the Absolute, in some indescribable dual unity, which is beyond any comprehension of the mind.

PART IV

UNIVERSAL MAN

Chapter Thirty-Nine

The
Diamond Pearl

The Nonconceptual Nameless Reality is the same as Nondifferentiated Pure Being, but realized beyond mind. The Absolute
is the same as the Nameless Reality, but now realized beyond
consciousness. This means it is the nature of all existence, it is all existence, it is everything and it is beyond everything. Hence it is the
ultimate nature of all differentiated aspects of Being. There can be
perception of differentiation, which here means difference and
variety, but not separation. There is absolute oneness of all that appears to perception; however, it is not conceived of as oneness,
since there is no conceptualization. There is unity as the nature and
essence of all.

To understand how functioning occurs, or is perceived, at this level,
is to understand functioning that transcends the individual. We alluded
to this in discussing functioning from the perspective of the dimensions of Absence, the Nameless and the Absolute; the totality of existence functions in unity, as a oneness of existence. However, this is
difficult to understand since functioning has so far been equated with
the mode of operation of the Personal Essence, which is an individuated and distinct—although not separate—presence.

It is possible to comprehend such functioning from the perspective
of a dimension of Being we call the Logos. It is one of the formless
and boundless dimensions, but is quite distinct from the other dimensions we have discussed so far, which are all experienced as the
presence of Being. They are different manifestations of Being, where

Being is a stillness, an existence, a thereness, a presence. There is no movement of Being here, or functioning.

The Logos, on the other hand, is the presence of Being in a boundless manifestation that has a distinct dynamic quality to it. It is experienced as Being in flow, in movement. The flow and movement are not haphazard, but coincide with the changes we see as the occurrence of events in the totality of the whole universe. In other words, all changes are perceived from this dimension as the flow of substance and beingness of the Logos. The world is perceived, in some sense, as alive and living, as one infinite and boundless organism of consciousness. It is not merely the presence of Being or consciousness; this dimension of Being is experienced as a living organism, boundless and infinite.

Movements, changes and transformations in the universe are then perceived as the functioning of this dimension. The whole universe is perceived to move, change and transform as a unity. This is universal or cosmic functioning, not related to a distinct entity in the world. This is admittedly rather mysterious, even unbelievable, when not experienced directly. It is the basis for the Western prophetic tradition's concept of a God that creates and runs the universe. The Sufis, for instance, differentiate God in his unity and absoluteness, "Dhat," the Absolute, from his creative and functioning manifestation, the dimension of manifestation of Being they call "Wahdat," One, where functioning is due to this dimension possessing the attribute of power:

> Thus there was first the *Dhat*, the unknown and unknowable of Herbert Spencer. . . . This is the stage of *Ahadiyat*. Then four *itibarats* (imaginary relations or hypostases) are found, knowledge of self, existence, light, and power. This is the stage of *Wahdat*. [Sirdar Ikbal Ali Shah, *Islamic Sufism*, p. 128]

The Sufis associate this dimension, the Logos, with the prophet of Islam, Mohammed, just as Christianity associates it with the Christ: "*Wahdat* is the reality of Muhammad; and the world is a manifestation of that reality." [*Ibid.*, p. 130]

True knowledge regarding this dimension is rare in the modern world although it is the spiritual reality emphasized by the Western traditions of Hellenism, NeoPlatonism, Sufism and Christianity. Christianity actually

476   makes this dimension, the Logos or the Word, its main source, and sees
       Christ as its personal embodiment, as in the following excerpts from the
       Gospel of St. John:

> In the beginning was the Word:
> The Word was with God
> and the Word was God.
> It was with God in the beginning.
> Through it all things came to be,
> not one thing had its being but through it.
> The Word was made flesh,
> it pitched its tent among us,
> and we saw its glory,
> the glory that is its as the only Child of the Creator,
> full of grace and full of truth.

It is beyond the scope of this book to discuss this reality further, except for two points. The first is related to functioning beyond the individual. The flow of the beingness of the Logos is seen as cosmic functioning. It is the same as the process of continual creation, which is a manifestation of all existence from the Absolute.

> The Creator gives up his immobility, his stillness, and points—through the Word—to creation. In pointing with the word, he shows himself, and is revealed. This is the primal revelation, creation itself. [Georg Kühlewind, *Becoming Aware of the Logos*, p. 26]

This kind of functioning can be perceived or experienced in different ways, depending on what formless dimension we are perceiving this flow from. In the following report, James, a student we mentioned previously, writes of his experience of the flow of the Logos from the Absolute, that resulted from working through some ego structures in a group meeting:

> My experience of working with you was one of working from the inside out. It felt like my deep images of self and object relations were at the cellular level, imprinted into my soul, that became tarnished. This work tonight felt like dissolving the images and assumptions at this deep-seated level. It felt like an exposing and revealing from the inside out. My deep beliefs and assumptions about my personality were seen for just what they are, beliefs and assumptions. Seeing the truth, I felt fear of losing control, sadness about losing an old friend and a going beyond these feelings, a dissolving of identity.

I began to experience myself as a flowing continuation of everything without my previous desire to hold onto identity and control. My perception was one of seeing everything unfolding, a moving transparency. What I saw was no different than myself. It was a sense of nothing, but yet contained everything. I felt relaxed with no desire for an identity, an allowing to see reality as it truly is without my mind. I felt dissolved and bathed in a moistness, vastness and richness beyond words, a sense of being united and immersed in this rich blackness.

The main ego structure James had to let go of in this experience was his sense of self and identity. Specifically, it is the fixation inherent in this ego structure and all others that becomes the main barrier against the experience of functioning as a flow of Being. So any rigidity in the personality, which is an expression of the ego's need for a lasting and unchanging structure, becomes a psychodynamic issue at this level.

The second point is that the dimension of the Logos is integrative in nature, and can be experienced as the totality of all dimensions, except for the Absolute. Hence, it is often seen as the totality of existence, termed sometimes "creation," or as the Sufi puts it: "This is such a station that here every station that has been mentioned before should be seen and observed as one." [Ibn 'Arabi, *Kernel of the Kernel*, p. 6] It is difficult to explain what this means, but it must suffice for our purposes here to state that the Logos brings about the capacity to see that all aspects and dimensions of Being can be perceived as one, as the manifest part of the Truth, contrasted to the Absolute which is the unmanifest Truth.

The realization of the Logos completes the process of personalization, which makes it possible to experience and understand the objective Personal Essence. To understand what this means we need to remember that the personalization of the various aspects of Essence leads at some point to the integration of all these personalized aspects. We have called this overall synthesis of all aspects in the presence of the Personal Essence the "Complete Person," and discussed the objective and formless dimensions of Essence just enough to see the main processes needed for this overall synthesis.

Just as the personalization of the aspects of Essence leads to the synthesis of all such personalized aspects, the personalization of the

478   various dimensions—the objective dimensions of Essence and the formless dimensions of Being—leads ultimately to the synthesis of all such personalized dimensions. This complete integration and synthesis of all aspects and dimensions into the presence of the Personal Essence, which is the same as the personalization of the Logos, makes the latter now objective in a very real sense of the word. This is the station of the objective person, who is not only complete but universal. One is a person, a personal presence, in all dimensions. The person is now the expression and embodiment of Reality, in all its aspects and dimensions. This objective realization, which is the fruit of the overall process of personalization, manifests in various ways and leads to many capacities. We will describe only a few:

- There is self-respect and dignity, which manifests also as respect for all other human beings. Others are perceived, as is oneself, as the expression of the Absolute Truth, and its differentiation into the various dimensions and aspects.
- Teaching becomes mainly the impact of personal contact. The action of the objective and real person is seen to be the corrective, orienting factor in the teaching relationship. The objective Personal Essence is seen, thus, to be the station needed for teachership.

Of course, this does not mean that to be a teacher of essential realization one has to be purely, completely and always the objective Personal Essence. Rather, the more this realization is established and integrated the more effective and capable is the teacher. It is a certain state of Being that will arise at some point, and will become more established and expanded throughout the rest of life. There is no end to its expansion, because there is no end to the human potential. However, this state of Being must be available for an individual to function as a teacher with the capacity to guide students toward the integration of all levels of reality.

Here we will digress to discuss the teacher and his role. One can work with others and teach them only what one has realized. This means one must be able to embody an essential aspect or dimension, at the time of interaction with the student, to be able to work with him effectively on that particular aspect or dimension. Just to know intellectually about the state, or to have had some experience of it, is not enough. This is partly because all states of Being are beyond the usual faculties of the mind, and hence cannot be used or known merely through the aid of memory. Also as is the case with any psychological state, if one cannot experience an essential aspect or dimension when it is needed, it must be due to the presence of barriers against it (usually unconscious). Such a barrier will then render the teacher unable to work with the student in relation to that aspect or dimension.

Thus, in order to be a teacher of Essence, one must work to realize himself on the dimension of the Personal Essence. His effectiveness as a teacher will depend on the extent of his realization. He is most effective if he is realized to the point of not needing or wanting, even not actually receiving, any personal gratification from the function of teachership. This is difficult to understand as long as one does not know selflessness from direct experience.

- The objective Personal Essence is the presence and life of the mature and adult human being. The principles and values governing the personal life and conduct are those of the Absolute Truth and its various differentiated manifestations.

- The sense of selflessness, service and giving, is second nature. One does not think of helping or try to help. It is one's nature to help, love, give and serve. One does not even know one is helping or serving. It is one's nature, just as it is the nature of the sun to radiate light, and the nature of the rose to give off fragrance. One is naturally and spontaneously in harmony with the totality of existence.

- Doing or functioning is not separate from Being. Functioning is the flow of Reality, spontaneous and completely non-self-conscious. It is a spontaneous response to situations, integrated action that implicitly takes into consideration the perspective of all aspects and dimensions, plus the Absolute source of them all. Functioning sometimes emphasizes specific aspects, when it is the particular need of the situation. This happens spontaneously without the interference of the mind.

- The mind, heart and body are completely integrated and redeemed. The mind is not experienced as an impediment, but functions as an instrument that has its own functions. The heart and body, too, function freely and are integrated in one total functioning.

- The personal conduct and behavior expresses the dignity, integrity and objectivity of the mature human being, the embodiment of Reality. The human being is seen to be the expression of all dimensions of

480   reality, and, hence, is the being who has all dimensions of reality available to his direct experience. He is a personalization of all planes of reality: physical, mental, energetic, essential and beyond.

This is different from the Indian model of liberation where one is supposed to have no vestiges of ego personality left. According to our understanding, the condition of the objective Personal Essence is one that includes the personality, for it is one of the dimensions of reality. It is true that it is now refined and developed and can be completely absorbed into Being, but it is still available in experience. It is transformed more and more into the experience of the aspect of the Soul, the individual consciousness that had been structured as the ego individuality, and is now experiencing its nature as Essence. In other words, the personality is still experienced, but perceived as the superficial part of oneself. Its refinement knows no end. To understand more what we mean here by the aspect of the Soul is beyond the scope of this book; we will come back to it in a future study of personal consciousness.

- There is perception, experience and understanding not only of the various dimensions, but of the mutual relationships between them. We are not claiming that one who is realized thus is aware of all such relationships; but that whatever specific awareness is needed for a situation is easily available to him.
- One's life is no longer governed by the dichotomy of pleasure and pain. The value of life is seen to lie beyond them, while including them.
- There is more understanding of one's personal work and life. One's personal life is experienced as not separate from the rest of existence. One becomes objective about one's work, role and contribution. In fact, the objective Personal Essence can be experienced as one's personal and unique actualization of the human potential.
- There is a direct intuitive knowing of the heart of any situation without analysis or perception. Knowing is direct, without knowing how one knows. Communication becomes also direct and to the point.
- The perspective is complete in the sense that all dimensions of reality are included at once. So the perspective does not come from one dimension, not even from the nonperspective of the Absolute. There is the understanding that there are different ontological

dimensions, of increasing reality and truth, culminating in the 481
Absolute Truth.

- One can function efficiently while being completely oneself. In other words, one experiences one's nature as that of the Absolute, but interacts with others on the level appropriate and understandable to them. This is a measure of maturity that most of us cannot tolerate, for it indicates a selflessness that is not even desired by most. Ibn 'Arabi writes of the individual who has attained to this condition, which he equates with the station of the perfect man, the ideal of Sufism:

  > His exterior universe is close to the people. His interior universe is conjoined inseparably to God. To understand this person is very difficult because people think and judge a man by his visible devout attitude and his exterior actions, and they think it is the devout man who is evolved. However, the Perfect Man's development cannot be seen with the eye of the senses. To be able to see him, you have to have the eyes that have reached him. [*Ibid.*, p. 23]

- It might appear in our discussion that this particular attainment is similar to other parts of the process of personalization, but deeper. In fact this particular integration is a whole process on its own, that commences after one attains to the Absolute and its personalization. It is what is referred to sometimes as the journey of descent, starting after the journey of ascent that culminates in the entry into the Absolute. It can be a difficult and painful journey, for it is felt frequently as leaving home, the peaceful majesty of the Absolute. It is the third and last journey in the Sufi path, according to Ibn 'Arabi.

  > This journey starts from Him, but at the same time it is the station of remaining (*baqâ*) with Him. That is to say, it is the journey from the Reality (*haqq*) to the Many (*khalq*). That is to say, having found the Universe of Oneness, he passes into the state of separateness. The man on this journey is for helping others to know, for clearing a way for others with a spiritual descent, and he puts on the cloak of manhood and comes down from his state to be among the people and mingles with them. [*Ibid.*, p.23]

- On the psychological level, this realization requires the abandonment of all internalized object realizations. In fact, it requires the abandonment or transcendence of the concept of object relations.

482   We are discussing this realization only briefly, for the sake of completeness of our study. It is by no means exhaustive. This is also true of our discussion of the objective and formless dimensions of Being. We do this out of a need for completeness and a need for clarity and brevity.

We see in this completely personalized state a total synthesis of the universe of the man of spirit and the universe of the man of the world. This is the true, mature human being, who is neither worldly nor otherworldly, neither personal nor impersonal. He is the potential for everything, the expression of all, the miracle of miracles. Here, man is truly the microcosm, reflecting the totality of all of existence, of all its ontological planes, expressed and embodied in one unique human being. No wonder that some of the wise have thought of him as the isthmus, as the viceregent of the Absolute, and as the expression of the image of God, of the totality of all that there is.

We can appreciate now that the human being is a treasure, incomparable and inconceivable. His objectivity has been likened to a precious diamond, and his personhood to a pearl beyond price. When his personhood becomes objective he is then the rare Diamond Pearl.

Chapter Forty

Epilogue

We have discussed the human potential as universal to all human beings. All humans know, or can know, sadness, pain, anger, joy, love, effort, surrender, aloneness, individuation, identity and other such qualities. Actualization of this potential involves universal processes, states, landmarks and transitions. Any human being who explores deeply into his nature will be confronted with the question of personhood and identity. If he goes deeper he will invariably come upon, for example, the transition from being an individual limited by body boundaries to boundless and formless modes of experience and being.

The experiences, realizations and perceptions we have discussed in this book are universal to all human beings, for they are manifestations of the human potential. This does not necessarily mean that all those who undergo the process of inner realization will experience all we have introduced, or go through the process in the order we presented, or even experience it in the forms we have described. Each human being is a unique expression of the human potential, and his realization of that potential will be unique to him. He might experience the Personal Essence, or any aspect or dimension of Being, in the ways we have described, or in similar or in quite different ways. The succession of experiences for him might reflect the order we have presented or it might significantly depart from it.

However, we expect there will be more similarity than dissimilarity, more points of convergence than divergence. While each rose in a

484   rose bush is unique and different from the other roses, they are all roses, and the fact of being a rose is more fundamental than the differences between roses.

The simultaneous universality and uniqueness in human experience is something to remember and respect, especially in the process of inner realization. It is this manifestation of the universal and unique in the Personal Essence that requires that one approach the work of realization with openness and respect toward oneself and the process, integrity in how one approaches one's experience, and sincerity in staying with exactly what one actually experiences. One need believe nothing about reality or oneself. One only needs enough integrity and sincerity in approaching the truth, which is always the truth of one's personal experience, and the Truth will invariably reveal itself. It will reveal itself within the specific individual as a unique actualization of the human potential. And the beauty of it is that this uniqueness will reflect the true unity of both humanity and all of existence.

APPENDIX

Nomenclature

We have tried to adhere in this book to a simple terminology, that is descriptive and also gives some of the relationships between the various major concepts. The terms Essence and Being are frequently used. Often we use them interchangeably, to indicate that basically they mean the same thing: the fact, experience and perception of true nature. We are referring to the ontological nature and suchness of consciousness, which is ultimately the nature of everything.

The difference between the two in our usage in this book is due to the fact that the experience of true nature can be of oneself as an individual being, or can be of the totality of existence. So when we want to make this distinction we use the term Essence to refer to the true nature of the human individual, and Being to refer to the true nature of everything. Still Essence is of the nature of Being; for the human individual is part of everything.

We must point out that we do not use the term Essence the same way that Gurdjieff and some of the Sufis, like Idries Shah, use it. These authors use the term Essence to refer to what is termed in Western languages the Soul. They are translating the Arabic word "dhat," which means self, identity, nature, essence, soul, all in one. We have not used the word "soul" in this book, except in passing, because we did not want to emphasize this manifestation, but it is implied when we refer to the human being as consciousness, or the consciousness, or the individual consciousness, or the personal consciousness. Sometimes we use the term psyche in this sense as the soul, even though the term psyche as it is used these days signifies only one manifestation of what is called the soul. Ego in fact is also one manifestation of soul, as indicated by some of the Sufis using the word ego to refer to soul.

Thus Essence is seen as the essence of the soul, its deeper nature, and ego as its external manifestation. Being is then the experiential

486   nature of Essence. This means that some authors mean both soul and Essence when they use the term Essence, without differentiating the two. We used the terms in the same way in our previous book, *Essence.*

We must also mention that we do not use the term Being in the way it is used in everyday language, nor exactly the way it is used in philosophy. We use it to refer to an actual experiential category, that of ontological presence; it does not refer to a philosophical concept or to the everyday concept of existing.

We acknowledge the fact that Being manifests in many and various dimensions, and Essence in many and various aspects. We capitalize a term when we use it to refer to an essential aspect or a dimension of Being.

We also use the terminology of psychoanalysis and psychoanalytic object relations theory to discuss ego states and structures and processes in some technical fashion. We define most of these terms as we go on in our discussions, but not all of them, especially not those common in psychological parlance.

REFERENCES

Alexander, Franz, M.D., *Psychosomatic Medicine,* New York: W. W. Norton & Co., 1950.

Ali, A-Hameed, "Essence and Sexuality," *Energy and Character—The Journal of Biosynthesis,* Editor: David Boadella, Dorset, England, Vol. 14: No. 2, August 1983.

al-Jîlî, Abd al-Karîm, *Universal Man,* Sherborne, England: Beshara Publications, 1983.

Almaas, A. H., *Essence—The Diamond Approach to Inner Realization,* York Beach, ME: Samuel Weiser, 1986.

Almaas, A. H., *The Void—A Psychodynamic Investigation of the Relationship between Mind and Space,* Berkeley: Diamond Books, 1986.

Almaas, A. H., *Diamond Heart Book One: Elements of the Real in Man,* Berkeley: Diamond Books, 1987.

Aurobindo, Sri, *The Life Divine. Vol. 1 and 2,* Pondicherri, India: Sri Aurobindo Ashram, 1973.

Avedon, John F., *An Interview with the Dalai Lama,* New York: Little Bird Publications, 1980.

Balsekar, Ramesh S., *Pointers from Nisargadatta Maharaj,* Durham, NC: The Acorn Press, 1983.

Blanck, Gertrude and Rubin, *Ego Psychology: Theory and Practice,* New York: Columbia University Press, 1974.

Blanck, Gertrude and Rubin, *Ego Psychology II: Psychoanalytic Developmental Psychology,* New York: Columbia University Press, 1974.

488   Blofeld, John, trans., *The Zen Teaching of Huang Po,* New York: Grove Press, Inc., 1959.

Blum, Harold P., M.D., editor, *Psychoanalytic Explorations of Technique,* New York: International Universities Press, Inc., 1980.

Cannon, W. B., *The Wisdom of the Body,* New York: Norton, 1932.

Cecil, Robert, editor, *The King's Son,* London: Octagon Press, 1981.

Conze, Edward, *Buddhism: Its Essence and Development,* New York: Harper and Row, 1959.

Corbin, Henry, *Creative Imagination in the Sufism of Ibn 'Arabi,* Princeton, NJ: Princeton University Press, 1977.

Corbin, Henry, *The Man of Light in Iranian Sufism,* Boulder, Colorado: Shambhala Press, 1978.

Davis, Madeleine and David Wallbridge, *Boundary and Space,* New York: Brunner/Mazel, Inc., 1981.

Eliade, Mircea, *Yoga, Immortality and Freedom,* Princeton, NJ: Princeton University Press, 1973.

Eliot, Charles W., M.D., editor, *The Harvard Classics: Sacred Writings. Vol. II,* Danbury, CN: Groller Enterprises Corporation, 1980.

Fairbairn, W. Ronald D., *Psychoanalytic Studies of the Personality,* London, Henley and Boston: Routledge and Kegan Paul, 1984.

Gellhorn, Ernst, *Autonomic Regulation,* New York: Interscience, 1943.

Govinda, Lama Angarika, *Foundations of Tibetan Mysticism,* New York: Samuel Weiser, Inc., 1971.

Greenberg, Jay R., and Stephen A. Mitchell, *Object Relations in Psychoanalytic Theory,* Cambridge: Harvard University Press, 1983.

Grotstein, James S., *Splitting and Projective Identification,* New York: Jason Aronson, 1981.

Guenther, Herbert V., *The Tantric View of Life,* Berkeley and London: Shambhala Press, 1972.

Guntrip, Harry, *Psychoanalytic Theory, Therapy and the Self,* New York: Basic Books, Inc., 1973.

Guntrip, Harry, *Schizoid Phenomena, Object Relations and the Self,* 489
New York: International Universities Press, Inc., 1969.

Gurdjieff, G. I., *Views from the Real World,* New York: E.P. Dutton, 1973.

Gyatsho, His Holiness Tenzin, The XIVth Dalai Lama of Tibet, *The Opening of the Wisdom-Eye,* Theosophical Publishing House: Wheaton, IL, 1981.

Gyatsho, His Holiness Tenzin, The XIVth Dalai Lama of Tibet, *Kindness, Clarity and Insight,* trans. Jeffrey Hopkins, Ithaca, NY: Snow Lion Publications, 1984.

Halevi, Z'ev ben Shimon, *The Way of the Kabbalah,* New York: Samuel Weiser, Inc., 1976.

Hartmann, Heinz, *Ego Psychology and the Problem of Adaptation,* New York: International Universities Press, Inc., 1945.

Herbert, Frank, *Children of Dune,* New York: Ace Books, 1967.

Horner, Althea, *Object Relations and the Developing Ego in Therapy,* New York and London: Jason Aronson, 1979.

Ibn 'Arabi, Muhyiddin, *Kernel of the Kernel,* London: Beshara Publications.

Ibn 'Arabi, Muhyiddin, *"Whoso Knoweth Himself . . .",* London: Beshara Publications, 1976.

'Iraqi, Fakhruddin, *Divine Flashes,* Ramsey, NJ: Paulist Press, 1982.

Izutsu, Toshihiko, *Sufism and Taoism,* Berkeley: University of California Press, 1983.

Jacobson, Edith, M.D., *The Self and the Object World,* New York: International Universities Press, Inc., 1980.

Johnston, William, editor, *The Cloud of Unknowing,* New York: Image Books, a Division of Doubleday & Company, Inc., 1973.

Joshi, Vasant, *The Awakened One: The Life and Work of Baghwan Shree Rajneesh,* San Francisco: Harper and Row, 1982.

Kernberg, Otto F., M.D., *Internal World and External Reality,* New York: Jason Aronson, Inc., 1980.

490   Kernberg, Otto F., M.D., *Object Relations Theory and Clinical Psychoanalysis,* New York: Jason Aronson, Inc., 1979.

Kühlewind, Georg, *Becoming Aware of the Logos,* New York: Inner Traditions/Lindesfarne Press Book, 1985.

Lal, P., *The Dhammapada,* New York: The Noonday Press, 1967.

Lu K'uan Yü, *Taoist Yoga,* New York: Samuel Weiser, Inc., 1970.

Mahler, Margaret S., *On Human Symbiosis and the Vicissitudes of Individuation,* New York: International Universities Press, Inc., 1968.

Mahler, Margaret S., et al., *The Psychological Birth of the Human Infant,* New York: Basic Books, Inc., 1975.

Moyne, John and Coleman Barks, *Unseen Rain—Quatrains of Rumi,* Putney: Threshold Books, 1986.

Muktananda, Swami, *Guru,* New York: Harper and Row, 1971.

Neisser, Ulric, *Cognition and Reality,* New York: U. H. Freemas and Company, 1976.

Ni, Hua-Ching, trans., *The Complete Works of Lau Tzu. The Shrine of the Eternal Breath of Tao,* Malibu, California: College of Tao and Traditional Chinese Healing, 1979.

Nisargadatta Maharaj, Sri, *I Am That,* North Carolina: The Acorn Press, 1981.

Ouspensky, P. D., *In Search of the Miraculous,* New York: Harcourt Brace Jovanovich, Inc., 1949.

Price, A. F., and Wong Mou-Lam, trans., *The Diamond Sutra and the Sutra of Hui Neng,* Colorado: Shambhala Publications, Inc., 1969.

Progoff, Ira, *The Death and Rebirth of Psychology,* New York: McGraw-Hill, 1973.

Rajneesh, Bhagwan Shree, *The Psychology of the Esoteric,* New York: Harper and Row, 1979.

Reich, Wilhelm, *The Function of the Orgasm,* New York: Pocket Books, 1975.

Roberts, Bernadette, *The Experience of No-Self,* Boston: Shambhala 491
Publications, Inc., 1982.

Satprem, *Sri Aurobindo, or the Adventure of Consciousness,* Pondi-
cherry, India: Sri Aurobindo Ashram Press, 1973.

Shah, Idries, *A Perfumed Scorpion,* London: Octagon Press, 1978.

Shah, Idries, *Tales of the Dervishes,* New York: E.P. Dutton, 1970.

Shah, Idries, *The Sufis,* New York: Doubleday, 1964.

Shah, Sidar Ikbal Ali, *Islamic Sufism,* New York: Samuel Weiser Inc.,
1971.

Stewart, Mary, *The Hollow Hills,* New York: William Morrow and Co.,
Inc., 1973.

Trungpa, Chogyam, *Cutting Through Spiritual Materialism,* Boulder,
Colorado: Shambhala Publications, 1973.

Winnicott, D. W., *The Maturational Processes and the Facilitating
Environment,* New York: International Universities Press, Inc.,
1980.

Zimmer, Heinrich, *The King and the Corpse,* ed., Joseph Campbell,
Princeton, NJ: Princeton University Press, 1957.

INDEX

About the author—

A. H. Almaas' background is in physics, mathematics and psychology. He is a teacher and author who for the last twelve years has guided students and groups in Colorado and California using his unique method of personal realization called the Diamond Approach. Almaas teaches courses to psychotherapists and has trained many teachers in the Diamond Approach.

The Diamond Approach work described in this book is taught in group settings in California and Colorado, and occasionally elsewhere.

For more information, write:

Ridhwan
P.O. Box 10114
Berkeley, California 94709

Ridhwan School
P. O. Box 18166
Boulder, CO 80308-8166